COLLECTOR OF GENIUS
A Life of Sir George Beaumont

COLLECTOR OF GENIUS

A Life of Sir George Beaumont

FELICITY OWEN & DAVID BLAYNEY BROWN

PUBLISHED FOR
THE PAUL MELLON CENTRE
FOR STUDIES IN BRITISH ART
BY
YALE UNIVERSITY PRESS
NEW HAVEN & LONDON · 1988

FOR GRACE

Set in Linotron Garamond by
Best-set Typesetter Ltd, Hong Kong
Printed and bound in Great Britain at
The Bath Press, Avon

Library of Congress Cataloging-in-Publication Data

Owen, Felicity.
    Collector of genius: a life of Sir George Beaumont / Felicity
Owen & David Blayney Brown.
        p.   cm.
    Includes index.
    ISBN 0-300-04183-7
    1. Beaumont. George Howland, Sir, 1753–1827.   2. Art patrons—
Great Britain — Biography.   3. Great Britain — Nobility — Biography.
4. Great Britain, National Gallery.   I. Brown, David Blayney.
II. Title.
N1090.094 1988
709'.2'4—dc19
[B]   87-26114
                                                                      CIP

Frontispiece. Thomas Lawrence: *Sir George Beaumont* (Paris, Musée du Louvre). Detail of Pl. 42.

iv

CONTENTS

ACKNOWLEDGEMENTS

FELICITY OWEN, a descendant of Sir George Beaumont, having devoted several years to studies of his life and art, met David Brown on common ground during their researches, from different points of view, into the background of those two extraordinary and libellous publications, the *catalogues raisonnés* of the British Institution of 1815 and 1816. The present book arose from ensuing exchanges about these intriguing episodes in the history of British art, but the work has since acquired other dimensions and become in the fullest sense a collaboration. It is now difficult to remember who wrote what; and, indeed, neither could have written the book without the other.

It is a pleasure to recall and acknowledge the assistance received from friends and colleagues: above all Sir Francis Beaumont has been unstintingly patient and generous in making available material remaining in the family collection, and John Crocker has been indispensable for deeply researched information about the Coleorton estate. Evelyn Mitchell Howe shared her knowledge, and the late F.A. Whiting left his transcripts of Beaumontiana. Jonathan Wordsworth gave help and advice on the poets' chapters. Sir Michael Levey supported research into the origin of the National Gallery.

For the loan of archive material, a special debt is due to the following: the Duke of Northumberland for Beverley papers; the Earl of Normanby for the Mulgrave correspondence; the Dove Cottage Trustees and Robert Woof for letters to Wordsworth; and Heather Godfrey for letters to J.C. Ibbetson.

For further documents and records thanks are due to Sir Brinsley Ford for the proceedings of the Society of Dilettanti; John Bensusan-Butt for countless forays into Essex history; Bill Ellis for Grosvenor Estate records; Howard Colvin for information relating to the building of Beaumont's gallery, and W.R. Hakewill for family papers; Ian Fleming-Williams for material and advice on J.B. Malchair and on Constable, and Graham Reynolds for contributions to the saga of *Jacques and the Wounded Stag* ; Nicholas Penny for Beaumont's links with Reynolds and Payne Knight; Hamish Miles for connections with Wilkie; Pat Andrew for deciphering Jacob More's letters; Sybil Rosenfeld for her invaluable material on the eighteenth-century stage; Kenneth Garlick for help with identifying Lawrence's portrait of Beaumont; Gertrud Seidmann for Beaumont's commission to Nathaniel Marchant; Susan Morris for her notes on Beaumont's Girtins; Gerard Vaughan for details of Beaumont in Rome; Frank Simpson for locating letters to William Smith; Michael Chapman of Wade & Davies for Beaumont documents.

Help is gratefully acknowledged from David Alexander, Brian Allen, Miriam

Allott, Joan Bailey, John Maturin-Baird, Hugh Belsey, Peter Bicknell, Pierre Bourrit, Noelle Brown, Herbert Cahoon, Gloria Cavendish, Margaret Christian, David Dallas, David Davenport, John Edgcumbe, Judy Egerton, Lady Elton, Henry Ford, Cyril Fry, Tom Girtin, Peter Goodchild, Christopher Hall, Michael Harvard, Francis Hawcroft, Luke Herrmann, Ralph Holland, Sheila Huftel, Sidney Hutchinson, Michael Kitson, John Leighton, Gillian Malpass, James Miller, Frances Moysey, Evelyn Newby, John Nicoll, Patrick Noon, Denys Oppé, Leslie Parris, Deirdre Paulley, Michael Pidgley, Anthony Lowther-Pinkerton, Geoffrey Rowell, Charles Rhyne, Kim Sloan, Dudley Snelgrove, Felice Spurrier, Lindsay Stainton, Dorothy Stroud, John Sunderland, David Thomason, Cornish Torbock, Henry Wemyss, S.C. Whitbread, Scott Wilcox, Pat Womersley and Christopher Wright. Thanks are due also to British Coal, the present owner, for its hospitality at Coleorton Hall.

For their support and constructive criticism the authors are most grateful to Doreen Brown, Caroline and James Knox, and Charles Owen.

BEAUMONT SOURCES

Coleorton records. Up to 1938 there remained in the library at Coleorton letters from the Wordsworths, Coleridge, Southey and Walter Scott, edited versions of which appear in Knight's *Memorials of Coleorton.* There was also a very large number of letters from Uvedale Price and others, including the Archbishop of Canterbury (Charles Manners Sutton), Abercorn, Ashburnham, Miss Baillie, W.L. Bowles, Englefield, Farington, W. Gilpin, Jackson, W. Smith, West and Wilkie, and the Commonplace Book into which many of Wordsworth's poems sent to the Beaumonts were transcribed. These were all held by the Beaumont Trustees and handed over to Sir Ifor Evans for study, as the result of which he wrote two articles for the *Times Literary Supplement* in 1935. Although the papers were entailed, with one or two exceptions they found their way to the Pierpont Morgan Library, New York (MA 1581).

Extracts from the letters copied out by members of the family and friends remain in the Beaumont Collection, together with a large number of drawings by the 7th baronet. Other drawings and paintings catalogued by A.C. Sewter for the 1938 exhibition of *Paintings and Drawings by Sir George Beaumont* at Leicester Museum and Art Gallery have been given to that Museum or purchased by it, but some are untraced. The works remaining in the Beaumont Collection after Sir George's gift to the National Gallery was made have largely been dispersed over the years (see Luke Herrmann and Felicity Owen, *Sir George Beaumont of Coleorton, Leicestershire*, Leicester Museum and Art Gallery, 1973). Works referred to in the text are still in the Beaumont Collection (B.C.), unless otherwise stated.

The contents of the library at Coleorton had been available to scholars when Evelyn Mitchell (now Evelyn Mitchell Howe) wrote her MA thesis, 'Sir George Beaumont and his Contacts with English Romanticism', London University, 1938. Mr F.A. Whiting, intending to write a Beaumont biography, also transcribed some of the letters and he kindly handed over the material before his death.

Leicestershire Records Office holds some Beaumont material, including a report on the Coleorton estate in 1827 and on the attempt to impeach the right of G.H. Willoughby Beaumont to the baronetcy.

The whereabouts of the letters from Beaumont to Price is unknown.

INTRODUCTION

For John Constable's biographer and fellow painter, Charles Robert Leslie, Sir George Beaumont had been quite simply 'the leader of taste in the fashionable world'.[1] So he had, for some thirty of the most crucial and eventful years in the history of English art and letters. But he was more than this. Spent as much in the service of others as in the pursuit of his own interests, Beaumont's life has not until now been fully appraised. He has lived mainly through his friends and protégés, a peripheral if tantalisingly attractive figure in their own more familiar stories. Today Beaumont's monuments, though numerous and varied, may often go unrecognised. In literature he is enshrined in the poetry of William Wordsworth and Samuel Taylor Coleridge, and in the diaries and autobiographical writings of Benjamin Robert Haydon and Joseph Farington. His own paintings and drawings can, sometimes with difficulty, be found in public galleries. In the Royal Academy, Michelangelo's marble tondo of the Virgin and Child with St John, brought by Beaumont to London in 1822, has pride of place as one of the most precious works of art in the capital. In the National Gallery and in the Tate, paintings from his gift rank among the most important in the collections, and indeed the National Gallery is itself his greatest monument, for it was his presentation of sixteen major paintings to the nation during his lifetime that provided its nucleus.

His friends and beneficiaries were not always kind to Beaumont, and a life devoted to genius, or to pretenders to the muse, as his had been, was bound to bring tribulation as well as reward. Although Haydon drew comfort from his memory in the hours before his tragic suicide, he had in 1810 made Beaumont the subject of one of the most sustained passages of vituperation he ever committed to his diary; accused of caprice, empty flattery and, worst of all in Haydon's terms, of meanness, Beaumont emerged from the pages first as monster, then as a pathetic figure scarcely worthy of pity. Beaumont's reputation as *arbiter elegantarium* and chief supporter of contemporary artists then seemed to Haydon a chimera. The charm and flattery could turn to neglect or dismissal as boredom succeeded shallow enthusiasm. Far from being the ideal of the noble and disinterested patron, 'anxious only to advance the Art, to raise it to the highest pitch of excellence for the intellectual gratification of the world', Beaumont appeared 'the clog of English art — as one who hates Modern Art, as one who would rather have blood wrung from him than money'.[2] And as Haydon had written a few days earlier, 'Sir George never comes to Town, but he brings Doubt, Irresolution & Misery in his train, to let loose upon every Artist, as his whim directs and his fancy excites — he is one who has been unsettled always himself, is unsettled now, who unsettles everybody else, and settles nobody, whose specious, fascinating, syren advice will bewilder, enchain and distract the firmest mind, with whom it was impossible to resolve, or determine, till you were without the magic circle of his manners.'[3]

Between the generous friend recalled in the tragic euphoria of Haydon's last hours, and the fickle, emptily charming enthusiast portrayed in 1810, we must seek the real Beaumont. Though Haydon came to regret bitterly his earlier assessment, he was never uncritical. Nor was he the only artist to censure Beaumont. While his own dispute was raging, another, centring around Beaumont's antipathy to J.M.W. Turner and his followers, was gathering momentum, and in the following years Beaumont was to find himself vilified in pamphlets vicious even by the standards of the day. Even Constable, great friend and frequent guest though he was, had no illusions about what he regarded as the limitations of Beaumont's mind and taste; and it should be remembered that Beaumont, for his part, never acquired a single one of Constable's original pictures. Even so, Constable expressed a debt that many artists must have felt: writing of Beaumont to their mutual friend Wordsworth in 1836, he said: 'I feel that I am indebted to him for what I am as an artist.'[4]

It is perhaps the fate of a patron to be controversial in his lifetime, since he is bound to excite the anger of those he chooses not to support as well as the gratitude of those he favours. Beaumont was no exception, and his quixotic nature and capacity for swift and sudden enthusiasm laid him all the more open to criticism. He himself admitted he was capricious; as he told William Gilpin, he 'ranged from flower to flower', and his wife, he added, was as 'inconstant' as himself.[5] It is true that he was speaking of his tastes in the old masters, but undoubtedly there was a certain justification for James Northcote's remarks to Farington that young artists tended to be given exciting rides on what he graphically described as Beaumont's 'flying coach', only to be thrown off when Sir George became bored with them. More often, however, consistent loyalty and generosity were displayed by Beaumont even when, as in Haydon's case, his patience was sorely tried.

Again, Beaumont could sometimes be accused of conservatism. While he was quick to recognise the genius of Wilkie and was unswerving in his support of it, he was entirely blind to that of Turner, often mystified by Constable, and peculiarly negligent of the generation of watercolourists who built on the foundations laid by friends of his youth like J.R. Cozens and Thomas Hearne. Wilkie himself admitted the backward-looking aspect of Beaumont's taste but, since he was himself in later years hardly less critical of his painter-contemporaries, he was more sympathetic than some of them to Beaumont's views. For Wilkie, Beaumont was 'the only one left among us of the school of Reynolds, of Wilson and of Gainsborough, of the primitive time, and what I fear, in respect to the present, must now be called the golden age of British art. It was to this his eye was turned — this he adhered to.'[6]

Had Beaumont then lived beyond his time? Certainly he was very much a man of the eighteenth century; but within the parameters of his background, his eyes were in fact remarkably wide open. At the same time, his nature contained not only a reverence for the values of the past — whether they were the intellectual standards enshrined in Reynolds's *Discourses* or certain niceties of social behaviour — but also a propensity for nostalgia that rendered them all the more attractive. Even inclined as he was to hero-worship, he once told Uvedale Price that he had met few people in later life, apart from Antonio Canova, who could compare to the personalities who dominated his youth — whether Reynolds in painting or Garrick on the stage. Younger friends, while being understandably fascinated by Beaumont's links with a vanishing age, may also have felt themselves being measured by exacting standards. Meeting Beaumont in Rome in 1822, the young Joseph Severn found him 'always recurring to the great artistic days which had passed. His accounts of Gainsborough, Romney, Lady Hamilton, Nelson and so forth were delightful, but all were made to centre round the pivot of Sir Joshua Reynolds who was top of his admiration both as a man and as an artist.'[7]

It was a heady mixture, and more than most, Severn's reminiscences convey something of the range of Beaumont's interests. For Severn, Beaumont was not a patron — nor even a potential one — but 'a famous amateur artist', the scope and quality of whose work must not be forgotten. The leading amateur painter and draughtsman of his day, instructed by a distinguished succession of masters including Alexander Cozens, Thomas Hearne, J.R. Cozens and Girtin, and advised by Reynolds, Gainsborough, Wilson and Constable, he could have achieved professional status were it not for his rank in life, and certainly he came near enough to it to be mentioned as a successor to his friend, Benjamin West, as President of the Royal Academy. On the other hand, the names of Nelson and Lady Hamilton open up worlds wider than that of art. At Beaumont's table in Rome, Severn was able to meet Samuel Rogers and talk of Keats, pointing to the literary sphere in which Beaumont was equally at home. His associations with Wordsworth and Coleridge are fascinating chapters in his life, friendship with the former, in his own words, being one of its 'prime blessings'. Similarly, Haydon had been thrilled by his stories of Garrick and by introductions to Mrs Siddons, testimony to Beaumont's love of the theatre that had made him perhaps the most talented amateur actor of his generation.

One senses from Severn, as from Constable and Haydon, the glamour that Beaumont must have had for his artist-friends: that of a man who was at once one of them, and at the same time belonged to other and greater worlds. Despite his informality when at home and in sympathetic company, Beaumont was nothing if not a man of his class, totally different — and obviously more fascinating — in manners and tastes from men like John Sheepshanks and Robert Vernon who derived their position from commerce and were doing so much to support the arts by the 1820s. Yet Beaumont's most attractive trait by far — and the one that sets him apart from many of the most cultivated of his contemporaries — was the way he sought to bring his own worlds and those of his friends together for their mutual benefit. This embraced not only single gestures of largesse such as that which offered Wordsworth the chance (little appreciated) to live with Coleridge at Applethwaite, but smaller and more subtle acts of tact, discretion and consideration designed to bridge social and economic gaps. In associating himself with the best interests of his protégés, he could occasionally behave with an undeniably patrician high-handedness, but, more often, he took infinite pains to overcome any imputation of condescension or obligation.

This book seeks to illuminate fascinating patterns of artistic and literary relationships extending over many years and spanning fundamental changes in taste, and to acknowledge the outstanding personal qualities of a man who deserves much more than the footnotes he has so far received — let alone mockery as the pedant who advised Constable to paint a brown tree. When Haydon once called Beaumont 'an epitome of the world',[8] he meant it insultingly, as if in Sir George were combined all the whims and frivolities of fashionable life. But in another sense the phrase is most effective, for Beaumont was indeed a perfect mirror of his fast-changing times, reflecting not only traditional values — even prejudices — but also an open response to the new, the civilised breadth of an aristocratic culture at its best, and that disinterested generosity that has since been eroded by a harsher history. To know Beaumont is to know the better faces of his period, and its leading creative spirits, more clearly. In the end none recognised his claim to memory more than Haydon. It was fitting that he should recall him in his last hours, but his greatest and fairest tribute was written just after Beaumont's own death. It cannot be bettered as both an introduction and a challenge to this book:

> Sir George was an extraordinary man, one of the old school formed by Sir Joshua — a link between the artist and the nobleman, elevating the one by an intimacy which did not depress the other. Born a painter, his fortune prevented the necessity of application for subsistence, and of course he did not apply. His taste was exquisite, not peculiar or classical, but essentially *Shakespearian*. Painting was his great delight... His ambition was to connect himself with the art of the country, and he has done it for ever... His loss, with all its faults, will not easily be supplied. He founded the National Gallery. Let him be crowned.[9]

I
FROM ESSEX TO ETON

THE FIRST GLIMPSE of the family life of George Howland Beaumont is at Dunmow, Essex in the summer of 1759 when he was five years old. The new curate of Thaxted, the Revd William Cooper, describes being introduced at Dunmow Bowling Green Inn by Viscount Maynard into the local circle of gentry and clerics which included Beaumont's father Sir George Beaumont, 'who afterwards became my intimate and particular friend'.[1] The hospitable sixth baronet and his wife Rachel, several years his senior and the youngest daughter of a neighbouring landowner, Matthew Howland of Stonehall, Little Canfield, lived with their son, born on 6 November 1753, in an Elizabethan brick mansion which stands today little changed on the road north from Dunmow to Thaxted, the old Dunmow Causeway (Pl. 1). This was no treasure house — in fact it is doubtful whether the Beaumonts owned one good picture — but a rambling, inconvenient old place with Dutch gables, mullioned windows and a wooden clock tower dating from 1651. It has none the less consi-

1. T.H. Barfield: *The Clock House, Dunmow* (detail), 1856 (B.C.).

derable quiet charm and its position on rising ground in the flat Essex countryside is one of its best features. To the east the Beaumonts enjoyed a rural view down to the handsome fifteenth-century church, while behind the stableyards lay the deer-filled park of Easton Lodge, the seat of Lord Maynard who, as *grand seigneur* of the district, was revered for his benevolence and good works.

Dating from Saxon times, Dunmow was a well-ordered market town with its own doctors and lawyers and a trade in wool cloth — say and bay — which, together with a tannery, employed a large percentage of the population of some 1,800 people. George Howland Beaumont's great grandfather, William, had come to the district in the second half of the seventeenth century, to be joined by his elder brother Thomas who was vicar from 1678 to 1715. In 1738 George Howland's father, the sixth baronet, had succeeded at the age of twelve to the one title remaining in the family after the six sons of the main Leicestershire branch had failed to produce an heir — a recurrent problem for the Beaumonts — and Thomas's sons had died young. With the baronetcy went the Leicestershire properties centred on Coleorton, the hall itself, surrounded by coalmines and in a dilapidated state, not having been occupied since the death of Viscount Beaumont in 1702. The attraction of this inheritance must have been largely financial to an Essex Beaumont, but the sixth baronet appears to have developed into a conscientious landlord. In 1757 he appointed Joseph Boultbee, a member of a well-known Leicestershire family, as manager of the estate, and, three years later, granted him a twenty-one-year lease of the colliery, farm and woods. In 1761 Sir George was in Leicestershire to serve as high sheriff, but he did not live long to enjoy his opportunities in the two counties, for the following year opened ominously with his making his will at Dunmow and, within a month, at the age of only 36, he was dead. Under the marriage settlement of 1751 Dame Rachel was already entitled to £250 a year from the income of the Leicestershire estate. To this her husband had added a further £100 a year and, until his son became twenty-one, the benefit of all his Dunmow property. George Howland Beaumont was to receive the income from Parsonage Farm, Dunmow, a manor held on lease from the Bishop of London.[2]

It is little wonder that Beaumont was accustomed to speak of his childhood as a solitary and somewhat melancholy one, for the loss of his father followed the death in infancy of two younger brothers and the household was soon to mourn his favourite uncle and trustee, William, a lieutenant colonel in the Surrey militia. This left another uncle, Thomas, of Buckland in Surrey, as the only surviving male Beaumont apart from himself, and there appears to have been little love lost in this relationship.

Dame Rachel was fortunate to have a host of Howland relations within a thirty mile radius, including Isabella, who was painted by Thomas Gainsborough in about 1768 as the personification of a well-to-do lady.[3] But none of the Howlands was young Beaumont's contemporary and although John Henniker, son of the Member of Parliament for Sudbury and a close neighbour at Newton Hall, was the same age, only Charles Maynard, son of Sir William Maynard and later to inherit Easton Lodge, appears to have been a friend. The two boys were dispatched in the autumn of 1762 to preparatory school, Beaumont going to Luton. When he returned later in life, not even the building remained, and the eighteen months spent there are unrecorded. He transferred to Dame Prior's house at Eton in May 1764 during the last years of Dr Barnard's headship, which had been enormously beneficial, the number of boys increasing to over 500. A true showman, Barnard turned his farewell speech in 1766 into a great event and his successor, Dr Foster, had literally a hard act to follow. Discipline deteriorated fast and the first year of the new régime was distinguished by a battle between the boys and the butchers of Windsor in which the future politician, William Windham, performed so effectively that he was obliged to leave Eton. Faced next with the rebellion of nearly 200 senior boys, who walked out considering themselves slighted by the new head, Foster did not have a happy beginning to his tenure of office and Beaumont was lucky that most of his time was under the mild and lovable Dr Dampier in the junior school, where riots were likely to mean extra 'holydays'. Having taken a good place in the second form on entry at the age of ten, he made little progress in the last two years and was removed from the bottom of the fifth form in 1769, before he reached sixteen. His contemporaries Maynard and Henniker did far better. Whether events at home were responsible for this poor performance or whether it was owing partly to a dislike of a mainly classical curriculum which involved construing Homer and Virgil and learning the Greek testament by heart, it is difficult to know. Certainly Beaumont cannot really be described as a late developer, for he did well enough out of school, and took full advantage of the various instructive diversions Eton offered in addition to its formal classes, ranging from amateur theatricals (later to become a favourite pastime) to lessons in drawing, French and fencing, the latter given by the Italian parent of one of Beaumont's younger fellow pupils, Henry Angelo.

With a certain romantic licence — and the benefit of hindsight — Angelo re-membered George as being both spirited and solitary: 'Sir George, though as lively as his compeers, was fond of wandering alone in the sequestered spots adjacent to the College, and doubtless there felt the charm of those poetic effects which abound at sober eve, where all is rich in those attributes of art and nature, which constitute the picture — ancient towers and turrets, woodlands, glades, and water.' More down-to-earth are Angelo's recollections of Beaumont's twin passions at Eton, swimming and drawing. There were several delightful bathing places along the Thames at Eton, such as Cuckow Ware (also famous for Moody's hot rolls and cheese), Head Pile and Pope's Hole, and Beaumont made full use of them. As a boy he was overweight, and, like many fat children, an excellent swimmer, 'so buoyant, that he could, and frequently did, remain in the water for one or two hours; and having been persuaded that the frequency of bathing would reduce him in size, he for one period might be said to be amphibious, living almost as much in as out of that element'.[4] Hence he acquired his Eton nickname of 'Otter'.

Hardly less time was spent above Cole's, the barber's shop, where the drawing master Alexander Cozens kept a room for evening drawing classes. Cozens had first come to Eton probably in 1763; he is recorded as an extra drawing master in 1766 and so remained for a number of years while building up his fashionable teaching practice outside the school. Mild and painfully shy, he seems to have been greatly loved by his pupils, although their antics must have tried him sorely. Angelo, perhaps romancing again, recalled being protected by Beaumont while the boys pelted bread at each other and the easy-going Cozens left them to learn by copying etchings. Some method, however, prevailed in the madness and in retrospect it is clear that Cozens's teaching was a crucial formative influence on Beaumont, even at such an early age. Certainly the boy was quick to learn. His first drawing book to survive must date from his earliest studies with Cozens, and although the outline sketches of Eton Chapel, and of various figures, who are presumably masters and fellow pupils, as well as a Scotsman in a tam-o'-shanter, show only minimal talent, there are others that document more clearly Beaumont's connection with his master. A study of a standing man in Russian costume, obviously copied from a print or drawing, is fascinating evidence that Cozens showed his pupils material surviving from his own remote Russian beginnings, while schematic drawings of landscape features and compositions correspond to some of Cozens's systems and can be matched in his own manuals and in drawings by other pupils at Christ's Hospital. A favoured and genuinely interested pupil such as Beaumont was obviously able to pick up some of Cozens's methods, even though at the time it must have all seemed like a game. Angelo remembered him at a more advanced stage when he 'distanced all his compeers' and was the only one among Eton's 'incorrigible blotters' who could make anything of Cozens's speciality — the conversion of blots of ink cast at random across the paper into a landscape composition. Unfortunately, none of Beaumont's Eton blots survives, but there are two later drawings founded on the same method.[5]

Cozens's teaching was also fundamental in a wider sense. There can be no doubt that Beaumont's taste was first formed in landscape. It always remained his greatest love, the field in which he held his most pronounced opinions, and the branch of art he practised himself. The highly selective, schematic approach that he favoured in his drawings, his preference for sober and monochromatic tones, and the general tendency of his taste to seek support in precedents can all, perhaps, be traced back to Cozens, whose teaching, like Reynolds's, was academic and rested on principles of imitation and appropriate selection. Just as Reynolds was to advise the students at the Royal Academy to amass a stock of compositions and expressions, so Cozens counselled his pupils to acquire a 'plentiful store of ideas of forms' through reference to suitable models at least as much as from nature. These were, as often as not, from the classical tradition of Claude and Gaspard Dughet, and Cozens's pupils were set to copy and trace examples of their work before independent drawings were encouraged. In any case, Cozens was no great advocate of study from nature. For Beaumont, that would come later. For the time being, Cozens's tutelage bred into him his own formal, disciplined, theoretical approach to landscape, and his ability to suggest the romance and mystery of the natural world by tone rather than naturalistic colour.

Cozens's other star pupil at Eton was Maynard, who excelled at drawing groups of horses. With him and Henniker Beaumont could share the journey home to Essex for the holidays which were a month at Christmas, two weeks at Easter and the whole of August. Dame Rachel, a forceful character, was adored by her son and when she broke the news that she was to marry again in the summer of 1768, the shock must have been considerable to a sensitive boy. Beaumont's obesity may well have been due to overeating in compensation for having to adjust to the abrupt changes that followed his father's death. Accustomed to his mother's undivided attention in his own home, he was now faced with the prospect — which must have seemed appalling — of joining the family of 'John Gates Esquire of Dedham' and his four daughters by a previous marriage. The match may have come through an introduction from Dame Rachel's sister, Hannah Pattrick, the widow of a prosperous farmer, who lived at Marks Tey not far from Dedham.

The existence of Mr Gates has been effectively erased from Beaumont family recollection, and yet he was a gentleman of considerable property with a musical inclination. His business interests included the mills at Higham and Wake Colne, which he was kind enough to leave to his stepson, together with £50, when he died in May 1787. From that date the name of Gates disappears, except on legal documents (his wife had probably always retained the title Lady Beaumont). Beaumont's effacement of his stepfather may have reflected a Beaumont's dislike of a connection with trade rather than any personal antipathy, for Mary Gates, the future Lady Palliser, recalled many years later the pleasure of Beaumont's visits to Langham Hall where the Gates family spent some of the years between 1768 and 1786.[6]

Whatever Beaumont's feelings may have been, after his early removal from Eton there was the problem of his education in the interval before he could follow in his father's footsteps to New College, Oxford, where his grandfather had been proctor from 1717 to 1729. This was solved by the introduction of a Cambridge scholar, the Revd Charles Davy, as his tutor. This cantankerous old man, whose wife was soon to leave him, brought up his own, slightly younger sons in a rough and ready way, forbidding them his own artistic tastes as a waste of time. Yet for Beaumont he was to become the affectionate father-figure missing from the young man's life. Rector of Benacre and Henstead under the patronage of Sir Thomas Gooch, his Henstead house in the north-east corner of Suffolk was within walking distance of the sea, where Beaumont was able to swim to his heart's content, disappearing towards the horizon with a rope attached at one end to his wrist, and at the other to a servant deputed by the anxious Davy to stand guard on the deserted beach (still deserted today). Long hours were spent too in reading Chaucer in a favourite 'sequestered humble station', and Beaumont's love of Shakespeare's plays, some of which he knew by heart, may have dated from this peaceful interlude with Davy, who treated him with the certain deference due to a baronet, or perhaps to a Beaumont. Such an attitude was welcomed by Beaumont throughout his life, though the conceit this implied was tempered by a genuine humility about his own accomplishments and an ability to forget himself when sharing an enthusiasm. Pride in his ancestry was attended by a sense of duty to those less fortunate and his own values were reflected in the choice of Francis Beaumont, the Elizabethan dramatist, as his favourite forebear.

This was no empty compliment, for the Beaumonts were a family of great antiquity and the first English baron to whom George could trace his line was Henry de Beaumont, a grandson of the King of Jerusalem and son of the duc de Brienne, who was close to the French throne. Originally soldiers, from the reign of Edward I for whom Henry de Beaumont fought in Scotland, the Beaumonts spread their tentacles across the land from Devon to Suffolk and north through Leicestershire to Yorkshire, establishing themselves in government and in the judiciary. Disadvantaged repeatedly by lack of a male heir, titles came and went. The literary gene of which George was so proud entered the Leicestershire branch in the late sixteenth century with the birth of Francis and his elder brother John at Gracedieu. Sir John confined himself to poetry now almost forgotten, but Francis gained lasting fame through his collaboration with John Fletcher. Although their plays were rather coarse for mid-eighteenth-century taste, George identified himself with this artistic talent, and the proximity of Gracedieu to the other Beaumont seats at Stoughton and Coleorton was a palliative in later years as he sought to become reconciled to living in Leicestershire. Meanwhile it gave him an appetite to find his own form of creative expression.

2. Gabriel Stuart (engraved Caroline Watson): *William Woollett* (Oxford, Ashmolean Museum).

3. (facing page left) Beaumont: *Charles Davy and Pupil, at the Rectory, Henstead, Suffolk*, 1770, pencil (B.C.).

4. (facing page right). Beaumont: *Self-Portrait*, 1771, pencil (B.C.)

It was the action of Davy, who took his pupil to London for six weeks in the spring of 1771 and introduced him to a number of artists, that fuelled the spark of a passion for art that was to transform the young man's life. A visit to the engraver, William Woollett (Pl.2), in his garret at 11 Green Street, Leicester Square, was particularly successful and was repeated nearly daily. This was an even more auspicious meeting than that with Cozens, for not only was Beaumont older and more receptive, but for the first time he could actually watch artists at work. Woollett enjoyed a reputation, in Thomas Jones's words, as the 'first Landscape Engraver in the world', owed in large part to the most splendid of the eight prints he made after Richard Wilson, that of *The Destruction of the Children of Niobe*, published ten years earlier in 1761. It was probably no accident that Beaumont was later to buy that picture, and to seek out Wilson as one of his chief artistic mentors; indeed it may well have been Woollett who was to provide the introduction. Woollett was also a landscape draughtsman, as was his pupil Thomas Hearne. Hearne was later to become one of the leading topographical watercolourists of his generation, but, at the time Beaumont met him in London, he was in his final year of apprenticeship and employed in etching a picture, *Morning* by Herman Swaneveldt, which Beaumont was also to acquire later. So enjoyable were the meetings at Woollett's that the engraver was persuaded that he and Hearne should visit Davy at Henstead that summer. There followed another intensely happy six weeks in Suffolk and Norfolk, and, as Beaumont later told Dr Monro, 'the remembrance of this happy year never fails. . .to cross my mind like a gleam of bright sunshine'.[7]

This summer of 1771 marks Beaumont's real début as a draughtsman in his own right; as he wrote to Monro, 'we sketched all day'. Not surprisingly, he was still highly impressionable, and at this period it was Woollett whose style made the greatest impact, to judge from a drawing of that year, *Ruined House and Abbey*. J.B.

Pouncy and 'old' Smith (presumably John 'Warwick') joined the group at Henstead at some point. Painstaking studies of Castle Acre from the same year demonstrate Beaumont's cautious and rather halting attempts to emulate the professionals. Thus far he was working without wash or watercolour. At the same time he was making some figure drawings that display the bent towards caricature he had first shown at Eton. From as early as 1770 is a small oval sketch in pencil in which a boy, eager and elegantly dressed, reads or presents a book to a stern and somewhat dropsical clergyman who sits behind a desk, while another middle-aged man watches apprehensively, his chin resting on the head of his cane (Pl. 3). Surely a skit on one of Davy's tutorials, perhaps with one of his sons, this is drawn much in the manner of the caricaturist Henry William (Harry) Bunbury, himself a Suffolk man and certainly known to Beaumont later on (although at this time the stylistic similarity must have been largely coincidental as it was only in 1771 that Bunbury returned from the Grand Tour and commenced exhibiting at the Royal Academy). Of the following year is perhaps our first image of Beaumont — a head and shoulders done quite freely and expressively in pencil, this time with neither satire nor flattery: a reflective, quite mature head, inclined to be plump, but with a long and well-shaped nose, deep lower lip and sharply etched mouth, and bright, challenging eyes (Pl. 4).

Also from 1771 dates Beaumont's love of the old masters, and the beginnings of his connoisseurship. Woollett's London engraving practice ensured ready access to pictures: 'We talked incessantly of pictures', Beaumont told Monro, 'and my love for painting was completely confirmed.' Back in East Anglia, there was a first visit to Houghton Hall (but not, it seems, to the other great local collection at Holkham, so rich in Claudes). Even so, for the time being it was the company of living artists — always thereafter essential to Beaumont's happiness — that counted for more than the masters of the past; as he told Monro, 'I was young and ardent, and admiration — the most pleasing of sensations — I enjoyed in the highest degree. I thought Woollett and Hearne the greatest artists that ever existed, and if anyone had presumed to say that Claude or Gaspar knew half so much of the matter, I should have considered it as ignorance or prejudice.'

Later that year, following the completion of his apprenticeship, Hearne accepted an offer to travel as draughtsman to the newly appointed Governor of the Leeward Islands, Sir Ralph Payne. Beaumont would not see him again until 1776, when the two young men were together once more, sketching with Woollett at the Spaniard's Inn in Hampstead. Their association was to be lifelong. 'Since that time,' Beaumont told Monro in 1816, 'Hearne has risen daily in my esteem, a man of purer integrity does not exist.' Woollett also remained close. Between them, with Davy's encouragement, they had fostered the love of art that was to be the chief force in Beaumont's life. It was to receive still further, and more practical, stimulus at Oxford where, after his release from Davy's tutelage, he matriculated into New College in May 1772.

II
THE EDUCATION OF AN AMATEUR

WHEN BEAUMONT WENT up to Oxford, the sleep of reason had yet to give way to Romanticism, and the world of learning could usually be found in a torpor, rousing itself more often for pleasure than scholarship. Without the Beaumont family tradition, New College would not have been the obvious choice for George since it was at that time properly reserved for those who had been to school at Winchester College. Recently, however, a limited number of noblemen and gentlemen commoners had been admitted to expand the College and afford a better chance of preferment for the senior fellows, and there had been changes and improvements not entirely typical of the University in the second half of the eighteenth century. The library had been re-modelled, as had the chapel, though this had yet to receive the controversial window of the Seven Virtues painted by Jervis after Reynolds. As well as handsome accommo-dation, the College had many beauties. Its garden had been admired by the pioneer of the Picturesque, the Revd William Gilpin, when an undergraduate at Queen's Col-lege. Beyond, on either side of the old city wall, lay a decorative and atmospheric tangle of shrubs and trees that in 1776 was to be the subject of drawings by the Ox-ford drawing master, John Baptist Malchair; while the serenity that prevailed in the Warden's garden had been captured most evocatively by Michael Angelo Rooker's design for the Oxford Almanack of 1769.

Now adjusted to his changed family circumstances, and encouraged by Davy's habit of treating him as an adult, Beaumont had emerged as a thoroughly uncomplicated young man who no longer sought sequestered spots and spent less time in solitary introspection. His old pleasure of swimming he could pursue alone in the many bathing places around Oxford, but in other directions he appears increasingly gregarious in the 1770s, and, with London placed between new Oxford friends and old connections in East Anglia, the early years of the decade were rich in opportunity. It is difficult to know whether scholarship played any real part in his life. Like many of his contemporaries he did not achieve a degree, but this carried no stigma and there remained a thoughtful side to him which Davy — full of erudition himself — must have fostered.

None of Beaumont's Oxford teachers seems to have succeeded in assuming Davy's role of moral tutor as well as friend, and it was his advice that Beaumont sought on ethics and metaphysics, for in May 1773 Davy wrote to him at New College to reassure him that 'Strange as it appears to you, it is by no means an unusual thing, to meet with many worthy persons who are unwilling to believe the doctrine of a par-ticular Providence, whilst they allow that it is extended to the whole system.' Warning Beaumont against the false humility of a pernicious French author who denied the individual 'any place in the attention of the Supreme Being', he insisted that 'the Creator must be as much present in one place as another at every point of time,' and offered the comforting, if unoriginal, philosophy that 'all who make a proper use of those talents which the Creator hath imparted and endeavour to conform their lives in due obedience to the precepts...given...will be certainly in some degree protected and rewarded in this life, so far as it may be consistent with their better and superior interest in another'. This letter, of which its author was evidently proud, was to be published by Davy in 1787.[1] That Beaumont should have looked to him for guidance is not surprising; his unusually wide connections gave him an authority hard to match at Oxford. The scope of these connections is indicated by the long subscription list, containing the names of the majority of the leading artists, a host of clerics and a sprinkling of noblemen, that appeared in 1775 with his son's translation from the French of Marc Théodore Bourrit's *Journey to the Glaciers in the Dutchy of Savoy* — a translation that Davy himself had supervised. As for his advice, Beaumont interpreted it somewhat liberally, but at least he avoided some of the dissipations all too readily available to rich and heedless undergraduates, whilst at the same time establishing his reputation as a good drinking companion.

Beaumont was fortunate in going up to Oxford at a time when the drawing school run by Malchair was at its height. This genial and talented man, a native of Cologne and by profession a violinist, had arrived in Oxford in 1759 to lead the band at the Music Room, and since his marriage had supplemented his income by instructing the gentlemen of the University and the local gentry in drawing. In the process he had developed an advanced method that, unlike the one employed by Alexander Cozens, placed as much emphasis on study from nature as from established examples. His pupils copied old masters such as Claude, the Carracci and Rembrandt — as well as their own contemporary, Richard Wilson — and drew on-the-spot studies of Oxford and the neighbouring countryside which they inscribed with date and time of day. Malchair's own drawings — other than those in which he played down to his pupils' level and, to paraphrase his own words, 'drew like a child while teaching a child'[2] — show a concern for light and atmosphere that is ahead of its time and anticipates the Romantics. These qualities he sought to inspire in his pupils, and, after giving them a thorough grounding in draughtsmanship, he took them out into the country for whole days of sketching — outings that they christened 'Eggs and Bacon' or 'Pork Griskin' expeditions.

Naturally Beaumont sought out Malchair and, together with Lord Aylesford, who was at Oxford rather earlier, he was his most celebrated pupil, as Malchair himself was to acknowledge. Unfortunately, none of the resulting drawings is known today. Although some may survive unrecognised among the many pupils' drawings preserved in albums at Oxford,[3] the absence of identified examples is puzzling, and, still stranger, only a few caricatures mark the years between 1772 and 1777, in which latter year a visit to the Lake District with Hearne and Joseph Farington stimulated him afresh. Malchair's teaching may have needed time to assimilate, but it is hard to believe that Beaumont ceased drawing, least of all in the summer of 1773 when he stayed with Davy and met Farington for the first time. Already an important topographical draughtsman, Farington was in East Anglia with the publishing magnate Josiah Boydell to make drawings of the Walpole collection at Houghton for a series of engravings. Beaumont accompanied them on a visit to the house for which Davy had

5. Oldfield Bowles: *Self-Portrait in Van Dyck Costume*, early 1770s (Private Collection).

assembled a large party; as Thomas Coke was of its number, perhaps there was also a visit to Holkham, his future seat. Farington was to be a key figure in Beaumont's association with artists, not only becoming a friend and an avid chronicler of his doings and opinions, but also influencing his style as a draughtsman. Above all, as a pupil of Wilson, Farington formed another link with the painter who was to become one of Beaumont's two or three most important artistic mentors.

Among Beaumont's many pleasures at Oxford was the company of the Bowles family at North Aston, north-west of the city. Despite his rotund and rustic name, and appearance to match, Oldfield Bowles was a worldly and sophisticated man, very comfortably off, with estates in Jamaica as well as in Oxfordshire, and a cultivated amateur of the arts. Fourteen years older than Beaumont, he was a friend of Malchair's and shared all Beaumont's love of painting. A supposed self-portrait (Pl.5) illustrates his artistic interests, showing him in Van Dyck dress with one of his own pastiches of Richard Wilson on an easel. He divided his life between London and North Aston, where, in addition to farming and horticulture, he had collected pictures, a notable library and musical instruments — in exchange for one of which Gainsborough was to give him a landscape[4] — and had fitted up a painting room.

North Aston was a model for the future Coleorton, a convivial meeting place for professionals and amateurs from the world of arts and letters, but it was probably more welcoming as there were three generations of Bowleses to make it informal and a little eccentric, whereas Sir George and Lady Beaumont would have only themselves. Above all, it offered a private theatre, the host's solution to the problem of entertaining his guests in the dull Oxford countryside. North Aston gave Beaumont perhaps his first chance to relax in mixed company — it was in 1773 that Davy referred approvingly to the 'young ladies of North Aston'[5] — and it became virtually his second home for some years, providing him with many friends and, a little later, with his wife.

An *habitué* of North Aston was Wilson's other pupil, Thomas Jones, whose *Memoirs* provide the clearest picture we have of the agreeable hospitality and sometimes rather demanding entertainments Bowles offered his guests. Life was not without its dramas, Jones being despatched out hunting despite his inexperience, and, having survived that ordeal, being nearly asphyxiated by the fumes from the unfamiliar paints he had to use for stage sets in Bowles's theatre. Jones first visited North Aston early in 1772 as Bowles's painting tutor, and Bowles, given 'a little cooperation and assistance', made such progress that — slightly to Jones's chagrin — he was judged to have 'surpassed his master' in paintings exhibited at the Society of Artists in the spring of 1773.[6]

October 1772 found Bowles's friends fitting up the theatre for its opening and the following year Beaumont's name appears in Jones's list of 'principal visitors who made a temporary Residence at North Aston this Season', together with a note that he was among the chief performers on the stage.[7] Guests included Bowles's two fathers-in-law, Sir Richard Bampfylde and Sir Abraham Elton, and their families, as well as his sister and brother-in-law, the Grahams. Among the spectators were Sir Charles Cotterell from Rousham, and Mr Page, the Member of Parliament for Oxford. The players, mostly the younger generation like Beaumont, came prepared for their parts and the three programmes comprised the most popular pieces currently playing in London. When all was ready, local farmers and neighbours were invited to a dress-rehearsal of *The West Indian* by George Cumberland with a short accompanying piece, *The Upholsterer*; and at full moon on 6 January 1774, 'the Theater was opened to the Nobility and Gentry of the surrounding District...above twenty carriages attended upon the Occasion... The Oxford band of Musicians who had been with us during the holydays, began with a grand Overture, and when the Performance was over, a genteel cold Collation was provided for the Company, who departed highly pleased and gratified.'[8]

The band was presumably Malchair's, and it must have been a cheerful party over Christmas and New Year with hunting available for those who enjoyed it. Theatricals continued ambitiously, much attention being paid to scenery and costumes. The new standard of staging set by Philip James de Loutherbourg at Drury Lane Theatre for David Garrick was probably a spur, but it comes as a surprise to learn that the amateurs also copied the professionals in offering two plays in an evening, following their opening programme with *The Merchant of Venice* and Garrick's *Lethe*, and then Nicholas Rowe's *Fair Penitent* with Samuel Foote's *Mayor of Garrett*. The next season was more modest, *The Mayor of Garrett* being performed again as well as Ben Jonson's *Every Man in his Humour*. Members of the University and local gentry were sent tickets for a performance on 23 December 1774, six weeks after Beaumont's coming-of-age.

Gentlemen Artists at their Studies

6. (?) George Dance (ascribed to Beaumont): *Gentlemen Artists at their Studies*; *Caricatures of Beaumont and Bowles*, pencil (Yale Center for British Art, Paul Mellon Collection). Caption on facing sheet reads: 'That Artist sure can never fail, / Whose lip is longer than his tail. / For fame that Artist bids most fair, / Whose eye brows rise into his hair.'

For Beaumont life at North Aston revolved around the stage and the painting room. Not only was his host already a gifted painter, a status to which he now aspired, but there was the added attraction of Jones on hand as a teacher. The lively caricature sketch of *Gentlemen Artists at their Studies* (Pl.6), probably by George Dance, must surely refer to this period when Beaumont slipped away to Bowles's painting room whilst his contemporaries went hunting. Jones himself was remarkably active, producing during this period some nineteen pictures, including a commissioned view of Rousham for Sir Charles Cotterell, a copy after Wilson, and his masterpiece of historic landscape, *The Bard*, which he presented to Bowles as what he called 'a retributory offering' for all the kindnesses he had received (Pl.7). It was about this time that Beaumont first began painting in oils, presumably in a Wilsonian manner, and although, as with his early drawings, the evidence is lost, it was no doubt the recollection of a familiar style that prompted Wilson's pupil, Farington, to remark some years later that the best oil he had seen of George's was one of 1775.[9] Certainly Jones approved whole-heartedly of the young man who was thrown so much into his company, for a long time afterwards he recalled their meetings to Uvedale Price with obvious affection. 'Do you know Squire Jones of Penkerrig?' Price asked Beaumont teasingly in 1795. 'He knows you though, and very well too, and has been a great deal in your company, and sees you act, and paint and do a great many clever things...you saw him at North Aston.'

7.   Thomas Jones: *The Bard*, 1774 (Cardiff, National Museum of Wales).

Beaumont could hardly have forgotten Jones, that 'honest Welch runt', in Price's words, 'who was a pupil of Wilson's and his face as red as his master's'.[10] In fact, as Jones's *Memoirs* establish, Beaumont's first meeting with Jones occurred most probably in London in June 1772 when Beaumont 'bespoke a picture' of Jones,[11] apparently his earliest purchase from a living artist. In 1775 he made another acquisition from Jones, *Storm with a Scene from The Winter's Tale*, painted in collaboration with the artist's close friend, the history painter John Hamilton Mortimer, and intended originally for the dealer Weston.[12]

The extent of Beaumont's association with Mortimer himself is, like many aspects of that tormented artist's life, a mystery. Yet just as most of Beaumont's early artist-friends — Mortimer included — provided him with a lead to Wilson, so it is striking how often Mortimer tends to crop up alongside them. Certainly Mortimer, who had been made Vice-President of the Society of Artists in 1770 and was to achieve its highest office four years later, enjoyed greater *réclame* in London than did Jones, or even Wilson by this time, and would have come to Beaumont's attention at exhibitions and gatherings. Probably his studio was one of Beaumont's ports of call during his stay in London with Davy in 1771; and later, Beaumont, Davy and Mortimer — and indeed also Hearne — would have a mutual friend in James Jefferys, who was Woollett's pupil with Hearne that year. Both Mortimer and Jefferys shared Beaumont's love for the theatre, and the former's flamboyant personality and precocious talent might well have been attractive. But both men died young and Beaumont seems rarely to have spoken of either in later years, although in 1812 he did lament the lack of a biography of Jefferys. Davy would remain a link with Jefferys, but in the

18

8. John Hamilton Mortimer: *Salvator Rosa*, c. 1775, pen and ink (photo: Sotheby's).

end the main evidence for Beaumont's connection with Mortimer remains the sheer number of the artist's works in his collection — twelve drawings, all datable to the mid-1770s and presumably acquired at the same time. Together with the Jones/Mortimer *Storm* (perhaps bought with Mortimer's interests as much in mind as Jones's, the purchase being made a couple of days after Mortimer's marriage), the Mortimer drawings were among the earliest of Beaumont's acquisitions from a contemporary artist.

The drawings, formerly kept in an album and all known today, are fine and characteristic examples of Mortimer's sharp, sinewy manner in pen and ink.[13] They include two remarkably portentous and significant works, companion portraits of a capricious and emotive character, both of artists — the one the young Salvator Rosa (Pl.8) and the other the aged Gerard de Lairesse. They were among the first European representations of artists of earlier times and their interest for Beaumont must have been partly art historical, since Rosa was then passionately admired by the connoisseurs and Lairesse was the author of that famous book on artistic practice and theory, the *Groot Schilderboek*. Rosa is portrayed as a bandit, and four more of the Beaumont drawings were of *banditti* and another of their captives, while four others were examples of Mortimer's other speciality, monsters. Finally, there was a drawing of a fishing boat beached in a gale, an exercise in the Sublime in the style of Rosa and C.J. Vernet, not to mention the young Wilson. With hindsight the Mortimer purchase — or was it a gift? — reflects a tendency on Beaumont's part towards the grotesque and extravagant that was typical of the taste of the time; but also a certain historicism that is rarer and altogether more advanced.

In later years there was to be something of this historical sense in Beaumont's deliberate references back to the examples of Wilson and Reynolds, part of a conscious and calculated pride in his status as a link with the past. For the time being, however, Wilson and Reynolds were natural lodestars in the circles Beaumont was moving in. Mortimer certainly knew them both, being 'intimate' with Wilson, according to Angelo;[14] and it cannot be chance that his drawings in Beaumont's collection formed the subjects of four out of the fifteen etchings published after Mortimer and dedicated to Reynolds in 1778.[15] Another contact with Wilson, besides Woollett, Jones, Farington and Mortimer, was Bowles himself, who owned several of Wilson's paintings and painted in Wilson's manner under Jones's instruction. Exactly when Bowles acquired Wilson's sketchbooks, one of which he gave to Beaumont in 1784,[16] is not known, but he may well have been the 'gentleman' whom the portrait painter William Beechey took to visit Wilson just before he left London for his retirement in Wales, and who bought 'all his sketchbooks' in order to provide the painter with means for his journey. 'Young man,' Wilson declared, 'I may never see you again, but depend upon it you will live to see my pictures rise in esteem and price.'[17] If there is any substance at all in this prediction, its realisation must be largely due to Beaumont, to Farington and a handful of other sympathisers.

By an early date Beaumont owned at least three oils by Wilson: *On the Arno, Strada Nomentana* and *Lake Nemi with two Friars*; and there was also the *Lake Avernus* he gave Constable in 1812.[18] Wilson's biographer, Thomas Wright, claimed that Beaumont was actually a pupil of Wilson, but this is unlikely in any literal sense. Beaumont's reminiscences of Wilson focus more on the artist than on the man, and he knew him well enough to tell him that he thought him a better painter than Claude — evidently Beaumont was then hardly more cautious in judgement than when he had preferred Hearne to Poussin — and to hear Wilson's tributes to Claude and Cuyp in reply.[19] At some time in the 1770s, probably around the middle of the decade when Wilson became Librarian of the Royal Academy, Beaumont made the caricature of Wilson now known only from an etching by Thomas Hastings (Pl.9). The painter appears in profile to emphasise his swollen, bibulous nose, but the satire is kindly rather than cruel, like the teasing Wilson was subjected to by students such as Rowlandson and John (Jack) Bannister — both then studying at the Academy before the latter had embarked on his theatrical career. Bannister later gave Beaumont a perfect mimicry of Wilson at his post in the Library: 'The librarian's voice was no less gruff than his manner. Wilson, hobbling round the Library table and suddenly stopping. "What are you about, Sir? What are you doing?" "I am sketching Sir." "Sketching! Take your hands off the book, boy." "And what are you about?" (addressing another). "Drawing from this print." "Drawing! Don't paw the leaves, Sirrah. You'll spoil the book. What — have you got eyes in your fingers, boy?"'[20] Certainly Beaumont was allowed no illusions as to Wilson's love of the bottle. No mean drinker himself at this time in his life, he had, as other humorous drawings show, an earthy frankness about such indulgences — there is a sketch of an artist vomiting in his studio, a landscape

9. Thomas Hastings: *Caricature of Richard Wilson*, 1824, etching, lettered: *traced from an original sketch made from life by Sir George Beaumont now in the Possession of R. Ford Esq.* (London, British Museum).

abandoned on his easel, that seems hard to reconcile with the mature Beaumont — and he would later entertain a more polite generation with such stories as Mortimer's insulting, and surely scarcely sober, remark to Dr Arne (told to him by Wilson), that the composer had eyes like 'two oysters just opened for sauce put upon an oval side-dish of beetroot'.[21]

*   *   *

By the mid 1770s Beaumont was spending more time in town, having taken lodgings in Bond Street. A London life was expected of a gentleman of his background, and he enjoyed the fashionable pleasure-grounds like Ranelagh and Vauxhall as well as the regattas and masquerades then in vogue. There were also the lures of the exhibitions at the Society of Artists and the Royal Academy and, even more powerful perhaps, of the theatre. 'You know the passion I always had for the stage,' Beaumont wrote to Bannister in 1820; 'the stage, therefore, with all its appendages, stands prominent among my most pleasing recollections. Garrick, Grand Seignor, stands at the head.'[22] Throughout his life Beaumont was to be accused of having heroes, and Garrick was always his *ne plus ultra* on the boards. He was already a lover of Shakespeare and Garrick's interpretations, as he told Joseph Cradock in 1826,

> made such an impression on me then that at the distance of half a century, every look, attitude and gesture is here before me; every tone and variation of his rapid and energetic voice rings in my ear at the present moment. In short for the last seven years of his bright career, I never missed seeing him if it were possible. His Lear, Hamlet etc; are so impressed upon my memory, that I can see him perform them in my 'mind's eye' with almost the effect of actual presence.[23]

And two years earlier, Beaumont had written in a similar vein to George Agar Ellis:

> Garrick is before me at this instant; I see his quick eye, and hear the electric tones of
> his piercing and rapid utterance. Other actors are men of slow proceedings; but he
> was like the lightning. It is quite impossible to form an idea of the sensations he
> conveyed, whether he chilled you with horror, or convulsed you with laughter.
> Other actors may be compared to Otway or Rowe; but Garrick alone was
> Shakespeare.[24]

When Beaumont was in London with Davy in the spring of 1771, Garrick was ill
and did not perform until the following year, but Beaumont may already have seen
him in his Shakespearian entertainment *Jubilee*, devised for Stratford and brought to
Drury Lane for the winter season of 1769–70, when it ran for a record ninety
performances. Two more of Beaumont's early stage favourites were Charles Holland,
whose last role was as Richard III in *Jubilee* in 1769, and Holland's close friend James
Powell, part-owner of Drury Lane, who played the lead in John Hoole's *Cyrus* before his death in May of the same year. This is probably evidence enough to date
Beaumont's first London theatre season to the year he left Eton, and throughout his
life he never faltered in his interest in the leading players. Ned Shuter, a member of
the rival company at Covent Garden and perhaps the greatest comic genius of the day,
was prone to invite so many people backstage that they got in the way of the actors,
and it is tempting to imagine Beaumont in the throng. With only two theatres
licensed for the winter season it was never easy to get in at all, so Beaumont would
bribe the attendants to admit him early to the pit and, when the doors opened, would
pretend to be as hot and bothered as those who had pushed their way through.

In 1771 Beaumont could also have seen Charles Macklin in his favourite role as
Shylock before the actor departed for a prolonged stay in Ireland. Other names that
occur in Beaumont's reminiscences are Thomas King (then a principal in Garrick's
Drury Lane company and later, in acknowledgement of help given when he had ruined
himself by gambling, to remember Beaumont in his will), James Dodd, Charles
Bannister, William ('Gentleman') Smith and William Parsons. The latter, like the
younger Bannister, Jack, was also an artist — in 1773 he exhibited a London view at
the Society of Artists — and joined Beaumont on the occasional sketching trip like
the one to the Spaniard's Inn, Hampstead, early in 1776, when they were accompanied by Woollett and also by Hearne, who was just back from his sojourn in the
Leeward Islands.[25] Although Beaumont met Smith briefly at Woollett's, this fellow
Etonian, who made a controversial marriage to a peer's daughter, became a friend only
after retirement, when Beaumont's letters to him at Bury St Edmunds reveal
Beaumont's overriding passion for Garrick and preference for the 'old school', and for
'Garrickean galvanism' compared to the 'measured steps, superexalted looks and
something approaching recitativo' of later performances.[26] As for actresses, Beaumont
took little notice of them until Mrs Siddons at her peak proved more attractive than
her brother, John Kemble. Although Beaumont made a sketch of the young Kemble,
in his eyes perhaps only Edmund Kean managed to take over Garrick's mantle — an
achievement Beaumont must have intended to mark quite literally when he presented
him with a Spanish cloak in 1814.

Beaumont knew Garrick in his last days at Drury Lane when his appearances were fewer and further between, especially in the Shakespearian roles that were taxing for a man approaching sixty and suffering from gravel and the stone — quite apart from the nervous strain of constant off-stage dramas with his termagant leading ladies. But when in 1774 Beaumont and his fellow amateurs from North Aston were preparing Jonson's *Every Man in his Humour*, he would surely have taken the chance to see Garrick at his best as Kitely, with King and Parsons in supporting roles, and, in 1775 when Beaumont played Hamlet, it was through his good offices that Garrick intervened personally, not only lending his own dreadful adaptation of the play that 'suited their small force better than the original',[27] but securing them a box for his own performance on 29 November when he was 'never better' in the part. Beaumont must have studied his hero's every move, and was tempted on occasions to identify himself with Hamlet, taking more pleasure in meditation than action,[28] while Smith was later to refer to reports of Beaumont as 'a perfect dramatic representative of the Prince of Denmark'.[29]

The following year, 1776, 'Old Drury' theatre saw Garrick for the last time in all his most famous roles. The young Mrs Siddons joined him on several occasions to a chorus of disapproval, and it is doubtful whether Beaumont was among the minority who recognised her talents so early. Certainly he would hardly have missed a performance, least of all Garrick's final Hamlet (with Mrs Smith as Ophelia) on 30 May, when tickets were required even for the pit and sold at a guinea instead of the usual three shillings; or his rather eccentrically chosen valedictory as Don Felix in Mrs Centlivre's *The Wonder* on 10 June. Tears flowed throughout the house as Garrick struggled with his farewell speech and Beaumont was not alone in thinking that so heady an experience could never be matched. He was to meet Garrick just once more, the following May at a performance of *School for Scandal*.

When Old Drury was demolished in 1791, Beaumont tried to obtain a piece of board from Garrick's stage on which to paint a picture, but as he told Jack Bannister, 'some unlucky Marplot found out the stage had been new floored since his time, and the thing dropped'.[30] However, in the spring of 1776 there had been an opportunity not only to secure a better memento of Garrick, but also to commemorate his own amateur performance in Garrick's *Lethe* at North Aston. When a pair of paintings by Johann Zoffany of scenes from *Lethe* in its 1776 revival appeared at Christie's — surely a shrewd move on the part of the vendor — Beaumont bought them. One shows Garrick as Lord Chalkstone, Ellis Ackman as Bowman and Astley Bransby as Aesop (Pl. 10), and its companion shows Bransby in the same role, Walker as the Servant and Beaumont's other friend Parsons as the Old Man. These, probably Beaumont's second major acquisition of English paintings, were bought for their subject rather than their artistic quality — considerable though that is — and remained for some time rather isolated in his collection. At some point he acquired another Zoffany, of Macklin as Shylock, but if one discounts the incident from *The Winter's Tale* introduced by Mortimer into Jones's *Storm* which Beaumont had obtained the previous year, and Haydon's altogether exceptional *Macbeth* with which Beaumont became lumbered in 1817, only Robert Smirke's two oils of scenes from Foote's *Taste* and from *The Taming of the Shrew* could count as fit companions to the Zoffanys.[31] It may seem curious that one so infatuated by the stage did not add more examples of theatre genre to his collection, but even Thomas Lawrence's and Reynolds's portraits of players in character apparently failed to tempt him. His explanation was quite simple: he had

10.   Johann Zoffany: *David Garrick as Lord Chalkstone, Ellis Ackman as Bowman and Astley Bransby as Aesop in 'Lethe'*, c. 1766 (Birmingham City Museum and Art Gallery).

seen so many interpretations that it was difficult to settle for any one of them; hence, as he told Haydon in 1807, his own struggles in painting scenes from Shakespeare.

*   *   *

The 1776–77 season at North Aston opened in a new theatre. To release space in his house for his growing nursery of children (eventually to consist of seven daughters and one long-awaited son), Bowles had moved his stage to a nearby barn, and the result was 'very spacious and elegant — with Scenery, Decorations and Habits... uncommonly splendid and entirely new'. Beaumont spoke a prologue by the Poet Laureate William Whitehead, catching both the enthusiasm and the inevitable bathos of ambitious amateur theatricals:

> Sure some infection hovers in the air!
> For every man and woman is turn'd play'r.
> No age escapes it — antiquated dames
> And reverend Romeos breathe fictitious flames;
> Pale misses antedate love's future force,

And school-boy Richards lisp — 'A horse! — a horse!'
No rank escapes it — with a Garrick art,
Right honourable Hamlets stare and start...

For the occasion the company offered 'a novelty indeed — a virgin play'. This was *The Siege of Scutari*, a tragedy by Edward Taylor, a somewhat precious character who from the age of thirty had spent his life at Steeple Aston in the pursuit of 'elegant literature'. Beaumont took the role of Cadwallah in the companion piece, *The Author*, by Samuel Foote, who had played the role that summer at the Haymarket with Aickin and the elder Bannister, Charles. Once deflowered, Taylor's play was never heard of again and the praises it drew sound faint compared to the adulation so often accorded to amateur productions. But, unlike the London pit, this audience came to enjoy rather than crab an entertainment that was offered by friends whose dress was as elegant as the setting, and that, at worst, provided an amusing talking point during the ensuing 'collation'.

This year and next Bowles's theatre season began earlier, and on 7 November 1777 Beaumont played in *The Merchant of Venice* and *Lethe* followed by a revival of *Hamlet*. On 21 November Rowe's *Jane Shore*, with Mrs Bowles in the title role, was accompanied by Garrick's *Bon Ton*. Not content with this, the amateurs also gave *Macbeth* and it was when Beaumont took the title role that he caught sight of his future wife in the audience. Margaret Willes, one of the three daughters of Bowles's neighbour John Willes had come over from Astrop Manor for the play. The romance blossomed and the following spring they were married.

The young man who embarked on courtship in 1777 was much changed from his earlier self. Since his coming of age in 1774, the house at Dunmow had been his together with a small increase in income, and with adequate means he was free to indulge his interests. His success on the stage had also given him confidence, for anecdotes of the mid-decade show him in quite a new, if fleeting, light as a practical joker and wit. One such anecdote, related by the artist James Northcote, involved Beaumont's advertisement of a new method of portraiture discovered by a German, whereby the sitter's likeness was purportedly taken on glass that had been heated sufficiently to take an impression. Having given the address of a perfumer's opposite his Bond Street lodgings, Beaumont spent the day watching credulous callers until the shopkeeper lost patience. In another story, he went with friends to dine at a tavern, and while the waiter held open the coach door, lighting the way with a candle, those who got down first slipped round in the shadows and climbed back into the coach from the other side, eventually terrifying the servant with the seemingly limitless numbers emerging from the vehicle.

It was probably one of Beaumont's fellow jokers, George Huddesford, who fostered the remaining and greatest blessing of his youth, the friendship of Sir Joshua Reynolds. As a boy, Beaumont may have met Reynolds during the holidays with his mother, for, in August 1767, the painter had visited Lord Maynard at Easton Lodge. Huddesford, a fellow of New College in 1771, would have been in a position to sustain this link, as he was briefly Reynolds's pupil. Besides painting portraits, Huddesford experimented with still life, examples of which display his talent for painting peaches. He was afterwards to presume a little on his friendship with Reynolds, flattering him almost to mockery in a satiric poem, *Warley*, published in

1778 ostensibly as a review of the militia in Essex. Dedicated to Reynolds, 'the first ARTIST in Europe', it showed a gift for poetry vulgar rather than pretty, and, though typical of the robust humour of its day, offended the more sensitive souls in Reynolds's circle. Huddesford was not altogether an attractive character but, perhaps because he never quite grew up, he was charming and funny and apparently as ready to take a joke against himself as to mock others. His features, which so resembled a horse that the wags of the day fed him oats through his letterbox and sent him to George Stubbs for his portrait, are preserved by Reynolds himself in a double portrait of 1779.[32] Huddesford's companion is his friend, the ill-fated poet, John Bampfylde, who was afterwards forbidden Reynolds's house for his unwelcome pursuit of the painter's niece, Mary Palmer, and was later to become bankrupt and insane, only regaining stability while dying of consumption in the 1790s. Beaumont knew him as a brother of Charles, a fellow actor at North Aston and kinsman of Bowles by his first marriage, and Lady Beaumont later wrote of him: 'a more artless unworldly soul never breathed'.[33] Reynolds shows him reflective and sensitive, whereas there is something sardonic, even sly, in Huddesford's equine face.

It seems ironic that Beaumont's friendship with Reynolds could have come through such a source, but it flourished none the less. For Beaumont, at first, it was probably attractive for social reasons, since through Reynolds he could meet many of the leading intellects, actors and literati of the day, as well as a number of other admiring lordlings; but he soon transcended the role of young admirer and entered Reynolds's deeper confidence. According to John Croker, for example, Reynolds gave Beaumont a manuscript copy of his squib, *Johnson and Garrick*, a satiric recreation of their manner of conversation that was later published—surely a memento of times spent together.[34] Beaumont would always retain his regard for Johnson, even amusing friends like Samuel Rogers by writing an epitaph in the manner of Oliver Goldsmith's *Retaliation:*

> There Johnson reclines in this grave, den or pit
> The bugbear of folly, the tyrant of wit...
> And if modestly silent, his censure to balk,
> He exclaim'd in a fury, Sir, why don't you talk?
> If you said black was black, still his answer was, no, Sir,
> And thundering arguments follow'd the blow Sir,
> For tho' lies he abhor'd from the days of his youth
> Yet the doctor lov'd victory better than truth...[35]

But by the date of this composition (1805) Coleridge had persuaded Beaumont that Johnson's writings were outdated and so much 'verbiage'.[36]

Although usually very secretive in such matters, Reynolds undoubtedly discussed aspects of his technique with Beaumont and advised him on his own painting, and more anecdotes survive of such talks with Reynolds than with Wilson. But the conversation was sometimes frivolous and it was probably only later that Reynolds began to take Beaumont seriously. 'Mix a little wax with your colours,' he is supposed to have advised Beaumont; 'But don't tell anybody.'[37] On another occasion when Beaumont had remarked that some medium recommended by Reynolds would crack, the great man retorted: 'All good pictures crack.'[38] And there is also Haydon's story which originated from Beaumont of a deluge of soot falling on a picture left by the fire

11. Joshua Reynolds: *Miss Bowles*, 1775 (London, Wallace Collection).

to dry, whereupon Reynolds, declaring 'A fine cool tint', scumbled it into the flesh tones.[39] In short, Beaumont could better learn technique elsewhere; and far more than his studio practice, regarded as dubious even in his lifetime, Beaumont soon came to value Reynolds's historical judgement, which he could observe in evolution since these were the years when Reynolds was delivering his Discourses at the Royal Academy. It was Reynolds who had the intellect to interest Beaumont in cultural history, and over the years he became a conscious disciple of the master, imbibing his tastes and his hierarchical, rather Olympian approach to the history of art, and adopting his mission to establish a British school of painting in the tradition of the old masters.

Fittingly, it was on Reynolds's behalf that Beaumont first exercised entrepreneurial artistic judgement of his own by persuading Bowles that Reynolds should paint his small daughter Jane. Inclined to favour George Romney because of the reputation of Reynolds's pictures for fading, Bowles was convinced by Beaumont that this was a small risk compared to the acquisition of a masterpiece; and so it turned out. The child was introduced to Reynolds at a luncheon in London in the spring of 1775 and was charmed by his amusing ploy of hiding her plate and smuggling it back again when she was looking away. Reynolds caught her gleeful expression perfectly and the finished picture is among his finest child-portraits (Pl. 11).

27

12. Thomas Hearne:
*Beaumont and Joseph
Farington sketching a
Waterfall*, c. 1777, pen,
ink and wash (Dove
Cottage Trustees).

1777 was Beaumont's last year as a bachelor and he again joined his old friend
Hearne, who was now working with William Byrne the engraver on a series of views
for *The Antiquities of Great Britain*. J.C. Brooke reported to the antiquary Richard
Gough that 'Hearne travels with Sir George Beaumont, a young Leicestershire
baronet, who has a great taste for drawing.'[40] In fact, no Beaumont drawings survive
from this tour and some idea of the itinerary must be gained from Hearne's numerous
subjects in Yorkshire and Cumbria, where Farington was now living. They got as far
as Warkworth in Northumberland before returning through Yorkshire and Notting-
hamshire. This was Beaumont's first sight of the Lake District, which, in the coming
years, was to win his heart. He was again working in oils, as we know from two
drawings by Hearne, formerly in his collection, of him and Farington painting the

28

waterfall at Lodore (Pl. 12). Painting *en plein air*, on the substantial canvases Hearne shows, was then distinctly unusual and could only have been inspired by the example of Wilson and perhaps of Jones.

Apart from the advanced practice recorded here, Hearne's drawing might appear to show the archetypal gentleman-amateur of the eightenth century, and under certain conditions this is just what Beaumont would have become — what his father's generation would have called a virtuoso, a man of many parts, with artistic and literary tastes, and respectable but forgettable talents. Such, in the end, was Oldfield Bowles. That Beaumont became so much more than this, putting his abilities and patronage to work in a committed and even passionate manner, and developing art-historical discrimination and connoisseurship as refined as any in his generation, must be owing most of all to the subtle, sophisticated, but friendly guidance of Reynolds of whom he was to see more and more in the coming years. Reynolds gave Beaumont's life its purpose, and lent pattern and context to the various interests and friendships he had discovered thus far. It was a revelation. No wonder Reynolds remained his hero of heroes; and well might Wordsworth, in the lines commissioned from him for the cenotaph Beaumont raised to Reynolds's memory at Coleorton, describe Sir George as

> From youth a zealous follower of the Art
> That he professed; attached to him in heart. . .

But these things come slowly, and for the time being Beaumont's heart was engaged elsewhere.

13. Joshua Reynolds: *Lady Beaumont*, 1780 (Collection of the Helen Clay Frick Foundation).

III
AFFAIRS OF THE HEART

WHEN SIR GEORGE and Lady Beaumont walked down the aisle of St George's, Hanover Square as man and wife on a May day in 1778, it was the beginning of a long and devoted partnership that was to bring most of life's blessings except children. Society weddings were quieter in those days and no newspapers recorded them, but the marriage certificate and the wordy marriage settlement — ironically dedicated largely to providing for the next generation — furnish the names of the main supporting cast. The Revd Charles Davy took the service and on the bride's side were her parents, Frances and John Willes, John being the son of the former Chief Justice of the Common Pleas, Sir John Willes. This controversial figure, who was satirised by Hogarth in *The Bench* and whose manipulating character is revealed in Thomas Hudson's portrait,[1] owed his advancement to Robert Walpole but switched allegiance to the Pelhams and then to the elder Pitt in an unsuccessful bid for a hereditary title. His two elder sons followed him into the law and Parliament, and Horace Walpole records admiringly the manner in which John, in defence of his father's interests, put down an overheated Mr Pelham in a Commons debate of 1748. A filazer for Middlesex in the Court of Common Pleas, John had married Frances Freke, a Bristol heiress, and enjoyed a life divided between Astrop, near his first constituency of Banbury, and 29 Grosvenor Square, a house, long since demolished, at the south-west corner, now part of South Audley Street. While his son, John Freke Willes, was to inherit Astrop manor, his daughter Margaret, 20 years old at her marriage, was one of three girls each to receive £5,000 in their father's will, an advance of £2,000 now being made to her, together with £200 for 'wedding clothes and ornaments'.

Acting for Beaumont was Thomas Bridge, an elderly Dunmow solicitor from a firm that survives in the same premises today. Beaumont's contribution to the marriage settlement was £3,000 held on trust, with a provision for his widow of £400 a year from the Leicestershire estate, then producing an income of some £1,100 on which his mother already had a claim. John Freke Willes was joint-trustee with Bowles, who had virtually assumed the role of elder brother in the bridegroom's life, while Sir Edward Willes and Beaumont's uncle George, who enjoyed the Howland propensity for long noses and longevity, were also signatories.[2]

The wedding party gave Dame Rachel an opportunity to meet some of her son's London friends. By all accounts he was now a popular young man and had been a distinctly eligible bachelor, for he did not drink so obsessively as his bottle-companion, Charles Howard, the future Duke of Norfolk, nor gamed like Sir Charles Bunbury, nor considered himself to smell of violets like 'the omniscient baronet',

Sir Henry (Harry) Englefield; and his talents on the stage had brought him recognition as a leading amateur actor and a good deal of female admiration. His family must have been grateful that he had been spared the fate of his boyhood friend and neighbour, Charles Maynard, who was absent from the wedding having recently made a notable *mésalliance* soon after inheriting the title from the first viscount. His choice of partner, Nancy Parsons, or Mrs Horton as she had mysteriously become, was bizarre in that she was nearly twenty years his senior, had enjoyed attachments to divers dukes, including Grafton and Dorset, and had already lived for some time as Maynard's mistress at Takely on the Easton Lodge estate. During the winter of 1778 on honeymoon in Naples, 'poor simple Lord Maynard', as Horace Walpole dismissed him, enlisted the help of the first Lady Hamilton in a vain attempt to get his wife received by the Queen of Naples, herself sufficiently *galante*. Where pleasantries failed, powders succeeded, for by dispensing the English cure-all, James's mixture, during an aristocratic epidemic, the Maynards established themselves in favour at the Neapolitan court. Even so, the marriage was an awful object lesson, its *dénouement* surpassing the most pessimistic forecasts, with Nancy eventually eloping to France with her husband's valet who later murdered her for the Maynard jewels.

The new Lady Beaumont was a refreshing contrast: pretty and rather fragile in her portrait by Reynolds of 1779 (Pl. 13), she was a great trier, for not only did she join in the next North Aston theatricals but was later described by Miss Mary Hartley to her friend, the Revd William Gilpin, as a 'young woman with some genius and a prodigious eagerness for knowledge and information', who was 'always learning something' but was 'not negligent of her toilet'. Fluency in French and Italian was to be amongst her accomplishments; she was a lover of literature and it was quite a feather in her cap when she could claim friendship with the learned Mrs Elizabeth Carter; and although she never developed powers of composition, she was able to sketch a likeness and copy drawings. Her eagerness, sometimes open to ridicule, was to remain her principal characteristic and she shared most of Beaumont's enthusiasms, for, as Mary Hartley continued rather cattily, 'her greatest object seems to be the preservation of her husband's affection'.[3]

She need hardly have worried, for she was to be nearly the perfect companion. Her upbringing had been less provincial than Beaumont's but probably stricter, and she matched traditional Tory inclinations with an upright morality and strong faith that sometimes verged on the prudish. Yet there was already a hint of that freer spirit that Wordsworth and Coleridge were to appreciate — one that could swiftly soar beyond its bounds and tremble with romantic ardour. She told Coleridge that, as a girl, before saying her prayers, she had tried to think of 'a mountain, or a river, or something *great*, to raise up her soul and kindle it', and the need to be stirred never left her. She dreaded the commonplace as only those brought up to it can, and, as Coleridge told Wordsworth, 'one may wind her up with any music, but music it must be, of one sort or other'.[4] Her husband could show her new worlds, and must have known she was made to share them; in fact, he was sometimes surprised how eagerly she grasped them, for she had the nervous energy that he lacked and an intensity that sometimes embarrassed him.

Before the young pair met in November 1777, Sir George had already planned an excursion north with Hearne, who was to continue his drawings of castles and abbeys, and this now became a honeymoon. Most of the time was spent in the Lakes, travelling in a post-coach-and-four with Lady Beaumont's maid and a footman in attendance. Hearne joined them at the end of June, for he told J.C. Brooke in September that they had all been away two months. They had moved on to Scotland, visiting Dumbarton, Glasgow and Edinburgh during August and September; Stirling was probably their final stop, and Hearne was to dedicate his view of the windings of the Forth from Stirling Castle, published in *Antiquities of Great Britain*, to Beaumont. His text recalled what must have been a favourite spot: 'The extraordinary views... are not to be described in words...they are magnificent and sublime.'[5] Hardly any Beaumont drawings survive from this tour save for one made at Ambleside in June and some feeble wash sketches of Glasgow and Dumbarton dated the end of August. But no doubt Farington, who was working on a series of drawings for his *Views of the Lakes*, published in 1784, provided encouragement as Beaumont continued his struggle to paint from nature in oils, and from this visit developed the *View of Keswick* that Beaumont sent to the Academy as an honorary exhibitor in 1779.[6] This picture, exceptionally large for him, was so severely criticised that it was fifteen years before he could bring himself to show again.

The summer was such a happy one for the Beaumonts that they were to return again and again to the Lakes, which later became the scene of some of the most intense friendships and experiences of their lives. Although there was now a steady stream of visitors to the area — 'the Tour of the Lakes', according to the *Monthly Magazine* in 1778, being 'the *ton* of the present hour' — this was still far from the conventional holiday it was to become, and Hearne, Farington and now Beaumont were among the earliest artists to devote sustained attention to the district. Although roads had improved, the tribulations of travel were still considerable and Lady Beaumont's aversion to inns, to which Uvedale Price referred later, probably dated from her honeymoon. In 1769 Thomas Gray had fled from Ambleside where the best bedchamber was as 'damp and dark as a cellar', but, fortunately, for a longer stay it was comparatively easy to rent a house. For their honeymoon the Beaumonts were at Lodore Inn near Keswick but in later years they took and furnished Old (then Low) Brathay, a small house near Brathay Hall, which itself was then only a farm dwelling. Old Brathay belonged to Mr Braithwaite who lived on Esthwaite, which Sir George was to draw in 1780. The approach to this southern end of the Lakes was from Hest Bank, north of Lancaster, across the sands to Kent's Bank and Allithwaite — a route with magical views to the Langdale Pikes north of the estuary, whose shifting sands added a spice of danger to keep the traveller alert when the soft seabed might have induced slumber after days on the bumpy road. From Allithwaite there was a good route alongside Coniston to Brathay, or alternatively west through Flookburgh to Holker Hall, the seat of an older friend, Lord George Cavendish, whose park was the starting point for another four-mile journey across the more treacherous Levens sands to the Furness peninsular with its abbey and Conishead Priory, both sketched by Beaumont and Hearne. The delights of the priory are evident from Thomas West's description in *The Antiquities of Furness* of Wilson Braddyll's house, built on the site of the ruins, with pleasure grounds sloping down to the sea. And if it should rain, there was 'the London of Furness' in the shape of Ulverston, only two miles away.

Beaumont, conditioned to the flat countrysides of Essex and Oxfordshire, found the Lakeland scenery astonishing, with it swiftly changing light — mist and rain giving way to gleams of revelatory sunshine with a suddenness that sharpened the vision. The mountains were to become his friends as the solitary side of his nature searched to identify itself with their mysterious majesty, and in these early years he was simply in his element. Lady Beaumont's pleasures were probably more literary: she would surely have read William Gilpin's *Observations*, printed only in 1786 but widely circulated in manuscript from 1772,[7] while Gilpin's tutor, Dr John Brown, had earlier offered a dramatic enough description to stir expectation: 'the full perfection of KESWICK consists of three circumstances, *Beauty*, *Horror*, and *Immensity* united...to give you a complete idea...would require the united powers of *Claude*, *Salvator*, and *Poussin*'.[8] Lady Beaumont's poetic tastes would have led her besides to Gray's *Poems* and his 1769 *Journal in the Lakes*, published with William Mason's memoir of the poet in 1775. This latter work greatly pleased Farington who, in 1800, staying with the Beaumonts in North Wales, was to make drawings from Gray's itinerary. In their honeymoon year Thomas West brought out his *Guide to the Lakes* which was to remain popular well into the next century, editions being revised by William Cockin. West took viewing the Lakes seriously, providing a list of 'stations' and promising tourists that they would get 'in miniature an idea of what they are to meet with there on traversing the ALPS and the APPENINES'.[9]

The incipient literary tradition of the Lakes as England's most sublime and Arcadian scenery must have been as powerful as the evidence of their own eyes as the Beaumonts explored and drew the district, little aware how soon it was to be transformed by the arrival of settlers from more sophisticated parts of England, notably Lord William Gordon and Joseph Pocklington, and of others who flocked there for the season. In 1798 Beaumont was to sketch the unobstrusive, single-storey house built by Gordon on Derwentwater[10] as the sort of design he would adopt himself if he built on Loughrigg Tarn and Gordon's good taste was in marked contrast to Pocklington's bombastic schemes, the first and most famous being his buildings on Vicar's Island (inevitably renamed Pocklington's Island).

According to Robert Southey, who knew them in later years, it was in 1778 when the Beaumonts had quarters in the little inn by Lodore Falls that Sir George embarked on one of his first and most remarkable acts of patronage. Hearne had been making some large and impressive drawings of the Lakes — *Derwentwater from Skiddaw* is a fine example[11] — which inspired Beaumont to commission him to paint a panorama of Derwentwater and the Vale of Keswick. That summer, Southey recalled, Hearne made 'a sketch of the whole circle of this vale, from a field called Crow Park. Sir George intended to build a circular banqueting room, and have it painted round the walls. If the execution had not always been procrastinated, here would have been that first panorama.'[12] The view from Crow Park, much admired by Gray and the subject of a large print by Thomas Smith in 1761, was indeed a specially beautiful one, but Beaumont's project was nevertheless an extraordinary tribute to both artist and landscape, for it was some time before the vogue for panoramas became established, the only immediately comparable scheme, William Locke's commission to George Barret for Lakeland decorations in a room at Norbury Park, coming several years later. Perhaps this was an intended commemoration of the honeymoon; certainly it was expensive, for Beaumont's account at Hoare's Bank, kept from 1777, shows an exceptionally large payment of £100 to Hearne in September 1778, presumably for his preparatory drawing which Southey described as 'preserved on a roll more than twenty feet in length'. Where the banqueting room was to be built is far from clear, as the humdrum rural life the Beaumonts were about to resume at Dunmow would scarcely have justified such luxuries. Not for the last time Sir George's heart had run before his head, but it had also placed him at the forefront of patronage and taste.

*   *   *

For Sir George the return to Dunmow after the honeymoon must have been his happiest homecoming since his mother's remarriage; and his bride was probably too excited to indulge any misgivings about her new life in Essex. She was already accustomed to living in a dark, Elizabethan house, but the Beaumont house was also haunted. The terrible death at the Tyburn stake of Ann Line is part of Dunmow history and the double chimney still exists in which she sheltered Catholic priests until her arrest during the celebration of mass on 2 February 1601. It is said that her presence continued in the house to the discomfort of its occupants up to the day of her recent canonisation, but her ghost, like Mr Gates, appears to have been a forbidden subject: none of the Beaumonts' visitors mentioned anything untoward, and even Coleridge, who would surely have made the most of such a phenomenon, found in the house 'nothing remarkable but its awkward passages'. It was a fairly cheerless place, with a whiff of the nearby tan-yard, and little changed since the lifetime of the previous baronet. Sir George, in love and delighted to have his wife all to himself, cared about little else than his painting room at the top of the house, and it was here in future years that he spent most of his time at Dunmow apart from riding in Maynard's park. This had now absorbed the Howland property, Stonehall, which was in due course to serve as a convenient woodland retreat for Edward VII and his friends staying with the Countess of Warwick at Easton Lodge.

It was as well for the Beaumonts that the Maynards were now in Naples, for, despite their husbands' friendship, Lady Beaumont could hardly have received the present viscountess. However, local company was even duller than in the previous generation, most of the good houses in the district being owned by prosperous city merchants who found it a convenient distance from the metropolis. Dame Rachel had been wise to forsake Dunmow for Dedham, a rich village only four miles from Colchester, with its own assembly rooms and more sophisticated entertainments. Joseph Gibbs, the Ipswich organist and friend of Gainsborough, belonged to the Gates circle, as did Joseph Eyre, a gentleman composer, and another interesting character was the picture collector, Jacob Hinde of Langham Hall. It was here that Sir George may have taken his bride when the Gateses leased it from its owner, who preferred a London life. While Dedham was some thirty miles east from Dunmow across the onionfields of Essex, other duty calls lay to the north — the Howlands fifteen miles away at Haverhill and Davy at Onehouse near Stowmarket, the smallest parish in England, to which he had moved in 1776. His younger son had died in India, but Charles junior, a fellow of Caius College, Cambridge in 1781, was introduced by Beaumont to the Ashburnham family who much later, in 1817, appointed him to the parish of Barking in Suffolk. Although old age at Onehouse was to be as lonely as it sounded, the old parson may have been fit enough to accompany Beaumont to the Lakes in 1777, for Hearne drew him amidst the ruins of Lanercost Priory, but a stroke was to reduce him to a cripple. His mind remaining unimpaired, he amused himself writing, and composing oratorios, one, *Balaam* of 1782, being dedicated to Lady Beaumont —

not a particularly auspicious gift for a young wife but then, nor could her husband have greatly enjoyed *Conjectural Observations on the Origin and Progress of Alphabetical Writing,* inscribed to him by Davy ten years earlier.

Fortunately, even during the early years of the Beaumonts' marriage they were able to enjoy many absences from East Anglia. In mid-April 1779 they were in London and Sir George, following the gruesome dictates of fashion, sketched 'from nature' the corpse of the unfortunate Revd James Hackman, hanged at Tyburn for shooting his beloved Martha Ray, the mistress of Lord Sandwich, in Covent Garden Piazza. A more attractive event was the Royal Academy exhibition. Even though Sir George's painting was ill received, there was Sir Joshua's portrait of Lady Beaumont, praised by the *Morning Chronicle* 'for the wonderful effect [that] excites fresh astonishment at the magic power of pencil of this artist'. Later, in July, the Beaumonts travelled through Leicestershire on their way to the Lakes but the sight of Coleorton apparently did nothing to attract them; it was, in fact, noticeably desolate to another traveller, John Byng, later Lord Torrington, who in 1789 remarked on the absentee landlords in a countryside blackened by pits. On this tour the Beaumonts spent 'many delicious hours' at Conishead Priory, while in September Sir George made a drawing of Borrowdale.

Lanercost was probably the most northerly point of the journey. By the middle of October they were again at Astrop, conveniently within reach of North Aston, where, after a break of a year, the theatricals resumed with a revival of *Jane Shore* and *The Author*, Lady Beaumont now joining the cast. These were played in the middle of December with tickets issued as before to house parties in the district and to members of the University.

1780 was to prove a more testing year. Mrs Willes became seriously ill at Astrop and died towards the end of February, her burial taking place in the parish church, King's Sutton. This left John Willes with his two unmarried daughters, and the Beaumonts were more welcome than ever, both in the country and at Grosvenor Square. Times were hard everywhere: while half the population of Dunmow was unemployed because of the decline of the East Anglian cloth industry, and the rector, the Revd John Howlett, became a leading pamphleteer, using his own experiences to counter the ruthless arguments of the political economists, in London a society long used to stability faced the traumatic experience of the Gordon Riots. A mob, which had first gathered on 29 May in support of Lord George Gordon's anti-popery petition to the House of Commons, besieged Parliament, then reformed on 6 June to begin a destructive surge through the city. Fortunately, Grosvenor Square was outside the danger area, but, as Charlotte Burney wrote to her sister Fanny in the middle of June, there was 'dreadful havoc and devastation in all parts of the town...everybody is wandering about in order to see the ruins of places that the mob have destroyed'; however, 'two camps, one in St James's, and the other in Hyde Park...together with the military law, makes everyone think he is safe again. I expect we shall all have "a passion for a scarlet coat" now.'[13] According to Horace Walpole, writing to Lord Harcourt, greater despair 'no mortal pen can describe, that has not seen a city taken by storm: yet who ever saw a capital of the size of London in flames in more than a dozen places and its own inhabitants rioting in every barbarity?'[14] Whereas his friend, Lord Algernon Percy, distinguished himself in defence of Northumberland House, Beaumont, who had no stomach for violence, appears to have avoided any form of fighting commitment, even though many young members of the nobility were already in the militia, having responded to the threat of invasion from France. Meanwhile, the American War of Independence dragged on, gaining little more than a despairing mention in many a diary filled with more pressing fears.

Valour apart, marriage had not diminished Beaumont's taste for male company nor for new experience, and he maintained his connections with artists of all sorts, partaking of some of their cruder entertainments which were to die out as society became more civilised and artists learnt to assume the manners of their patrons. 1779 had seen the premature death of Mortimer, his health broken by the irregular life he had lived a few years before, but Beaumont remained in touch with their mutual friend Jones, and in the autumn of 1781 Jefferys, Mortimer's other friend and disciple and Woollett's old pupil, was staying with Davy at Onehouse. The ailing clergyman's latest project to relieve the monotony of his life was an extra-illustrated version of the Prologue to Chaucer's *Canterbury Tales* for which he prepared the text and Jefferys made a series of drawings depicting most of the main characters. If Davy intended to burst into print again, the scheme foundered, only one of Jefferys's drawings being engraved; but the original volume was later owned by Beaumont and survives today.[15] Beaumont would have seen more of Jefferys when he returned to London, for the artist was then at Hearne's address, 1 St Martin's Street, Leicester Square. The distinctive style as a draughtsman and fondness for the bizarre that Jefferys shared with Mortimer were the stimulus to Beaumont's own occasional fantastic and caricature drawings, such as the placid Lakeland scene of 16 September 1780 in which a knight in armour advances to the rescue of a man in the grip of a viper, while a bear watches from behind a rock. (Pl. 14) Presumably this was in response to some romance such as Ariosto's *Orlando Furioso*, for evenings in the country were often passed reading poetry or plays.

14.   Beaumont: *A Soldier confronting a Man in the Grip of a Viper*, 1780, pen and wash (B.C.).

Beaumont had evidently never lost contact with Alexander Cozens, for he was a subscriber to the artist's *Principles of Beauty relating to the Human Head* published in 1778. Wilson was still in London, and friendship with Reynolds was deepening. In 1779 Sir Joshua accorded Beaumont the special mark of favour reserved for his richest patrons and best-loved friends, taking him as guest to the Academy dinner. In later years Beaumont was rarely to miss the occasion, but that night, as he watched his host in his presidential robes, he could scarcely have guessed that one day he would be spoken of — however lightly — as a potential candidate for the same office by the Academician, Richard Cosway, in 1807, and by the banker, Henry Hope. In 1778 and March 1779, Lady Beaumont sat to Reynolds (Pl. 13); her husband did not follow suit till 1787 (Pl. 25), but in 1780 he had his portrait taken by Daniel Gardner for ten guineas.[16] By now, the engraver John Raphael Smith was also a dining companion — a welcome one because he knew many of Beaumont's actor-friends such as Parsons and Bannister, and also kept an excellent cellar — and it was he who engraved Lady Beaumont's portrait in mezzotint. Smith's reputation was at that time far from pure and Lady Beaumont, who must have been shocked by the antics of her Dunmow neighbours, the Maynards, may well have looked askance at such bohemian friendships in London. But she remained outwardly sanguine, while like Gainsborough, whom he was also coming to know well, her husband allowed no prejudice to restrict a wide acquaintance. With Gainsborough there may have been an early and irreproachably respectable family link through Beaumont's older relative Isabella Howland, whose portrait he had painted in 1768. A common East Anglian background now drew them together in London, but their friendship seems to have ripened fully a little later, after the Beaumonts' return from the Grand Tour. Meanwhile, Beaumont must have enjoyed Bowles's visit to the artist's studio to select a painting in exchange for a violin, the landscape chosen having been exhibited at the Academy exhibition of 1781.

Lady Beaumont's readiness to throw herself into her husband's interests — since it was clearly not a sign of shallowness or foolishness — was a boon. Far from diminishing, Sir George's artistic career took on a new lease of life in the early years of his marriage. He was drawing more and more, not least in the Lake District where the couple returned in 1780 and again the following year, having rented Old Brathay. Society no longer consisted of only a few entrenched local families, and even these were probably better company than the moneyed merchants of Dunmow, for they cared deeply about the area and several were contributing as much as any outsiders to the growth of its Arcadian reputation. The Knotts at Rydal Mount — though they were to let the estate in 1782 — were cultured people who had in the 1770s planned to enhance the classic views from their house by building an obelisk on top of Orrest Head and a pyramid on Loughrigg, while nearby at Rydal Hall Sir Michael Fleming jealously guarded his ascendancy in the district. So sensitive was he that he was later to fall out with the Beaumonts over the purchase of land by Loughrigg Tarn, but for the time being he welcomed and entertained them. A pencil sketch by Beaumont of a lane and stone cottages, *Near Sir Michael Fleming's*, was dated 1781, and Rydal Hall, a many-gabled white house, appears in drawings by Beaumont (Pl. 15) and Farington, evidently taken from the same viewpoint and perhaps drawn side by side. Farington's drawing, in black chalk and stump in a distinctly Wilsonian vein, is dated 1781[17] and another of the same large size and technique depicts Rydal Lower Fall;[18] it is evidently

15.   Beaumont: *View of Rydal Hall*, 1780, pen, ink and wash (B.C.).

contemporary, and then, as in previous years, Farington probably stayed with the Beaumonts.

Farington's large drawings, together with Hearne's panorama from Crow Park, were no doubt the inspiration for several extensive Lakeland subjects by Beaumont, but more typical are those of modest size, showing a mastery of monochrome washes and a deft touch of the pen to heighten detail. These drawings are preserved in an album once belonging to Bowles,[19] who had perhaps joined the Beaumonts at Brathay while alterations were being made to North Aston by John Yenn, and they represent a period of intense activity between 22 and 31 August 1781. Unfortunately, none records Pocklington's first regatta on Derwentwater which took place on 28 August, perhaps because the weather was so appalling that its highlight, the mock attack on Pocklington's Island, fortified with cannon, by a fleet of rowing-boats and musket-carrying marines, was rained off till late evening. The opposing forces displayed the respective colours of the English and Dutch in commemoration of a recent battle off the Dogger Bank and, with the guns echoing round the lake, the spectators can have found little difficulty in experiencing the intended sensations of terror and horror before the defenders ended the 'attack' with a jolly victory salute. The Beaumonts may have been present at an even more ambitious performance in 1786 when they were based at Holker Hall at the southern end of the lakes, but the Pocklington era was over by the time they stayed at Keswick in the late 1790s, and his taste for sham heroics and ostentious buildings had become the object of some derision.

The winter of 1781–82 saw the last of the North Aston theatre company, Beaumont playing Jaffier in *Venice Preserv'd* to Mrs Bowles's Belvidera; and on 15 April both families were among 'the polished and refined audience from the Metropolis' who attended a performance of *The Mourning Bride* at Sir William East's private theatre at Hall Place near Birchetts Green in Berkshire. Among other keen 'dramatic amateurs' present was Harry Bunbury, who since schooldays had acted on yet another private stage, Wynnstay. The owner of Wynnstay, Sir Watkin Williams Wynn, was also present at the Hall Place party and a few nights later was himself one of the performers. On the evening the Beaumonts attended, an epilogue, written by 'the macaroni of the day', Captain Edward Topham, a popular wit and incorrigible gossip, was delivered by him in his characteristic, affected voice. A friend of Reynolds, Topham was later to keep a sharp but sympathetic eye on Beaumont's activities in his newspaper, *The World*, recording among other things the final eclipse of his acting career. But for the time being the evening at Hall Place is the last glimpse of the Beaumonts in England for more than a year, for they were already preparing for the Continent.

IV
THE GRAND TOUR

ITALY MUST HAVE been an enticing prospect for the Beaumonts in the early months of 1782, for spring came late, delayed well into May by cold east winds, and the news throughout the winter had been uniformly bad. Lord Cornwallis's surrender at Yorktown the previous November had signalled the loss of the American war, and after surviving a long period when nothing went right on land or sea, the Prime Minister, Lord North, appeared only too anxious to hand over the reins of government. The new Rockingham administration, taking over in late March, now had to recognise the independence of the former colonies and to recapture prestige by pursuing more vigorously the war against France, Spain and Holland. Then came the turning point in British fortunes: in the very week in mid-May that the Beaumonts sailed for the Continent, news arrived of Sir George Rodney's victory in the West Indies on 'the glorious twelfth of April'. The defeat of a French fleet by the overstretched British navy was so unexpected that a 'delirium of joy'[1] swept the country. In August Sir Samuel Hood was to capture more French ships, ensuring the safety of Jamaica, while in the Mediterranean Gibraltar was relieved. Peace negotiations took place while the Beaumonts were abroad.

Impetuous in his enthusiasms, Beaumont was slower to act, and it was characteristic of him to leave his grand tour until rather late when, under the influence of Reynolds and inspired by the recollections of Wilson, he might have set out for the Continent at the earliest opportunity. Nevertheless, the timing was to prove happy: not only were Thomas Jones and other friends also in Italy, but, having made progress with his own painting and drawing, he now went to Rome as much the aspiring artist as the incipient connoisseur. With his wife at his side, he was the very antithesis of the boisterous young Englishman who regarded travel as an opportunity to drink his way round Europe in company with his fellow countrymen. The Beaumonts looked forward to their tour both as an enlivening experience and as a second honeymoon. After four years of marriage, and with no offspring, their round of East Anglia, London, the Lakes and Oxfordshire was becoming a trifle monotonous, and Sir George had made no effort to involve himself in the business of his Leicestershire estate — an omission he was later to regret.

The Beaumonts' route to Switzerland, where they planned to spend the summer, may have reflected the uncertain times: instead of the short journey to Calais, they took the packet to Ostend. After a wait at Dover for a favourable wind and tide — a process that could take up to a week — the passage of twelve or fourteen hours began. For Beaumont it proved a traumatic one that laid a shadow across the rest of his life. The trip was rough and windy and, as he told David Wilkie in 1807, 'I caught a cold. . .and I verily think I feel the effects of it to this day; certain it is a fever succeeded which reduced me to a mere skeleton, and I could not entirely get rid of it all the time I was abroad.' He paused to recuperate at Ostend, a pleasant enough town, although William Beckford, who also arrived 'in piteous condition', had condemned it as a 'scurvy place'. Probably because they had brought their own carriage, the couple continued 'the land-way' rather than by canal to Bruges and Ghent, reaching Antwerp by 21 May. Here they stayed at the Bear where the land-lord 'studies to oblige the English', and Beaumont drew 'the fine and large crucifix of brass on a marble pedestal',[2] one of the features near the inn in the great street or *Mère* along which carriages paraded in the afternoon. If confined to his room, he would still have been able to see what little life there was in a town that struck many visitors as uncannily quiet; but, guided by a *valet de place*, he probably struggled to see some of the pictures recommended by Reynolds from his 1781 visit, including Rubens's *Descent from the Cross* in the cathedral.

To reach Antwerp the Beaumonts had crossed the Schelde by ferry after travelling through country reminiscent of the Romney Marshes, and the road on to Brussels, running alongside the canal, was just as pleasant with views of Villevoorden Castle, where the Duke of Cumberland had camped in the 1770s, and of the villas in the neat Flemish countryside. The entrance to the city was through a tree-lined avenue that led to the Grande Place. The Beaumonts would have had introductions to the best collections, which they were to see during their 1785 visit, and the playhouse was recommended; but they were in no mood to tarry. On 25 May they were in Brussels and by 5 June they had reached a point on the Moselle between Pont à Mousson and Metz. Few drawings by Beaumont exist to indicate their route there, but they did follow the well-trodden road through the university town of Louvain to Liège and thence to Chaud Fontaine, 'a romantic spot in the style of Matlock' and in similar country. Perhaps they paused briefly at Spa, where the English assembled ostensibly to take the waters, but also to gamble; by 17 June they were in Schaffhausen, some three miles above the Falls of the Rhine, which Beaumont drew that day. Whether owing to his illness or to his natural reaction to this 'hell of waters', as *Murray's Guide Book* was to describe them in 1838, his sketch is but a weak rendering of a water-splash, and there are no more drawings until 5 August when the Beaumonts were in Lausanne on their way to Geneva.

In a normal year Geneva would have been an early port of call, for Marc Théodore Bourrit, a minor artist whose *Glaciers in the Dutchy of Savoy* had been introduced into England by Davy, was precentor in the cathedral. That June, however, the republic was in a state of revolution until two of her protecting powers, France and Berne, intervened to restore the old patrician oligarchy; and Bourrit, who liked to call himself grandiosely 'historiographer of the Alps', and whose eccentricities included sleeping under a walnut tree in his garden with a fur coat in July and coatless in January, may well have been at his chalet in Chamonix as, in 1782, he was writing up a journey to the Great St Bernard.

Bourrit did not aspire to the level of the scholarship that was being contributed to geological studies by his aristocratic rival Professor Horace Benedict de Saussure, but he was accepted as the first artist to record the mountains accurately. Strangely, however, it had been a young Englishman, William Windham (later to marry a Dunmow widow and to father William, the politician) who had first aroused the

Genevese to take an interest in their own mountains by an adventurous journey to the glaciers above Chamouni in 1741. In the wake of subsequent explorations by de Saussure, Bourrit and others, Chamouni had been transformed from an isolated Savoyard settlement into the first mountain tourist village, with inns to house hundreds of visitors each summer.

Whatever Beaumont's opinion of Bourrit's paintings, which by all accounts bore the stamp of the miniaturist, he would have been flattered by the reception the alpinist reserved for the English aristocracy — evidently the precentor was something of a snob — and infected by his genuine passion for the Alps. The Beaumonts may even have had his company for part of their excursion from Geneva — made by chaise through Bonneville to Sallenches. Here it was necessary to transfer to a *char à banc*, a simple plank contraption, designed for the narrow road that had now left the Arve valley and was contained by mountains rising perpendicularly on each side. As they made their precarious progress, Sir George could have reflected on nature's supremacy over art, while Lady Beaumont found the mountains — the *'great* things' of her childhood imagination — realised before her.

Chamouni was the centre for expeditions, a favourite one being to the source of the Arveiron in the Glacier de Boisson, where an astonished Miss Berry, Horace Walpole's friend, 'stood upon blocks of ice that had fallen. . . from the great body of the glaciers which rose on one side like an immense wall. . .while on the other the river rushed from under its blue cave over masses of rock and ice'.[3] More strenuous was the ascent of Montanvert (at that time considered a mountain), which, if the weather were kind, afforded superb views of the surrounding peaks, including L'Aiguille de Dru and Mont Blanc. During Beaumont's second visit to Switzerland in 1819, it was these 'Gothick towers', and the Mer de Glace, that inspired some of his finest drawings, and to Wordsworth he described Mont Blanc as 'glory in the abstract', surpassing even his memory of earlier years.

August was the ideal month for such excursions and the Beaumonts must have enjoyed being in the vanguard of the tourist invasion, for they were already connoisseurs of mountains, Sir George at least viewing them with quite a modern eye and conceding little to the current preoccupation with the Sublime and the consequent passion for horror and terror. In any case, not only Bourrit, but also the Alpine views taken by William Pars that Beaumont would have seen being engraved by Woollett in 1773, had prepared him for something of what he was seeing. Nor was Lady Beaumont one to cower before precipices and cascades when taken to explore isolated mountain villages, though she was probably relieved to find country-house life on the shores of Lac Leman quite familiar, for society there included many English families attracted by the mild climate and — if, as often, they were invalid — good doctors. The prospect of crossing the Alps always aroused apprehension (even though the only English casualty that century seems to have been Horace Walpole's spaniel, snatched by a wolf), but even this part of the route had improved immeasurably in the past forty years.

The Beaumonts were in Chambery, the point of departure for Italy, on 24 August, having visited Aix to inspect the baths or try the waters, which one traveller had found had 'a sulphurous smell not much less disagreeable than Harrowgate'. Beaumont's strength had not been properly restored by his two months in Switzerland, and he was still liable to succumb in hot weather. Whether or not his chill had been connected with the epidemic of 'flu' that swept Europe that year and often developed into a pleurisy, fevers and malaise recurred for most of his life. Old age was to bring some relief, but meanwhile his debilitated system appeared to respond best to change, be it of doctor or scenery. In the event he survived well the journey into Italy, the first part of the trip over the Alps to Turin being completed in the customary seven or eight days.

The smaller Savoyard villages through which they passed were bywords for poverty and overnight stops were far from enjoyable. Transport also now became more arduous: near Modane the road grew exceptionally steep with 'a tremendous precipice on one side' and then, in the words of an earlier traveller, Lady Anna Miller, zig-zagged like the 'lacings of an old fashioned stomacher'. At Lanslebourg, a village that appeared as 'if by some vast concussion a number of entire cottages had been thrown against the mountains',[4] a carriage could go no further and had to be stored against the day of return, or dismantled and carried by mule. The tourists themselves were conveyed at dawn by porters who ran rather than walked, outpacing any Englishman who preferred to trust his own feet. Having started at five in the morning, by eight they reached the plain, remarkable for the variety of its flowers, though the cold often made breakfast a more pressing prospect. Certainly Beaumont allowed little time at Mount Cenis for his sketch of the inn, La Grande Croix, which was famous for trout from the lake and good mountain wine. At this isolated spot there was also the house of a hospitable priest where Beaumont's friend, Lord Algernon Percy, had spent the three summer months of 1770 in search of health, with only a horse and some sporting dogs for company. In those earlier days travellers such as Lady Anna had felt decidedly nervous on the descent but, by the 1780s, although steep, 'the way was wide enough to admit half a dozen chairs or mules abreast', and the threat of being bumped off by a beast of burden no longer prevented enjoyment of the 'sublimely beautiful' views. At Novalese carriages were reassembled, post-horses hired with *vetturino* and the journey continued into Turin on a good road across cornfields planted with mulberry trees until a fine avenue of elms led into a large and bustling city.

The Beaumonts would have had all the introductions they wanted in Turin from Louis Dutens, who had divided his recent years between the Duke of North-umberland's family (he had conducted Lord Algernon Percy round Europe in 1768) and Lord Mountstuart, envoy at Turin. Apart from the Italians' 'odious custom of making use of the corners of landing places', most of the English enjoyed Turin, finding the palace of the Dukes of Savoy, with its ornamented front, impressive, whereas, at this time, the King's palace appeared unfinished for want of stucco. Beaumont made a drawing of the Capuchin monastery and no doubt had time to admire the theatre, which was grander than anything in England but unfortunately had performances only during the carnival.

Armed with Lalande's *Voyage en Italie*, one of the popular travel books of the day, the Beaumonts may have bypassed Milan whose cathedral was described by Lalande as 'd'un gothique assez laide' and where Leonardo's *Last Supper* was in a wretched condition. By 15 September, having taken the direct route through Piacenza and Parma, they had completed the journey of some 200 miles to Bologna, then as notorious for its thieves as for Italy's other leaning tower. Here Sir George made some slight copies after Guido Reni, including one after his *Apostles Peter and Paul*.

From Bologna the Beaumonts faced the journey across the bleak Appenines, often made from Pietramala by moonlight, then at last they found themselves descending into the lush groves and vineyards of Tuscany. Surprisingly, they allowed themselves less than a week in Florence, despite the attractions of churches and galleries, and the legendary hospitality of Sir Horace Mann, the British envoy in Florence, for they were soon off again through Perugia and Spoleto, where Beaumont made a quick sketch on 25 September.

The Beaumonts were now intent on getting to Rome as fast as possible, exhausted by changes of frontiers, currency and post-horses, quite apart from bug-infested beds and indifferent food in roadside inns. Sir George probably sighed with relief as he sketched a 'Post house 3 posts from Rome', and the final lap of the journey was completed with all possible despatch. Like most visitors from northern Europe, the Beaumonts' first real sight of the Eternal City was the vast arena of the Piazza del Popolo with its twin churches, obelisk and overhanging gardens of the Pincio, crowned with stone pines and still swimming in the glow of late summer. Thence it was but a short ride to the English quarter around the Piazza di Spagna, and nearby, under the Pincian Hill, was Margherita's, lodgings, popular with the English, which the Beaumonts made their headquarters.

They were doubtless too tired to embark at once on a full exploration of the city but Sir George relished the opportunity to walk round an area rich in artistic associations, to find in the Caffé degli Inglesi at the foot of the Spanish Steps such artists from England as were then in Rome. But the heat proved too much for him and the existence of only one, rather limp drawing of the Forum or 'Campo Vaccino', done after his arrival on 7 October, speaks volumes. The Beaumonts wisely decided to defer Rome a little longer, and by the 17th they were higher and cooler, at Albano in the Alban Hills.

A fortnight here among these picturesque slopes, their sides covered with olives and vines, or with dense, evergreen forest, and descending at intervals to the lakes of Albano and Nemi, or to the dry valley of Ariccia, was a marvellous tonic. Beaumont was busy drawing — his old teacher Malchair was later to be greatly moved by his sketches of Ariccia — and he had regained strength enough to swim. Nemi indeed, was almost his undoing, for so eager was he to dive to its depths that he plunged in with a stone attached to himself by a rope to further his descent, and, having hopelessly underestimated the depth of the water, would have drowned had he not managed to unhook the rope before losing consciousness — hardly the act of an invalid.

Back in Rome around the end of the first week of November, the Beaumonts settled in their lodgings for the winter. Margherita's, well placed for English neighbours, enjoyed panoramic views across the rooftops of Rome towards Trajan's column and the dome of St Peter's. This was a skyline Beaumont drew from his window on two occasions the following spring (Pl. 16). Rome itself was by no means an unmixed blessing. In an advanced state of decadence, it was a city in which *virtù* was rarely synonymous with virtue, and it was apt to appear squalid, smelly and mean as often as it impressed by its grandeur and scale. Poverty was rife in the Papal States, and the splendour of the Vatican could scarcely conceal the incompetence and corruption of its administration. The Roman patriciate, also, was in sad decline, the ceremony maintained by a few families like the Borghese standing in sharp contrast to the ignominious decrepitude of lesser noblemen who eked out existence in cold and

16. Beaumont: *Rome, 'from the Window at Margaritta's . . . April 19–[17]83 Saturday*, pencil (B.C.)

battered palaces, letting rooms, selling pictures and even, as we know from Thomas Jones's *Memoirs*, pimping their daughters. But none of this could detract from the splendours of art and antiquity, and for the Beaumonts, as for all their countrymen, Rome worked its magic in the end.

Good company helped. Society was more important for the Beaumonts than for some of the younger Englishmen who passed through Rome with their tutors and were as likely to escape, when heated by Roman wine, to Casanova's brothel as to more respectable evening entertainments. For the sprigs, the language barrier was hard to surmount; if grand enough, they might be invited to the great Roman houses, but there they often huddled in groups, carping at the company, and on their walks on the Corso, they mainly met each other. The Beaumonts probably looked indulgently on their *gauche* ways, for fortunately they had their own circle. The had now met for the first time John Hamilton, already describing himself as D'Hamilton, Comte Héréditaire d'Abercorn.[5] This pompous personage, who later inherited a splendid house in Grosvenor Square, was to share Beaumont's interest in politics, and at Stanmore Priory offered the most elegant theatricals of the early 1800s. Old friends in Rome included Lord Algernon with his wife, much liked, who was to produce a daughter in the following winter, and Lord St Asaph, destined to become the Percys' son-in-law some twenty years later.

These proved excellent companions for the Beaumonts, and as Lady Beaumont made it her business to master Italian and Sir George had become a passable speaker

46

they could enjoy also evening *conversazioni* in Roman society. To these they were more suited than the young Englishmen, for unmarried girls and any refreshment stronger than ices and lemonade were excluded, while cards were played only at the *conversazioni di seconda sera*. But if these gatherings suggest extraordinary restraint, the Beaumonts soon found it disproved it at the opera, for here the rich Romans behaved abominably even by London standards, arriving late and chattering when not amused by their favourite *castrati*.

The artistic interests of the English in Rome were looked after by a group of self-appointed guides. Often failed artists — Gavin Hamilton was the notable exception — they acted as bankers, agents between patrons and other painters, and *ciceroni* to the monuments and antiquities. Nearby in Piazza di Spagna lived James Byres, as erudite as he was boring; and more grandly on the Corso — at least when not at his spring residence at Castel Gandolfo — was Thomas Jenkins, more likeable but perhaps less honest; there was little to choose between them. Although Jenkins was the more amusing, he had recently been largely ostracised by travellers and by the English artists for whom he used to give huge Christmas dinners, having been caught trying to sell some dubious drawings by his late friend Anton Raphael Mengs at greatly inflated prices; 'since then, *he* has been invisible to almost all the English', one of them observed acidly of him. Byres was also later to tarnish his reputation by some slightly shady practice over the sale of Poussin's *Seven Sacraments* from the Boccapaduli family to the Duke of Rutland.

Contemporary morals were flexible, of course, and none of this impugned the very real connoisseurship that men like Byres and Jenkins had built up. Gavin Hamilton was shortly to publish his important contribution to art history, the *Schola Italica Pictura*, and, in so far as the Beaumonts fell into the hands of any *cicerone*, it was probably his, for years later Sir George was to remember him above the others when talking to Charles Eastlake in Rome, recalling especially Hamilton's memories of the painter Orizzonte, who, in turn, claimed to remember Claude. However, Beaumont also saw Rome with Jacob More, a landscape painter as renowned in England as in Rome, thanks partly to assiduous self-promotion — even Reynolds being persuaded that More was the finest painter of air since Claude. More knew everyone in Rome; as well as painting, he was remodelling Prince Borghese's gardens — part of a grandiose redevelopment of the Villa Borghese which also included Gavin Hamilton's redecoration of a room with a series of pictures of the Trojan War. More's picturesque landscapes with their Claudian overtones and suffusion of Italian light made perfect furnishing pictures. Beaumont lost no time in reserving one, and his accounts show payments to More maintained into the 1790s, long after his return to England, while the artist continued to send him advice on painting. As his taste matured, Beaumont grew tired of More's work, and his private admission that he thought Robert Freebairn, who also worked in Rome for many years, a better painter, seems the *reductio ad absurdam* of More's exalted self-esteem. But for the time being More was an ideal companion for a visitor to Rome who wanted to paint as well as to learn, and as he loved to work in the open air, Beaumont could accompany him on his painting expeditions.

Beaumont's taste still inclined first to landscape and, apart from Hamilton, he made little attempt to seek out subject painters, of whom there were fewer than in the previous decade when the brilliant generation who centred around Henry Fuseli was working in Rome. In his sketchbook Beaumont continued to cast the odd wry glance at comical priests or elderly ladies — thus unwittingly preserving the bent for caricature that had infected the English in Rome from Reynolds to Thomas Patch and was more often directed against their own kind than against the natives — and even attempted the academy figure, perhaps at the French Academy in the Villa Medici which held good life classes. More seriously, he did his duty looking at the Carracci, Raphael and Michelangelo (later he was to kindle the enthusiasm of the young Thomas Lawrence by his account of his own first impressions of the Medici Chapel) and he must have watched Hamilton working on his pictures for Prince Borghese. But fundamentally he did not change his taste. Standing before Domenichino's *Last Communion of St Jerome*, what struck him was 'the finest landscape background in the world',[6] and the impression, which remained for many years, is telling.

Like Jones before him, Beaumont saw Italy first through the eyes of Wilson, but there were others besides More who could refresh or modify that vision. Among them was More's friend Philip Hackert, whose classic landscapes with atmospheric lighting were no less celebrated throughout Europe than More's. Although Hackert was generally despised by English painters, his friend Goethe recalled him always surrounded by English people, leading groups of amateurs on sketching expeditions, and holding evening drawing classes around a lamplit table when 'all competed in handling the lead pencil and sepia', while an *abbé* stirred their imagination with readings from Tasso.[7] Beaumont may well have been part of this most agreeable of academies, and his earlier trip to the Alban Hills may have been made to follow up an introduction to Hackert, who 'readily admitted' foreign visitors to his house at Castel Gandolfo.

The freer and looser handling of some of Beaumont's drawings from later in his Roman stay suggests that he also knew the landscapist and topographer Carlo Labruzzi, whose contacts among the English were to lead to a commission from Sir Richard Colt Hoare in 1789 to accompany him along the Via Appia and record the sites *en route*. Labruzzi, like More, was a committed *plein-airiste*, and, unlike More's, his drawings showed it. Another and very different painter, who certainly gave Beaumont lessons in Rome, was the Venetian, Antonio Zucchi, husband of Angelica Kauffman. In a letter to Uvedale Price, Beaumont recalled how 'this great castle-maker' worked:

> His mode [was] to draw first a bold and raised outline of the rocks, mountain or eminence on which the castle was to stand [then he] added his castle; you will be surprised to find how the image is assisted by this practice and what towers, battlements and projections are suggested by it...I always observed that his building was more varied and picturesque in exact proportion to the taste and happiness [with which] the foundation was struck.[7]

Here, then, was a pull in a more old-fashioned direction, and in some respects an echo of Alexander Cozens's teaching — an evocation of a capricious and decorative landscape that had little to do with real nature.

Apart from More and Hamilton, the most eminent British artist resident in Rome was Allan Ramsay, by now retired from portrait painting and absorbed in archaeology and pamphleteering. During the winter the Beaumonts and their friend St Asaph saw quite a lot of him, and it was Ramsay's precocious thirteen-year-old son who recorded

17. Beaumont: *An Antique Sarcophagus, 'Palatine Hill'*, pencil (B.C.)

in his diary in December the arrival of the watercolourist who was to be perhaps the greatest formative influence on Beaumont, Alexander Cozens's son John Robert. J.R. Cozens had with him three volumes of drawings, made in Naples where he had been working for William Beckford. Beaumont had plentiful opportunity to study them, and from this period dates his lifelong admiration for Cozens's work. Its impact was soon to be diffused into his own; he was to acquire some important Cozens water-colours as well as tracings after a number of his compositions and at least one rare oil; and he would later support Cozens during his sad final days.

Under these benign if varied influences Beaumont spent the winter agreeably enough, drawing and sketching around Rome when the weather allowed. The number of surviving drawings is not particularly large, but if this suggests a leisurely passing of time rather than any real commitment, the impression would be unfair. Beaumont still showed more dedication than natural talent and may well have felt rather bedevilled by the various styles to which he was being exposed. Hardly surprisingly, his Roman views fluctuate between them, sometimes tight and finicky, at others loose to the point of vapidity; on the one hand the product of serious looking, and elsewhere adhering to picturesque formulae. The common denominator is almost always monochrome, none of Beaumont's Roman mentors having managed to lure him into confident use of watercolour; and generally the most effective of his drawings from this period are those which still recall Wilson, whose own dislike of coloured drawings was axiomatic. The unaccompanied use of chalks or pencil in Beaumont's drawings is often very Wilsonian — as in a study of a sarcophagus (Pl. 17) — and this is combined with Wilsonian composition and staffage in a group of larger drawings in pencil and wash, of uniform size and on prepared grey-washed mounts, such as *The Banks of the Tiber*, drawn on 23 February 1783. The date on this and similar drawings like *The Palace of Nero*, made the previous November, implies study from nature, but the subjects are brought firmly within the classical conventions.

Some carefully prepared but evocative drawings, which suggest a more serious attempt to preserve a finished record for himself, rather of the kind that Wilson had

49

prepared for Lord Dartmouth or Cozens had made for Beckford, show Beaumont at his most committed (Pl. 18). It must have been under Cozens's influence, perhaps combined with that of yet other landscapists, such as Louis-Rodolphe Ducros, then working on paper on a giant scale, that Beaumont graduated to a few very large landscapes in blue and grey washes, among the finest of which is an undated view of Tivoli from the following spring (Pl. 21), displaying a breadth of handling, freedom from outline, and sensitivity to Italian light that mark a distinct advance.

A few oils also survive from during or just after this Roman stay. They are very consistent in style, based on Wilson in their broad, saturated brushwork, and from time to time on Claude in composition. They usually developed from drawings, as in the case of the effective and atmospheric *View of Rome from the Villa Mellini*, dependent on a squared drawing dated 6 March 1782. Some smaller oils, however, such as a pair showing Ariccia and S. Lorici, have the appearance of being sketched from nature. These Italian scenes served for many years as subjects for pictures; as late as 1806, Beaumont exhibited a *Lake of Albano* that must have been based on his sketches made there in October 1782, and the exact chronology of his Italian oils is impossible to establish.

Hard as Beaumont worked at his art, there were many distractions in Rome quite apart from the winter chills and rain that kept even professional artists confined to the brazier at the Caffè degli Inglesi. There was picture-gazing in galleries and churches, and some attempts at purchase — at least once on a grand scale, for, through More, Beaumont attempted to buy certain of the Claudes that belonged to the Barberini family. Like most of his generation, he had conceived a passion for Claude while in Rome, treading in his footsteps as an ardent pilgrim and even copying his memorial inscription in Sta Trinita dei Monti — actually a piece of serendipity, for when he later returned to Rome, he found the tablet gone. Prince Barberini seemed amenable to a sale and had already despatched at least one of his Claudes, the great *Seaport with the Embarkation of St Ursula*,[8] to England, but a further deal was frustrated by the machinations of some Italian middle man, for later, when Beaumont did succeed in buying his first example of the master, More wrote admitting he had discovered the Barberini sale was 'an intended trick which is too much the practice in this country; Mansotti must either be a fool or concerned in it'.[9] Instead Beaumont contented himself on this occasion with less ambitious acquisitions, prints of Piranesi and — like many of the English who passed through Rome — a gem by Nathaniel Marchant, in this case a 'head of Castor' based on one of the antique statues of horse-tamers on Monte Cavallo.[10]

There was no lack of social life. Beaumont sketched the Portuguese Ambassador, and in mid-December, when the duc de Chartres visited Rome, and the great cross in St Peter's together with much of the rest of the church and its piazza were specially illuminated, young Ramsay observed the Beaumonts watching the spectacle with Lords St Asaph, Algernon Percy and Shaftesbury and 'almost all the English'; and, when early spring brought the climax of the Roman season, he glimpsed them at balls and masques like the Festino at the Aliberti theatre when the Pope's niece was 'dressed in a Turkish habit and had a great quantity of jewels in her Turban'.[11] On this occasion the Beaumonts were accompanied by St Asaph, Hackert and Cozens. They were also present at the various ridiculous masquerades in the Corso when it was the custom to 'throw a handful of little white balls...full into the faces' of friends,[12]

18.   Beaumont: *View of Rome*, pen, ink and wash (B.C.).

competing carriages entering into pitched battle; the carnival terminated in the race of riderless horses down the Corso.

The English community thrived on scandal and gossip, when not creating them itself. The Beaumonts were deprived of the antics of the Bishop of Derry who happened to be in England in 1782, but were on hand to watch the romance between the poet Vittore Alfieri and Louise of Stolberg, Countess of Albany, who had deserted her husband, the Young Pretender, Charles Edward, and was living under the protection of her brother-in-law, Cardinal York, at the palace of the Cancelleria. The Cardinal's belief in the innocence of the association was shattered by what he learned on a visit to his furious brother in Florence in April, and Alfieri found it wise to leave Rome. Artistically this was no great loss in Beaumont's view, for, having attended some of Alfieri's tragedies written on the day of performance, he found them 'pedantic and uninteresting'.[13] It was the man rather than his work that was attractive and the English were fascinated by his role of *cavaliere servente*, Lady Beaumont and her friends preferring to see it as entirely one of *convenance*; while distaste for the bloated wreck of a man who, but for divine providence and paternal stupidity, might have been their king, warmed them to the Countess. Only a few years ago it had been unwise to be too closely associated with the Stuarts in Rome for fear of being dubbed a Jacobin spy, but events had overtaken these prejudices.

News from outside Rome was sporadic and came mainly through Mann in Florence. English papers were slow to arrive and were passed eagerly from friend to friend. Lord

North's speeches on American independence and the signing of the Peace of Versailles bringing peace at last between France and England, caused a stir, but Italian news usually had the more immediate impact, particularly when it was as dramatic as that of the appalling earthquake and floods that struck Calabria in February. The Beaumonts were particularly alarmed, for they planned to visit Naples in March. Reports were confused but spoke of tremors in the city and the Neapolitans fleeing their homes, and although the real zone of destruction lay far to the south, the Beaumonts were apprehensive as they set out from Rome. But the journey, across the Campagna over the Alban Hills and down the coast past Terracina and Gaeta, was a beautiful one, and on 8 March Beaumont drew Naples spread before him untouched and basking in the spring sun.

In the autumn on the Bourbons, Naples was usually an alluring city, larger and more metropolitan than Rome, once again with an established English community, presided over by Sir William Hamilton. The envoy's first wife, cultured and kind, had long extracted a certain decorum from the mixed bag of expatriates, refusing to receive Lady Maynard and restraining the passions of Beckford; but the previous August she had died, leaving her disconsolate husband to pursue his archaeological researches and his obsession with the eruptions of Vesuvius. Emma Hart had yet to enter his life and Neapolitan society was uncharacteristically calm, only the horrific news from Calabria, which Sir William was about to investigate for himself, shaking it with rumour of ghastly deaths and miraculous survivals.

As the Beaumonts allowed themselves little more than a week in the city, they had scant chance to cultivate acquaintance with Sir William, but no doubt they paid their respects to this most hospitable of diplomats at his villa; and in Naples they found Jones and delivered a packet sent with them by Cozens. Once again Beaumont had an old friend to guide him, and the day before he left Naples, he and Jones 'went

19.   Beaumont: 'Near the Scola Virgilio – coast of Pausilippo', wash (B.C.).

20. Beaumont: *Tivoli April 27 {17}83'*, pencil and wash (B.C.).

21. Beaumont: *Tivoli*, pencil and wash (B.C.).

together by Sea to Marechiaro, Gajolo, &c on the Coast of Pussilippo [*sic*] to take Views and make Studies', some of which survive, Beaumont's drawings being similar to those of his companion (Pl. 19). In Jones's painting room Beaumont 'took a particular fancy' to an unfinished view of Velletri, painted earlier at Rome, and asked for a companion piece;[14] Jones gave him the former, but asked to be excused from the commission until he returned to England, for he was suffering from the 'Swiss Malady'. Another day, attracted as ever by the mysteries of deep water, Beaumont had sketched Lake Avernus during a visit to the Phlegrean Fields, and he must also have visited Agnano which the King of Naples kept covered with wildfowl for hunting, and near which was a site popular with tourists, the 'Grotto del Cane' with its 'cruel and silly experiment performed on a dog'. Inevitably the Beaumonts made an expedition to the foot of Vesuvius, of which Sir George made a drawing, but they may not have had time to climb by mule and on foot across the lava fields and up to the crater; instead Sir George paused again to draw on the way back to Portici, where there was a museum of relics found nearby at Herculaneum, which, like Pompeii, was a great attraction.

The Beaumonts left Naples on 23 March, thus missing two more earthquake shocks five days later; it was probably the threat of these that had decided them not to tarry, and indeed instead of its usual entertainments the frightened city had already been offering 'the head of S. Gennaro exposed at the Cathedral with other marks of public humiliation' to ward off disaster. Halfway back to Terracina, Beaumont stopped to sketch the ferry over the Lirio, and on the next day, 24 March, Terracina itself with its brooding cliffs. By the beginning of April they were installed again at Margherita's.

Beaumont had been particularly busy with his pencil in Naples, and now, aware that time was running out, he was hard at work in Rome. During the first fortnight in May, the Beaumonts removed to Tivoli (Pl. 20) where the Villa d'Este with its glorious gardens and the Villa Adriana were favourite subjects, and he drew a panoramic view from the window of his room as he had at Margherita's. His Tivoli studies led to the large wash drawing already mentioned (Pl. 21), replete with the influence of Cozens who was at Tivoli at the same time.

To avoid the full heat of summer, the Beaumonts at last set out for home near the end of the month, their parting made more bearable by anticipation of a few days in Venice. Save for Beaumont's sketch dated 27 May, there is little enough to record their first impressions of a city of which he was to write most movingly in his later visit in 1821. Like most tourists, they completed the homeward journey much more briskly than the outward; sketchbooks were hardly produced at all except at Como and Constance, where perhaps they paused as much for swimming as for the scenery. The Alps loomed before them as a powerful reminder of the journey ahead, and Beaumont seems not to have put pencil to paper again until aboard the boat from Calais to Dover — proof that the return crossing at least was calm.

V
THE DISCIPLE OF SIR JOSHUA

THE BEAUMONTS WERE not to return to Italy until 1821, when Sir George was acting *cicerone* to his heir. With hindsight it is hard to over-estimate the effects of his first European tour in sharpening his critical standards and imbuing him with a golden vision of the old masters, but for the time being the memories and impressions of more than a year of travel needed time to assimilate. They did not immediately change his life.

The last vestiges of his provincial upbringing had disappeared, but their passing brought an insistent question. With many advantages, and more absorbing interests than many acquire in a lifetime, Beaumont yet lacked direction. Had he paused to think as he landed at Dover in July 1783, he might have felt that his return marked the end of his youth but that the future was hard to discern. Spared the need to make fundamental decisions, he continued to be happy enough to respond to events as they came along. In the next few years he added some important pictures to his collection, but perhaps in only one respect would he act decisively — in divorcing himself from his commercial interests in East Anglia as completely as he had ignored his property in Leicestershire. For one thing at least was clear: the position that fate might have prepared for him, that of unpretentious country gentleman, was no longer enough. Life had henceforth to be more metropolitan, closer both to the great world and to the heart of art and letters.

If the Beaumonts shared a weakness it was the tendency to be as easily bored as they were excited, and *ennui* could lead to depression. They returned to England with a double cloud across their lives: family pride was natural to Sir George and with few enough Beaumonts in the world it was understandable that he should feel the continuing failure to produce an heir no less keenly than the loss of his own health. Lady Beaumont was just as concerned, and in the years ahead both would seek fresh stimuli to keep the shadows from lengthening. Those who admired them — and especially Sir George — for their enjoyment of the world, were not always aware that a certain effort went into it. Fortunately, new opportunities would rarely be lacking, but at least in the autumn of 1783, the Beaumonts had little option but to resume their familar round with a tour of East Anglia, visiting the Gateses, old Davy and the Howlands, and getting as far as Yarmouth where Beaumont made a fine drawing. For Christmas they repaired as usual to North Aston.

This year there were no theatricals. *The Provok'd Husband* had been mentioned but dropped — perhaps Bowles was already beginning to suffer from the rheumatic illness that plagued him several years later — and instead the party amused themselves drawing and sketching. Beaumont had brought his Continental drawings and

22. John Baptist Malchair, after Beaumont: *The Villa of Diocletian*, 1784, chalk and watercolours (Oxford, Ashmolean Museum). Copied at North Aston, 18 January 1784.

Malchair, often a fellow guest, was delighted by his progress, telling another of his old pupils, John Skippe, that Sir George was now 'a very capital drawer of landskipp', and asking, 'Pray where is L'Arici', for 'there wer [*sic*] some drawings of and about that place which beat anything I have ever seen'. He was impressed enough to copy some of them (Pl. 22) and told Skippe that while 'there were many things in his collection done by Piranesi and others before, yet Sir George had made them new and interesting by giving them in different points of view, but his chief things are his representations of the country, his landskipps, they are capital I assure you.'[1] Lady Beaumont was also trying her hand. On 2 February, probably as a farewell present, she gave Malchair a copy she had made of a Caylus etching of a tree, after Annibale Carracci. Malchair kept and inscribed the Beaumonts' drawings,[2] and Sir George for his part remained devoted to his old teacher, this year joining with Skippe and other former pupils to provide him with an annuity for life.

With Italian memories still fresh, returning to Dunmow in the depths of winter was drearier than usual, and only the prospect of a London season made the wet Essex fields bearable. In early spring the Beaumonts were again at 29 Grosvenor Square — a property that was to become their own that same year. In London as in the country, politics continued to occupy everyone's attention. In December the precarious coalition of Lord North and Charles James Fox, formed under the nominal leadership of the Duke of Portland some months earlier, had collapsed after the defeat in the House of Lords of Fox's India Bill and the personal intervention of the King, who bitterly resented Fox's apparent encouragement of the Prince of Wales's extravagances — already the talk of London and something that Beaumont, with many others, was to condemn strongly. Amidst general derision William Pitt, with a great name but little experience at only twenty-four, accepted the task of forming a new ministry.

There followed a trial of tactics between two very different men who were to dominate political life for the next twenty years — Fox, impulsive and charismatic, Pitt, calculating and masterful; neither prepared to serve under the other. With the

56

King behind Pitt, Fox found his support dwindling as the 'country gentlemen', who would have preferred a coalition, deserted him — a process that accelerated sharply after Fox's friends attacked Pitt's coach in an unpleasant incident in St James's. On 24 March Pitt was ready to dissolve Parliament and during a dramatic general election one hundred members, mostly 'friends of the late administration', lost their seats. Pitt was now relatively secure.

In London electoral interest focussed on the battle for Westminster, for which Fox was standing against Lord Hood and Sir Cecil Wray. The campaign took place amid unprecedented riot and frenzy, with Covent Garden and Leicester Fields, near Sir Joshua Reynolds's house, swarming with mobs. Amid torrents of abuse and lampoons, Fox was in the end re-elected, but not before Pitt and Wray had delayed his return by a scrutiny, both sides gaining thereby a somewhat Pyrrhic victory, for if Fox's support had been eroded, Pitt would have appeared vindictive in questioning it.

Beaumont, watching the run up to the election in Oxfordshire and Essex and its rough dénouement in London, knew that for better or worse his allegiance lay towards the centre, with the 'country gentlemen'. If politics was not yet an option he had considered for himself, it was soon to come his way and the 1784 election was an opportunity to review his priorities. In later years he was to strike some of his younger friends as the most old-fashioned of high Tories, but this was a misunderstanding. The chameleon character of English politics in the aftermath of the American war demanded an open mind, and even in the face of the French challenge a few years later, and after the Terror had divided the friends of Freedom, Beaumont always remained, as Allan Cunningham remembered, a 'lover of liberty', at least in theory. He could stomach the passionate idealism of Coleridge but not the reasoned radicalism of William Hazlitt, and republicanism, when it appeared in friends like Wordsworth and acquaintances like Richard Brinsley Sheridan, appalled him. Later he distanced himself from politics, and if his conservative attitudes appeared to harden, it was probably because, as Uvedale Price was to appreciate, he shared Montaigne's belief in the *status quo*, especially in hard times. In fact Lady Beaumont's views were the more extreme, Henry Crabb Robinson finding her in old age 'bitter against the whigs' and 'disposed to be as intolerant as politeness would allow'.[3]

For the time being, Beaumont sometimes found himself drawn towards the Whigs. Fox's charisma he readily conceded, believing his heart to be in the right place; Reynolds was also often thought to have Whig sympathies, and so too had been Lord Algernon Percy's father, the Duke of Northumberland. Latterly, however, the Duke had become more and more of a maverick politically, had 'openly talked opposition in all companies' during North's administration and had resigned from his position as Master of the Horse in 1780. Beaumont's friendship with Lord Algernon, now deepening into intimacy after their companionship in Rome, drew him into a world of fluid political attitudes that perhaps flourished best on an eminence of wealth and position. The Percys put family first, close friends second and all others far behind, and tempered their views to serve their purposes. Lord Algernon was now a Pittite and had long ago reached an accommodation with the 'country gentlemen' who had not challenged him in his constituency of Northumberland, while his old tutor, Dutens, was connected to the Prince of Wales's Foxite circle. In 1786, on his father's death, Lord Algernon abandoned his seat in the Commons to enter the upper House as Lord Louvaine. Perhaps he was already retreating from the world, for Walpole was complaining that he was rarely seen in public and his later years were to be spent mainly in seclusion on the Continent.

Romantically susceptible and extravagant as a young man — his complacent father, presented with his bills of £60,000 for a single year abroad, had merely expressed the hope that the time had passed agreeably — Lord Algernon had impressed Dutens as being also exceptionally sensitive, and the Beaumonts responded to this introspective side. They were entertained at his house in Portman Square, in the country at Hitchin Priory and later at Orwell Park, and also at Syon, where they met his father and Dutens, who became a friend. This was a glittering circle to be drawn into, and through its lively talk of art and letters were woven the Duke's astringent comments on the contemporary scene. Dutens was to remark the 'judicious manner of bestowing favours' which made the Duke appear more generous than he was, and whether or not the Percys had already marked Beaumont down as a coming man, it was their patronage that would soon procure him a Parliamentary seat, and it was with Lord Algernon that he later took the temperature of liberty in France.

*   *   *

A particularly busy London season afforded some relief from politics. The highlight of 1784 was the Handel commemoration, and at the overwhelmingly crowded events in Westminster Abbey and at the Pantheon in late May, the Beaumonts coped as stoically as the rest. Now was the time to establish themselves among *le tout Londres*, and although there is no evidence that they were particularly musical, save Beaumont's later assertion that music improved the Academy dinner, they rallied to support the organiser, Dr Charles Burney, who was now a friend. Charming and travelled, Burney was an ornament of London's innumerable *conversazioni* and a favourite of their blue-stocking hostesses. The Beaumonts too were constant guests, for they were not yet in a position to do their own London entertaining. Lady Beaumont was young to be a true 'blue' — later Byron would have her qualify — but she was probably ingenuous enough to enjoy the various gambits. Not Mrs Vesey's insistence at her 'chaoses' on chairs placed back to back, nor Miss Monckton's refusal to notice the arrival of her guests, let alone to introduce them, nor Mrs Montagu's desperate anxiety to be a leader in all things, nor their indigestible offerings of tea, lemonade and cakes from seven o'clock onwards deterred the town, and at their gatherings the Beaumonts could hear most of the lions of Georgian London in full roar — save for Dr Johnson, who was to die that very summer.

But neither of the Beaumonts was made for society alone. Relatively new as they were to the great world, they were grateful for friends with more modest tastes. In later years Sir George was to appear a very glamorous figure to his painter friends, but for the moment he felt at least as at home in their company, and probably in truth more relaxed, than at the grandest dinners and routs, and his commitment to their world gained fresh proof that summer when he and Bowles formed a dining club with Farington, Hearne, and a relatively recent friend, Benjamin West. The conversation was serious, mostly of painting, as on the evening at Farington's house in April when West made a drawing to show them the composition of Titian's *St Peter Martyr*.[4]

The same year, on the strength of his Italian tour, Beaumont was elected to the Society of Dilettanti. Although Walpole admitted that the meetings, at the Star and

23. Thomas Lawrence: *Uvedale Price*, 1799 (Courtesy Museum of Fine Arts, Boston; Gift of Robert Jordan from the collection of Eben D. Jordan).

Garter tavern in the early months of the year, could be as hard on the liver as on the intellect, the membership was distinguished and Beaumont came into contact with many more interesting personalities. His proposer was the Secretary, the naturalist Sir Joseph Banks, who was also President of the Royal Society and an enthusiastic supporter of artists, including Hearne and Paul Sandby, while his fellow members included Reynolds, Englefield and two Whigs who, despite their politics, were to be among his closest friends and rank with him as arbiters of taste — Uvedale Price and Richard Payne Knight.

Price (Pl. 23) he already knew, for they had met at Roma's the picture dealer's, and had immediately hit it off. Beaumont must have brought Price back to dine at Grosvenor Square after this meeting, for, as Price later reminded Lady Beaumont, her husband was 'an older acquaintance of mine by at least three hours' — but as he assured her, she was 'last but not least in love'[5] and there was indeed to be an almost romantic feeling in his affection for the Beaumonts. Although, much to his sorrow, their contact was later mainly by correspondence, Price was among their most intimate friends; Cranston, the Herefordshire landscape gardener, remarked that he never knew two people who thought so much alike as Price and Beaumont, and for the Beaumonts, Price's worldly manners, literary tastes and passion for landscape gardening proved irresistible. He had travelled widely, had studied Italian in Florence and visited Voltaire at Ferney with Fox. They moreover shared friends in Malchair, Bowles, and Gainsborough, who had painted his father and visited his estate at Foxley in Herefordshire.

In contrast to Price, with whom he was to engage in vigorous debate on the Picturesque, Payne Knight's origins were commercial and his character pugnacious. But he had a sharp eye for pictures, was soon to begin his important collection of antiquities, and was already working on his account of the worship of Priapus that was to embroil the Society of Dilettanti in scandal. Beaumont's views on the affair are not recorded, but it was in the year of his induction that the Society voted to print the investigation into Priapic rites surviving in Italy, originally submitted by Sir William Hamilton. When Knight's version appeared in 1786,[6] Beaumont was not among the subscribers, but he was most probably amused by the ensuing rumpus. The two men began seriously collecting the old masters around the same time, and meanwhile Knight, like Beaumont, was much interested in living artists. His tastes were often remarkably similar, for he too had a *penchant* for Mortimer and the younger Cozens, and had just commissioned Hearne to produce a series of watercolours of his estate at Downton, as well as copies of drawings made on his expedition to Sicily in 1777. Beaumont and Knight were to complement each other admirably as collectors and patrons, competing in friendly rivalry that was occasionally laced with — but not soured by — envy of each other's *coups* or amusement at each other's special fads.

Among their fellow Dilettanti were Charles Gore, an amateur draughtsman who was a friend of Goethe and Hackert and had been Knight's companion in Sicily, and another proponent of landscape theory, Thomas Johnes, whose grounds at Hafod, like Price's at Foxley and Knight's at Downton, were to be a key document in the Picturesque. These men formed the nucleus of a circle of like minds, and the following year Knight seconded Beaumont when he moved to expand the Society by proposing Bowles as a member. Bowles, however, was to be conspicuous by his absence from meetings, thus incurring heavy forfeits and, like most members, including Beaumont, being 'done' for 'face money', after failing to submit a portrait of himself to the Society.

Charles Townley joined the Society in 1786, as did Philip Metcalfe, following Beaumont's seconding of his sponsorship by Reynolds. In 1789 the same partnership secured the election of the mineralogist and collector, Sir Abraham Hume, whose daughter Amelia was to challenge Beaumont's supremacy as the leading amateur artist and was to marry Charles Long, a prominent Pittite with a fondness for Dutch pictures who would be Beaumont's ally in his campaign for a national gallery. In 1787 the Society collectively proposed the election of the bibliophile collector, the Revd Clayton Mordaunt Cracherode. Beaumont was undoubtedly playing his part in encouraging the upsurge in *virtù* that characterised the Society in the 1780s. Later, he was also to bring more artists into its ranks, proposing West for membership, seconded by Hume, in 1792. The Society was a first and most revealing insight into the potential of patronage by committee, and the proving ground of the influence that Beaumont was to wield with men like Knight and Hume on the Committee of Taste.

The Beaumonts now needed an independent London base where they could further develop their circle, and it was to come almost as soon as the wish. In June 1784, John Willes witnessed the marriage of his eldest daughter, Frances, to Henry Fermor of Fritwell near North Aston. Willes may already have been a sick man and he died at Astrop on 24 November. His main bequest was to his son, but Lady Beaumont received £3,000 with which she and Sir George were able to acquire for themselves the lease of 29 Grosvenor Square (Pl. 24). In their hands the house was to become

24. *Grosvenor Square, London*, c. 1731 (engraved Sutton Nicholls) (Courtesy of the Parker Gallery). No. 29 is at the bottom left corner.

comfortable and purposeful, with Lady Beaumont as proud of her library as her husband of his pictures, and, instead of grand parties, they preferred quiet dinners for a few close friends from various walks of life, at which actors and artists — not just Reynolds, who was in universal demand, but also the Hearnes and the Faringtons — would find themselves meeting writers and talkers as well as old intimates of the Beaumonts like Bowles.

The company was largely male, it not yet being the custom to entertain 'a jumble of pairs like animals entering the Ark', and the wives of those not socially equal seldom qualified, for this was an era when each guest was expected to contribute to the entertainment. The transition from actor to raconteur came naturally to Beaumont who contrived to keep a straight face however amusing his anecdotes, which were to become prized by wits such as Samuel Rogers. Beaumont was to maintain his eighteenth-century style through the years and his flat statements and refusal to engage in argument later contributed to the frustration of artists unable to make him justify himself. Meanwhile, he was quite a handful for his wife who, apprised of her husband's youthful drinking prowess (judging by his letters, Price for one enjoyed making teasing references to this), took in her stride his continuing forays into the coffee-houses of Mayfair. The Mount was an especial favourite, and in later years Beaumont loved to reminisce of rakish scenes, such as Harvey Ashton's winning a bet of fifty guineas by persuading a famous Irish duellist to stand barefoot before him — Ashton having caught him off guard by declaring that the Irish, being born in bogs, were all web-footed, so that the furious Irishman pulled off his shoes to disprove it.

61

In Beaumont's London circle Gainsborough and Reynolds continued to be the artistic lodestars. They offered him the attraction of opposites as well as individual charm and distinction, representing the poles of his own personality. Reynolds appealed to his sober side, Gainsborough to the old light-heartedness that had only recently out-grown practical joking and still delighted in caricature. Beaumont knew both men well enough to appreciate the differences that kept them apart, but his affection for each enabled him to bridge the gap. If he learned to penetrate Reynolds's somewhat stuffy exterior, his impressions of Gainsborough are proof that he saw beneath that surface also. Gainsborough once confessed to him: 'I am considered a sad fellow and I do talk in a wild, sad way, but 'tis all *flash*',[7] and he never hesitated to reveal his melancholy, unstable side to the Beaumonts, not least at dinner one night at Grosvenor Square when he fell into a depression, announced he was going to die — 'I know it — I feel it — I have less time to live than my looks infer' — and begged one worthy man' to accompany him to the grave, only perking up when Sheridan agreed.[8]

Whether or not the Beaumonts shared Gainsborough's passion for music — and Beaumont was later to react violently to an unfair suggestion by the artist's biographer, William Jackson, that Gainsborough was naive enough to suppose more merit in the instrument than in the performer[9] — they had the theatre in common. Besides Sheridan, the actor Henderson was a mutual friend, and Lord Algernon heard him give one of his inimitable readings one night at Grosvenor Square. It seems odd that Beaumont did not acquire directly from Gainsborough any pictures more important than two small oils of his favourite dogs — especially when the artist's house was lined with unsold landscapes — and Gainsborough, who was usually suspicious of gentlemen unless they produced their purses, must have noticed the omission. In later years Beaumont liked to talk with a tinge of regret of notional commissions to both Wilson and Gainsborough that would have displayed their different characters: 'Both were poets; and to me, The Bard of Gray, and his Elegy in a Country Churchyard, are so descriptive of their different lines, that I should certainly have commissioned Wilson to paint a subject from the first, and Gainsborough one from the latter.'[10] But neither project had materialised. Beaumont's major purchases of the artists' work were made posthumously, and Constable, another unquestionably great painter of his acquaintance, was to suffer a similar lack of concrete support.

In fact, there was now a lull in Beaumont's collecting of modern art. In March 1785 he roused himself to send £36 to Jacob More in Rome, but a year later More, who had actually fallen out of favour but did not realise it, was wondering why his patron was not more concerned about the picture — still unfinished — that he had commissioned in Rome. Jones could have asked a similar question, for the companion piece to his *Velletri*, if painted, was unclaimed and evidently forgotten. Inconstancy was a patron's privilege, of course, but the truth was that in the aftermath of his Continental tour, with an enhanced income and a house to furnish (the Willes taste had been plain and the walls of Grosvenor Square were mostly bare save for family portraits and the modern pictures Beaumont had added himself), his attention was now fixed on the old masters.

There was much to encourage a collector. Although the greatest dispersals of Continental collections lay several years ahead, the London market was very active, with Benjamin Vandergucht in Upper Brook Street and Joseph Desenfans holding

25. Joshua Reynolds: *Sir George Beaumont*, 1787 (Collection of the Helen Clay Frick Foundation).

splendid exhibitions of their stock. The latter's sale in May 1785 and his exhibition at 125 Pall Mall a year later were important for the connoisseurs, and the autumn of 1783 brought an equally significant event on the Continent, a sale in Brussels of pictures from dissolved monasteries and similar old collections at the behest of the Emperor Joseph. Reynolds spent over £1,000 at the sale, and a vogue for Dutch and Flemish painting — in which Desenfans was also greatly interested — now joined the long-established taste for the Italianate.

Reynolds's own collection, and the profound, if hieratic, connoisseurship made plain every other year in his Discourses, were familiar to Beaumont; but he was far from a slavish follower of Reynolds's ideas. He was eager to learn but insisted on using his own eyes, which led to the occasional argument. As Allan Cunningham recorded, 'On his return from abroad, Sir George spoke with much freedom of the excellences and defects of the great masters of Flanders and Italy: this was reckoned heresy by some of the English painters; and by none more than by Reynolds, who was never willing to see any thing but perfection in the conceptions of Michael Angelo and the colouring of Titian.'[11]

Cunningham perhaps overstates the case, for not only did Reynolds encourage independent judgement, urging Beaumont to 'Do something to provoke criticism',[12] but Beaumont learned Reynolds's maxims faithfully enough to hand them on to a younger generation of painters. And if Reynolds's aesthetic philosophy was, as Gainsborough complained, 'all adapted to form the History Painter', while Beaumont was still unshaken in his preference for landscape, even Reynolds in his Discourse for 1786, turned his attention to landscape more pointedly than ever before. That year he spoke of the virtues and varieties of interpretation in art and, as if to acknowledge just how broad a church it was, contrasted 'nature represented with all the truth of the camera obscura, and the same scene represented by a great Artist', be it Poussin who 'transports us to the environs of ancient Rome, with all the objects which a literary education makes so precious and interesting', Sébastien Bourdon who 'leads us to the dark antiquity of the Pyramids of Egypt', or Claude who 'conducts us to the tranquillity of Arcadian scenes and fairy land'.

Reynolds saw his own collection as a source of models for his painting, and must have urged a budding painter-collector to do the same. He lent Beaumont his picture by Jacques Foucquières[13] — a great rarity — to work from, and was to bequeath him his Sébastien Bourdon, The Return of the Ark (Pl. 30). In a similar spirit, Beaumont was now in pursuit of a Claude and a Poussin. If he were to form a serious collection, Claude above all was indispensable and the failure to secure any of the Barberini pictures still rankled. It was not only that he had grown to love Claude for himself, nor that he was still nostalgic for Italy: Claude was a passion he shared with his mentors, just as he would wish to share it with the new generation of Turner and Constable. For as he told William Gilpin, 'My friend, Sir Joshua, was full as warm in his admiration of Claude as myself;' and 'As to Wilson, he was such an enthusiast, that he would not suffer Claude to be criticized in any degree...."I'll tell you what", said he, "all I know of the matter I learnt from Claude, who is the only person that ever could paint fine weather and Italian skies, and if you will study him, and get acquainted with him, you will be of the same opinion. There is one picture of his (and I think he named 'The Doria Claude' with the temple) which makes my heart ache. I shall never paint such a picture as that, were I to live a thousand years"'.[14] Wilson had

26. Claude Lorraine: *Landscape with Hagar and the Angel* (London, National Gallery).

27. Claude Lorraine: *Landscape with Goatherd and Goats* (London, National Gallery).

died in 1782, but his words still rang in Beaumont's memory and fuelled his desire. Probably in 1785 and certainly by the autumn of the following year, it was to be splendidly fulfilled. In October 1786 More, writing from Rome, was 'glad to hear you have purchased a fine Claude'.[15] This must have been the small *Landscape with Hagar and the Angel* (Pl. 26) that was apparently in the sale of Matthew Duane on 23 April 1785. Thus Beaumont's favourite among his old masters — the picture he loved so much that he carried it with him on his travels and recalled it, alone among his pictures, from his gift to the National Gallery to keep with him for the remainder of his life — was probably the first to be acquired. It was, however, very soon joined by another, for in June 1787 More was again congratulating Beaumont on finding an 'excellent Claude',[16] the early *Landscape with Goatherd and Goats* (Pl. 27). The larger *Landscape with Narcissus and Echo* was added in 1790.[17] More, echoing Reynolds's practical sentiments, thought the pictures would 'be to you a fine guide (if they are in good preservation)'.

Never one to be modest, More was full of news of his own doings and anxious to win Beaumont back as a patron. He had employed an engraver to translate a *Moonlight with Diana and her Nymphs* and a *Morning Chase with Diana*, and had painted a *Storm by Night with a Shipwreck*, 'thought the best thing I have done yet. An Italian gentleman has made it the subject of a poem...I would send it to you if you have not forgotten your Italian.' He was also eager for news of Beaumont's own work: 'Mr Hamilton has reported your welfare and great progress in painting...I should like confirmation from you.'[18]

Reports had been over optimistic, for Beaumont later admitted he had neglected his easel and only one oil, *Caister Castle* of 1785,[19] survives from this period. With Wilson dead and Jones retired in Wales, most of his friends, apart from Reynolds and Gainsborough, were now among the draughtsmen. There were times when he felt the lack of professional instruction. When Reynolds offered technical advice it tended to be dangerous, while the shortcomings of the master's practice were already becoming apparent. Beaumont was happier to accept the goodwill of other friends like the topographical draughtsman, J.T. Smith, who, to encourage him in his monochrome drawing gave him a piece of bistre, safer than ink-based sepia which could eat into the paper; it had come from a larger lump given him by Paul Sandby, who had got it from the hollow trunk of an ancient beech in Windsor Park.

*   *   *

Christmas at North Aston remained an institution and the Beaumonts had returned again at the end of 1784, Sir George receiving a further spur to his artistic ambitions in the shape of Bowles's gift of a sketchbook used by Wilson in Rome in 1751.[20] Like most of the *ton*, the Beaumonts avoided London for much of the second half of the year. In 1785 they returned briefly to the Lakes, journeying back through Liverpool to spend the latter part of August in East Anglia, and in November they were at Salisbury; in this as in other years, their itinerary can be reconstructed from the drawings. The following year they added spas to their round, spending February at Bath, where Beaumont gave Gilpin's correspondent, Mary Hartley, 'a very masterly little sketch' that quite won her heart. She was no mean judge, for although hampered by a stroke, she had been a talented draughtswoman and etcher. Gilpin and his friend, William Mason, who usually had a horror of 'clever and ingenious misses or learned Ladies', admired her greatly, and her wide acquaintance, transparent goodness and questioning mind — her father was the philosopher David Hartley — made her one of the *doyennes* of Bath.

The Beaumonts next took the waters at Tunbridge Wells before staying with Sir George's fellow Dilettante, William Mitford, at Exbury in Hampshire. He was working on his *History of Greece* which, although admired by many contemporaries, was somewhat pedantic and clumsy, and lent dubious distinction by anti-Jacobin passions that jaundiced his view of Athenian democracy. Mitford, already a Member of Parliament, may have stirred, if not altered Beaumont's political views. He was later to succeed Beaumont as Member for the constituency of Bere Alston.

The 1786 stay in the Lakes was spent in a house lent by a well-established political figure, Lord George Cavendish, the 'father of the House'. The property was probably his own Holker Hall, as he was frequently away. Gilpin, after seeing Beaumont's Italian drawings, had high expectations of what he would produce in the Lake District and confirmed Miss Hartley's good opinions: 'I dare say he will bring away some fine sketches. . .I know of nobody who sketches in so intelligent and easy a manner as he does or has the art of conveying so much meaning in so few strokes.'[21] Miss Hartley was delighted: 'you think of [his] sketches as I do. The commendation you give. . .of freedom and intelligence is exactly what I admire so much in him.'[22] Evidently Gilpin felt he had little to teach this particular amateur, and indeed the discipline first learned from Hearne and Farington, tempered by the breadth of handling he had

66

28.   Nicolas Poussin: *Landscape: A Man washing his Feet at a Fountain* (London, National Gallery).

admired in Cozens, was now bearing fruit in an expressive and quite individual monochrome manner.

The spring had found Beaumont again Reynolds's guest at the Academy dinner, an especially splendid one at which one of the guests of honour, the duc d'Orléans, sat beneath his new portrait by the President. The Beaumonts had seen him, as duc de Chartres, in Rome. He was now rumoured to be drunken and slovenly but was at least Anglophile, and Reynolds found him — or claimed he did — gracious and easy, with much dignity as a sitter. That year also, Reynolds's house was a focus for the connoisseurs when Poussin's *Seven Sacraments* arrived there from Rome, sent by the Boccapaduli family which, through Sir Joshua, was selling them to the Duke of Rutland. There had been much competition to buy them and the future Lord Mendip, Welbore Ellis, was, as Reynolds said, 'very much what the vulgar call *down in the mouth*' at missing his opportunity. Despite his current enthusiasm for collecting, this great series was not for Beaumont who had no space for it and would have found the price of £2,000 steep. However, the pictures' presence in Reynolds's house may well have spurred him to acquire a more modest example of the master, and the following year William Pether was able to engrave Poussin's *Landscape: A Man washing his Feet at a Fountain* (Pl. 28), now in Beaumont's collection and probably the object of

67

his payment of £200 to Vandergucht in 1787. This would make sense as its presumed pendant, the *Landscape with a Roman Road*,[23] was in London in the collection of the rival dealer Desenfans; presumably the pair had recently been divided. The stern dignity of the Poussin, contrasted with the mellower pastoral of the two Claudes, provided a noble focal point in Beaumont's growing collection; Constable, looking at it at Coleorton in 1821, would find it 'a solemn, deep, still, summer's noon... the most affecting picture I almost ever stood before'.[24]

But Beaumont was also casting his net wider. Reynolds had urged him to study his landscape by Foucquières, recommending it, as Constable was later to recall, as 'an excellent model on which to form his style' and advising him to 'adapt its fine principle especially that of colour (which he said "was equal to Titian")'.[25] Thus far at least Reynolds was trying to coax Beaumont back to his easel; and when he did return to it, it was indeed with the example of Northern masters as much in mind as Claude or Wilson. In 1785, after the great Brussels sale, James Northcote had noticed that 'a trip to Flanders... became fashionable among the lovers of the fine arts, who were all anxious to possess some of the exquisite specimens of the great Flemish masters'.[26] Beaumont was no exception, and in the autumn of 1786 planned a visit of his own. Consulted for advice, Reynolds replied rather off-handedly on his way out to dinner — 'I am sorry I have not more time to recollect myself' — but recommended Rubens's *St Bavo* in Ghent Cathedral; the 'once famous crucifixion of Vandick [*sic*] almost destroyed' in St Michael's Church; Mr Orion's pictures at Brussels ('difficult to be seen'); Rubens's *Last Supper* at Mecklin; Rembrandt in Amsterdam; a Van der Velde at 'the office of the commissary of the warfs [*sic*]', should be seen, and Beaumont should 'take particular note of a picture by Vander Elst'; at Antwerp the 'chapeau de paile in the Cabinet of Mr Van Haveren' was a must, but 'I fear you will not be able to see Mr Peters Pictures as I hear he is dead'.[27]

How useful all this was can only be conjectured; Beaumont made no copies of the pictures he saw on this trip and his sharpest impression in his sketchbooks is of 'A great epicure' who 'had eaten pickled herring till he was sick, but still held one in each hand'. However, it must have been at this time that the Beaumonts discovered their love for Rubens, whose *Château de Steen* (Pl. 61) was to be one of the glories of their collection. Back in London Beaumont lost no time in discussing Rubens with Reynolds, who remarked that the pictures of Rubens appeared much less 'brilliant' than they had done on the former inspection; this, Reynolds went on to explain, was because when he first saw them he had his sketchbook in his hand and by the eye passing immediately from the white paper to the picture, the colours derived uncommon 'richness and warmth'; for want of this foil they afterwards appeared comparatively cold.[28] Beaumont himself had no reservations about Rubens as a colourist, and the painter's luxurious and sensual style came as a revelation. However, the Northern picture that Beaumont bought during or shortly after his visit to the Low Countries was an exercise in the more familar Claudian pastoral — the *Rocky Landscape with Peasants and Pack Mules* by Jan Both that was engraved by William Byrne as in the Beaumont collection in May 1790.[29]

*　　*　　*

If 1786 was remarkable for the number of miles the Beaumonts travelled, it was

68

29. G.B. Campion
(engraved J.C. Armytage):
Dedham, Essex, 1832.
Lady Beaumont's house
was opposite the church.

also the last year in which they spent much time in Dunmow. In May 1787 John Gates died and they naturally repaired to Dedham to comfort his widow. For the next ten years Dame Rachel's handsome, tall brick house in the main street at Dedham (Pl. 29) became the focus of the Beaumonts' summers, the gathering place for friends brought down from London for country air and sketching holidays, and an alternative springboard for visiting Davy at Onehouse and other East Anglian relatives and friends. The somewhat complex affairs of Mr Gates were in the competent hands of his executors, two local worthies, Golding Griggs and John Round. Beaumont was happy to leave them that way and he immediately put up for sale the two mills bequeathed to him. Later he was to refuse the Parliamentary seat of Colchester because of its proximity to Dedham and for once in his life he appeared unusually decisive. His mill at Higham run by Stephen Harris continued to do good service until destroyed by fire in 1821, its linseed being used by local artists, including Constable; but far from hob-nobbing with fellow mill-owners such as Constable's father Golding, Beaumont in future years descended on Dedham as a star from another firmament, and C.R. Leslie in his *Memoir* of Constable perpetuated this view of Beaumont by obligingly omitting the fact that Mrs Constable had known him as a boy. That Mrs Constable and the erst-while Mrs Gates belonged to much the same local circle could have been a bond, but in fact it was to create an ambivalence, at times even a barrier, between patron and painter.

*   *   *

In London Beaumont followed the theatre as avidly as ever. To a devotee the pit audience was part of the show and when alone he often took advantage of the custom of going in at half price after the first act. The Beaumonts had missed Mrs Siddons's triumphant return to Drury Lane in 1782 but were back in town for her brother John Kemble's début the following season. His declamatory style was little to Sir George's taste, being the antithesis of Garrick's; moreover Kemble was supplanting old familiars, the portly Henderson and Smith, in the leading roles. Until his early death in 1785, a strong body of opinion favoured Henderson as Hamlet, and Beaumont enjoyed adding his own voice. He could draw on personal experience, for this had been his own role and, until challenged by Lord Henry Fitzgerald in 1787, he retained his reputation as the best gentleman-actor at a time when the conceit of this amateur was fed not only by sycophantic newspaper critics, but also by Walpole, who went so far as to declare Garrick a monkey compared to Lord Henry in the romantic part of Don Felix. Beaumont's friends, who included the dramatist George Colman as well as Jack Bannister and the older King, now manager of Drury Lane, would have saved him from such prejudice as Walpole's, had his own sensitivity failed him, for the professionals understandably took a jaundiced view of private theatricals which might lure smart audiences from the public theatres.

Fashion was fickle, however: in 1784 a mania for hot-air balloons had gripped society and this was evidently to Beaumont's taste, for he followed the adventurous Vincenzo Lunardi, an attaché at the Neapolitan Embassy, to Liverpool in August the next year to make some lively sketches of the crowd surrounding the balloon. Lunardi had made a successful flight from Moorfields, accompanied by his cat and dog, the previous September, but the Liverpool ascent was destined to failure. 'Balloonacy' lasted another season as 'Herschel's planetary discoveries stimulated the fashionable passion to turn "air-go-naut"'.[30] Beaumont never courted danger, except in water, but several of his acquaintances risked their necks, their enthusiasm diminishing only when an attempt to cross the Channel from Boulogne ended precipitately with two Frenchmen being dashed to death. Such pursuits of the sublime were succeeded by the ridiculous, with a rage for performing dogs, this mercifully yielding in 1787 to a renaissance of private theatricals — now very private according to a reluctant member of the audience at Blenheim, the professional actor F.R. Reynolds, who found the performers inaudible. The Duke of Richmond's company, which performed in the Privy Gardens, was thought to eclipse all its predecessors, but competition was at best uneven.

The possibility of the theatre at North Aston reopening was mooted in *The World* that autumn. Old hand though he was, Beaumont was pronounced reluctant — 'when a gentleman gets married...he does not act...so much as formerly' — but by November there were rumours of a joint production with Blenheim, Lord Grandison being hailed as the newest attraction. Nothing came of it, but the following year the Beaumonts and the Bowleses, having attended the Blenheim dramatics in late October, were expecting to play in *Catharine and Petruchio* as well as *The Nabob* at North Aston the next month. This performance, however, was suddenly cancelled when news came of the King's illness. In February there was further talk of Beaumont playing Nabob to Janus performed by Sir John Aubry or Lord Malmesbury, but this time Bowles himself became ill. Not surprisingly, the theatre fell into disuse and all that came of a final attempt in 1791 was a wistful and sardonic prologue, written by Beaumont to echo Whitehead's earlier one and preserved in *The World*:

> The sleeping Thunders now forget to roll,
> The Spider spins within the poison'd bowl;
> My useless Helmets garrison the Bats —
> And all my Wigs are eaten by the Rats.
> The grand Cascade which flash'd upon the Drop,
> Is now a Floor-cloth in the Barber's shop...

> Dan Whitehead's prophecy is out 'tis plain,
> And my Barn's now almost a Barn again...

Amateur dramatics were a young man's fancy and both Beaumont and the older Bowles had outgrown them. Bowles's rheumatic illness had been serious enough to keep him from London for a time and he abdicated altogether from the Society of Dilettanti. Although his recovery was to be complete, the passing years left him sometimes eclipsed by Beaumont's new friends. But the intimacy between the two families persisted and extended to most of the numerous Bowles daughters and their husbands, as well as to Charles, the long-awaited son, for whom Sir George stood sponsor at his christening in the summer of 1785 — no doubt a poignant reminder of the Beaumonts' own childlessness.

North Aston's reaction to the illness of George III in November 1788 reflected concern not only for the sovereign but for his government. After five years under the leadership of the younger Pitt the country was stable and the King's virtues had become more widely apparent the longer people considered the alternative — an extravagant and amorous Prince of Wales who would replace Pitt with Fox and the radical Whigs. Anxiety was exacerbated by rumour, doctors having pronounced the King insane while they disputed the prognosis. A regency looked inevitable, but then the King made a surprise recovery. By mid-February 1789, after seventeen weeks of misery, he was calm enough to talk to Pitt, and on St George's Day he endured a five-hour Thanksgiving in St Paul's. A political showdown thus averted, attention returned to Westminster Hall, where the trial of Warren Hastings, on charges of corruption in India, had been proceeding for a year. This 'fine show', as Fanny Burney's younger brother heartlessly described it, was compulsory viewing for a fashionable audience, who had each other to quiz when the speeches dragged. The novelty wore off long before Hastings's acquittal seven years later, but in the early stages Beaumont was as attracted as anyone else; the trial produced brilliant speeches from Fox, Sheridan and Edmund Burke and appealed to his sense of theatre if not of justice.

Indirectly, however, it brought a great personal sadness, for it was while watching one of the sittings that Gainsborough, recently troubled by a cancer, suffered a sudden deterioration. He died on 2 August 1788 after a short but painful illness. Reynolds and Sheridan — just as he had begged at the Beaumonts' table — accompanied him to his grave in Kew churchyard. The Beaumonts were out of London and, whether or not they returned for the funeral, Sir George never ceased to feel his loss. Reynolds too was ageing, and the decline and death of these mentors of his youth brought the sense of the ending of an era, and perhaps also an urge to find a more characteristic voice of his own. His collecting apart, the last decade had slipped by largely in frivolous pursuits better suited to a younger man, and these no longer seemed entirely appropriate. By the close of the decade he was ready for public life, but when he entered it, he did so as a man whose truest interests lay elsewhere. The love of art, and the practice of it, remained central to his being; it already set him apart, and in time he would dedicate his life to it. Even now, it was apparent that a 'new race of fashionable young dilettanti' had taken the stage in London, and that Beaumont, with his friends Hume and Englefield, were its stars. Beaumont was to excel the others by far, but a different experience was needed before he could recognise where his future really lay.

VI
ART AND POLITICS

THE FALL OF THE Bastille on 14 July 1789 was welcomed, albeit somewhat cautiously, in England — any misfortune that befell the traditional enemy being considered grist to the English mill, while for the democrats in particular it struck a magnificent blow against oppression. In the first days of the Revolution Beaumont was not alone in feeling more curiosity than alarm and when Lord Beverley — as Lord Algernon Percy had become — proposed a visit to Paris, he was happy to join in to see for himself what was going on in France. Thus, in the spring of 1790, two Englishmen who could share the epithet 'mild and aimable' set off armed only with the usual introductions, including one to the painter, Jacques-Louis David, a member of the Jacobin Club. But, if Beaumont hoped to take his first critical look at the French School, he was disappointed. The visit was abruptly curtailed, for, as Allan Cunningham described, 'one day the two friends were out walking when the "sovereign people" came forth and seized a victim, whom they hurried off to execute *a la lanterne*'. The Englishmen's 'looks of astonishment and horror...were understood as well as words and deeds by the friends of liberty; and Sir George and his companion were in a fair way of being hanged as unceremoniously as the man they pitied, when a sympathetic citizen fixed a tricoloured cockade in their hats, and aided their escape'.

This was bad luck, for many English visited France unharmed up to 1792, before the worst days of the Terror — the French, as Haydon would put it with rich irony, being 'not inclined to assassination' — and the experience made a deep impression on the two travellers. Each kept his tricolour as a memento, and the order for post-horses dated 31 May 1790 also survives. Beaumont, who disliked upsets, swore not to leave England again until the Continent was safe — and waited nearly thirty years. His more phlegmatic companion was not deterred for long, setting out again at the Peace of Amiens in 1802 and paying the penalty of internment near Geneva in 1804.

By Percy standards the Paris excursion was a modest one, two drafts for £50 on the French banker, Perregaux, appearing in Beaumont's bank account of June 1790. Moreover it may have brought Beaumont an unexpected dividend. Beverley had inherited from his father the rotten borough of Bere Alston, about twelve miles north of Plymouth, which, although a tiny constituency of some thirty voters, returned two Members to Parliament. John Mitford, a cousin of the Percys, was already one, but when the second seat fell vacant at the general election that June, his brother William was unavailable owing to family illness and Beaumont, conveniently on hand to keep the seat warm, found himself promoted to candidate. Election Day was 19 July and, though it was usual for candidates to be on the spot for an expensive celebration, Beaumont seems not to have made the long journey across Dartmoor but to have left the honours to John Mitford, to whom he later sent a contribution of £50. He himself was occupied sketching in the neighbourhood of Dedham that month, before paying the Beverleys a long visit at Hitchin Priory in September. Meanwhile his return to Parliament was duly recorded and the Opening took place on 25 November.

Beaumont entered the House when the leading protagonists, Pitt and Burke on one side, and Fox and Sheridan on the other, achieved heights — and lengths — of oratory that have seldom been equalled. Pitt, 'that wonderful young man', was over-optimistically anticipating a peaceful future and Beaumont, along with most of his fellow Members, did not expect his duties to be particularly arduous. After a quiet first session which broke up on 30 December, Parliament reassembled at the beginning of February and, almost immediately, the Loughborough and Leicester Canal Bill began its passage through the House. Beaumont had subscribed to the original petition for this canal, which was intended to increase the profitability of the Leicestershire coalfield, and the Bill may even have influenced Beverley's determination that his friend should enter the House, but there is no evidence of his playing an active role before it became law in May. Meanwhile his co-Member, John Mitford, a tough-speaking lawyer, had steered through a bill which brought relief to dissenting Catholics by removing restrictions on their rights. While this was generally welcomed, the same liberality did not extend to Scottish dissenters, and Beaumont was listed amongst those against extending the repeal of the Test Act to include Scotland, a Whig proposal that was duly defeated. His name also appears on the committee considering the East India Judicature Report which was to meet intermittently during the next two years and bring him into closer contact with some distinguished Members, including William Windham and the future Foreign Secretary, Lord Grenville.

It was not until the end of March that Beaumont saw the House spring to life with Fox at his most brilliant. Pitt, having in a rare error of judgement almost involved the country in war with Russia over a piece of land on the Black Sea so remote that few people had even heard of it, deserved to be the butt of the bombardment and, though the administration survived the Ochakov Affair, the evident reluctance of its less committed supporters and the independent Members to vote with Pitt caused him to trim his sails and change course to safer waters. A man of Beaumont's temper was far from dismayed at seeing the majority greatly reduced and rather could congratulate himself on the contribution of the 'country gentlemen' to the triumph of common-sense.

Besides Mitford and his old friend Lord George Cavendish, now 'father of the House', Beaumont's mentors at Westminster were Windham, who as an admirer of Burke was gradually moving away from Fox, and another Etonian, the staunchly Tory Henry Phipps. Succeeding as Lord Mulgrave in 1792 on the death of his brother Constantine, Phipps was the closest friend of the three and introduced Beaumont to White's, the club which was now the Tory stronghold in St James's. Pitt himself was at that time often to be seen at dinners and gatherings there, but in the ensuing years Beaumont was to notice how the cares of office distanced him from his friends. Phipps was politically to the right of Pitt but had his trust. He was an uninhibited, jovial man, 'a complete John Bull',[1] whom Beaumont relished for his 'uncommon vein of humour' and, while still an active soldier, he took an interest in theatre and art; later, with his younger brothers Edmund and Augustus, together with Augustus's wife, Maria, he was to form with Beaumont a significant caucus of connoisseurs. In these

30. Sébastien Bourdon: *The Return of the Ark* (London, National Gallery).

early years, however, his perception was somewhat limited, for, opposing with Beaumont in 1791 William Wilberforce's motion for the abolition of the slave trade, he claimed that, during a year spent in Jamaica, he had never seen a slave ill-treated. The following December he was looking for evidence of subversion in his own country, and, having noted the seditious publications available on the bookstalls, he made a sensible speech, very much in tune with Beaumont, in support of the Aliens Bill. Parliament had been specially assembled to approve the calling out of the Militia and to debate the Bill, which was amongst the first of a number of repressive measures taken to contain rising discontent. With reform in the air, spread through the country by the 'corresponding societies', fear of being 'overrun by French principles' was uppermost in the minds of leading politicians (other than Fox, who perversely welcomed them) and Mulgrave, writing to Windham in December 1792, agreed that the difficulty was 'the timid disinclination' of others 'to be first. . . to exert themselves in defence of their rights'.[2] Beaumont, who had actually seen the savagery of a revolutionary mob, was never likely to be guilty of this, although he felt no embarrassment at consorting with conspicuous Whigs like Price and Knight — or even with Fox

74

. Claude Lorraine: *Landscape with Narcissus and Echo* (London, National Gallery).

himself — with whom he found debates on the Picturesque or the theatre more challenging than political argument.

Amid the gathering clouds of 1792, Beaumont suffered a great personal sadness. Reynolds had been ailing during the winter and on the evening of 23 February he died. Beaumont, much affected, was among the gentlemen who followed the family and members of the Academy in the funeral procession from Somerset House to St Paul's on 3 March; his friends, Abercorn, St Asaph, Burney, Hume, Knight and Townley were also there. In Reynolds's will Beaumont was left the Bourdon *Return of the Ark* (Pl. 30) — but not the Foucquières *Landscape* he had borrowed. The picture came at an opportune moment, as if to christen the picture gallery he had just built at Grosvenor Square. He had decided to build a lofty gallery over the lumber room two years earlier, having just added another Claude, the sombre and melancholy *Narcissus and Echo* (Pl. 31) to his collection. Hearne had bid up to £525 for it in the sale of Peter Delmé in February 1790. This expenditure, together with that now provided for the alterations to Grosvenor Square, was quite substantial for a man of Beaumont's means and signalled his determination to form as fine a collection as he could.

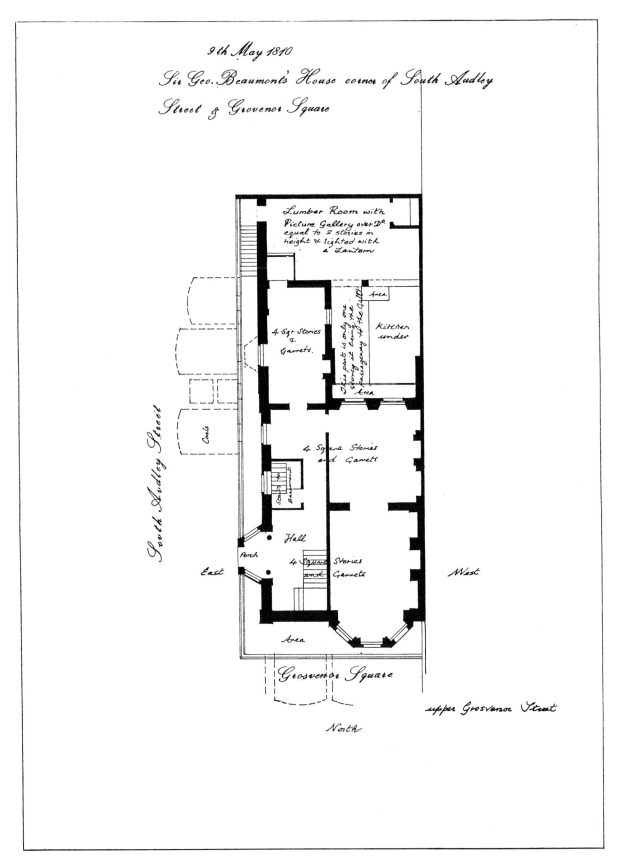

Plan of the Beaumonts' Grosvenor Square House including the gallery or 'Picture Room' (Courtesy of the Grosvenor Estates).

Beaumont's conduct of the project for his gallery was characteristic if not entirely admirable. He turned to John Hakewill, a fellow actor from the earliest North Aston days and now active in London with various building schemes, but also approached James Playfair, who produced one design to cost £355, and another a month later in June 1790, together with an 'Estimate for Executing Sir George Beaumont's design as given in by Hakewill £380'. Meanwhile at the Academy that year Playfair had optimistically exhibited a 'Design in perspective of a gallery now erecting'. Little did he know his client's genius for prevarication which was to plague George Dance at Coleorton, for in the end, having plagiarised Playfair's designs and discussed them with various friends, it seems that Beaumont built his own and Hakewill's version, Playfair having to content himself with three guineas for his own design and two for the estimate.[3]

Hakewill did not live long enough to see the completion of the gallery, announced in *The World* of 13 March 1792. Lit by a lantern in the roof, it had a fifteen-foot frontage on South Audley Street and ran some thirty feet to the back of the house — a typically modest affair, built by a true amateur without thought of ostentation (Pl. 32). Of the pictures described there by Coleridge in 1804, only the two Claudes, *Narcissus and Echo* (Pl. 31) and *Hagar and the Angel* (Pl. 26), and Poussin's *Landscape: A Man washing his Feet* (Pl. 28) could be hung at once, but the Bourdon was soon to join them and it was probably around this time that Beaumont acquired several large canvases appropriate to a gallery, among them a radiant Venetian Canaletto, *The Stone Mason's Yard* (Pl. 33), perhaps a Willes family picture, and that early masterpiece of historical landscape by his old friend Wilson, *The Destruction of the Children of Niobe* (Pl. 34). Of the latter he was to write to William Gilpin with the highest praise, noting its 'vigour of mind and hand'; Wilson's 'fine taste for lines and a classical feeling' would always 'commend him to those who are capable of relishing beauties of this kind. For my own part, I have no hesitation, as far as my own judgement goes, to place him at the head of the landscape painters of this country.'[4] Beaumont conceded the rivalry of Gainsborough and he too would soon be admitted to his gallery. Some of Beaumont's own paintings, in Coleridge's words, 'undishonoured' in comparison, also hung here, among them perhaps the 1775 landscape that Farington preferred of all Beaumont's works. What Beaumont chose to call his picture room served — as Coleorton in a cultural desert never could — to attract kindred spirits happy to sing the praises of the old masters and the growing number of successors in the British School.

*　　*　　*

It took the execution of the French King Louis XVI in January 1793 to prove that revolution was no game; but even after France had declared war on its one implacable enemy, Fox and his fifty-odd followers in the House persisted in their refusal to condemn 'the friends of liberty' across the Channel. Such was Fox's charisma that it was to be more than a year before Windham and like-minded 'old Whigs' would finally desert their leader to join Pitt, and by then the situation had greatly deteriorated. The winter of 1792–93, following a bad harvest, saw not only the beginning of a war which was to last almost without interruption for over twenty years but of a new

33. Antonio Canaletto: *'The Stone Mason's Yard'* (*Venice, with Campo S. Vidal and Sta Maria della Carità*), (London, Nationa Gallery).

era in Britain when dearth lead to dissatisfaction and the constitution itself seemed threatened.

The outbreak of war gave new impetus to the loyalist associations which were springing up all over the country in answer to the radical 'corresponding societies', and even Fox joined Beaumont's neighbouring Hanover Square parish association, although also a member of the dubious Friends of Freedom. At Dunmow a meeting was held in January 1793, chaired by Maynard's younger brother, Henry, to confirm the town's 'zealous attachment to the Constitution', but Beaumont must have been appalled to hear that Coleorton was one of the areas affected by the riots and he conveyed to Farington 'his great apprehension about the times' the following January as Parliament reassembled after a seven-month recess. Summer was to bring only one break in the bad news, Lord Howe's victory at sea on the Glorious First of June; and even then the French merchantmen managed to evade the blockade. It was as well for Pitt that there was no alternative to his administration, Fox having put himself out of court with his advocacy of republican principles, and the Prime Minister was relieved

34. Richard Wilson: *The Destruction of the Children of Niobe*, (?) 1766–7 (New Haven, Conn., Yale Center for British Art. Paul Mellon Collection). Version of the picture in the Beaumont Gift destroyed in World War II.

when the Duke of Portland at last decided to rally the old Whigs to his support, allowing a reshuffle in the autumn of 1794 with much-needed changes at the Admiralty and War Office, where Windham became Secretary of War with a seat in the Cabinet. By now Beaumont shared with Mitford 'a mixture of rage at the triumph of the Jacobins, of mortification at our disgrace' abroad as the war threatened to develop into an allied retreat. Before Parliament rose in June, Beaumont had had enough and went first to Cheltenham on Dr Pitcairn's advice, and then on a sketching tour of the Wye Valley accompanied by Hearne. Chepstow Castle, shortly to appear in one of his pictures, much impressed him — 'superior to Conway' — and there was also time to visit Bath and Lord Radnor at Longford Castle to see the Claudes. After a lull of a couple of years, he was painting again and must have been grateful that the House did not reassemble until December.

At the beginning of the new Session Pitt had the mortification of hearing one of his closest friends, William Wilberforce, urging overtures for peace. Wilberforce's proposal was made with the best intentions but, to Beaumont, it was a stab in the back and he told Farington that 'great mischief' had been done to the British cause, blaming it on Wilberforce's listening too much to the dissenters; quoting Windham he added that the motion had 'encouraged our enemies and discouraged our friends'. Ever prepared to excuse Fox, whose company he was enjoying more and more, Beaumont's forgiveness did not extend to Sheridan nor to the upstart, John Courtenay, when Windham told him 'Fox is *not* a republican', but that 'in spirit' the other two were, and he felt the greatest indignation that a Tory should do the most damage.

There was also growing dissatisfaction with Pitt amongst his supporters, epitomised by Mitford, now Solicitor-General, who in January 1795 accused Pitt of involving himself with honours and jobs instead of 'preserving the integrity of the administration', and noted 'a languor in every department' with colleagues 'who only bring you weakness'. Receiving no answer, he tried again to impress the truth: Pitt's 'conduct of late has turned some warm friends into cold friends, or perhaps bitter enemies', for he no longer appeared his 'own master'.

In this, Mitford certainly spoke for Beaumont, who was to find Pitt's deportment increasingly 'dry and rejecting' and never felt at ease with the Prime Minister as he did with Fox and Grenville. His own solution would have been for Windham to have remained out of office, 'as with his abilities at the head of the country gentlemen at this crisis he might have had great effect against the opposition';[5] but Portland had wished it otherwise. Beaumont heard Windham reply to Wilberforce's second motion for peace with France, which was rejected by 201 votes to 96, and the Secretary of War, who was already showing the strain of office, was also to disappoint his admirers, for he was not a natural leader and something of an embarrassment as a speaker. Whatever his failings as a war minister, it was Pitt who wound up this debate, and again and again he was to carry the House, although his health was beginning to fail under the pressure of a string of misfortunes.

*   *   *

In many ways these were halcyon days for Beaumont, despite the background of war and discontent. Although he would have denied it, he prospered under pressure and his political cares had in no way diminished his zest for art; indeed as the political situation deteriorated, art was the more welcome as an escape. Not only had he built his gallery in anticipation of his collection, but he was taking painting more seriously again. For the first time it is possible to speak of him as a real artist of genuine promise, and if it is sometimes surprising that his contemporaries did just that and paid serious attention to his work, it must be remembered that in the period between the death of Wilson and Gainsborough, and the emergence of Turner and Constable, the landscape field was unconquered territory, dominated only by topographers like Farington or pasticheurs like Sir Francis Bourgeois. Without going so far as the critic of the *Monthly Magazine*, who, reviewing the 'present State of the Manners, Society, &c &c of the Metropolis' in 1800, declared that the 'landscapes of Gainsborough, Turner and Sir George Beaumont, may, without peril of comparison, embellish the same gallery with those of Claude de Lorraine and Carlo Maratti',[6] it is evident that Beaumont's competition with his contemporaries was, for a time at least, perfectly legitimate. As an amateur painter, he still occupied a somewhat anomalous position,

35. John Robert
Cozens: *View of
Langham, Essex*, c. 1790,
watercolour (Private
Collection).

and it took little to provoke even friends like Farington to reassert their profes-sionalism when his work threatened to impinge on their own. As a connoisseur, however, he was on surer ground. His position was the stronger for being no longer overshadowed by Reynolds, and his opinions gain a new ring of authority in the 1790s. 'Ventus Beaumontianus', as Gillray was to characterise it, was beginning to blow.

Beaumont was keeping a sharper eye than ever on contemporary painting, probably because Parliament kept him more often in London. Artists as diverse as Nathaniel Dance, C.-J. Vernet, Francis Wheatley, Thomas Stothard, Thomas Daniell and Luigi Mayer were attracting his attention beside old-established friends who were regularly entertained. Julius Caesar Ibbetson probably stayed at Dunmow early in the decade, and during the Beaumonts' visits to Dedham, Hearne and J.R. Cozens had been among the first guests, the latter drawing a view of the Langham hillside around 1790, not long before his lapse into insanity (Pl. 35). Beaumont himself was busy sketching during his summer expeditions, and he was constantly on the move during the Parliamentary recess, for the house his mother had leased at Dedham was even more confined than Dunmow. In 1792 the Beaumonts took Dame Rachel, Anne Willes and their friends Sir Henry and Lady Harpur of Calke Abbey, Derbyshire, to spend the short season at Lowestoft, where Sir George made a drawing that was later copied by Hearne. That summer he worked again at his favourite ruins of Castle Acre and the following year he made his first tour of North Wales, visiting Llangollen, Caernarvon, Conway — later another favourite spot — Anglesey, Harlech and Dolgelly between July and the end of August. Some impressive drawings exist from this trip, one, of Conway Castle, being among his most effective essays in the manner of Hearne (Pl. 36); and it was with Hearne that he made his tour of the Wye in 1794, after which he began a large view of Chepstow on a canvas over four feet by three. Farington thought it 'a very agreeable proportion', the size having been re-commmended by Benjamin West, who, as the new President of the Academy, was to see a great deal of Beaumont.

Beaumont had not exhibited at the Academy since 1779 and had been diffident about showing his Dedham subject that spring, but Farington 'confirmed him in a re-solution to exhibit'[7] and the picture was generally admired, John Singleton Copley going as far as to say it 'wd. have done credit to any artist in any country'.[8] Anthony Pasquin, however, was less enthusiastic, his 'Liberal critique' recommending a study of Waterloo to 'lead the student to a simple and proper choice of nature. . . in which this Gentleman. . . is more deficient than in his handling'[9]. In fact, if a contemporary and possibly related Dedham subject of a picturesque cottage painted as a wedding present for Charles Long (Pl. 37) is any guide, Beaumont was already falling under the spell of the Dutch masters and beginning to explore the notions of variety and contrast that Price, Knight and Gilpin held essential to the Picturesque aesthetic. Nor was this an accident, for in June 1794 Beaumont had been among the friends to whom Price sent his *Essay on the Picturesque* — it was the subject of discussion with Farington at Dedham — and the author was anxious that Beaumont should 'now and then look over my head and advise'[10] on the passages dealing with painting in the forthcoming *Letter to Humphrey Repton*, the landscape gardener having intervened with a *Letter to Uvedale Price*. Fox was consulted for his general reactions and Abercorn for the 'expression', and even the radical Horne Tooke joined the ranks of advisers — strange company indeed for Beaumont at this period. In fact he proved a less than diligent correspondent — Price complained that for him 'laziness serves in lieu of method' — but when he did put pen to paper it was to such effect that Price, who knew how to flatter as well as to chide, 'wished you would turn author'.[11]

Reading the *Letter*, Beaumont found much in common with Price, sharing his preference for 'accidents of nature' and his desire that landscape gardeners study the old masters and, like a painter, 'make the best use of the materials. . . in real nature'. Price's earliest surviving correspondence with Beaumont, of 28 November 1794, acknowledged a communication on Titian and Claude '& the reasons for their choice of subjects', and in return he sent his pages on 'prospects & on views down steep hills on both of which we agree', accepting criticism 'not only with docility but with thankfullness'. A week later Beaumont was asked to read 'with attention and all his acumen criticum' the final passage on 'the general and confined sense of beauty' which included a quotation from Knight's *Landscape, a Didactic Poem*, intended to flatter this friend and rival into accepting Price's definition.[12] Beaumont had dis-covered from the printer John Robson that Repton was agreeable to his *Letter to Uvedale Price*, criticising both Price and Knight, being reprinted with Price's reply, but when these were published early in 1795, it was left to Lady Beaumont to thank Price for a copy she had read on her own — an unusual occurrence in a household whose master was '*un grand dupeur d'oreille*', adept at 'slurring over the weak and im-pressing the strong parts of a book'.[13] Thereafter nearly three years elapsed before Price resumed the despatch of his manuscript, but he had not been idle: in 1796 he published a new edition of his *Essay* with additions approved by Abercorn and Knight, and had begun a second volume including an *Essay on Architecture and Buildings* on which Beaumont was again consulted before it appeared in 1798.

Determined not to neglect his own art, Beaumont was glad of advice himself when, in September 1794, Farington (Pl. 38) spent ten days at Dedham. It rained most of the time and Farington busied himself washing-in some of his drawings for Boydell's *History of the Thames* while his host worked on his Chepstow picture. Over dinner the Beaumonts relayed the Beverleys' Court gossip, and Farington vastly enjoyed the

36. Beaumont: *Conway Castle*, 1793, pencil and wash (Bolton Museum and Art Gallery).

37. Beaumont: *Landscape with a Cottage*, c. 1794 (B.C.).

38. Thomas Lawrence: *Joseph Farington*, 1790, pencil (London, Thomas Agnew and Sons).

39 (facing page). Rembrandt: *The Descent from the Cross* (London, National Gallery).

insight into the high, or high-spending life (Lady Beverley's father was 'distressed' on £18,000 a year), but relates little of local affairs save the visit of a Roman Catholic priest from Giffard Hall. It was a quiet, or working, holiday: 'Dined at 4, drank tea between 6 & 7 — and then went to bed at ½ past 10... the usual hours of the family which is very comfortable.' On fine days Beaumont and Farington rode or walked, and there was an expedition 'in the carriage to Mistley, and the village of Thorn, and crossing a bridge... through Bergholt and Stratford'. Farington thought the country-side 'a rich English landscape, the distance towards Harwich particularly beautiful',[14] while Beaumont was quite inspired, returning to London with two fresh pictures which 'He thinks are better than those He was working on before'. To Farington he admitted 'His hand was not in before owing to his having been many months from painting', and in the New Year, that he was 'so out of practice that it is only lately that He began to feel tolerably certain in his execution'.[15]

*   *   *

It was a bitter winter that year, with more unrest at Coleorton and warnings from the Revd Howlett at Dunmow that the government was not doing enough to relieve the poor. Bread was scarce and expensive, and while Lady Bessborough responded to threats of famine by giving up powder and forbidding 'pies and puddings out of patriotism', to the labourer it could mean starvation. The squalid conditions suffered by his colliers were later to be a factor in persuading Beaumont to take over his Coleorton estate, but as yet he was more concerned with subversive activities in the metropolis and in February, with Mulgrave, he visited the prophet Brothers, who described himself as 'nephew of the Almighty'. Formerly a naval lieutenant, this

prodigy's lineage was a puzzle, as he expected shortly to be revealed as 'prince of the Hebrews' and ruler of the world, but his small following already included at least one Member of Parliament. Beaumont and his friend saw him rather differently, 'mad' but an instrument of the democrats advising submission to the French, and a fortnight after their visit he was arrested and certified.

There were other concerns that spring. With Knight and other friends, Beaumont found time to raise a subscription for Cozens, 'now paralytic to a degree that incapacitated him';[16] with Lady Beaumont he had virtually adopted the painter Ibbetson's daughter Mary after her mother's death in 1793; and in March he advised on reserve prices for the collection of Reynolds's pictures, drawings and prints, which the painter's niece, Lady Inchiquin, was selling at Christie's. He had balked at intervening in any private sales, for 'of picture dealers in general I have no high opinion & I have little reason to think there is any regard lost between us',[17] but bought for himself two small Dutch pictures, a Brouwer,[18] and Rembrandt's oil sketch of *The Descent from the Cross* (Pl. 39). Rembrandt was not a new enthusiasm for Beaumont, and the painter was a positive passion of his friend Knight who placed him on a par with the greatest Italian masters and already owned several examples of his work, while Price could write to Beaumont: 'I most heartily join with you in wishing that Rembrandt was among us in flesh and blood'.[19] Yet the purchase is interesting as an instance of Beaumont's own growing taste for the Netherlandish schools with all their implications, whether expressed in landscape or subject painting, of painterly execution, contrasted texture and chiaroscuro lighting. He had already absorbed much of this from Reynolds's Foucquières. The Rembrandt was a connoisseur's tribute to the Picturesque, and in his collecting as well as in his painting, Beaumont was beginning to reflect a fashionable range of ideas. Meanwhile, Price, earlier that year, had recommended a Rubens landscape at Vandergucht's in terms which allowed even Claude's supremacy to be challenged. Having escaped the attentions of an expensive dentist, Beaumont should 'lay out half the money so saved in purchasing the little landscape by the greatest *dupeur des yeux* that ever existed' and never mind talk of Rubens's 'splendid impositions' or 'meretricious style', for while 'I love such chaste & genuine nature as we see in Claude, yet I equally dread a great deal of cold, honest matter of fact under that name, which in reality is the grossest of all impositions'.[20]

Encouraged by the praise for his 1794 exhibit, Beaumont sent two landscapes to the Academy in 1795. He was in his element at the Academy dinner where the top table seemed like his private party, blending art and politics just as he was doing himself: Farington sat opposite with Townley, Knight, Wilberforce, Hume and Long, and on Beaumont's side were St Asaph, Abercorn, Mulgrave, Windham, John Mitford, Beverley, Lord Inchiquin and the Dance brothers, as well as Sir John Call, whose constituency was near Beaumont's. The following day Farington, who had been largely responsible for the arrangements, breakfasted with Beaumont and the two friends resumed their exchanges of information. Neither held office in his own sphere but Farington was increasingly considered the power behind the throne in the Academy, while in the political world Beaumont, widely respected for his talent as an artist, was well briefed on Parliamentary affairs.

The summer of 1795 brought a spate of meetings called by the London Corresponding Society to condemn the war and whip up anti-government feeling. The first, in St George's Fields before Parliament was dissolved in June, created such tension that Members expected to be recalled, although the date was later postponed to October. Beaumont kept mainly to Essex and Suffolk, trying to paint, although there were also two weddings to celebrate. Elizabeth Bowles was married that summer, and Beaumont's happiest task was to propose the offer of his friend, St Asaph, now thirty-nine years old and a widower with four children, to Lady Charlotte Percy, only nineteen. The marriage took place on 25 July at Orwell Park, some fifteen miles from Dedham, where Beverley had moved in 1794. Its peaceful riverside shore and magnificent views provided a new sketching ground not only for Beaumont but also for Hearne, who numbered Charlotte and her sister, Susan, among his most proficient pupils. It was a happy solution that Hearne should find a welcome with the St Asaphs, for he was soon to feel over-shadowed by Beaumont's younger protégés.

*　　*　　*

Beaumont's name will always be associated with Dedham on account of his fateful meeting with John Constable there around 1795. Constable's own version of the occasion, which had been engineered by the 'anxious and parental attention' of his mother,[21] is too well known to quote, but the charisma and authority with which Constable immediately invested the visitor from London is a reminder of how far Beaumont had grown beyond his own East Anglian origins. To impress, Constable showed Beaumont not his juvenile sketches made on a recent trip to Norfolk, but painstaking copies after Dorigny's engravings of Raphael's cartoons. Beaumont was kind and admired them, in return showing Constable his Claude *Hagar*, which as usual had travelled with him to the country. Thereafter it was rarely out of Constable's mind, and thus began a long and for many years distant, but in the end happy and fruitful friendship that is part of the personal history of British art, and the first of a series of relationships in the course of which Beaumont deliberately sought to mould a painter's life and work.

In August Beaumont left Dedham and Farington reported: 'He has begun pictures since He went into the country, but not satisfied himself and only finished a small one. — He cannot be satisfied if transparency & elegance of execution are not conspicuous.'[22] After a few days in London he went on to Boldre in Hampshire with Sawrey Gilpin to stay with the Revd William Gilpin. These brothers were to be Beaumont's lifelong friends and kindred spirits. He was much impressed by the parson's good works in the neighbourhood and, in 1801, when William Gilpin decided to raise more money by selling his drawings, Beaumont became his most active puffer. He recommended to him the auctioneer James Christie as 'the best *orator*' in 'the present state of that sort of pulpit-eloquence'.[23]

Beaumont might long to concentrate on painting, but the political situation was too distracting even were his hand more certain. In October his nervous disposition had its worst fears confirmed when a London mob, inflamed by the government's failure to provide bread or victory, surrounded Pitt and the King on their way to open Parliament. The Seditious Meetings Bill, rushed through to contain such disturbances, he considered a 'strong but necessary measure', and was further convinced on 12 November when he ran into a mob outside Copenhagen House in Islington on his way to Dunmow and was forced to turn back. For the Whigs, however, the legislation was an infringement of liberty, and protest meetings were held in New Palace Yard and later in Marylebone Fields. While Beaumont felt there was little to fear from the crowds there, 'the agitation of the publick mind ' could not be denied, and he was by turns bored and upset by the disputes the Bill had provoked in the House. On its first reading, he was complaining 'attendance on the debates becomes tedious, with little entertainment. . .you are prepared to expect much of what. . .the speakers will say';[24] but on 21 November Price warned him that Fox was about to 'exert himself', and 'the altercation was more violent and desagreeable [*sic*]' than ever before, with Windham 'so warm that He did & frequently does commit himself by unguarded expressions'.[25] A new star on the government benches, Sir William Grant, was soon to impress him by a brilliant performance that eclipsed even Fox and allowed Pitt to resolve, as Lord Mornington told Beaumont, to 'Let the debate rest here on our part' — and when the Bill came to the vote Fox could muster little support against it. But Beaumont had seen the unpleasantness of politics and already seemed 'not to wish to be in another Parliament'.[26]

*　　*　　*

April 1796 brought a further sale of the Reynolds estate, and Beaumont bought several works, including a fine and broadly treated sketch of the head of a negro (Pl. 40) that, when he lent it to the Reynolds retrospective that he helped to arrange at the British Institution in 1813, he would identify as the painter's 'black servant', and the head of a melancholy bearded man (Pl. 41),[27] said to be the model, George White, a paviour from Yorkshire, who had sat for Ugolino in the picture of 1773. Beaumont had also been painting again, and whatever his difficulties the previous summer, had brought three pictures to London in February 1796, of which two were intended for exhibition. Farington, consulted as always, urged more attention to chiaroscuro — 'the colour of his lights is too much the same...a want of contrast in the tones'[28] — and typically, Beaumont sought comfort from the old masters, 'very strenuous for the necessity of painters occasionally copying...a great source of improvement'.[29] With West he visited Hampton Court to see the pictures and, still eager to train his hand in the new language of the Picturesque and convinced it was best expressed in a Dutch accent, painted an imitation of a Ruysdael in West's collection, as well as a copy of Sir Abraham Hume's Rembrandt. Farington lent him his *Maecenas's Villa* by Wilson to have beside him while he worked, the previous year having assisted in Beaumont's purchase of another version of the subject by Wilson from Vandergucht. Beaumont had already, for at least two years before that, owned *The Destruction of the Children of Niobe* (Pl. 34), but Wilson had ceased to be the fount of all knowledge for him and his eye remained more firmly fixed on the Netherlands. Comparing Farington's Ruysdael with two of his Wilsons, Beaumont declared that 'in Grandeur & stile Wilson greatly surpassed; but in strength & clearness...Ruysdael [was] superior'.[30] At the exhibition of the Orléans collection in May it was Rubens of whom he was speaking in 'rapurous terms', and by 1797 it would be obvious to Oldfield Bowles that Beaumont 'in his mode of painting had for some time quitted those views of the Art which were the effect of studying Wilson's pictures. That he looks for a dashing effect without making out parts, — and has so narrowed himself to this kind of execution that He cannot paint a large picture.'[31]

The loss of Beaumont's Academy exhibits of 1796, and the rarity of his oils from that decade, make it difficult to assess what was evidently a conspicuous change of style. Reviews of that year, however, indicate that he had succeeded in at least some of his aims. The *St James's Chronicle*, observing that 'Last year Sir George exhibited the best picture in the Exhibition', noted that his contributions were now 'rather sketches, than finished', while the *Morning Herald* went furthest to point to the fresh inspiration of his work at this period: 'pure nature charmingly designed and wrought up with all the magic glow of the Flemish School', and 'all the brilliant beauties of Ruysdael, without his formalities'. It is clear that the pictures were a success, and Beaumont

40. Joshua Reynolds: *Study of a Black Man*, (? Frank Barber) c. 1770 (Houston, Menil Foundation Collection).

41. Joshua Reynolds: *Head of a bearded Man*, c. 1770 (London, Tate Gallery).

found himself reviewed not just as an amateur of above-average talent, but as a leader of his school, 'unquestionably at the head of the Landscape' according to the *Oracle*.

Beaumont might well be content at this recognition, coming as it did at a time when he was having still graver doubts about pursuing a political career. Personal divisions upset him and seemed irrelevant to his own concerns. In May it was from Knight's dinner party for Fox — rather than from some Tory stronghold like White's — that he went to the House to hear General Smith press for the expulsion of a fellow Member for alleged misuse of recruiting funds, and with Long and many others he walked out of a debate that brought only embarassment. More important, but more difficult still, was the debate the next day following Fox's motion on the war with France. The indictment was grave: with Holland lost, the French King executed and the Republic more powerful than ever, the government had failed on all counts. Pitt knew it all too well, but it was clear there was nobody to replace him. With Pitt's colleagues convinced that omens for a general election were favourable, Parliament was dissolved on 19 May.

Bere Alston, which had been a gift in every sense, was now claimed by William Mitford. Despite his reservations, Beaumont seems to have considered another constituency, for that spring he drew £7,000 out of his bank account. Moreover, he had earned the offer of a ministerial seat, but characteristically, made his acceptance conditional on not being 'bound to support all measures or to be precluded from exercising his judgment'. This did not go down well, and 'when Principals were referred to, the proposal was not renewed'. The constituency was Colchester, and 'the probable expense not more than 5 or 600', but its 'being in the neighbourhood of Dedham', convenient as it might seem, 'made an objection'.[32] His prevarication 'perplexed' George Rose who wrote to Pitt on 11 April that 'Sir George concurred, but I afterwards learnt that he was suiting with Malmsbury, if he has not actually agreed';[33] and it was presumably Malmsbury, with only thirteen voters but expensive ones, that decided him to 'make his congé to Parliament being not disposed to give the price which seats sell for'.[34] Up to the last moment he was trying to see the party manager, Long, who was overwhelmed with work (a more persistent suitor who 'forced himself upon him' found him seated at a table buried under 500 letters), but Beaumont could summon no real enthusiasm for discussing yet another alternative, and his success in the Academy can only have confirmed that his heart was in art and not politics.

Beaumont's reluctance to accept a ministerial seat had also been touched by his growing disillusionment with Pitt. It was true that politics tended to appear a distraction from his real interests in painting and collecting, but even his artistic concerns served to highlight the contrast between the reserved Pitt and Fox, whom he often saw socially. While Fox regularly attended the Academy dinner — in 1796 he sat between Price and Knight — Pitt was conspicuous by his absence. It was remarked that Lord North, whose own problems had been taxing enough, had always found the time, and Farington went so far as to complain to Long that 'Mr Pitt possessed everything but taste'.[35] For Beaumont, who put personality above party, such things went deep. Pitt struck him as arrogant as well as aloof and uninterested, while he could not help being impressed by Fox, who 'converses like a man who wishes to learn' and 'expresses himself doubtingly, as if He desired to be determined by others'. He told Farington that 'in these respects Mr Fox differs from Mr Pitt...He courted opportunities to address Mr Fox or Lord Grenville; but always felt a difficulty when He sees Mr Pitt'. Lord Beverley, dining with him at Grosvenor Square, went furthest to point the contrast with Pitt's manners, striking a note of patrician disdain: the Prime Minister's 'deportment...& his neglect of their applications' having 'disgusted' the nobility, 'Lord Beverley said, His education had been confined, and his associations of a common kind, which had given a turn to his mind, that made him unfit to conciliate the affections of people of rank as well as others'.[36] Thus have Tory noblemen often squirmed under the brilliant outsiders who have led them.

For Price and Knight, differences with Pitt were thoroughly political, and if their Whig web did not completely ensnare Beaumont, it was a force in his life. Price was to become a 'crop' in November 1796, as evidence of his disapproval of the government, and reported to Beaumont the cutting of Knight's pigtail by his rabidly Whig mistress, Lady Oxford, who, he added, was anxious to meet him but would like to cut off the heads of all Tory friends. Price defied the Beaumonts to be angry as he sent them his own 'somewhat splenetic' epigrams on 'his Majesty's Improvements in private and public':

> Windsor! thy injur'd towers, parks, forests groan,
> England! thy wealth, power, freedom, are all flown.
> What various ruins from his pretty tricks,
> Whose taste was form'd by Brown; by Bute his politics

or on Pitt whose

art, oh learn its power to dread,
Transmutes each nobler metal into lead.

He feared Lady Beaumont's wrath more than Sir George's, but he was not altogether in jest and added, 'I do believe this transmutation has undone the country'.[37]

Beaumont, who prided himself on being 'a liberal sort of fellow', took all this in his stride; he could always find refuge, if needed, with the robustly Pittite Mulgrave, and their correspondence displays his continuing respect for the leader the two friends christened 'The Modern', even if Beaumont had to admit that Fox was the more generous in adversity and always spoke of Pitt 'as a great man, and this when some of Fox's party are inclined to undervalue him'. On the other hand, Mitford, though once a critic of Pitt, pointed to some of Fox's failings at dinner in Grosvenor Square in March 1797, when he was very 'talkative': 'Fox never makes a speech...without something escaping him which destroys the intended effect'; and 'Fox has more general knowledge than Pitt but is not so good a Politician'.[38] Beaumont showed his true colours when voting for Sir Alan Gardner rather than Fox in the 1796 Westminster election, and time was to reconcile him completely to Pitt: in 1806 he wrote to Mulgrave 'how every hour brings fresh conviction to the minds of all the wisdom of Pitt...All the brewers and bakers and tailors upon earth will never fill the space that was occupied by his little finger.'[39] But Beaumont was no less certain that he wanted no part in politics, and through Lady Mulgrave in 1811 he sent her husband the advice he took himself in 1796: 'the contentions of politics are irksome and injurious to the health — I wish he would give them up'.[40]

42.   Thomas Lawrence: *Sir George Beaumont* (Paris, Musée du Louvre).

VII
PROVIS, PRICE AND THE PICTURESQUE

IN 1793, OVERCOMING his dislike of having his portrait taken, Beaumont had sat to Lawrence. The picture was apparently intended for Mulgrave, but neither it nor a subsequent attempt in 1808, were much approved and it would be some time before Beaumont learned to appreciate either the artist or the man. He quarrelled unintentionally with him over his portrait of the Duchess of Gordon's daughter, the Duchess having used Beaumont's verdict that it was a poor likeness to reject the picture, and Lawrence's unctuous manner was 'always making him uneasy, his compliments forced';[1] perhaps he felt a certain reserve before a promising young man he had thought to encourage but who turned out to be bumptious. Lawrence's only portrait of Beaumont known today is in the Louvre (Pl. 42) and could be either the 1793 picture or its successor. It shows nothing of Beaumont's acknowledged charm, but is otherwise a perspicacious picture of him in mid-life. The face is handsome, authoritative, sensitive, but with a hint of something else — indolence perhaps, or the fatigue of indifferent health. It is not the face of a completely happy man.

The last five years of the century were uneasy ones for Beaumont. He missed the stimulus of politics, and the enforced timetable of the Parliamentary year, more than he cared to admit. Though still a member of White's, he had removed himself from the golden circle of government and was dependent for news on friends such as Long, Mitford and Mulgrave whose steadily advancing careers now contrasted pointedly with his own. If he had hoped to devote himself to painting, even this made no great strides. Two small oils appeared in the Academy in 1797 but he sent nothing the following year, and when he resumed exhibiting in 1799, it was with a subject conspicuously outside his usual range. In the Lakes in 1798, he recovered his touch as a draughtsman, but it would be a year or two before the experience was reflected in his painting. The inspiration that had flowed freely under pressure was fading — or must be forced — now that he was thrown back on his own resources. Wavering and worrying, he lost both health and strength, and something of his judgement too, falling victim in quick succession to quacks both of art and medicine.

There was little joy in the Beaumonts' backyard. The Coleorton agent, Boultbee, later to be found guilty of 'scandalous imposition', would be given notice in 1797, and with his colliers ever rough and ready to riot — he had spent £50 towards their prosecution early in 1795 — Beaumont's faint heart sank at the thought of his neglected inheritance. These problems at least could no longer be shelved and there is evidence of a new broom sweeping through his affairs. A London lawyer, John Philpot, now appeared frequently at Grosvenor Square and at Coleorton a local surveyor was hired to assess the extent of Boultbee's dishonesty. This soon became too much for Beaumont and it was not only the search for the elusive qualities of Dutch painting that left him unable, as Oldfield Bowles reported, to finish a large picture at Dunmow that summer. It was a sensitive time, and it was particularly unfortunate that Beaumont should at this point turn from Holland to Venice to revive his flagging inspiration. He would not be alone in falling prey to the 'Venetian Secret' now being hawked by Thomas Provis, but the affair would prove highly embarrassing to one whose artistic judgement, if not always his talent, was winning respect in the highest quarters. But dogmatic as he was, Beaumont could also be easily led. Recently he had been taking his cue from Benjamin West, borrowing both his certainty of expression — 'the finest picture in the world', West declared of Sebastiano del Piombo's *Raising of Lazarus* one night at Grosvenor Square[2] — and many of his ideas. Farington had heard them both in full cry in 1796, fresh from the Laborde and Orléans collections, and phrases like 'rapturous terms' (Rubens) and 'extraordinary merit' (Annibale Carracci)[3] preserve in his diary the echo of conversations that never fought shy of hyperbole. Scarcely outdone by his wife as a singer of praises, Beaumont was sometimes no less impressionable, and the 'Venetian Secret' was another enthusiasm he owed to West.

Like many of his generation, Beaumont was sufficiently the disciple of Reynolds to be constantly curious about technical nostrums and potions. Reynolds's habitual secrecy and private experiments had bred an attitude to the craft of painting that was as undisciplined as its stylistic and formal language was controlled. The potent appeal of the 'Venetian Secret' lay in its combination of mystery and historical revivalism. Just after the Christmas of 1796, West showed Beaumont a picture he had painted using the recipe 'discovered' by Provis which purported to create the effects achieved by the great Venetian painters. West was soon to run into trouble over the 'secret', not least with his fellow artists, who suspected him of trying to pirate it himself; but for the time being he had agreed to test it on behalf of the Academy. Beaumont thought the trial picture he saw did produce a rather Venetian effect, and was soon all too thoroughly converted. At first he was sensibly cautious, reluctant to part with any money to purchase the recipe — which Provis was selling on condition that purchasers swore to uphold its secrecy — as he thought 'it might be done on honor'. Unfortunately he changed his mind; not only would he 'know the process on the conditions prescribed' but went further and, 'though advised by those on whose judgement he relies not to grant a Bond...He offers...to pay double'. The Cassandras had been Knight and Windham, who, as a harassed Secretary for War, must have been rather surprised to be asked for his opinion on this matter. Both were worried lest Miss Provis, who was now managing the discovery for her father and was, not surprisingly, 'willing' to accept Beaumont's offer, were to change her status, perhaps by marrying an unprincipled man; and Beaumont himself was unsure how to react if other friends pestered him about the method and its price. It was left to Farington to use his usual diplomacy. By 11 March the dust had settled and Beaumont took his first lesson. His teacher was Miss Provis herself and he pronounced himself 'delighted'.[4]

It was not long before doubts returned. Neither a white nor a dark ground seemed to produce quite what was expected, and samples of the method painted by Thomas Daniell and Henry Tresham were not promising. Beaumont believed the process 'true', but wondered whether Provis had it complete. Turning to West for reassurance, he was greatly encouraged in April by his friend's large *Cicero at the Tomb of Archimedes* (Pl. 43), painted partly in the Venetian manner and partly in bodycolours.

43. Benjamin West: *Cicero at the Tomb of Archimedes* (photo Christie's)

Beaumont may have suggested the picture himself, for the previous summer West had given him an oil sketch of the same subject,[5] and now he was thrilled by the finished version — 'superior He thinks even to the landscapes of N. Poussin. — For grandeur and variety, and entertainment, it is remarkable, — and on the whole the best of West.'[6]

Both West and Miss Provis were consulted over Beaumont's two small landscapes, one a *Twilight*, intended for the 1797 exhibition. These must also have been experiments in the 'Venetian' method, for *The Times* and the *Morning Chronicle* spoke of their 'old manner' and 'old system'. Other reviews suggest that Beaumont was still moving towards freer execution, the *Morning Herald* observing that 'nature is his model', although his style still struck its critic as Wilsonian, as it did also the writer in the *True Briton* who considered 'the general touch seems to be in the manner of Ruysdael, combined with the manly force of Wilson'. Samuel Rogers, on the other hand, thought the pictures 'spotty & touchy', and a hostile note was sounded by the *St. James's Chronicle* which was sorry to observe that 'Sir George Beaumont not hindered by the scourge of necessity, has lately moved retrograde'.[7]

Beaumont had again dithered about exhibiting. He was unhappy with the pictures, left out a third one that Francis Bourgeois had particularly urged him to include, and sent the other two in late, which caused a distinct coolness with Farington whose own exhibits were moved to accommodate them. Farington, his patience wearing rather thin, 'thought this very unhandsome treatment...to alter an arrangement which was approved to accommodate him who did not for many days determine whether He wd. exhibit or not, was unreasonable'. All the more galling for Farington to hear 'The Nobility say Sir Geo: Beaumont is the only Landscape Painter'; his barbed comment, 'The Amateurs imprudently credited', betrayed his resentment.[8]

Even Beaumont sensed an atmosphere and moved quickly to reserve one of Farington's landscapes in the exhibition. This was more a matter of diplomacy than of the 'classic taste' praised by the *True Briton* when reporting the purchase, but Farington was not easily mollified and a tinge of acid now crept into his remarks about Beaumont. Old friends though they were, Farington was becoming irritated by

95

Beaumont's perpetual recourse to others to solve problems he lacked the imagination to deal with himself. Catching him painting with West's Hobbema and a small sketch by Rubens at his elbow, and 'pleading the advantage of having such pictures to constantly throw his eye upon', Farington 'did not dispute the point, but think[s] it shackles the powers of an Artist. The observations shd. be in the mind.'[9] And as a dedicated professional, he could hardly be other than exasperated to find Beaumont another day 'all for Salvador — Old pictures only true models, they having been proved by time, — fashion may make moderns pass.'[10]

Ever readier to pronounce on others, Beaumont was still troubled by his own lack of direction, the more obvious now that his art was his main resource. His painting and his health were both suffering, poisoning each other in a vicious circle. In April, after two 'attacks', he was induced by the Bishop of Gloucester to seek relief for 'bilious complaints' from a Revd Mr Barclay of Manchester Buildings, and was put on a strict régime forbidding 'web-footed animals', red meat and milk, and concentrating instead on 'Large Cod, — whitings, soles, Haddocks, — Turbot'. All these were supposed to 'regulate the Bile...the great object of life', but Farington had also noticed that 'Sir George often labours with Phlegm'.[11] Lady Beaumont had paid Mr Barclay £7 for 'Specific' — made up for 'Persons of fortune' — cordial, pills and advice, but she was sceptical of their power and complained of the expense, and in July the patient was no better, having 'gout in his feet' which made him 'peevish' as never before, unable to attend meetings or make the journey to the Lakes.[12] Instead, he was confined to Haverhill and Dunmow, where Dame Rachel had returned after giving up the Dedham house. He had never done his best work at Dunmow unless inspired by a visiting artist, and Farington, looking over some recent studies, saw rank confusion and 'frankly told Him that picture which He painted in 1775 was his best',[13] thus dismissing twenty-two years of progress. But he was little dismayed, and his critic was soon to find him 'more attached to painting than ever'.[14]

Meanwhile, another 'Rembrandt' had arrived at Grosvenor Square, bought from Lawrence for 200 guineas, although the painter claimed to have given 400 for it. This was the *Jew Merchant*, now considered mainly studio work but then regarded as a considerable masterpiece.[15] Short of money as he often was, Lawrence had offered it at 150 guineas provided, if he chose, he could have it back at 200. Beaumont had no wish to set up business as a pawnbroker and delivered a diatribe against Lawrence's manner — 'the over-reputation he had had was a dangerous temptation to overset his judgement'[16] — but he badly wanted the picture in whose rich texture and shadowed tones he found the stronger meat he now sought in painting. The previous year he had bought two theatrical pictures by Robert Smirke out of the Academy[17] and a small sketch from the impecunious Francis Wheatley as 'an accommodation under his present circumstances',[18] but his witty dismissal of de Loutherbourg's exhibit of 1797, a scene of bandits attacking travellers in Germany — 'pity so much fine writing on such nonsense' — suggests boredom with lightweight narrative painting.[19] Nothing, however, would more clearly display his vacillating mood than his own recourse to this genre for his single exhibit of 1799, the result of his summer spent at Dunmow (Pl. 49).

There was little cheer that autumn. A sudden change of government in France had dashed all hopes of peace and inflation was making life intolerable for much of England. At Dunmow the vicar, Howlett, who was no revolutionary and looked to the

96

44. Beaumont: *An Ox Roast at Dunmow, 15 November 1797, to celebrate the Victory at Camperdown*, pen and wash (B.C.)

labouring classes as suppliers of services to the better off, had written of the 'famished countenances' and 'shivery limbs' of those Pitt had failed with his half-hearted proposals for poor relief. Beaumont was thankful that Henry Maynard took the lead in local affairs, but did his best to break the gloom, commissioning a production of *The Provok'd Husband* at the Dunmow theatre, and, after Admiral Duncan's victory at Camperdown, spending £80 on an ox roast when 'many hundreds partook of the cheer of eating and drinking'[20] — festivities that produced a spirited sketch (Pl. 44). At Coleorton Boultbee's removal was troublesome, and there were family cares besides, Mr Howland, now over ninety, dying of cancer at Haverhill, and Beaumont himself still beset by mysterious maladies. The Duchess of Gordon, whom he relished for her 'humour & entertainment like that of Foote the Comedian' — exactly what he missed in his ardent but earnest wife — had amused him with her quip about her ailing physician: '*since He was ill*, our family have been very well'.[21] But, alas, he failed to take the hint, trying every doctor until one Ewer matched his own weathervane moods by diagnosing 'a degree of induration' and then doubting it. His mercurials, however, were taken through into the spring, not surprisingly leaving Beaumont more 'nervous' than ever. To make matters worse, the 'Venetian Secret' was now finally exposed as a canard and it can have done little to speed the patient's recovery to see himself portrayed in a caricature by James Gillray as a fat, puffing putto, fanning the flames of seven Academicians and a host of hangers-on as they solemnly pursued the elusive genius of Venice (Pl. 45).

* * *

45. James Gillray: *Titianus Redivivus — or — The Seven Wise Men consulting the new Venetian Oracle, — a Scene in ye Academic Grove,* 1797, engraving (London, British Museum). Beaumont is one of the flatulent putti whose wind puffs the Venetian Secret; his wings are inscribed VENTUS BEAUMONTIANUS.

Price had briefly relieved Beaumont's depression by an unexpected and welcome visit to Dunmow when a 'little Ruysdael scene near the house' was on the easel.[22] Lady Beaumont was evidently the better company, for many years later Price was to remind her of the 'lively conversation, rides to Domesday oak' and 'your looking so remarkably well that if I had had a grain less of love & regard for Sir George, I should have felt very much disposed to "teach my lovely scholar all I knew"'.[23] That it took years for her admirer to dare such a confession reveals something of Lady Beaumont's primness and she was becoming increasingly disapproving of society's lax morals, to which Sir George, in later years, considered 'Fox had contributed more than any other...by introducing Mrs Armstead His Mistress, a woman who had been very common, into Company after he married Her'.[24] Price, whose own wife was no paragon of virtue, loved to escape from home, and after his happy interlude at Dunmow, the south room at Grosvenor Square was always available to him.

But ailing, moody and indecisive, Beaumont had given his guest pause for thought, and that December Price wrote, partly in jest but also in some concern, to tell him he was

> Yet indeed a perpetual blister on my back! You officious skipping, pragmatical, gate-opening knave, go to! Marry I'll tell you what you are, & I hope there be truths. You are a person who being thoroughly acquainted with all the country through which I am travelling, out of pure friendship to me, having no business of

your own to call you out, accompany me the whole way, keeping me out of bogs and quagmires...and shewing me a number of beautiful parts I should not have discovered...What a lucky thing it would be for you if your friend could say with the great poet,

> He can requite thee, for he knows the charms
> That call fame on such gentle acts as these:
> And he can spread thy name o'er lands & seas,
> Whatever clime the sun's bright circle warms.

Nothing of this kind can I do for you, & if you have a mind to get into the temple of Fame, you must 'eer shake off your indolence, & knock boldly on the gate yourself.[25]

The charge was plain: Beaumont must cease leading a vicarious life. It had needed saying for years. But Price continued to contribute to the problem by seeking Beaumont's advice on his own book, once again pursuing him with queries and proofs to London, North Aston and Dunmow, and when Beaumont reacted for once with untypical force, he did not altogether like it. Reeling from a 'philippic against parentheses' — thus had Beaumont poached on Abercorn's stylistic preserve — Price wrote tartly: 'Don't use me like a certain Jack Daw, & strip me of my borrowed plumes, for I am very proud of them.'[26] It was all the more galling when Beaumont did not pay attention to the content, mistaking where acacia trees should be planted. Price put it all down to the Boultbee affair and the 'Billion of account books haunting you'.[27]

During the winter of 1797–98, staying at Sonninghill, Price was in easy reach of the Beaumonts in London was well as Fox at St Anne's and Abercorn at Stanmore Priory. His writing prospered. Fresh from Grosvenor Square he was full of praise for the recent acquisitions. The 'Rembrandt' portrait 'makes my mouth water' (Lady Beaumont had approvingly pointed out the dirt in the sitter's finger nails), and as for the little Brouwer, 'what tinds! as poor Malchair said'.[28] For his book he decided to write up the Bourdon *Return of the Ark* (Pl. 30) as 'an instance of the great judgment with which he has introduced picturesque circumstances, when the subject & the general style of the picture is grand & solemn'. His description, 'written *con amore*', was sent to Dunmow in January in the hope that the 'excellent' copy that Lady Beaumont had painted would be there for comparison;[29] it was duly approved with only slight alterations. Price had already congratulated Beaumont on his contribution on the 'town in Tivoli' and 'Zucchi's mode of castlemaking',[30] and had agreed with both Beaumont and Fox on the elimination of Gabriel Perelle, who 'has no business to be mentioned with Gaspar'.[31] In return, the Beaumonts were given his completed essays on *Artificial Water* and *Decorations near the House*. Seldom can an author have engaged such a chain of critics, for Price's next submission on 'the motion in a bridge' — 'an idea that requires some better sanction than the author's own'[32] — was taken by Fox to read to Mrs Armstead, then to Paul Sandby, to Englefield for his 'omniscience', and finally to Beaumont, though Abercorn too may have been waiting in the wings; and it was even conveyed to Repton who, not knowing its originator, also approved. When Price's book incorporating this essay on *Architecture and Buildings* came out in March 1798, Price left Beaumont in no doubt of his special place in its pages: 'how do you like yourself in print? don't you think all that part about sculpture

& painting in Mr Price's preface uncommonly ingenious? somebody will ask you; a devilish good account that of Wouverman's picture: is it not Sir George?'[33]

*   *   *

Howland died in February 1798, a year after old Davy, and the Beaumonts' East Anglian round was no more, save for the Beverleys at Orwell Park. There was talk of building on to the 'Haverhill villa', Price recommending his 'little friend, Nash' who was 'very docile'.[34] This was none other than the great John Nash, later the vastly successful, but prodigal and unreliable, architect of George IV, and even at this early stage of his career his estimates needed checking. Beaumont, however, postponed any decision until peace should be declared and also dropped negotiations for a new lease at Grosvenor Square. Although his Howland legacy was almost £100,000, other members of the family had a life interest and he pleaded poverty when Price offered a trial, with an option to buy later, of his new house built by Nash on the sea at Aberystwyth in a truly picturesque setting. This caused Price some mirth — surely some of the breeches Sir George had found at Haverhill had money in the pockets? — but although the Beaumonts talked of a house in Wales, they were not to be enticed; a return to the Lakes was well overdue and they could make a brief inspection of Coleorton *en route*. A busy season in town had included several evenings with Townley, and there had been old Tom King's benefit at Drury Lane, as well as a dinner at the London Tavern with Dance and Farington at which Bannister proposed setting up a club to dine at each other's houses, Mulgrave, John Hoppner and Colman being the additional members. Bannister, who gave his 'excellent imitations of Kemble, Colman, Bensley etc', took them on to see his performance in the new farce by John O'Keefe, and they all ended the evening at the last act of *Castle Spectre*.[35] In early July Beaumont was ready to depart for Holker Hall. Casting aside his cares, he had written by the 9th to Poole the colourman 'for a pound of wax and many colours';[36] sketchbooks he must have taken with him for it was to be a long and active tour.

Lord George Cavendish had died in 1794 and Holker, which held so many happy memories, was now owned by his brother, Field Marshal Lord Frederick. There were changes too at Conishead Priory where Braddyll had run through his money. The Beaumonts gravitated naturally northwards, and on this visit they bought the ideal site for a 'summer-house' on Loughrigg Tarn, just above Brathay and on the back road to Grasmere — only for their vision of a peaceful haven to be destroyed by Sir Michael Fleming's resentment of their invasion of his territory, so that within a few years the land was resold. After spending much of July and August in the neighbourhood of Keswick where they visited Squire Bertie and Lord William Gordon, the Beaumonts, still dissatisfied with Sir George's health, travelled south and took a house in the Crescent at Bath where Lady Beaumont's sister, Frances Fermor, joined them in December.

As winter approached, Price felt neglected: 'I know no more about you & Lady Beaumont than if you were in the moon' — and aware they had been in the Lakes he wrote asking, 'have you been working hard, as you said you would, at the detail of light & shade, & effect? No one can do it so safely as you, for that grand principle of breadth is so rooted in you, that you can never sacrifice it.'[37] If Price expected Beaumont to overcome his recent difficulties and more happily assimilate the classical and the Picturesque, it is unlikely that he would have been disappointed by the fruits of the summer. Beaumont had not exhibited at the Academy that spring and his Lake oils are so difficult to date that it is scarcely possible to pin any down to this year, but a number of wash drawings are sufficient testimony to the quality of his work in 1798. Free from his cares, he had found himself again in the observation of his beloved scenery. Modest as they usually are, his sketches had attained a completeness of design that lifts them beyond immediate impressions into more developed works of art. Sometimes there is an echo of Italy, but it is the Picturesque that is pre-eminent. From 1798 and the following year date series of Lakeland subjects in broken blue or grey washes in which irregularly formed trees, rocks and boulders animate what remain essentially Claudean vistas.

Such sketches were later elaborated in chalk-and-wash drawings in an album that Beaumont used from 1802,[38] and in some oils which, though seldom more than sketches, are characterised by a vivid impasto and dramatic cloud and light effects that can be reminiscent of Cozens, and sometimes of the bold touch of Samuel William Reynolds under whose spell Beaumont had fallen after Reynolds had entered his life as an engraver in 1800. Beaumont's thrall to this Reynolds would be yet another example of his tendency to work best under the guidance of a mentor. Recently his prompter had been Ibbetson, whose technical methods were at least as interesting as his style, and since the failure of the 'Venetian Secret' Beaumont had been looking to him as the purveyor of another old-masterly effect, his so-called gumtion, a variety of darkening glaze based on magilp. Beaumont was to pass the recipe on to Farington, but, as his letters to its inventor show, it could bring disappointments of its own.[39]

Well-known as they were, Beaumont's borrowings had yet to impugn his own sway over the younger professionals, and his Lakeland drawings were also assimilated and developed by a much greater artist, Thomas Girtin. It was once widely believed that Girtin was the Beaumonts' guest in 1798, and although this now seems unlikely, a sketch of the mid-nineties drawn near the Suffolk village of Nacton,[40] and his 1799 Academy exhibit, *A Mill in Essex*, might suggest that he had visited them at Dedham or Dunmow. Versions of sketches of Wathenlath and Culloth Force (Pl. 46) are among several adaptations from Beaumont known today, but it is most likely that Girtin worked on these in London. The professional and the amateur were certainly close by 1799 when Beaumont became an associate member of Girtin's Sketching Club, an evening drawing society that met to sketch subjects from literature and would attract most of the best young draughtsmen. In the spring of 1798, West had been 'full' of both Girtin's and Turner's watercolours over breakfast at Grosvenor Square, and Beaumont would also have come into contact with Girtin through Dr Monro, with whom he was on friendly terms and involved over the affairs of Cozens. Beaumont was rather impressed by Turner's earliest exhibits in oil, but although there was as yet no sign of his later antagonism towards the artist, it was to Girtin that he felt personally drawn. It seems certain that he entertained him at Conway in 1800, and he collected some thirty examples of his work,[41] his most extensive accumulation in the field of watercolour that he was later to spurn. It was to be Beaumont's habit to share his protégés with Mulgrave, and Girtin also visited Mulgrave Castle that summer. Girtin's early death in 1802, too soon to take advantage of Beaumont's suggestion of a cure in Madeira, deprived the two friends of the first artist they had encouraged together. Beaumont continued to treasure Girtin's drawings and was later to show them to Constable — now about to re-enter his life — as 'examples of great breadth and truth';[42] while S.W. Reynolds dedicated his posthumous mezzotint of Girtin, after John Opie (Pl. 47), to their mutual patron.

*   *   *

Beaumont had lost none of his old love of the theatre. Amongst the highlights of the 1790s had been the final performance at Old Drury in May 1791, when devotees of intimate drama bade farewell to the stage of their youth, and, some seven years later, the nostalgic occasion of King's benefit on 15 May 1798 brought 'Gentleman' Smith out of retirement once again to play Charles Surface in *School for Scandal* (afterwards he was entertained by Beaumont, Mulgrave and Jack Taylor, the editor and critic). Less sentimental was the evening spent after the play with Malone and Kemble when the Duke of Leeds, who was 'too fond of low company' and 'talked too much', at least lived up to his reputation for 'late hours' and kept them up until three. Beaumont was always harsh on Kemble, whereas Malone, at a contentious dinner party at Grosvenor Square nearly a year later in March 1797, defended his performance as Benedict, although allowing he might fail as Macbeth or Othello. Such controversy was the breath of life to old stagers like Beaumont and Bowles, but there was no gallant to challenge Beaumont's declaration at a quieter dinner with Hearne, Dr Monro and, for once, both the Faringtons, that 'Mrs Siddons owes most of her fame to her figure, countenance and deportment'.[43]

In fact, it had not been a vintage decade for the stage, and when the Beaumonts accompanied Windham and the former beauty, Mrs Crewe, now rather 'en bon point', in May 1798 to see *Isabella* and *Blue Beard*, 'the house was thin and the performance flat, and they left before the end'.[44] New talent was at a premium and in 1799 the talk of the season was a series of plays written anonymously — actually the work of Miss Joanna Baillie, although it was some time before the mystery was solved. That January Beaumont and Price with their wives had met at Bath and Sir George read one of the plays, *De Monfort*, on the theme of hatred, to an appreciative audience. Price, ever eager to fan the flames of debate and temporarily tired of the Picturesque, now turned to the drama and there followed a lively exchange of correspondence, orchestrated *con brio* by Price and including a eulogy from Fox that ran to five pages and some verses by Mulgrave, who, assuming the author to be male, asked:

> How shall I judge his works, with hopes so rais'd,
> Compared to Shakespeare, and by Beaumont prais'd...[45]

Beaumont had never expected to meet such tragic passion in his own day and so electrified Miss Berry that she tried to obtain the written criticisms for her friend Mrs Cholmeley — 'the ideas of three very superior understandings and tastes, all struck with different beauties'[46] — but had to report that Price 'knows their value, keeps them in cotton'.[47] The following year Kemble and Mrs Siddons took *De Monfort* to Drury Lane, but despite a prologue by Frederick North and an epilogue by the Duchess of Devonshire, Miss Baillie's lack of stagecraft proved too obvious and the play ran for less than a fortnight. However, she continued to write with some success and her *Metrical Legends* of 1821 would include 'The Elden Tree', based on a chivalric story told her by Beaumont. He also did his best by Miss Berry: in 1812 his dining-

46. Thomas Girtin: *Culloth Force*, c. 1799, watercolour (B.C.).

47. John Opie (engraved S.W. Reynolds, with dedication to Beaumont): *Portrait of Thomas Girtin*, 1817 (B.C.).

club friend, George Colman, was persuaded to read *The Two Martins* and found it worthy of the Haymarket Theatre, subject to 'sundry touches, heightenings etc' for the '"Dutch Painting", as the Author terms it, wants some dabs of Distemper to produce those Candle-light effects which the present taste of the Town (False or true) deems requisite'.[48] Miss Berry came to Grosvenor Square to discuss the project, but her play never reached the professional stage.

Price had found Beaumont in excellent spirits at Bath, and sent a glowing account of his metamorphosis to Abercorn. He was always at his best when his interest was caught and back in London he was busy collecting and painting again. At Miss Gainsborough's sale in March he was 'agitated' at nearly losing one of the two pictures by her father that he coveted, *Cottage Door with Peasants smoking* (Pl. 48), to the Duke of Beaufort; but all was well and the picture became his, soon to be joined by a Gainsborough sketchbook bought jointly with George Hibbert to divide between them.[49] The *Cottage Door* may well have contributed to the painting Beaumont made ready for the Academy that spring. Based on sketches made in East Anglia, it was a picturesque portrait of a local character, Elizabeth Woods of Creeting Hills, Suffolk, who lived in the oven chimney of her tumbledown home. Soon to be engraved by S.W. Reynolds, (Pl. 49) it compounded Gainsborough's fancy pictures with both the Dutch tradition Beaumont had recently been studying, and the work of several contemporaries, chiefly some landscapes by Farington with figures by Robert Smirke; two of scenes of Falstaff particularly impressed him and in April, he was also 'delighted with Smirke's picture from the poem of the Hermit, imitated from Rembrandt'.[50] Nathaniel Dance, who had had high hopes of Beaumont's work a few years earlier, was disappointed by this experiment and disliked its bolder handling; he thought Beaumont 'falls off in his painting, — is all for painting pictures as a writing Master

48. Thomas Gainsborough: *Cottage Door with Peasant smoking*, c. 1786 (Los Angeles, University of California).

49. Beaumont (engraved S.W. Reynolds): *Elizabeth Woods, of Creeting Hills, Suffolk*, 1800 (B.C.).

would flourish, all by dexterity & slight', and 'confines himself to trifling subjects instead of exerting himself on some considerable composition'.[51] But most comments were favourable and Beaumont was eager to escape to the country and begin painting again.

Early in June he planned to 'stay at Dunmow a fortnight & endeavour to paint a picture before he goes on any excursion',[52] and later he was resolved to return to Conway, but not before he had had his fill of the important exhibitions in London that spring. In May he was among the swarm who gathered at William Beckford's house to see the Altieri Claudes, and was ready with his opinion: 'in Claude's cold manner, which He fell into as he grew old, His *golden warmer Manner* is preferable'.[53] Having seen the Orléans collection in Pall Mall, he pronounced Lord Carlisle's *Three Marys* by Annibale Carracci 'the finest picture of the size in the world', echoing the absolutes of West.[54] Fuseli's Milton Gallery was also in Pall Mall that year and Farington found Beaumont there with Bowles; all agreed the pictures were proof of a powerful mind, '*but the public wd. laugh*', and Farington urged the painter to 'get some ladies to attend his Exhibition to make it more general'.[55]

This was the last year that Beaumont attended more than the occasional Dilettanti Society evening — he resigned in 1802 — and he also played an active part as a Fellow of the Society of Antiquaries, supporting Englefield in order to keep Lord Leicester in the presidency, despite being canvassed by Samuel Lysons and Farington who, with many artist members, opposed Leicester's choice of Craven Ord as the new Director. The London season was spoilt for Beaumont by the news that Boultbee was fighting Beaumont's demand for compensation for mismanagement of his property. A legal action loomed and in April 1800, despite a new doctor's prescription of more meat and a daily pint of port, Beaumont was again weak, with his liver 'sluggish'. But his sights were still set on Cumberland, and the Beaumonts would descend from the hills only for Christmas at North Aston. After three months spent between Keswick and Ambleside, they leased a house in North Wales. Benarth, high above the Conway estuary among woods and with magnificent views, so delighted them that they returned there for the next three years. The following October Price, fresh from a tour of the Wye, was eager in join them. He was perhaps a little in love with Lady Beaumont and longed to see her again in a setting that he thought well suited her soul, 'amidst old castles, mountains, cataracts and sea'.[56]

VIII
COLEORTON AND ITS MUSES

NORTH WALES, several days' journey from London, was to provide a happy escape from the realities of the new century which had opened inauspiciously, not least for the Beaumonts. While the country and its leader, Pitt, were being worn down by the strains of war and now faced an enemy reinvigorated by a formidable First Consul, Napoleon Bonaparte, Beaumont had won his first battle with Boultbee. But the agent, knowing his ex-master's dislike of business and his lack of stamina, was leading him towards a costly dance through the law courts in an exhaustive attempt to avoid repaying the income he had fraudulently diverted to his own account. Represented by some of the best legal brains, Beaumont was to emerge the victor, but at the cost of no less than three recourses to Chancery at a time when he had become increasingly vulnerable to bouts of depression. For a man of such temperament he was now too reliant on his own efforts and, despite the lavish praise for recent pictures by peers and press and the companionship of younger artists who had the right aspirations, he had yet to find his own role in the development of the British School. With the Boultbee business always looming, Beaumont longed to get away from the bustle of daily cares, yet his conscience no longer permitted him to ignore the problems of Coleorton. It was to be largely from a sense of duty that he would make his future there, for his heir was his little-loved cousin, Thomas, who had a 1,500-acre estate at Buckland in Surrey. Thomas had married Bridget Davie, the sister of a Devon baronet, in 1799 and within the year produced George Howland Willoughby Beaumont whose first name indicates Sir George's acceptance of the *status quo*. That Sir George was not merely to survive the decade but, during it, reach the peak of his influence was, in great part, due to Lady Beaumont, who provided unfailing support, and whose sensitivity and enthusiasm lent impetus to friendships with the Lake Poets and transformed the creation of a new Coleorton from a penance into a challenge.

*   *   *

Like many important families with seats in the northern half of England, the Leicestershire Beaumonts derived much of their wealth from coal. At Coleorton their mines had been worked with varying degrees of competence since the fifteenth or sixteenth century, the most recent resident being the staunchly royalist third viscount who had rebuilt the earlier hall after its destruction in the Civil War. At his death in 1702 that title lapsed and a distant cousin, another Sir George, from the Stoughton Grange branch on the other side of Leicester, inherited as the fourth baronet, directing the Coleorton pits himself in the later 1720s and introducing two of the revolutionary

Newcomen 'fire' engines which pumped out water, making deep mining possible. Sometime before his death in 1737 his nephew, William Busby, acquired a lease and the operation became so run down that, by the time the Dunmow Beaumonts inherited, only a rogue or a fool would take on the colliery. Joseph Boultbee, appointed agent by the sixth baronet, was certainly no fool, and following a year's trial employment, during which he invested some £1,500 in a new 'fire' engine, in 1760 he agreed a new lease of twenty-one years.

Had Beaumont's father lived a normal span, Boultbee might have given good service in the dual roles of Coleorton agent and colliery tenant but, with only the Dunmow lawyer, Bridge, supervising as the principal agent, Boultbee's self-interest soon got the better of him and he began to acquire neighbouring pits and coal deposits, building up a successful business at the expense not only of the Beaumonts but also of Lord Ferrers and other local landlords. His epitaph in Coleorton church erected by his son, Joseph, at his death in 1789 — 'distinguished for Christian and moral virtues' — was an ironic tribute to Beaumont's misplaced trust, for, if Boultbee had indulged in philanthropy, it was often with his master's money.

There had been exchanges between the two parties towards the end of the lease in 1780, when Boultbee confessed to exceeding the annually permitted 10,000 loads of coal, but pleaded the difficulty of separating Beaumont coal from his own in adjoining seams. Having established Bridge's total ignorance of the subject, he put forward proposals favourable to himself for a renewal of the lease. In 1784 Beaumont, just back from the Grand Tour, instructed Bridge to refuse it, but by then Boultbee and his son, who was the real rogue, were acting as if they owned the estate and had opened a new mine, Coleorton Field, meanwhile keeping the Dunmow office quiet with slightly higher returns. This state of affairs continued until Beaumont, caught up in the new mania for canals, began to take an interest in the colliery, which was expected to benefit from the new Loughborough and Leicester Canal, the Charnwood Forest branch making the profitable Leicester market accessible. Beaumont, who had watched the enabling legislation through Parliament in 1791, took five £100 shares in the Leicester Navigation Company while Boultbee subscribed for twice that amount. If this did not cause comment, George Wade, the competent young lawyer who had taken over from Bridge, must at least have noticed that in Boultbee's accounts the Newbold Mine, leased at £50 per annum — a figure the agent had represented as fair — was assessed for Land Tax in 1790 at £220.[1]

In September 1791 the Beaumonts had combined a visit to the Harpurs at nearby Calke Abbey with an inspection of Coleorton. The signs of bad if not dishonest management were there for all to see; John Throsby had recently written of the 'lordship dirty',[2] the hall, which old Boultbee had occupied, nearly down except for one turret and scarcely a trace left of the park. Shocked further by the living conditions on the estate, Beaumont had to decide whether to let things stand and settle for a steady income of about £2,000 a year, or face the more troublesome alternative. He was in no hurry to involve himelf in business while Parliament absorbed him, but after some correspondence, Boultbee, now living in Bath, was summoned to London in 1793 by Beaumont's new legal adviser, Philpot, who later masterminded a series of surveys at Coleorton. It was obvious that the Boultbees had far exceeded their contractual obligation of 10,000 loads of coal and this was only one of many acts of fraud. Investigations were delayed by the bitter winter of 1794–95, when the already problematical Charnwood Forest stretch of the new canal lost its water level and hardship among the colliers led to riots. Boultbee handled Beaumont's part in their prosecution, while at the same time distributing charity from Lady Beaumont, and stouter hearts than Sir George's might well have wished to avoid confrontation with an agent who himself threatened to flood the colliery. But in March 1797 Boultbee was finally removed. In November 1798 a Bill of Complaint was issued against him and *Beaumont v. Boultbee* was listed in the Court of Chancery the following year.

The worry of Coleorton, where yet another riot celebrated the new century, was enough to send Beaumont to 'the silent hills' of the Lake District even in the middle of winter. After the usual December visit to North Aston and a period at Dunmow, he spent February 1800 painting at Ambleside before returning south for the season. Joseph Hodgkinson, a burly London surveyor who was now in overall charge at Coleorton, the lawyer Philpot and Mitford, now Attorney-General, all rallied to Beaumont's support. Still, Lady Beaumont knew that the best course was to get her husband away whenever possible, and they had already enjoyed a month at Benarth, their Welsh retreat, when at last the case came up on 15 July 1800. With John Mitford and the brilliant Samuel Romilly representing Beaumont, Boultbee with two provincial advocates was at last outmatched, and the Lord Chancellor, Lord Loughborough, found him guilty of 'gross abuse of unlimited confidence', refuting the plea that it was neglect by the plaintiff in not bringing the demand earlier, on the grounds that the defendant was also confidential agent. In a judgement complicated by allowance to Boultbee for various acquisitions and investments, he was ordered to pay compensation for the 'overplus' of coal and for various underpayments to the extent of some £20,000.

When this welcome news reached Benarth, the Beaumonts, who had already enjoyed the company of a group of young artists in June, were entertaining Knight and the poet and wit, William Robert Spencer, and these were followed by the Bowles family. Farington, the sole guest during September, found Beaumont in fine form, well able to ride twenty miles a day. His wife had died in February, and this time the guest rather than the host needed comforting. Farington wrote: 'Sir George very kindly talked to me on the subject of my health and situation & I was much the better for the conversation. He is convinced my bodily debility...encreases my difficulties by the effect it has on my mind'[3] — Beaumont's own experience.

Beaumont and Farington visited Conway, Bettws and Llanryst, and Lady Beaumont made up the party for a week's tour which took them through Bangor to Caernarvon, crossing the straits in the ferry to get the best view of that town. From their next inn they took '3 hours and 40 minutes in going 10 miles' to Harlech, the mountainous road requiring four horses to draw the chaise, to be rewarded by only 'bacon & eggs at a very bad Inn which afforded nothing else though it was Sunday,'[4] and no wine. With Beaumont a connoisseur of both port and cider, the fare at Benarth was no doubt more satisfactory and helped pass the long evenings when he read a Shakespeare play or Miss Baillie's *De Monfort*.

Benarth proved quite a magnet to the Beaumonts' friends who were prevented by the war from travelling on the Continent, and, in September 1801, after visits from the artist William Alexander and the Bowles family, Price, whose ill health now exceeded Beaumont's in severity, was at last fit for the journey, anticipating a warm tub and perhaps a sea bath too. That summer he had sent his friend a pair of special stirrups after hearing of Sir George's terrifying experience when he had been dragged along by his horse with his foot caught up, Lady Beaumont being a helpless onlooker. Price's affection for his hostess enabled him after this happy stay to mimic her, having first taunted her with their reluctance to return his visit: 'I stay at Foxley after this, no not a day, not if he would give me his woods; they may be very fine, but Boscathlin!!!...do you remember the ride we took Sir George, & the shed with ivy & the little spring!'

Price hoped they would settle at Foxley to sketch, without Lady Beaumont 'wishing to get it over',[5] but in October 1802, when they arrived in appalling weather, Sir George caught one of his chills — and perhaps a fit of jealousy — and, as soon as he was on his feet again, they left for a cure at Cheltenham. The return journey from Benarth in 1800 with Farington through Llangollen, Shrewsbury, Colebrookdale, Bridgnorth, Worcester and Broadway to spend a fortnight at North Aston had been a happier one, except for the artist, whose spirits remained low, despite the household of five Bowles daughters and William Delamotte, now drawing master at Oxford, who came to show his South Wales sketches. Laura Bowles had attracted a visit from the Revd Frederick Moysey, an amateur painter who excelled at seascapes and whom she later married, while Henry Hakewill, the son of Beaumont's old friend and now himself an architect, came over from Oxford. On some evenings Beaumont read plays by Foote or Farquhar while, on others, the company looked at Van der Velde and Wilson drawings. A reminder that the threat of invasion had to be taken seriously came when Bowles showed off his own militia troop in 'uniform dark blue jackets with silver trimmings', twenty-six strong, who fired their pistols for the first time. He was full of talk of a recent county meeting, having been amongst the minority of gentlemen who voted that the scarcity of bread was indeed 'real'.[6]

The Beaumonts were back in London on 1 November and after five months' absence they had to turn their minds to their own problems. There was bad news from Coleorton where Boultbee's prevarication at handing over the colliery, let alone the compensation, spelt trouble; Lady Beaumont's brother, John Willes, had suffered a paralytic complaint, his death in January 1802 coming as a merciful release; and, in the wake of this, to complete their gloom, came 'a more calamitous Event to the country than all the victories of the French',[7] the resignation of Pitt, who went out on the issue of Catholic Emancipation in Ireland, precipitating another bout of madness in the King, who had denied his minister this legislation. With Pitt's blessing, Addington formed an administration in March 1801 and, to the nation's relief, George III recovered. Addington, however, could never measure up to his predecessor and it was not long before Beaumont was commiserating with Mulgrave, one of the Pittites soon to press his leader to return.

*   *   *

In August 1802 the Boultbee case came up again in the Court of Chancery. John Mitford had been 'banished' as a reluctant Lord Chancellor of Ireland and Beaumont had to rely on lesser mortals. Boultbee's appeal was against the part of the verdict back-dating compensation to Boultbee's father's time: this was dismissed by the new Lord Chancellor, Lord Eldon, though Boultbee was allowed to convey his own Rotten Row mine in part payment. If Beaumont's victory had been final, it would still have

50. George Dance: *Self-Portrait*, 1795, pencil (Oxford, Ashmolean Museum).

been a pyrrhic one: he emerged the undisputed owner of a run-down colliery, the monetary compensation was reduced to some £15,000, a fraction of the Boultbees' gain, and there were high legal and surveyors' costs. In fact it was 1805 before the saga ended, Lord Eldon finally refusing Boultbee increased wages or legal costs but allowing Beaumont interest on underpayments only from 1798.

The Beaumonts meanwhile having decided to have their own country establishment, and that it must be at Coleorton, commissioned their old friend, George Dance (Pl.50), in the autumn of 1801 to design a house for about £8,000, Price and William Mitford being promised the sketches. Mulgrave, who shared Beaumont's resistance to joining the rush to the Continent following the Peace of Amiens, was at Benarth in the following July to push forward his own architect, William Atkinson, whose plans, the first to arrive, were acknowledged as 'ingenious'. The Beaumonts' friendship with the Mulgraves was now in full flower, for the 'Lady Partner' was a delightful person without grand airs, and Sir George was probably telling the truth when he wrote: 'I think I never passed a few days so happily as while you were with us.'[8] The following year it was the Beaumonts' turn to visit Mulgrave Castle, a long carriage drive across the Yorkshire Moors, and in such a situation on the coast north of Whitby that Repton had once preferred its prospect to that of Mount Edgcumbe on Plymouth Sound; it was a far cry from the workaday landscape that the Beaumonts faced at Coleorton.

Once the Beaumonts had decided to build at Coleorton, they were beyond persuasion, although one friend after another expressed dismay. Beaumont explained to Gilpin that he had little choice: 'the air is however fine and the prospect from the chosen spot splendid in point of richness and extent'. There is, in fact, an affinity between the adjacent Forest of Charnwood and the Lake District: there were the same knolls of oak, rocky outcrops, stone walls and bracken heathland, but Coleorton had 'no *river*, or lake, and indifferent roads',[9] nor, Beaumont might have added, mountains. Dance soon had reason to complain of the roads and he found the pitridden surroundings depressing. It was also ironic that, although Leicestershire was synonymous with the chase, sport was the last thing the Beaumonts enjoyed. Their intention, however, was not to create a residence that would tie them all the year, but a modest house that would act as 'a bait' to future generations so that the estate would never again suffer the neglect that had stirred Beaumont's conscience when he learnt of the 'many acts of oppression and injustice' done in his absence.

The Beaumonts expected that Dance would incorporate a corner of the existing house into the new one, the more recent additions being reduced to the dust they deserved. The earliest plans, dated 27 January 1803,[10] show a small, grim, two-storey castle, distinguished by the old octagonal tower at one corner and copies at the others. It appeared a simple and uninspired solution. Dance had already confessed his wish 'to steal' from his former pupil, John Soane, explaining: 'I have got a house to build in the country which plagues me to death tho' I am excessively eager about it',[11] and he was probably as disappointed with his first effort as the Beaumonts. The elevations that followed had all the variety of desperation as Dance, realising Beaumont's capacity for prevarication, tried to tempt him with prettier presentations of medieval castles in a woodland setting, classical mansions and even a building resembling part of a village, something his client had fancied for the Loughrigg site, perhaps following the example of Lord William Gordon on Derwentwater.

One reason for Beaumont's indecision was the resumption of war on 18 May 1803. The news occasioned less dismay than a yearning amongst Pitt's supporters for his return, and after the situation was debated in the House of Commons on 23 May, Beaumont told Farington that Pitt had 'shone with extraordinary lustre' before returning to his post at Walmer as Lord Warden of the Cinque Ports. The Beaumonts were in London until June, then, after the usual week at Dunmow, they set out for Coleorton, having invited Price to join them at the new Hall Farm, their makeshift headquarters, but refusing his counter-offer to bring Knight, on the excuse that additional advisers would sour Dance. They had talked of urgently needing 'a celebrated ground gardener'[12] and Price engaged his local man, Cranston, on very reasonable terms, sending him fully briefed. Cranston found Beaumont similar to Price, and his ten days at Coleorton were a great success as he staked out planting positions and the nursery garden, and began pruning and clearing with the help of six labourers. Price, laid up with excruciatingly painful piles, wrote in August of his delight at 'little Cranny's progress' now Sir George 'begins to take such an interest'.[13]

*　　　*　　　*

But Beaumont's heart was still in the Lakes, though on the journey north for a long-overdue visit this July, even he could not have guessed what a fateful meeting lay

51. George Dance: *Project for Coleorton Hall* (London, Sir John Soane's Museum).

52. George Dance: *Ground Plan of Coleorton Hall, as built* (London, Sir John Soane's Museum).

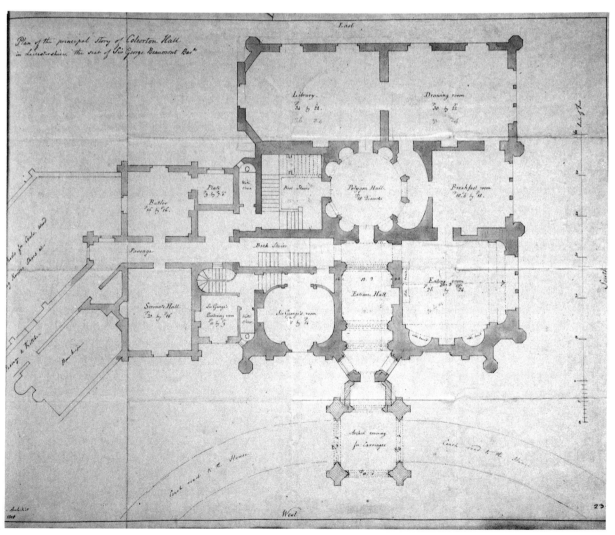

ahead. Before staying with Mulgrave's friend, Lord Lowther, to whom they recommended Cranston, the Beaumonts had settled into lodgings at Greta Hall, Keswick, which also housed the Coleridge family. Beaumont's first impression of the plump and garrulous Samuel Taylor whom he had met in London at William Sotheby's had been so unfavourable that he told Farington he had 'considered how He shd. shun him', but here in the mountains the poet's talk matched the sublime, and in November Beaumont reported him 'of great genius — a Poet, — prodigious command of words, — has read everything' and Wordsworth, who had just crossed the Beaumonts' path briefly, 'a rival genius', as Farington noted acidly.[14]

Nothing was more calculated to impress the Beaumonts than the thought of a muse shared between geniuses, and amongst Coleridge's themes was his absent friend, Wordsworth, to whom he wrote on 23 July, after having played on the high-strung sensibilities of his new friends with all his force:

> Sir G. and Lady B. . . are half-mad to see you — (Lady B. told me, that the night before last as she was reading your Poem on Cape RASH JUDGMENT, had you entered the room she believes she should have fallen at your feet).

It was probably only on the Beaumonts' day of departure that they saw Wordsworth, and they were not to meet again for nearly three years, but their friendship flourished by letter and was fanned by Beaumont's impulsive gift of land at Applethwaite, which was intended to bring Wordsworth closer to Coleridge. Beaumont wrote of his gift:

> I had a most ardent desire to bring you and Coleridge together. I thought with pleasure on the increase of enjoyment you would receive from the beauties of Nature, by being able to communicate more frequently your sensations to each other, and that this would be a means of contributing to the pleasure and improvement of the world, by stimulating you both to poetical exertions.[15]

Such an impractical purchase — even the poet of nature needed a habitable house or the money to build one — shows the euphoria to which the Beaumonts had been led by Coleridge's magical talk. Even before they realised it he had revolutionised their rather sober lives.

To overcome the disadvantage of having been thought a violent democrat — in Lady Beaumont's eyes a heinous sin — Coleridge, one evening at Keswick on their first acquaintance, had argued the case against the scurrilous Junius letters in such a manner that it was the less adept William Hazlitt, then making his way as a portrait painter and engaged to paint the poet, who found himself tarnished with the democratic brush, and lost a patron. In an impassioned dinner-table outburst, he upset his host so much that 'in disgust he never saw me afterwards',[16] and it was useless for Coleridge to try to repair the damage by stressing the common ground between them, or to write to Beaumont later of 'our friend Hazlitt'.

Hazlitt had already painted Wordsworth as 'a profound strongminded Philosopher', and Coleridge confirmed to Beaumont that the sitter was 'a great Poet by inspirations whose Poetry was your philosophy under the action of strong winds of Feeling — a sea rolling high'.[17] That August Coleridge also did his best to please his friends, in frenzied handwriting bewailing his early associations with democrats and Jacobins, and sending them parts of his ode 'Dejection', together with Wordsworth's 'Resolution and Independence' — perhaps to emphasise the relationship between the two poems. The Beaumonts particularly enjoyed the last four stanzas of the 'Ode to Tranquillity' which subsequently, in September, accompanied 'Mont Blanc' and 'Extempore', and they were to be delighted at the approval of Coleridge's poetry shown by Walter Scott and the poet and public orator William Crowe at Grosvenor Square in March. Meanwhile, Lady Beaumont, encouraged by Coleridge's reaction to her favourite *Provincial Letters* by Pascal — not quite sharing her gluttony for punishment he concentrated on the first part — sent him Dr Isaac Barrow's *Sermons*.

It was Lady Beaumont who turned the friendships into a vital element in all their lives. Coleridge brought out the best in her, for he recognised her streak of unworldiness and enjoyed her flights of fancy — already he had compared her to a miniature of Madame Guyon — and he was one of the few to appreciate her intellect and wide knowledge of literature. In return her frustrated maternal instinct came to the rescue when his mental and physical torments became evident, for it was not only his brilliance that appealed to her but his frailties — 'it is among my wishes to write my whole life to you', he had confessed within months of their meeting, and so he did, on huge scrawled sheets that hit the breakfast table like a lunatic newspaper, hiding nothing save the addiction to opium that was the root of his problem. It was the breath of life for the Beaumonts to hear of Wordsworth from none other than his close collaborator in the *Lyrical Ballads*, and they saw Coleridge as a sort of John the Baptist, heralding one greater than himself and oblivious to his own good. In this honeymoon period in their relationship Beaumont, whose melancholia was gaining on him, rushed headlong towards a kindred spirit in equal need of comfort and love. Such rapture could not last, but, for a few weeks at Keswick and Dunmow, when the talk was a torrent, Beaumont was both elated by his contact with true genius and warmed by the response of a fellow sufferer who knew despair.

By the time Coleridge came to Dunmow the following February, he could report back to the Wordsworths that the Beaumonts were so indoctrinated that Sir George talked of 'William, his domestic Happiness, and his height and uniqueness of poetic Genius, till the tears have been in his eyes, and on Lady Beaumont's Cheeks who verily has a soul in point to quick, enthusiastic Feeling, most like to Dorothy's — only not Dorothy's powers'. Coleridge's excuse for visiting Dunmow — where he 'went for 2 days and staid 10' — was to study his host's drawings, of which he promised '*translations*', possibly 'a moral-Descriptive-poem'. Sir George's gift of a drawing of a waterfall (Pl. 53), left behind for him after the Beaumonts' departure from Keswick, he had first seen through tears. Admiration ran as high as hyperbole in the volatile poet who, that February, told his correspondent, John Rickman, that Beaumont was 'an undoubted genius' after a week in which he 'learnt as much...respecting Pictures and Painting and Painters (as)...from any man in the same Space of Time', and added, perhaps a little wistfully: 'A man may employ time far worse than in learning how to look at a picture judiciously'. Overwhelmed, he found 'their solicitude and affection is enough to effeminate one' and he felt himself almost swooning, 'as an innocent young woman pleased and uncoy, the intelligible all of a lover's behaviour'.[18] He reported his host 'bewitching company', and learned to regard highly Beaumont's knowledge of Shakespeare, while the baronet was impressed by one who had 'read everything'. Sadly, nothing seems to have come of the 'translations' Coleridge had promised, although he had earlier written enthusiastically of 'the poems

on your sketches, dear Sir George! I hope this much that they will give evidence that the Drawings acted upon my mind as Nature does, in it's after workings; they have mingled with my Thoughts, and furnished Forms to my feelings.'

Aided by some 'rich & precious wines', Coleridge's health temporarily improved while at Dunmow. Beaumont probably preferred to ignore the hints Coleridge gave of his drug addiction, though details of 'night horrors', attributable to 'atonic Gout', are in the letters for all to see. His hosts encouraged him to try the year's absence in a warmer climate advised by his medical friends — the solution recommended to Girtin and later to Wilkie. Beaumont, who considered himself quite a connoisseur of illness, was interested enough to try some of Coleridge's own remedies: oxygenated chalybeate drops, or, if they failed, Davy's compound acid, both despatched later from London

54. George Dance: *S.T. Coleridge, 'March 21st 1804'*, pencil (DCT).

with 'Daniels Poems with the eminent Passages of the Hymen's Triumph. . .*marked*' (the latter presumably for Lady Beaumont).

Riding together one day in Maynard's park, Beaumont proved of little help when Coleridge fell from his horse, the animal galloping off wildly, only to be found later 'as mild as a lamb'. A month later in London, however, the Beaumonts rescued Coleridge from a severe attack of illness, Lady Beaumont showing, as Dorothy Wordsworth recognised, all the tenderness of a sister as he was nursed back to health. During this stay at Grosvenor Square, Farington and Dance were introduced to Coleridge, having probably heard enough before the meeting to be wary of poetic genius. After an 'evening was passed listening to a succession of opinions and explanations delivered by Coleridge', Dance sympathised with Farington, who was 'fatigued by that sort of confinement'. Dance had at least shared the limelight, deriding the 'prejudice of limiting Designs in Architecture within certain rules', and pronouncing that 'in his opinion Architecture unshackled wd afford to the greatest genius the greatest opportunities of producing the most powerful efforts of the human mind'.[19]

Coleridge was preparing in his muddled way for his departure to Malta. Lady Beaumont saw to it that his new portmanteau, in addition to food and drink, carried a grammar and dictionary, as well as the manuscripts of Wordsworth's poems lovingly transcribed by Dorothy and Mary, while a new writing desk housed a packet of James's Powders (but not, unfortunately, the aperient so necessary in the Mediterranean that a surgeon would have to board from another ship to provide relief). Sir George added a present of £100, delivered by his servant, for the poet had already 'mildly but firmly' refused two previous offers. As a reminder, the Beaumonts now had Coleridge's portrait, painted for them by James Northcote and Dance drew him on 21 March before his departure (Pl. 54).

Coleridge's obvious pleasure at being lionised by such 'good and elegant people' made his parting into the rough and tumble of a sea voyage quite poignant and at heart he was deeply conscious of his debt. It was of Lady Beaumont that he was thinking when, just before his departure, he wrote in his notebook that 'the Water Lily in the midst of the Lake is equally refreshed by the Rain, as the Spurge on the sandy Shore'.[20] Her husband's final letters, as Coleridge set off in a despairing search for health and peace of mind, reveal the contrasting aspects of his concern: a final instruction, as though for a small boy, to resist over-indulgence in the delicious fruits of the Mediterranean, and a farewell: 'God for ever bless you and restore you to complete health, and grant you a speedy return to those friends, who love and honour you and to a world which stands in need of your admonitions and instructions.'[21]

It was shared sorrow at the loss of the their friend, so much more agonising to the Wordsworths than to the Beaumonts, that brought the two families closer as they committed their worries to paper. Lady Beaumont's loving care of Coleridge during his illness that March had further endeared her to Dorothy, and soon they were corresponding in quest of news from Malta, while there was from the beginning a healthy frankness between the two men. Wordsworth in his first letter, acknowledging with some embarrassment after an interval of eight weeks the ill-timed gift of Applethwaite, had confessed to nervous sensations which gave him 'an aversion from writing'. This struck a chord in Beaumont who lost no time in admitting to his own nerves and his 'selfish' motive in giving Applethwaite, for, 'you very well know it is impossible to be acquainted with him, [Coleridge] without earnestly wishing to oblige him...and there was no means of doing this so effectively as by accommodating his friend'. Wordsworth had enclosed three sonnets and Beaumont, wishing to make these 'patriotic lines' 'more generally known',[22] arranged their publication in the *Poetical Register*:

> SHOUT, for a mighty victory is won!
> On British ground the Invaders are laid now...

and early in 1804 Wordsworth composed a special sonnet at Applethwaite:

> Beaumont! it was thy wish that I should rear
> A seemly Cottage in a chosen dell,
> This dids't thou plan for me that I might dwell
> In neighbourhood which One to me most dear,
> That undivided we from year to year
> Might work in our high calling...

Almost as pleasing, in the autumn, Dorothy gave the Beaumonts the credit for stimulating her brother to resume work on *The Prelude* when they sent him William Cowper's poem, 'Yardley Oak'. On Christmas Day 1804 Wordsworth outlined to Beaumont the plan for his 'poetical labour': first 'The Recluse', 'to express in verse my most interesting feelings concerning Man, Nature, and Society; and next, a Poem (in which I am at present chiefly engaged) on my earlier life or the growth of my own mind'. Beaumont hardly sensed their importance, nor that *The Prelude* was a masterpiece in the making, but he cared too much for these poems 'to throw any impediment in their way' by insisting on a hoped-for visit, and added rather lamely: 'your natural and beautiful lines on the wrens nest make us long to see it as well as the kind architect whose letters delight us'.[23]

The previous March Beaumont had spoken much of Wordsworth to Farington. The poet had 'chosen to forego professional views, preferring retirement upon something more than £100 a year with the gratification of indulging his imagination to any worldly advantages. — He has long been what he calls idle, *not writing*, finding that it affected his nerves.' At that time Wordsworth was concentrating on 'The Recluse', and Beaumont read Farington 'Tintern Abbey', which he thought 'exquisite and has read it 100 times', and 'The Beggar': 'Sir George said He was infinitely indebted to Wordsworth for the good He had recd. from his Poetry which had benefitted Him more, Had more purified His mind, than any Sermons had done. Coleridge has more learning — more reading than Wordsworth, but Sir George thinks Him not equal in poetical power.'[24]

While Beaumont had been able to embrace Coleridge with all his pent-up affection and desire to serve a man of such 'high calling', he realised that Wordsworth was made of sterner stuff and was content to keep in touch largely through his wife, who had found such an admirable correspondent in Dorothy. He much regretted missing the opportunity of acquiring portraits of the Wordsworths when Henry Edridge, whom he admired 'both as a valuable man and an ingenious artist' and who was later to paint Lady Beaumont,[25] took the poet's likeness early in 1805; but greater intimacy followed the death of Wordsworth's brother John, shipwrecked in his East Indiaman that February. On the 17th Beaumont wrote a letter of consolation, quoting, as so often, from Shakespeare and from his favourite 'Tintern Abbey': 'that presence which has heretofore "disturbed you with the joy of elevated thoughts" will I am confident afford you assistance in this hour of trial'; and with all the delicacy of which he was master, he offered help if the family finances had been affected. Wordsworth's long, reassuring reply increased Beaumont's admiration for a man with whom he felt on quite open terms, and it came naturally to the patron to enclose a small present of money, only for the poet to make heavy weather before reluctantly accepting. Beaumont, who valued 'that natural intercourse, that delightful equality, which is the joy, the life, the sunshine of friendship',[26] wished he had thrown the note into the fire, but it was a timely reminder of Wordsworth's independence of spirit, an attribute that was to save them both from the usual patron-protégé relationship so often fatal to friendship.

The Beaumonts' enthusiasm for the Lake Poets was to prove their salvation at a time when the prospect of a house at Coleorton, which privately filled Sir George with gloom, increased their mutual regret at being childless — something the occasional appearance of two small boys, the cousins, at Grosvenor Square did nothing to allay. Beaumont became increasingly unwell and suffered one of his fevers at Mulgrave in 1803 at the end of the northern tour. Patriotism was in the air and despite Mulgrave's reservations on the value of volunteers to meet the threat of invasion, Beaumont did the right thing by his country, raising a corps of infantry at Coleorton and one of pioneers at Dunmow, but excusing himself from participation on the grounds that 'the least fatigue or damp renders me useless'.[27]

*   *   *

While great progress was being made with the grounds at Coleorton under Lady Beaumont's watchful eye and with the help sent by Price, the problems of rebuilding on the old site had continued to be discussed during the early part of 1804 when the

55. J.R. Thompson after William Wilkins (engraved J. Stewart): *Donington Park, Leicestershire*, 1809.

question was whether to sacrifice view for aspect. Dance regretted that the principal rooms would face north/north-east which Price preferred to west — one of his tiresome interventions, though Dance agreed that the ideal aspect was south/south-east. An intermediate plan went to Price in January who complained that the model was so flimsy and glutinous that one tower stuck in the basement, and he awaited a summons when the estimates were ready. This came late, probably for early June, and hardly was Price back at Foxley than he learnt the plan to add two good rooms and offices to the old house, which he had 'recommended' and Knight had endorsed, was already threatened: 'if Mr Dance spoils my favourite composition from the eastern window of the bow in the drawing room...where the principal hill is seen between the Elms and the Wych Elm...I shall, do what would be very difficult on any other occasion, quarrel with him'.[28] Price could, however, save himself the trouble, for at the last minute the surveyor Hodgkinson conveniently declared what 'Sir George called the execrable old mansion fit for nothing but Offices'.[29] The new site, different by only a few yards, was an improvement and Dance, who on 19 July had told Farington 'he should rejoice to give £200 to have nothing more to do with it', rallied once again to draw up an entirely new design. The architect had so far been more successful with his portraits than his plans, drawing Price, Cranston and Hodgkinson,[30] and was soon to add Beaumont and the Earl of Moira, the Beaumonts' most desirable neighbour, to his gallery. It cannot have been a coincidence that the exterior finally chosen for the new house was, in effect, a smaller version of Donington Hall (Pl. 55), seat of this distinguished soldier and friend of the Prince Regent.

By the time the Beaumonts left Coleorton in late September the foundations were under way, the first stone having been laid on 21 August 1804. Lady Beaumont was now in her element in the role of Price's pupil, receiving pages on the construction of pools, the best variety of tree, underplanting and pruning, while advice went to Sir George, 'once such a great uncorker of bottles',[31] to cork the poor damaged wych elm. The view that Price cherished towards Bardon Hill — 'the Olympus of Leicestershire', as Throsby called it[32] — lay approximately east of the main rooms of the house, in front of which a terrace was to be built and, beyond new lawns, the ground sloped

120

away into a dip where a newly dug fishpond would serve as the lake. To the south of the house lay the dell destined for a winter garden which was separated by the carriage road until this was diverted in 1812 to the perimeter. Dance, with some sharp comments on both the practicality and the cost, was to save the Beaumonts from adopting a more elaborate arrangement of the surrounds of the house planned by S. W. Reynolds, Sir George explaining to his prime patron, Samuel Whitbread, that the artist lacked the necessary knowledge of surveying.[33]

Although the ugly brick houses of Coleorton village were allowed to remain in the view and the stone used for building was chosen in line with Sir Joshua Reynolds's maxim that it should match the local soil as nearly as possible,[34] the exposed site needed a solid mansion and Beaumont found himself making excuses to Wordsworth for creating 'too conspicuous'[35] a residence. It also dawned on Price that few of his conceptions were to be realised: there was neither bow window nor conservatory, but he made the best of it, rejoicing at the thought of an entirely new building and being able to step out of the library's north window into the grove where some fine trees had survived 'that husky Misodendron Hodgkinson'[36] and previous stewards. Nobody appears to have attached any importance to the humble offices, banished into an extension, despite the Beaumonts' having lived their lives in sensibly compact houses.

*   *   *

During the winter of 1804–5 Beaumont was more severely ill than usual, being laid up for most of January with painful rheumatism. The following month S. W. Reynolds was invited to Dunmow to engrave the Rembrandt, and no doubt the visit was intended as some compensation for the disappointment of not having his plans for Coleorton accepted. Reynolds, who spent time in France despite the war and was said to be a radical, had a way with him that caused his patrons to forgive him his sins, and his vitality was as welcome to Beaumont as his assistance with painting, 'his excellent eye to judge of a work when finishing'[37] being warmly commended by his host whose 1806 Academy pictures, including *Peele Castle* (Pl. 64), owed much to this artist's continuing influence.

There was no lack of novelty in Beaumont's life, for the boy-actor William Betty had made his début at Covent Garden in December and Beaumont, after seeing him as Young Norval in *Douglas*, was afflicted so badly by Bettymania that a few days later he and Lady Beaumont shared Thomas Lister Parker's outing with the boy to the Tower of London, Mulgrave joining the party afterwards. This was not quite the happy holiday anticipated, the young Roscius merely reacting against the sight of the monkeys kept in captivity there; but although the boy-wonder bore 'not a few marks of the spoilt child'[38] and cared little which character he played, Beaumont, who attended some of his rehearsals with his tutor, expected him to banish '*recitative acting*'[39] from the stage, an opinion reinforced in February by 'Gentleman' Smith. This retired actor, contrary to his fellow professionals and perhaps to spite his old adversary, Kemble, publicly pronounced Master Betty worthy of Garrick's seal, which had been entrusted to him until he found a successor who acted 'from Nature and from Feeling'.[40] Such a gesture appealed greatly to Beaumont, who could read Smith's effusion in the *Morning Post*, and he was soon up from his sickbed at Dunmow to add his voice to 'what makes the sole conversation of London'.

The climax of young Betty's career was his Hamlet played on 14 March to a house that included Lord Sidmouth, Pitt, Fox and George Canning, as well as the Duke of Devonshire and Lady Bessborough, who reported 'excessive applause'. Beaumont had seen him a second time in the part when he told Farington that Hamlet 'has never been so performed since the time of Garrick';[41] but he was soon to change his tune. The boy was discourteous to Parker, who pursued him everywhere until Smith wished Parker would profit by experience and advice — meaning Beaumont's. The following spring Beaumont was prepared to praise only young Betty's Norval, one of the 'skin deep characters' in which he remained unsurpassed.

Bettymania lasted long enough to see society to the threshold of two great sorrows, the deaths of Lord Nelson and Pitt, whose efforts to form an effective coalition against Bonaparte, now Emperor of France, had been in vain. The nation, in mourning for its lost heroes, was alone in effective opposition to a brilliantly led enemy, while being saddled with the so-called 'Ministry of All the Talents' under the lacklustre Grenville, with Fox, long past his best, as Foreign Minister.

Handicapped as the new government was by allies whom Beaumont graphically described as 'led by kings of such imbecility' that only the 'vainglorious Emperor of Russia' had 'any commonsense',[42] he wished it well, at the same time identifying himself with Mulgrave who had wept copiously at his old leader's funeral. None of Pitt's close followers was in the new administration, and the Beaumonts now had an open invitation to Mulgrave Castle. With the Beverleys lost to the Continent, the Phipps family circle became one of the Beaumonts' happiest retreats, Lady Beaumont, who numbered Edmund among her admirers, being amused by the many 'bardlings' in the family, amongst whom Mulgrave's second son, born in 1801, had been christened Charles Beaumont and made Sir George's godson in honour of the friendship.

Beaumont might share the patronage of artists with the Phipps brothers but none of the latter cared for the Lake Poets, even though Augustus and his wife were accused by Wilberforce of having 'a succession of Heroes', just like Sir George, 'who *must* have a Hero'.[43] In 1806 Lowther, now building a castle to a plan of Robert Smirke recommended by Beaumont, was rather piqued at playing second fiddle to Wordsworth and told Lady Beaumont: 'when you are tired of the Poet, you will come to us'.[44] The amount of time the Beaumonts devoted to talking of their new friends must have seemed extraordinary given that Coleridge, with typical misfortune, failed to get more than one letter through to them in two years, and that they had barely met Wordsworth. In May 1804 Beaumont had hoped to accompany to the Lakes Humphry Davy, who was one of Coleridge's introductions, but instead the brilliant young scientist called the following summer at Coleorton where he found Dance helping to pass the long August evenings by sketching from English proverbs while Beaumont, who later provided the architect with a stock of 'whimsical subjects', completed drawings of the neighbourhood. Wordsworth, who had decided not to come to London early in 1805 to see to the affairs of his dead brother, also contemplated a visit to the Hall Farm that August, having become alarmed at Beaumont's reports of dejection due to 'bilious obstruction' following the bad bout of rheumatism. But there was not sufficient room for his family and he had to rely on letters to keep in touch with his patron. These now flowed freely: they had already discussed at length Reynolds's Discourses and the young Roscius, and they turned to Southey's *Madoc*, Sir John Beaumont's poetry and the scant news of Coleridge. The Wordsworths were grateful for a print after North-cote's portrait of him — more pleasing if less like than Hazlitt's.

Beaumont, full of his own woes, had apparently again failed to rise to the occasion in June, when Wordsworth announced the completion of *The Prelude*, 'a sort of portico to the *Recluse*, part of the same building'; but he did at least apologise on 21 July: 'I have not half expressed the sympathetic pleasure I feel at your having completed your work'.[45] Wordsworth had by then sent his new poem, 'What, you are stepping westward?' with a brief extract from Dorothy's 'Journal of the Scottish Tour', and these 'exquisite lines'[46] understandably delighted his patron, whose literary comments were as brief as those on art where fulsome. An accompanying transcription from *The Prelude* was barely acknowledged, but no doubt Lady Beaumont made amends and the Wordsworths took pleasure in sending more poems, including 'To the Daisy (Sweet Flower!)', which became a favourite. William also presented Beaumont with a hand-some copy of Houbraken and Vertue's *Heads of Illustrious Persons*.

'The Character of the Happy Warrior', despatched in February 1806, did elicit a keen response, Beaumont, with his patron's instinct, suggesting that 'an effusion may be added more particularly addressed to him Nelson in which his name may be men-tioned with enthusiasm', for one 'so dear to the public will call the attention of everyone'.[47] Beaumont, whose patriotic feelings were very much to the fore in these anxious years, had already extolled Nelson's virtues, confessing: 'I never was so affected in the same manner by the loss of any public man'.[48] But Wordsworth considered 'the allusion sufficient', Nelson's death, in any case, being timely. Moreover, the poet saw little reason to regret Pitt's more recent demise. Beaumont accepted that 'it is not necessary for friends not to differ on any subject',[49] but must none the less have winced a little when the death of Fox, whose 'conduct and seces-sion during the mutiny'[50] he could never forgive, drew some fine tributary verses from Wordsworth a few months later.

The correspondence had been going on for more than two years before Wordsworth at long last met the Beaumonts again when he came in the spring of 1806 to spend part of eight weeks in London at Grosvenor Square. The poet could write of 'my Friends Sir George and Lady Beaumont' with some pride, for they were recognised as cultured people of great charm, with a position in 'the world' he affected to despise but found, at least for short periods, irresistible. For all his high principles and blunt manner, he had a proper appreciation of the uses of London society and took to it with ease. His brother Christopher was chaplain at Lambeth Palace and, with many other acquaintances in town, Wordsworth, who made Grosvenor Square his headquarters, enjoyed himself greatly and, like Coleridge, whose silence now caused mutual con-cern, was flattered by his hosts' attentions.

Beaumont's painting, *Peele Castle in a Storm* (Pl. 64), hung in the house before appearing in the Academy, which they visited together on the first day of the ex-hibition. The artist, in deference to his guest's feelings, had not drawn attention to it, and was subsequently 'not a little elated' to receive the 'Elegaic Stanzas', suggested by this picture, which were coloured by Wordsworth's grief for his dead brother:

> Then, Beaumont, Friend! who would have been the Friend,
> If he had lived, of Him whom I deplore,

> This work of thine I blame not, but commend;
> This sea in anger, and that dismal shore.
> O 'tis a passionate Work! — yet wise and well,
> Well chosen is the spirit that is here...

Beaumont, in his emotional letter of thanks, counted the poet's friendship amongst his blessings and hoped, despite 'the jarring state' of his nerves, that it would help him to 'the serenity which can never be attained but by that estimation of the future in preference to the present, which your works and conversation so admirably inculcate'.[51]

Confessions on this note were to recur frequently and are hard to reconcile with the teasing tone Beaumont adopted when writing to Mulgrave or even Price. However, Wordsworth's own sorrows made him sympathetic to his patron's innate melancholy hidden from more worldly friends, and he provided the warmth and wisdom missing from Beaumont's life since the death of his old tutor, Davy. The affection was mutual as patron and poet struggled to become reconciled to John Wordsworth's death. Beaumont's 'goodness' was evident to the grieving family, and earlier he had restated his faith, instilled by Davy in his youth, and which he felt Wordsworth shared:

> It is pleasing and awful to observe the great vessel of the universe steadily pursuing her course with undeviating serenity — because guided by the perfect hand which governs all and 'rolls thro all things'...nothing can be perpetrated but by his presumption.

In the face of the threat of invasion, which receded only when Bonaparte turned on Russia, Beaumont consoled himself also 'with the aphorism that partial ill will in the end produce universal good'.[52]

Such confidences exposing Beaumont's basic humility combined with many kindnesses in London transformed a relationship of mutual respect into an ever-deeper friendship which supported Beaumont for the rest of his days; for both it was a meeting of souls and Wordsworth's capacity for joy became a most precious gift. With Lady Beaumont compelling her husband's attention, the poetry grew on him too. She longed for a hero on whom to pin her literary ambitions; separated from Coleridge, she was fighting, like the lioness to which Price was to compare her, for Wordsworth and his work, sometimes appearing, in Sir George's words, 'as intolerant in her opinion as Bishop Bonner on religious matters'.[53]

Coleridge's return had long been a fading prospect until in March 1806 Dorothy Wordsworth conveyed a second-hand report of his having reached Naples. The Beaumonts had heard nothing more when they left for Coleorton at the end of the season, but they were looking forward to another visit to the Lakes. Deprived of this at the last minute by the illness of his favourite servant, Sir George tried to console himself with the thought that the Wordsworths, who had outgrown Dove Cottage, might accept his offer of the Hall Farm for the winter. He was 'labouring under a severe fit of...morbid dejection' when in August he received a second sonnet that Wordsworth had translated from Michelangelo:

> The prayers I make will then be sweet indeed
> If Thou the spirit give by which I pray:
> My unassisted heart is barren clay,

124

That of its native self can nothing feed:
Of good and pious works Thou are the seed,
That quickens only where Thou say'st it may,
Unless Thou show to us thine own true way
No man can find it: Father! Thou must lead.
Do Thou, then, breathe those thoughts into my mind
By which such virtue may in me be bred
That in thy holy footsteps I may tread . . .

Welcoming 'the glorious aspirations of M Angelo' as 'perfect cordial to the languid soul', Beaumont wrote of Coleridge, whose portrait by Northcote looked down from the chimney piece: 'he does indeed . . . put his friends to severe trials, yet we shall all forgive him, & I hope he will be able to forgive himself'. There was the sorrow too of the death after a cruel illness of Richard Palmer, whose 'angel of a wife' was the closest of the Bowles daughters. At a low ebb, from an access of affection, Beaumont wrote to Wordsworth in images worthy of his friend: 'the thought of accommodating you & yours strikes like a sunbeam on my clouded mind'.[54]

IX
A POET'S HEART

UNCOMFORTABLE AS THEY were in Dove Cottage with their growing household, the Wordsworths had hesitated to take the Hall Farm if it meant a winter in Leicestershire without seeing their hosts. The Beaumonts, however, could hardly contemplate sharing the farmhouse with three Wordsworths, Sara Hutchinson and the children, not to mention two maids. They therefore decided to call at Coleorton for two or three nights *en route* from Mulgrave Castle to London at the end of October when the Wordsworths had just moved in. Thus, at last the long-awaited meeting with Dorothy and Mary was effected and it more than lived up to expectations. Back in London, his birthday — though 'no day of exultation' — drew the best from Beaumont in a letter to Wordsworth:

> Were I to express to you how much our interest and if possible our regard is encreased by a personal knowledge of your family of love, it might appear like affectation...

and his description of the return to town was vivid:

> the day was delightful...a slight shower just sufficient to form a magnificent rainbow — Indeed the sun seemed kindly inclined to spread out all his treasures before us...such a setting! Such burning tints, such flakes of floating gold, among which the eye was led in from glory to glory in such a preternatural manner, that it brought to my mind that sublime passage in Milton you read the other night... where he describes his, the Messiah's coming as shining afar off...

Wordsworth in his reply, 'moved even to weakness' by Beaumont's letter, expressed 'a great happiness to be beloved by you', for 'I esteem the friendship one of the best gifts of my life'. As for Coleridge, Beaumont could only pray he might '"shake off this fever which thus shakes him"'.[1]

After the Beaumonts had left, Wordsworth began to interest himself in the dell, part of the projected pleasure grounds within sight of the house. He had discussed with them an article by Joseph Addison that Lady Beaumont had found in an early *Spectator*, proposing a garden planted exclusively with evergreens, and after giving it much thought, Wordsworth responded, on 23 December 1806, in the longest letter he had ever written with a complete plan. His vision, modelled on Addison's, was 'of a Spot which Winter cannot touch', screened on three sides and with a central 'cloistral alley'. The Beaumonts consulted Redesdale who, not being apprised of 'the sentiment of the Place', objected to Wordsworth's sunless walk, while Price regretted that it divided the dell down the middle; but Wordsworth won his point, and was soon taking the mile stroll from the farmhouse twice daily to supervise the labourers working in the winter garden. In February he and Craig, the head gardener whose nose was somewhat out of joint, borrowed a gig from the agent, Captain William Bailey, to buy plants from a nursery in Nottingham. While Lady Beaumont worried that Wordsworth would be deflected from his poetic labours, the garden provided a happy diversion from the problems that Coleridge had by now brought to the household.

At long last, this elusive friend, having more or less agreed a separation from his wife, had arrived just before Christmas bringing his ten-year-old son Hartley. The Wordsworths, who had seen little of him since his return in July, soon found him sadly changed. Though briefly solaced by the 'happy vision of beloved faces' and moved by Wordsworth's reading of *The Prelude* to celebrate 'high and passionate thoughts — to their own music chanted',[2] Coleridge became obsessed by Sara Hutchinson (who, for the second time, inspired a short but poignant poem, 'An Angel Visitant') and he was too unhappy to see his other friends. With his marital problems praying on him, his need for stimulants was hardly satisfied by the supply of health-giving Loughborough ale specially ordered by Lady Beaumont. Sir George, fore-warned of his state of mind, was sufficiently magnanimous to make the first approach, in writing, in February. It was a charming letter, as was his response to Coleridge's reply in which he assured the tortured 'runagate': 'Never for a moment suppose our love and esteem for you can be diminished because you are unfortunate', and for once Beaumont gave positive advice:

> when agreeable thoughts arise — cherish them, patronise that admirable painter your imagination whenever she is inclined to body forth the form of soothing fancies to your mind — remember there are two sides to all things...therefore do not torment yourself by turning the wrong side outward....[3]

The Hall Farm on the same bleak plateau as the big house was hardly an ideal winter retreat, but the Wordsworths made the very best of it, especially relishing the sunsets of which they had been deprived in their Lakeland hollow. Already housing the bailiff and dairymaid, the farm was full to the brim when Dance came in February, and Dorothy worried how to fit them all in, even Sir George's painting room being put to use. She was very much in charge, and, with ample domestic help, was enjoying a rare interval of comparative leisure. The family also did justice to the Beaumonts' favourite spot, Gracedieu, the patrimony of Sir George's poetic forebears — a forty-minute ride away, but much slower on the asses, one obstinate and the other obdurate, provided for the women by Bailey. The exterior of the new house was already completed and in December Dorothy wrote of the turrets which 'looked exceedingly well by moonlight'. Even if the turnpike road to Ashby was 'shocking' and, as William had complained, the church congregation, mostly old or untidy, obliged to listen to an unsuitable sermon on Gnostics — '*h*adversaries to Christianity and *h*enemies of the Gospel' — Dorothy's letters transmitted an air of contentment that must have been encouraging to her absent hostess whom she addressed as 'my dear friend'. The relationship between the two women had flourished during a period when Lady Beaumont had been deprived of the company of her favourite sister, Frances Fermor, widowed and isolated in Switzerland by the war.

At Coleorton Coleridge whiled away many hours in the Beaumonts' library to which, much to the Wordsworths' delight, they were constantly adding. In the margin of an old book, *The Emperor Marcus Antonius: His Conversation*, by the words 'Nobody ever fancied they were slighted by him; or had the courage to think themselves his Betters', the poet wrote: 'this reminds me of Sir G B'.[4] Yet it was April before Coleridge did at last bring himself to call at Grosvenor Square, taking Hartley, whose head Beaumont asked Wilkie to paint: 'my little piping friend' helped to break the ice but, although the Beaumonts were to encourage Coleridge with his lectures and publications and to help his family whom they pitied, in future Sir George in particular was to retain his reservations.

Wordsworth also was in London that spring of 1807, and briefly at Dunmow with the Beaumonts who were concerned at the poor reception of his *Poems in Two Volumes* published in May. They took a proprietorial interest, for some had been composed at Coleorton in the final flourish of what Matthew Arnold called Wordsworth's 'Great Decade' of writing. Amongst them, the poet had dedicated to his hostess:

> Lady! the songs of Spring were in the grove
> While I was shaping beds for winter flowers...

and Lady Beaumont can only have been enchanted with 'O Nightingale thou surely art', the second verse recalling spring in the grove:

> I heard a Stockdove sing or say
> His homely tale, this very day...

There were several more short poems, 'November 1806', 'Gipsies', 'The Subjugation of Switzerland', and 'A Prophecy' from this winter as well as the more important 'Song at the Feast of Brougham Castle', dedicated to Lord Lowther, for which Wordsworth had taken one line from Sir John Beaumont's best known poem, 'Bosworth Field'.[5] Perhaps the most moving was 'A Complaint'; Wordsworth had been suffering considerable anguish at the withdrawal of Coleridge — even at the farmhouse a lonely figure in their midst — when he wrote:

> There is a change — and I am poor;
> Your love hath been, not long ago,
> A fountain at my fond heart's door...

He had been careful to hide his sorrow from the Beaumonts who were deeply impressed by his courageous defiance of the savage criticism that greeted his poems. Especially pleasing was his condemnation, in his letter to Lady Beaumont that May, of Samuel Rogers, author of *The Pleasures of Memory*, to the class of the undiscerning who regretted that 'so many trifling things should be admitted to obstruct the view of those [poems] which have merit'. The Beaumonts and Rogers had felt a mutual antipathy when introduced by Farington at Conway, and there was some rivalry between them as Rogers's house in St James's Place, showing exquisite taste, began, in Burney's opinion, to attract 'the best company of talents and genius'. It was only in 1816, after he had been of service to Wordsworth, that the Beaumonts fully forgave Rogers such malevolence as when he 'dwelt particularly on the beautiful idea of the "Dancing Daffodils"' — thus playing off, in Farington's view but not posterity's, Lady Beaumont's 'want of judgement'.[6] Wordsworth had warned her, 'you have many battles to fight for me: more than in the ardour and confidence of your pure elevated mind you ever thought of'. In fact, Wordsworth the teacher was complemented by his eager disciple who, convinced his writing would 'be efficacious in making men wiser, better and happier', set to work to spread the gospel. Following an attack by Francis Jeffrey in the *Edinburgh Review* Sir George, too, was sufficiently concerned to spring to his friend's defence, adopting the stance which originated with Coleridge, that a great poet must create his own public; and when Lady Beaumont unwisely forwarded a 'friend's comments intended to be helpful' but based on an insultingly inaccurate transcription, her husband smoothed Wordsworth's ruffled feathers. The poet complained that the writer had given instances of what he disliked in a poem on 'a Daisy' — it should of course have been '*the* Daisy' — and 'on Daffodils *reflected in the Water*!' Beaumont replied:

> The criticism Lady Beaumont sent you was dispatched when I was particularly engaged, or I hope I should have prevented its journey...it was not fair to communicate what was written in a hurry & imparted in confidence — The truth is, my friend is a most ardent admirer of your works in general, & in common with us was nettled to perceive them not relished as they deserved, & so illiberally treated, his sincere wish is that they may become generally read, not only on your account but for sake of the good they are so well calculated to produce — this induced him to consider in his mind what could be the reason they were not more popular... whether you never were induced to select subjects so peculiarly your own observation that people in general could not feel their whole force & beauty without the advantage of your own conversation [crossed out] & illustration — If you were to see how earnestly Lady Beaumont & Mrs Fermor are now reading your poems in the next room & observe the delight in both their countenances it would make you some amends for this criticism which I hope as we had no right to communicate it, you will not suffer to go out of your family.[7]

In 1807, cutting short their London season, the Beaumonts hastened via Dunmow to Coleorton for a week with the Wordsworths before the two families made their separate ways to the Lakes. This summer the Beaumonts were again at Greta Hall where Robert Southey, his wife and her deserted sister, Mrs Coleridge, lived with their respective children. William and Dorothy came to stay at separate times and for the final fortnight the Beaumonts took lodgings at Grasmere to be near their dearest friends. At their first meeting at Grosvenor Square in 1804, the Beaumonts had not cared for Southey, but, as Dorothy had forecast, he grew on them. With his Tory views and commonsensical approach, he lacked only the capacity for enchantment which they sought in their heroes. Sir George had found difficulty in being 'much interested for *Madoc*', and though he pressed the author to write more poetry, he was happy enough with Southey's answer: 'it is impossible to make up one's mind to posthumous bread and cheese'.[8] At Keswick the families made the best possible neighbours; while the men walked and talked, Lady Beaumont took pleasure in the countless children, particularly the Coleridge trio, with Hartley her favourite.

The Beaumonts were lavish with small presents to their Lake friends — game, books for all the family and toys being quite acceptable; but, while Coleridge had ultimately been thankful to receive £100 on his departure for Malta, Wordsworth, despite Dorothy's practical approach — she had quietly accepted the hospitality handed out at Coleorton — preferred to remain in near penury. That July he was a fellow guest with the Beaumonts at Lowther Castle, whose owner was also anxious to assist him financially, but again he made it as difficult as possible and it took all Beaumont's diplomacy and patience in the role of go-between before Wordsworth accepted a small annual advance from Lord Lonsdale (formerly Lowther) in 1812 until the salaried post of Distributor of Stamps for Westmorland became available the following year and relieved his money worries. Beaumont's intervention in Southey's attempt to obtain the Stewardship of the Derwentwater estates — following his failure to obtain a university chair through his reluctance to subscribe to the Thirty-nine Articles — was just as frustrating and came at a bad moment. Explaining his failure, Beaumont admitted he had been unduly sanguine and had encouraged the poet not only 'in ill-founded exultation but in such corporal pain' that he hardly knew what he was doing. But at least Southey was not disappointed, for having discovered the onerous duties of the post, he declared he would 'rather live in a hollow tree all the summer and die when the cold weather should set in'[9] than undertake such employment.

To Wordsworth, ever a reluctant beneficiary, Beaumont learned to content himself with gifts of his own work. It was as well that even these were offered in all humility as a practicioner of the 'sister art', for the reaction was unpredictable. Beaumont's first drawing of *Applethwaite* gave pleasure but Dorothy plainly did not like *Conway Castle*, while the painting, *The Thorn*, after Wordsworth's poem, received quite a battering from William, who even quoted to Sir George the opinion of 'Old Molly', who admired the frame but could 'mak nowt on't'. Unaccustomed as he was to such candour, Beaumont went ahead with a sketch for *Peter Bell*, hearing the poem for the first time from the poet's lips at Grasmere, and at Coleorton he worked this up into what he called a 'tailpiece' (Pl. 56).[10] In 1814, 'wishing to do something which might record our intimacy',[11] Beaumont commissioned Alexander to make a print from this painting to accompany the poem, and though publication was postponed, that year the two octavo volumes of *Miscellaneous Poems* carried prints after *Peele Castle* and a trite *Snow Cottage*, while Beaumont had also produced a view of Bolton Abbey, complete with doe, to serve as frontispiece in the expensive quarto edition of *The White Doe of Rylstone*. Beaumont's pleasure at his contributions was tempered by the realisation that he was 'a poor hand at any thing which does not arise spontaneously',[12] and that he had difficulty in painting figures. In 1803 his diffidence had caused the poets William Lisle Bowles and Rogers to drop a proposal for an illustrated translation of Theocritus's *Idylls*. Bowles's father had been vicar at King's Sutton in Lady Beaumont's youth, and the fourth party in the Theocritus project, the scholarly William Howley, then tutor to Abercorn's family and later Bishop of London, was to become related by marriage, the alliance of Mary Howley with George Howland Willoughby Beaumont bringing the Beaumonts great joy in their last years.

*　　*　　*

Despite having Alexander as a painting companion for ten days in January 1808, Beaumont reverted to his usual low, winter state in Dunmow where, in deference to his ageing mother, not even Maynard was entertained. This boyhood friend, forgiven his follies, was now dismissed as being dedicated to horse and hound. Dame Rachel, who had impressed Coleridge in 1804 as 'a sort of miracle for beauty & clear understanding & cheerfulness', was at last losing much of her 'power of seeing & hearing',

56. Beaumont: *Peter Bell*, c. 1809 (Dove Cottage Trustees).

while hardly surprisingly, Sir George now looked pale and thin on his new diet of camomile and vitriol. The winter months were indeed quiet in the old house, starting with 'the fire laid in each Bedchamber at seven', shaving water brought in at eight, breakfast at nine, dinner, for which they dressed, at half-past four, tea at seven and roast apples before they retired to bed not later than eleven.

With such a dull life Lady Beaumont could be forgiven if all her thoughts — or rather, those not in flight with Wordsworth whom she now termed 'angelic'[13] — were of Coleorton. Her husband had refused to take any interest in the furnishings there, and Dance considered her taste appalling — a description which applied also to the cost, some £5,000 for the contents and £15,000 for the building, nearly double what they had intended. But for all his misgivings, Beaumont too was buoyed by the prospect of a house truly his own, and of hanging his pictures in a new light. At Dunmow in July his spirits were as high as they had been low in the winter, and William Owen, there to paint Dame Rachel (Pl. 69) now that her days were so clearly numbered, found his patron 'quite a different man from what He seemed to be in London, very entertaining — playful even Boyish!'[14] At last the new house was nearly ready and, although Dance, himself made ill by the smell of new paint, tried to deter them, the Beaumonts left Essex to take possession on 12 August, nearly four years after the first stone was laid.

131

Despite Sir George's sensible intention, relayed to Gilpin, not to 'over-house' himself, Dance had indeed provided a solid mansion, and an interesting one too. It did full credit to the architect's eclectic view, with its picturesque Gothic front, vaguely Tudor elevations on the garden sides and faint echoes of the Orient in the slender paired turrets at the corners; nor was patrimonial pride forgotten, the Beaumont lion bestriding a massive *porte-cochère*. Inside the most remarkable feature was the polygonal hall — inspired by Soane's plan of Tyringham — surrounded by pointed arches, its shadows aglow from stained glass in the gallery above. It was a romantic house — perhaps Dorothy Wordsworth was right to think it best by moonlight — and a painter's house, with a painting room at last worthy of the name. Its living quarters, where Gothic gave way to a severe and economical classicism, and main bedrooms almost walled with glass, were full of light and air — too full, for the draughts and chills were to be a perpetual curse, scarcely relieved by Dance's attempts at central heating. There was, however, no gallery, for in the country as in London Beaumont intended to live amongst his pictures.

Though Claude was soon to hang on its walls, Coleorton was no place to indulge nostalgia for the warm south. Spring and autumn brought out the best of the house, riding high above the Forest of Charnwood, the trees swept by the passing shadows of the clouds; but on a winter's day the gloom of a pit-pocked landscape exposed to the east wind was far from welcoming. Although the Beaumonts had been spending part of their summers in the farmhouse, there was still much to do when they took over. At Grosvenor Square William Seguier had checked pictures and frames for their journey to Leicestershire and their hanging would give the essential character to a house which was unusually plain within. Lady Beaumont, who had waited so long to be her own chatelaine, threw herself into the gardens to the extent that her husband feared she might 'take root herself'. Now he too took an interest in the grounds where ruined cottages were preserved near the dell — one covered with ivy was to be mistaken for an old abbey — and a rampart had risen like a miniature castle keep to retain the southeast lawn above the Wordsworth garden that, in Lady Beaumont's words, was to become 'a monument for his taste for the picturesque'.[15] Although not above the 'blasphemy' of criticising her favourite poet, Price had carried away affectionate memories of him and Lady Beaumont could write to Dorothy Wordsworth that

> he speaks with great pleasure of meeting your brother at Coleorton, we agree very much in our opinion of his genius tho' his heart may be less deeply affected than mine. . . *The Brothers* he thought faultless. . .his taste is good in all things, and were his morals pure, he would have a true relish for sublime poetry.[16]

* * *

The Wordsworths had departed, but their presence at Hall Farm, together with the poetic strains heard previously at Gracedieu from Sir John and Francis Beaumont, 'the ornaments of my pedigree', had been among the most propitious omens for Coleorton. An artist was the first guest in the new house, old friend Hearne, who set to work on a series of drawings of the exterior (Pl. 57) as well as a watercolour of the polygonal hall (Pl. 58). Hearne, who was not easily impressed in his old age, thought 'the stair a pleasing gloom' and 'the apartments handsome and well finished' though the outside was too plain.[17] Dance came to see that all was well, and Edmund Phipps called *en*

57. Thomas Hearne; *Coleorton Hall*, c. 1808, pencil (B.C.).

58. Thomas Hearne: *The Staircase at Coleorton Hall*, c. 1808, pencil and watercolour (B.C.).

route for Mulgrave, while in September the Bowles family arrived to stay for six weeks. Old Bowles was in fine form, worth a bottle a day and painting in the Wilsonian manner. Before winter set in, Beaumont's painting room, as always at the top of the house, had been well and truly christened; then, as if to confound the Job's comforters like Lonsdale who had consigned them to the country bumpkins, the Beaumonts set off on their normal round of London, North Aston, Haverhill and Dunmow, where they spent Christmas with Dame Rachel.

After a long interval the Wordsworths came to Leicestershire again in July 1810, but this time only William and Dorothy, for Mary was nursing her last child. Coleorton was now in full swing and Dorothy found it 'much improved'. There had been a flow of guests including Wilkie and Haydon the previous August who had roused Beaumont to a fury of painting, followed by Laura and Frederick Moysey who both sketched very much in his manner. But it was Wordsworth who made his friend's heart sing, and after their last meeting in the Lakes Beaumont had written: 'To desert those lovely Mountains with such friends at the foot. . .on such a lovely day, required a degree of philosophy almost bordering on insanity'.[18] Since then they had disagreed on the poet's opposition to the Covention of Cintra, Beaumont sharing the opinion of Lonsdale, who refused his support, that Wordsworth showed poor political judgement. Wordsworth, aided by Coleridge, again wintering at Grasmere and working on his periodical *The Friend*, still went ahead with a long Cintra pamphlet, published in 1809, which led their patron to caution Haydon against Wordsworth's 'democratic notions'. In June Farington reported Sir George vastly irritated, 'Lady Beaumont spoke of the Book as if she was *employed to sell it*. She sd. She Had caused the sale of some of them.'[19]

133

Sir George was becoming more astringent. Painters felt it and Dance too when the bills mounted at Coleorton — henceforth its owner was full of dire warnings against building — and the combined company of his wife and her two sisters sometimes tried him sorely. The youngest was so neurotic that two years later at Grosvenor Square she was unable to face Wordsworth, while Frances Fermor, the victim of a tragic life and as 'doleful as dull Tragedy', returned from Switzerland in a tense state of mind, longing for philosophic consolation. This Coleridge was to find to his cost when Lady Beaumont expected him to help her sister who, in order to consult him, had taken nearby lodgings at Bath in 1814; and he complained bitterly that June of 'a direful Burthen which the usual Wisdom and Delicacy of Lady Beaumont have imposed on me', declaring:

> Poor afflicted Dowager! she clings obstinately to the Faith, that the whole Source of her Sufferings is in her Head & Heart, tho' it is evident that the mischief lies a foot or two below the one, & 8 or 9 inches below the other —. For tho' 'alimentary canal' & 'lower digestive and eliminative organs' are handsome-looking synonimes for Guts, yet they cannot stand the competition with Desertion from Heaven, want of genial Grace, the *mind*, Sir! O the *mind* —

Lady Beaumont's sisters were staying at Coleorton when William and Dorothy arrived, to be mistaken for 'wandering Troupers'. After the initial surprise the welcome was overwhelming and Wordsworth found himself exhausted by the constant talk and never being alone. The four guests were taken on an outing to see the local wonder at Tutbury, 'the Woman who had lived 4 years without solid food, and nearly two without liquid'. The age of credulity had not yet passed, but Wordsworth at least was unimpressed and concentrated on the winter garden. Leaving Dorothy to spend a few more days at Coleorton, where she enjoyed listening to Chaucer's *Prologue* and *The Knight's Tale* and looking over Jefferys's drawings, before the Beaumonts surprisingly allowed her to make an unnecessarily rough journey to Cambridge, Wordsworth went on to Radnorshire, Sir George taking the opportunity to gain extra time with his beloved friend by accompanying him part of the way. During three days that Beaumont described as 'among the whitest of my life',[20] they visited the theatre at Birmingham — a pathetic performance of *Venice Observ'd* to an audience of twelve — and saw two estates, William Shenstone's Leasowes and Lord Lyttleton's Hagley, where there was a temple dedicated to the poet James Thomson and an urn to Alexander Pope, giving Beaumont the idea of lending character to Coleorton with similar ornaments.

Nearly twelve months elapsed after this before Wordsworth stirred himself to write; perhaps he was distancing himself a little as his wife — just as Mrs Constable was to do — encouraged him to refuse the annual invitations from the Beaumonts. However, his letter of August 1811 more than made amends by including a sonnet, 'Upon the Sight of a Beautiful Picture', inspired by Beaumont's *Coleorton Landscape*:[21]

> Praised be the Art whose subtle power could stay
> Yon cloud, and fix it in that glorious shape;
> Nor would permit the thin smoke to escape,
> Nor those bright sunbeams to forsake the day;
> Which stopped that band of travellers on their way,

> Ere they were lost within the shady wood;
> And showed the Bark upon the glassy flood
> For ever anchored in her sheltering bay.
> Soul-soothing Art! who, Morning, Noontide, Even,
> Do serve with all their changeful pageantry;
> Thou, with ambition modest yet sublime,
> Here, for the sight of mortal man, hast given,
> To one brief moment caught from fleeting time
> The appropriate calm of blest eternity.

He had also composed an 'Epistle to Sir George Howland Beaumont Bart. from the South-west Coast of Cumberland'. He was staying near Bootle in the faint hope that his delicate daughter, Catharine, would benefit from the seaside and the poem is wistful, with allusions to Coleridge, specially added for Beaumont:

> No tales of Runagates fresh landed, whence
> And wherefore fugitive or on what pretence...

and a stanza regretting his patron's decision not to build on Loughrigg Tarn, described as 'Diana's Looking-glass':

> A glimpse I caught of that Abode, by Thee
> Designed to rise in humble privacy,
> A lowly Dwelling, here to be outspread,
> Like a small Hamlet, with its bashful head
> Half hid in native trees. Alas 'tis not,
> Nor ever was; I sighed and left the spot
> Unconscious of its own untoward lot,
> And thought in silence, with regret too keen,
> Of unexperienced joys, that might have been;
> Of neighbourhood and intermingling arts...[22]

Beaumont's acknowledgement of the 'Epistle' is lost, but his obvious delight led to a flurry of letters as Wordsworth responded to a request for inscriptions at Coleorton. In 1808 they had planted a cedar there, as Wordsworth celebrated:

> The embowering rose, the acacia and the pine
> Will not unwillingly their place resign;
> If but the Cedar thrive that near them stands,
> Planted by Beaumont's and by Wordsworth's hands.
> One wooed the silent Art with studious pains:
> These groves have heard the Other's pensive strains;
> Devoted thus, their spirits did unite
> By interchange of knowledge and delight.[23]

More permanent monuments were now intended — a seat in the grove in memory of Francis Beaumont and an urn, at the end of an avenue of newly planted lime trees, dedicated to Reynolds, while a short inscription was required for a niche, hollowed out of the sandstone in the winter-garden bank by Wordsworth and his wife, whose contribution was acknowledged in the final lines of 'In a garden of the same'.

With help from female hands, that proudly strove
To aid the work...

The Beaumonts having relayed William Bowles's somewhat officious criticism, Wordsworth had altered and improved these lines.[24] With the homage to Reynolds all important — Constable who appreciated this was to perpetuate it in his painting *The Cenotaph* (Pl. 92) — Sir George worried about virtually assuming 'the merits of composing these exquisite lines' which began

Ye lime trees ranged before this hallowed urn
Shoot forth with lively power at spring's return

with the announcement in the first person:

Yet here may I
Unblamed, upon my patrimonial grounds
Raise this frail tribute to his memory...

Wordsworth tried 'a hundred different ways' to obviate this objection and suggested as an alternative:

Hence, an obscure Memorial, without blame,
In these domestic grounds, may bear his Name.[25]

He showed remarkable patience when Lady Beaumont, 'from redundancy of care', mislaid the first draft, which was the preferred version though with further slight amendment, and on 20 November, at the end of what had been a most enjoyable month for the Beaumonts, he sent them lines composed the previous morning after a walk with Dorothy, these in tribute to Francis Beaumont and intended for his commemorative seat in the grove:

Beneath yon eastern ridge, the craggy bound
Rugged and high of Charnwood's forest ground,
Stand yet, but, Stranger! hidden from thy view,
The ivied ruins of forlorn GRACE DIEU...

ending with a universal tribute to genius that was bound to thrill his friends:

Communities are lost, and Empires die,
And things of holy use unhallowed lie;
They perish; — but the Intellect can raise,
From airy words alone, a Pile that ne'er decays.

Wordsworth had always assisted Beaumont's preoccupation with his literary ancestors, encouraging him to republish the poems, 'elevated, pious & pure',[26] of Sir John Beaumont, provided that 'The Crowne of Thornes' could be traced; but Southey, to whom it had been entrusted, failed in this mission and the work remains lost.

Conscious of the trouble these exchanges had caused, Beaumont wished to make Wordsworth a small present of money, 'offered with all the frankness of a brother',[27] and he was extremely upset to find it again firmly rejected, though in the end the poet may have adopted the donor's suggestion of keeping it for travel expenses. It was the Beaumonts' intention to inveigle Wordsworth south to see the first sonnet he had addressed to Lady Beaumont made a feature of the 'circular gothic structure' that was to be erected in the winter garden; but owing to the Beaumonts' own delayed return, Coleorton was not on his itinerary when, in the spring of 1812, Wordsworth did leave the Lakes to deal with the unhappy breach that had arisen between him and Coleridge and had been festering too long.

The Wordsworths had been unbelievably tolerant when Coleridge had chosen to live with them in the years 1800–10, but William had warned Coleridge's next intended host, Basil Montagu, of his intemperate habits. Montagu's insensitive repetition of these home truths had fed Coleridge's sense of persecution and now he feared that Wordsworth's presence at Grosvenor Square would set the Beaumonts against him. In fact, Wordsworth, who loved Sir George for his 'delicate reserve', had spared him the more recent details both of Coleridge's addiction to drugs and of their rift. The Beaumonts had already placed Coleridge at a certain distance, Sir George relying on mutual friends like Southey to 'say anything soothing to poor Coleridge when you see him',[28] but the unhappy poet had relayed to them his agonies, as he 'earnestly wished to die' and was 'labouring under a depression of the spirits, little less than absolute'. Now he himself alerted them to the cause of his depression and so alarmed Lady Beaumont that she anticipated an attack on Wordsworth's 'literary merits' in his next set of lectures which she had sponsored with Thomas Bernard and William Sotheby. If this reflected a loss of faith, it also showed a wounding lack of judgement of the man who at Coleorton, after hearing *The Prelude*, had addressed to Wordsworth an effusive poem. This was now sent to Lady Beaumont, Coleridge rushing to assure the Beaumonts and anyone willing to listen that he was incapable of 'feeling vindictively' towards his fellow poet. For a moment it seemed he would be too disturbed to fulfil his lectures, already famed for their unpredictability. His outraged sensitivity contrasted with Wordsworth's cold exasperation made for an impossible situation and friends were greatly relieved when Henry Crabb Robinson volunteered to act as intermediary. Thanks to his tact, the estrangement between the poets ended a month after Wordsworth's arrival in London, but Coleridge retained a scar so deep he never again crossed Wordsworth's threshold. He seemed dogged by ill luck, for on the very day of their reconciliation there was the assassination of the Prime Minister, Spencer Perceval. Lady Beaumont was among the first to suggest a postponement of Coleridge's lectures, and when at last he did proceed, the subscribers numbered nearer fifty than the five hundred for which he had hoped. He had also been disappointed with the response to *The Friend*. He had consulted Beaumont and Sotheby over the prospectus, and this over-ambitious publication finally appeared in June 1809; but despite Lady Beaumont's success in enlisting her friends to subscribe, it ran for only twenty-six issues owing to his own erratic contribution. Sir George encouraged Coleridge in one more venture, the adaptation of *Osorio* with Colman and the Haymarket in mind. On this occasion the author was fortunate for Samuel Whitbread intervened with an offer and, under the title of *Remorse*, the play ran with some success at Drury Lane from January 1813.

The summer of Perceval's assassination was an uneasy one. Wordsworth, deprived of the pleasure of witnessing the murderer's execution for fear of the crush, was shocked at the intransigence and even the glee of the lower orders. In his letters to Mary he regretted not hearing more political talk and, as a literary lion, he now suffered from too many social invitations. He did, however, enjoy accompanying the

Beaumonts to dine with Mulgrave, where the Longs did not please, then calling in on Lady Crewe's rout for the Princess Regent. London life suited him and it would have been a dreary duty to continue on to Coleorton, but the Beaumonts were dissuaded from spending any time there by reports of riots at Nottingham, only twelve miles distant, and one of the Midlands towns being badly affected by unemployment. Instead, at the end of the season they went to Ashburnham Park in Sussex which their old friend Lord Ashburnham, the former St Asaph, had just inherited. Price, whose 'overgorging' had become noticeable, was prevented by illness from getting to grips with this Capability Brown landscape, but Dance came to plan a gothic appearance for the house. Ashburnham, whose collection of Italian pictures in London was visited by many Beaumont protégés, proved a difficult employer; Beaumont and Price enjoyed him for his humour although he was a man of few words, and, according to Hearne, the children of his first marriage, having inherited the trait, sometimes did not speak for a week.

Another host noted for his lack of small talk was the Beaumonts' neighbour, Lord Moira. His departure from Leicestershire was one of the unfortunate side-effects of the Perceval tragedy. As the Prince Regent's man he was asked to form a new government but failed, the majority of the previous ministers continuing under the Earl of Liverpool. In the autumn Moira, whose hospitality at Donington was as legendary as his debts, accepted the Indian command to restore his depleted exchequer and spent virtually the rest of his life abroad, leaving the Beaumonts the sole standard-bearers in an empty district. Of the remaining nobility, the Ferrers had an unhappy history and were invalids, while Harpur Crewe at Calke Abbey was a recluse.

The Beaumonts had settled down to a retired life at Coleorton; this suited Lady Beaumont but Sir George relied on visitors to break the monotony. Jackson and George Arnald, there for eight weeks around September 1811, had been delightfully amenable guests, although Arnald's *View of Coleorton Hall* suggested to Wordsworth that it was impossible 'to *excel* in *landscape* painting without a strong tincture of the Poetic Spirit', and that Arnald would be a better painter if he read more; but Beaumont paid him double his asking price, for 'Though he has not much senti-ment...he took great pains'.[29] In October 1812 Farington and Owen came for a fortnight to be present that fine, cool, last day of the month when, surrounded by workmen and servants, Lady Beaumont pronounced: 'May nothing but Time destroy this Monument', as each struck with a mallet the first stone of the monument to Reynolds. Heralded by two plinths, the bust of Raphael on one and of Michelangelo on the other, the severe sarcophagus still stands at the end of a 'darksome aisle' of lime trees.

Inevitably, samples of the lines written in tribute to Reynolds came up for discussion when other poems by Wordsworth were read of an evening. Farington was gratified when Sir George admitted: 'Wordsworth's reputation as a poet wd. have stood higher had the two volumes of His poems contained only those which would be generally approved', the critics making the most of such as were 'thought to be puerile in their simplicity'; but there was no gainsaying his declaration, after Lady Beaumont had read her husband's favourite poem, 'Tintern Abbey', that the poet was 'as much superior to Walter Scott as Claude to me'. Farington and Owen provided just the con-versation in which Beaumont revelled and to which he contributed more than his share. Regrettably, Farington failed to comment on the house during a discussion about taste in furniture, when Lady Beaumont complained that the splendour of Carlton House diminished its guests while Sir George compared Lord Grosvenor's more sombre apartments, filled with company, to a Venetian picture. On the first morning of the visit, Sir George had hurried up to take his old friend to another room 'to see a beautiful effect of Sun rising over a distant hill'.[30] This view towards Bardon, full of ancestral memories, was Beaumont's joy and now featured in many of his paintings (Pl. 59).

Outside Leicestershire the Beaumonts were leading quite a glittering life and in May 1809 the list of their dinner guests was printed in the *Morning Post*: 'HRH the Duke of York,...the Earls Bathurst, Camden, Chatham, Lord Mulgrave, Mr Secretary Canning and a large party of Noblemen'. Mulgrave's brother-in-law, Robert Plumer Ward — later to consult the Beaumonts about his very dull novel *Tremaine* — was among the politician friends who did not always impress Lady Beaumont, and might find themselves congratulated by her on ignoring the division bell of a House of Commons that 'turned them into Hottentots'.[31] Such acerbity may have been occasioned by their failure to appreciate the Lake Poets, but there were certainly converts, George Canning's associate, William Sturges-Bourne, who had married Anne Bowles, starting with *The Excursion* in 1814, while Lonsdale's family needed no encouragement. Of the literary ladies Miss Baillie was a friend and admirer of Wordsworth, as was Mrs Opie, but the mannish Miss Berry regretted that Beaumont was 'strangely misled by the dogmas of Coleridge, Wordsworth etc.', and, still more, that he was 'perfectly blind to the stature of Bonaparte', considering Cromwell 'a greater man'.[32]

Byron now included Lady Beaumont in the circle of 'Blues', whose 'Litterateur, the Oracle of the Colerics', was William Sotheby, aptly nicknamed 'Botherby' from his habit of pressing his writings on his friends. Surprisingly, Byron was a guest with Scott and Rogers at Grosvenor Square in 1815 (perhaps a reward for his kindness to

59. Beaumont: *Bardon Hill from Coleorton* (Leicester Museum and Art Gallery).

Coleridge, who had written to him for encouragement) and Wordsworth met him there briefly in 1812 when *Childe Harold* was the rage. For her part, Lady Beaumont had recognised in *The Giaour* and *The Corsair* 'some wild and beautiful flowers of poetry', but predictably deplored Byron's 'want of more lastingly devout principle', considering his intellect to be 'near derangement'.[33] When in 1823 Byron decided to publish his literary eclogue, *The Blues*, she can only have dismissed it, as in the end she dismissed the author. If this satiric work has any value, it is that it includes the glimpse of 'Lady Bluemount's' conversation, invoking her own Sir George to lend weight to her defence of 'Mouthy' and 'Wordsworthy'. There was indeed something pretentious in Lady Beaumont's manner, as is evident from her morally indignant but justified condemnation of Northcote's tasteless remarks on Pitt, which led Northcote to conclude that 'she is not strong enough in mind to be formidable', although 'Sir George is admitted to be everything'.[34]

*   *   *

Misfortunes with Coleorton agents had continued meanwhile. Bailey, who had married Mary Ibbetson in 1806, now proved unsatisfactory and was replaced by a jolly north-countryman, Taylor, recommended through Lonsdale to fill the position of 'emperor'[35] of the little colliery which produced £1,000 a year and could do better. After a period of euphoria, Beaumont was soon deploring the man's stupidity which was to cost his employer a great deal of worry and some £1,000 by the time he had been paid off to avoid a lawsuit. In the autumn of 1811 Wade was called up from Dunmow to deal with the dismissal after Beaumont complained of having 'never been so abused *out of the* street';[36] the Beaumonts must have wished that they had listened to some of the tittle-tattle picked up by Dorothy Wordsworth when there was talk of Taylor, amongst other idiocies, mistaking a field of clover for honeysuckle.

Another source of anxiety for Beaumont was his mother. There was no mistaking the depth of depression he revealed in his letters to Wordsworth as Dame Rachel approached her end in the early months of 1814. For a man of his temperament, the thought of death invoked a mood of introspection of which Farington too became aware. Inevitably, there were already many friends to mourn: Oldfield Bowles in 1810, his daughter Mrs Palmer in 1812, Lord Aylesford during Farington's Coleorton visit, Lady Beverley about the same time and, in March 1813, the unhappy Anne Willes, whose demise occasioned a long visit to Bath. But above all he dreaded the loss of his mother who, over the years, had provided the calm affection and approval he craved.

The Wordsworths, themselves having lost two of their beloved children within a year, were also in deep sorrow, particularly Mary. Dorothy's letter announcing Catharine's death had just missed the poet at Grosvenor Square in June 1812 on the day he left for Essex. Ironically, only a few weeks earlier, he had told Crabb Robinson that he was 'one of the happiest of men', adding: 'And no man who does not partake of that happiness, who lives a life of constant bustle, And whose felicity depends on the opinions of others, can possibly comprehend the best of my poems.' The description appeared to fit Beaumont who, however, was quite unconscious of any barrier between them, and in his turn he wrote confidently to Price of Wordsworth and Coleridge as 'sometimes apt to get into the clouds, but one can bring them down with a whistle'.[37]

To Beaumont's regret, Wordsworth was too busy taking up his duties as Distributor of Stamps to leave home in 1813, and the following year he made another Scottish tour. In June 1814 his patron consoled himself with the thought that 'the film which has so long blinded the public & prevented them being sensible to your excellence is gradually desolving'. Dame Rachel had died on 5 May and Beaumont tried to express his feelings in verses that were to feature on her memorial in Dunmow Church. 'Maimed by my bungling Muse', he had consulted Rogers before sending them to Wordsworth 'in a desperate fit of Valour':

> The dreaded hour is come — t'is come t'is past —
> That gentle sigh — dear Mother was they last —
> And now diffus'd among the blest above
> Glows the pure spirit of maternal love...

Always at his most maudlin around the date of his birthday — with 'such a shattered frame...I ought, were I not mad, to consider each succeeding year as my last' — his letter to Wordsworth of 20 November was primarily to thank him for 'the exquisite pleasure'[38] given by the recently published *Excursion*. Wordsworth, with great promptness despite toothache, relieved Beaumont's nervous anticipation with kind words of approval which were taken without a pinch of salt. Then it was Beaumont's turn to be generous: he had actually read *The Excursion* — or at least the first two books — and considered 'the vision near the end of the 2nd book' as 'the finest flowering of British poesy';[39] moreover he hoped, rightly, that the vision described was 'suggested by the marvellous effect we saw in returning thro' Patterdale amongst the mountains of Ullswater':

> Glory beyond all glory ever seen
> By waking sense or by the dreaming soul!
> The appearance, instantaneously disclosed,
> Was of a mighty city — boldly say
> A wilderness of building, sinking far
> And self-withdrawn into a boundless depth,
> Far sinking into splendour — without end!
> Fabric it seemed of diamond and of gold,
> With alabaster domes, and silver spires,
> And blazing terrace upon terrace, high
> Uplifted...
> By earthly nature had the effect been wrought
> Upon the dark materials of the storm
> Now pacified: on them and on the coves
> And mountain-steeps and summits, where unto
> The vapours had receded, taking there
> Their station under a cerulean sky.
> Oh, 'twas an unimaginable sight!
> Clouds, mists, streams, watery rocks and emerald turf,
> Clouds of all tincture, rooks and sapphire sky,
> Confused, commingled, mutually inflamed,
> Molten together...

In the autumn of 1814 Beaumont, expressing 'a strong ambition to attend you in your flight',[40] was worrying about his illustrations for Wordsworth's forthcoming collection of poems. Lady Beaumont's earlier postscripts to her husband's letters had been more demanding: she wanted to know 'why *The Excursion* is substituted for *The Recluse*, if it be part of that work', and wished publication to be delayed until the end of the year 'when the ferment of spectacles has subsided'.[41] When *The Excursion* came out nevertheless in August 1814 and sold only slowly, she checked like a good saleswoman that the price was not the cause — two guineas being quite average, she discovered. In full flow, her handwriting would deteriorate until it resembled, in Price's view, the work of a fluffy brush discarded by Rembrandt — he had already urged her to address her letters properly, for envelopes naming neither county nor town left too much to chance. But if her letters on the subject of Wordsworth's poetry were barely legible to the most diligent reader, none could mistake her message. In 1815 the new Dean of Bocking, Christopher Wordsworth, staying with his wife at Dunmow, reported his hostess's paean of praise for *The Excursion* and caused Dorothy to fear 'her zeal will outrun her discretion and prevent her aiding the sale'. Unfortunately the Wordsworths' letters to the Beaumonts from 1812 to 1820 are lost, but the poet, not averse to admiration, was probably satisfied with Lady Beaumont's verdict, expressed in one of her awkward phrases, that his work ensured 'encreasing fame and not popularity'.[42]

As the publication date of the *Miscellaneous Poems* and *The White Doe* approached, Beaumont, who was contributing a frontispiece to each, waited two weeks at Coleorton for the unreliable S.W. Reynolds to deliver the proof of *Peele Castle*. It appeared still too dark after retouching — to call it 'a libel'[43] was no exaggeration — and to save further annoyance, Alexander took Beaumont's newly completed picture, *Bolton Abbey*, to J.C. Bromley for engraving. This gave complete satisfaction, and the *Snow Cottage*, to appear opposite the poem of 'Lucy Gray' in the same volume as *Peele Castle*, was also well done by Bromley.

Having painted a 'tailpiece', Beaumont had chosen to have *Peter Bell* inscribed to him, but Wordsworth substituted the *Miscellaneous Poems*, emphasising in the dedication that, while some of the collection had been 'the means of first making us personally known to each other', upon others Beaumont had 'a peculiar claim, — for some of the best pieces were composed under the shade of your own groves, upon the classic ground of Coleorton; where I was animated by the recollection of those illustrious Poets of your name and family, who were born in that neighbourhood'. Wordsworth must also have appreciated his friend's deep comprehension of the spirit of his work, by now transcending such connections as these and arising from a shared vision of nature. It was no less a judge than Scott who would later commend Beaumont's understanding of Wordsworth: 'a rare thing, for it is more easy to see his peculiarities than to feel his great merit, or follow his abstract ideas'.

Nothing, however, could have given Beaumont greater pleasure than this tribute to his forebears, and for once he felt fulfilled. He wrote immediately, thanking Wordsworth for 'the affectionate manner in which you have dedicated the work to me — I dread a compliment from most people, it rarely fails to make me hang my head and blush — you on the contrary elevate it to the degree of dignity but place me on tiptoe — seriously I feel the honour done me, and the thought of descending to posterity as the friend of Wordsworth delights my imagination and warms my heart.'[44]

X
PATRONAGE

IN 1801 WILLIAM SOTHEBY dedicated to Beaumont a 'Poetical Epistle on the Encouragement of the British School of Painting'. No poetic genius, he shared his friend's high aspirations for the sister art, hoping Beaumont would use his influence with statesmen to 'counterbalance the effects of our ambitious rival to form the School of Art at Paris', and urging him to 'invoke the senate! bid the nation hear!' Sotheby knew he was addressing a man who had become one of the chief arbiters of English taste. By the turn of the century, Beaumont was striding the exhibitions and galleries of London with new confidence, never lost for an opinion. His enthusiasm might sometimes seem a little ridiculous, as when he was reported 'boring' the Archbishop of Canterbury and the Bishop of Durham about painting one night over dinner,[1] or had his remarks on the 'immense breadth of light and shade' in a picture at Bowood cruelly cut down to size by Sydney Smith, who hated 'coxcombing in the fine arts' and 'innocently said, "Yes; about an inch and a half"'.[2] But generally his judgement was acute enough to make amends. Noble collectors looked to him for advice on old masters and rising talents alike, knowing that his was also a painter's eye, and the politics of art were to absorb him more and more in the coming years. While he welcomed them as the destiny he had been seeking all his life, they were to prove sometimes as contentious and upsetting as Parliament, from which he had so delightedly escaped.

Beaumont was finding artists harder to please, and often less pleasing, than poets. Affectionate gratitude such as he had won from Wordsworth and Coleridge was a rarer commodity among painters, although in fact they seemed spoilt by comparison, beginning to charge high prices for their work and becoming fiercely jealous of professional pride, while poets laboured in solitude and for little reward. Farington would soon bestow italics on his host's statement one night at Grosvenor Square *'That Poetry was superior to Painting'* — a dictum that had silenced not only the diarist but his fellow painters Thomas Daniell, Henry Edridge and B.R. Haydon.[3] Painting was still Beaumont's first love, and its encouragement a continuing passion. A gallery of British art had been one of his earliest dreams for Coleorton, and nothing would have pleased him more than to garner the best of the moderns to hang beside their elders and the old masters. The pity was that he could now find so little to admire.

By 1803, Beaumont was quite distressed by the tendencies prevailing in art. His search for a more spontaneous and lively handling in his own painting had always been accompanied by a proper regard for the general effect, but now it seemed that younger painters were discarding the values of the past. To Farington he complained that 'the practise of many Artists has become very meretricious, "an influenza" has affected in a very high degree Westall, — Turner, — &, a little, Lawrence. — That harmony and modesty which distinguishes great masters is not seen, but crudeness and bravura are substituted';[4] and to William Bowles, who wrote five years later to commend the landscape efforts of the Revd Mr Merewether, he replied in mock despair:

> a strange taste prevails at present, this is the age of innovation in all ways, & our wiseacres of the present day have had the sagacity to discover that in politics, poetry and painting all that has hitherto been done is fit only for the flames — I hear the young Genii are in the habit of calling Titian Claude &c the black masters, warning each other with earnestness not to paint like them...the art is now beginning again and at the wrong end...any little master with his milk spoon in one hand and his palette knife in the other dashes away without knowledge or reason and produces the most disgusting nondescripts.[5]

Sotheby had well understood the fundamentally traditional taste of

> Beaumont!
> whose fond remembrance wakes thy tear
> That streams o'er these frail flowers on Reynolds' bier

and as much for his patronage or his own pictures, Beaumont had become known for his collection of the old masters, and of a past generation of British artists, Gainsborough, Wilson and Reynolds, with whom he had grown up. In Grosvenor Square and soon at Coleorton, his collection set a standard of comparison by which he measured new art and to which he aspired in his own pictures, of which examples also hung in his gallery.

It was now a wide-ranging collection. The Claudes, the Poussin and the Bourdon — Beaumont had now described the painter as 'the prince of the dreamers yet not without nature'[6] — represented the classical tradition in its pastoral and historical characters, the Canaletto the most lucid and lucent of topography, the Rembrandts the resonant tenebrism of the north, the Brouwer picaresque genre, the Gainsborough and the Wilsons the assimilation of north and south into English painting. Portraiture was manifested by Reynolds and Gainsborough, and Beaumont's growing interest in history painting — an aspect of his mature taste that was to be increasingly evident in the coming years as he adopted artists like Haydon and Washington Allston and responded warmly to Vincenzo Camuccini when he returned to Rome — was already fed by West's sketch for *Cicero* and now expressed itself more clearly in his purchase of an early and rather forbidding work by the artist, *Pylades and Orestes* from the *Iphigenia in Tauris* of Euripides (Pl. 60). Beaumont was to describe it as 'chaste and elegant'.[7] One of West's most severely neo-classical pictures, its frieze-like groupings derived alike from the antique and from the Raphael cartoons, although West himself was to recall he had painted it with his 'mind full of Correggio'.[8] It had been one of the painter's first successes in London at the Society of Artists in 1766 — Beaumont thought West's rapid rise to greatness, despite a provincial and colonial background, unprecedented in the history of art — and the expressions of its suffering characters had so impressed the physiognomist Johann Caspar Lavater that in 1775 he had published engravings of some of them in his *Physiognomische Fragmente*. Following an uncertain early history, the picture had returned to the artist by 1802.

Beaumont was quite fond of West and had learned much from him. He admired his

60. Benjamin West: *Pylades and Orestes brought as Victims before Iphigenia*, 1766 (London, Tate Gallery).

dedication, his classical taste and above all his pursuit of the old masterly, and no doubt he intended the purchase to signal his loyalty to an artist whom he as yet exempted from most of his strictures on the moderns, but who was becoming increasingly unpopular with his Academy colleagues. Beaumont could understand why, for he also thought him devious, not a little greedy — in particular he detected a tendency to work shoddily for the engraver — and apt to be crude in his speech; indeed he went so far as to paraphrase Pope in describing him, '"A man so very high, so very low"'.[9] Nevertheless, Beaumont and West shared common assumptions about the heirarchies of art — West's fellow painters were to be only too delighted when he was rebuked by the King himself for leading noble patrons too much towards the old masters at the expense of modern art — and West was entrusted with the restoration of Beaumont's most important accession of the new century (at least until his collection was crowned with the Michelangelo tondo), a masterpiece of northern landscape, Rubens's view of his own house, *The Château de Steen* (Pl. 61). This was a gift from Lady Beaumont who paid £1,500 for it out of a legacy of £2,000. William Bowles was moved to poetry by its affectionate portrayal of harmony and husbandry,[10] and Beaumont, who had often talked to Ibbetson of 'the light within' Rubens's paintings, soon succumbed to the temptation of stealing the credit for buying 'the finest landscape I believe he ever painted...a noble study and all alive with the *lumine*

145

61. Rubens: *The Château de Steen* (London, National Gallery).

dentro.[11] Never lost for an elegant phrase, he named Rubens 'the Shakespeare of painting',[12] anticipating Haydon, who would characterise Beaumont's own taste as 'essentially *Shakespearean*'.

The impact made by the Rubens, which was soon to be celebrated by Price and freely repeated in one of James Ward's most splendid paintings (Pl. 62), is proof of the importance that now attached to Beaumont's collection. Not only was it filled with works of high quality and very few mistakes, but above all it belonged to a man who could talk about pictures in a manner both honeyed and to the point. Even literary men admired him as a critic, for, as Scott remembered, 'he always made his criticisms intelligible, and used no slang'.[13] Yet Beaumont's collection was modest by some standards. He bought what he liked and could afford. Like his friend Knight, he was impatient of the inflationary prices being asked for important pictures and in the end it was estimated that his had cost only £4,000; only at the close of his life would he part with large sums, and then they were for sculpture. In 1802, thinking of his British gallery, he asked Farington to offer 600 guineas for Hogarth's *Rake's Progress*,[14] but backed away when the owner, the architect Soane, demanded more (of Hogarth he would content himself with two lesser works, one a sketch for the painter's large *Pool of Bethesda* in St Thomas's Hospital),[15] and he thought the Altieri Claudes, bought by Beckford, 'very fine but the price ridiculous'.[16] He was unaffected by the 'vanity' that the dealer William Buchanan noticed in the English in 1803, 'of possessing capital works of Art of a few favourite Masters . . . which have made a noise in the world',[17] and Mrs Jameson would be right to number him among those who collected 'for love, for companionship, for communion; to whom each picture, well chosen at first, unfolds new beauties — becomes dearer every day'.[18]

146

62.   James Ward: *St Donat's Castle, Glamorganshire, Bulls Fighting*, 1803 (London, Victoria and Albert Museum).

As he had hinted to Lady Inchiquin when she sought his views on the sale of her inheritance from Reynolds, there was much in the new commercial art world that Beaumont disliked, and it might well have shocked him to learn that Buchanan thought his friend West had been disappointed not to receive a percentage on the sale of the Rubens, 'although he was neither the introducer nor adviser of Sir George or his lady. Indeed it would be absurd to say that anybody was *Sir George Beaumont's adviser*.'[19] It was more usual to find Beaumont himself acting in this capacity, and, attempting to sell Claude's *View of Delphi* to Lord Wemyss, Buchanan was ready to 'beg' him to give his verdict 'for the inspection only of an old Gentleman in the country...in short to say whether he considers it as a *fine picture*'.[20] If temptations were implied, it is inconceivable that Beaumont succumbed, and in 1803 he was actually threatened with libel by another dealer, William Bryant, for complaining about his underhand methods in acquiring a valuable Titian from Lord Lowther, and went so far as to stand witness when Lowther took the case to court — a bold step for one who so hated contention.[21]

Such episodes emphasise Beaumont's importance in the art world at this time and the independent status that enabled him to say exactly what he thought. This would prove both his strength and his undoing, for he was laying down judgements and standards at a period when artists were highly conscious of their new-found professionalism and when dealers were beginning to proclaim superior knowledge, often fraudulently. But Beaumont's repeated recourse to his own taste and collection — however distinguished — as a model for others, involved a fundamental inconsistency. Though he assured William Gilpin during a lively debate on the merits of Claude in 1802, that he had not 'the least idea of calling your taste in question, because you do

147

not admire Claude as I do',[22] he must have known that his remarks would have just that effect. But at the same time, Beaumont's more fleeting enthusiasms tended to undermine his authority. Quite apart from the personal hurt his fickleness could cause, it was bound to damage his credibility. When convinced, the pedagogue in Beaumont demanded immediate agreement, but it proved harder to win as his followers realised he might later change his mind.

Others felt positively threatened, and a new and vociferous generation of artists and critics was soon to challenge the very right of a connoisseur to pronounce upon the professionals. Beaumont might seem at the height of his influence after 1800, but such a privileged figure, free to indulge his whims and confident of respect, belonged to a vanishing era. Even his taste seemed to prove it. Lawrence, ever the flatterer, would praise it as 'neither intolerant nor excluding',[23] but the reality could be rather different. It was true that Beaumont could be remarkably open-minded, the champion of some of the most original minds of his day, but he could also be obtuse, and to those unfamiliar with the sensitive understanding, tact and generosity he reserved for his real friends, he could seem more steadfast in his dislikes than in his affections; it was sad, but understandable, that his sustained hostility to Turner, contrasted with his passing fancies among the newcomers to the art, would prove as conspicuous as his numerous acts of kindness.

*   *   *

The difficulties his painter-friends sometimes felt in accepting his advice were mirrored in Beaumont's own painting, which continued to reflect many impressions without finding an individual style. His aim to 'work out something that shall have an original stamp founded on the observation of various excellence', described to Farington on his departure to the country in summer of 1803,[24] was a contradiction in terms, but it was one that would be resolved in the art of his young friend Constable rather than in his own. Beaumont was now coming to terms with his own limitations as a painter, but not with the attitudes that were hindering his progress. Around 1807 he took a major stride that would refresh his art, by spending much more time sketching in oil from nature, chiefly in the Lakes with which, inspired by Wordsworth, he professed himself more and more delighted; but at the beginning of the decade he was painting as derivatively as ever.

In 1800 Beaumont sent two landscapes to the Academy, one of which was presumably the picture he gave to his old University the following year (Pl. 63). The Vice-Chancellor of Oxford, Michael Marlow, wrote to thank him for 'one of the best Landscapes the present Age had produced'.[25] This was not yet a nonsense, for the picture is a competent essay in the fashionable Dutch picturesque manner that Beaumont had developed in the 1790s, although the painter Augustus Wall Callcott, attempting to denigrate him both as artist and connoisseur, would later accuse it of being copied from a picture by William Artaud.[26] This was highly improbable — and indeed Callcott may even have confused Artaud with George Arnald, one of Beaumont's protégés in landscape around this time — but comment on the baronet's art had turned sour long before this. His exhibits of 1802 were little admired save by their author, who considered one, an 'Evening' that he gave to Mrs Palmer, 'perhaps his best', and by the still impressionable Constable, Turner echoing most artists' view

148

63. Beaumont (engraved John Browne, with dedication to Beaumont): *The Forest*, 1800, (London, British Museum).

that they were 'made up'.[27] One at least of three pictures shown in 1803, *The Ghost, from Bloomfield's Farmer's Boy*, produced a chorus of disapproval. Robert Smirke thought all of them 'very well for an Amateur, but His moonlight He sd. was *trash*, — and the others rubbish when compared with what pictures should be',[28] and even friends like Farington and Dance, now at the height of his trials over Coleorton, felt in a difficult position when asked for their opinions, the former agreeing with Charles Long that 'I left it to others to speak their full...it cd. not be required of me to do more than not to prefer them to better productions.'[29]

Beaumont's drawings were now more widely admired than his oils. In Wales in 1802 he made a number of Benarth woods, in chalks on blue paper in the manner of Gainsborough, which were much commended, not least by Dr Monro, who drew in a similar vein.[30] Such elegant pastiche drew out the best in Beaumont, although the scenery he loved in Wales or the Lakes continued to find expression in more immediate and atmospheric drawings in broken monochrome washes that would be a formative influence on Constable. Otherwise, Beaumont was passing through a frustrating period in his art. His ineptitude with figures persuaded him to abandon his Theocritus subjects in 1803, and disillusionment with his recent oils led him back to his earlier work the following year; that spring he showed Farington 'many old pictures' he was taking to the country to 'revise',[31] and the reworking of former materials was henceforth as constant a feature of his practise as his recourse to the old masters. Once in a while, as in the case of *Peele Castle in a Storm* (Pl. 64), made ready for the Academy in 1806 and worked from drawings of around 1798 and a preparatory oil sketch,[32] this

149

64. Beaumont: *Peele Castle in a Storm*, 1806 (B.C).

could produce an image hardly less powerful than the original impression, especially when recollection was transfigured by the strong romantic mood to which Beaumont could sometimes rise. Peele Castle, like Conway, of which he showed pictures in 1804, 1810 and 1811, based presumably on the fine drawings he had made of it during his Welsh visits at the beginning of the decade, fascinated him and inspired some of his best work in which, to a degree hitherto rare in English painting, the Picturesque yields to the Sublime. In *Peele Castle* it is for once no matter that Beaumont has adduced so many impulses from art as well as nature — Cozens, Vernet and S.W. Reynolds can all be called to account — for here indeed are the 'strong winds of feeling, a sea rolling high', that Coleridge had admired in Wordsworth's poetry and the painter's 'philosophy'.

*   *   *

In 1803 Beaumont would 'give anything to see an accomplished Landscape Painter arise',[33] and the frustrating search for such a prodigy was by now a constant preoccupation. Through it all Beaumont would remain hostile to the one pre-eminently great painter of the day, Turner, and strangely blind to the genius of Constable, though this was nurtured under his very eyes. Otherwise he ranged far and wide, hardly troubling to distinguish between masters large and small — one of the more engaging features of his taste. A friend like William Gilpin could count on his support in promoting his work, Beaumont electing himself the 'puffer' for Gilpin's drawings in the saleroom in 1802; but others like Alexander, S.W. Reynolds and George Arnald were given their chances, each helping to guide his hand at his own easel, and amateurs were also followed eagerly. James Ward particularly impressed him early in the decade, and in 1803 Beaumont was 'in raptures' with his large imitation of the Rubens *Château de Steen*, a view of St Donat's Castle in Glamorganshire with bulls fighting (Pl. 62).[34]

None of these painters would prove to be truly outstanding, while Callcott, who caught Beaumont's eye around 1805, was to become an implacable enemy. Scarcely more successful in winning lasting favour were the young water-colourists who stayed with Beaumont at Benarth in the summer of 1800. Farington during this visit was asked to paint a 'view of this place...very picturesque owing to the accompaniments',[35] and Girtin made a watercolour of Conway, one of many commissioned by his host,[36] but other guests, including George Samuel, Thomas Underwood and John Samuel Hayward who were members of Girtin's Sketching Club and must have been introduced by him, were apparently less fortunate. No doubt Beaumont tried hard to like their work, but within two years he had turned against almost all watercolourists for the threat they posed to oil painting — with which he had already urged Girtin to experiment — telling Gilpin that, together with the lamentable English passion for portraiture, 'another cause impedes the progress of landscape, namely, the great encouragement given to tinted drawings almost to the exclusion of oil painting. Whatever beauty this branch of the art may possess, it is certainly inferior to the other.'[37] Later he would be highly critical of the flourishing watercolour exhibitions — 'such a want of harmony, such a *chattering display*'[38] — and Haydon would endear himself with his prophecy that the fashion would be over within three years.

Constable, who had been a regular visitor at Grosvenor Square since his arrival in London in 1799, was determined to succeed in oil. Beaumont was lavishing his best intentions on him, showing him his gallery, prescribing the Discourses, laying out drawings by Girtin and Cozens and putting him to copy pictures including the Claude *Hagar* and Wilson's *Maecenas's Villa*. Constable, who found it all a perfect therapy for his youthful 'melancholy', was grateful, but intractable. Returning from Dunmow at the end of February, 1801, Beaumont found Constable 'animated by the paintings' and ready to proceed 'with resolution',[39] but neither he nor the Royal Academy could deflect the student from his chosen path, and to his boyhood friend Dunthorne Constable wrote a famous letter the next spring, having 'just returned from a visit to Sir G. Beaumont's pictures', declaring his

deep conviction of the truth of Sir Joshua Reynolds' observation that there is no *easy* way of becoming a good painter...for these past two years I have been running after pictures and seeking the truth at second hand...I shall shortly return to Bergholt where I shall make some laborious studies from nature there is room enough for a natural painture.[40]

65. John Constable: *Dedham Vale*, 1802 (London, Victoria and Albert Museum).

66. (facing page). J.M.W. Turner: *Calais Pier, with French Poissards preparing for Sea: an English Packet arriving*, 1803 (London, National Gallery).

Lady Beaumont would misunderstand Constable's independent spirit, telling Farington he 'seemed to be a weak man',[41] but her husband knew better and persevered in case Constable should truly prove the Messiah he longed for. It would have been as well for his own art had he gone to the country in the same spirit as Constable, whose summer of 1802 would produce that wonderful conflation of the composition of Beaumont's *Hagar*, the intimate rustic detail of the *Landscape with Goatherd* — the 'little wood scene of Claude' that he preferred 'above all others' at Grosvenor Square[42] — and the real scenery of East Anglia: the upright *Dedham Vale* (Pl. 65). Beaumont, however, might well have thought its realism too prosaic, without the poetry he sought in paint, and he felt it his mission to educate Constable's taste. There were signs of hope, for Constable's manner was respectful, and, ironically in view of their shared preference for oil, he was absorbing much of Beaumont's own manner as a draughtsman in monochrome, Farington, for example, finding it hard to distinguish their drawing of trees.

By 1800 it must have been as obvious to Beaumont as anyone that Turner was one of the newcomers most worth watching, and Turner's friendships with Girtin and Dr Monro should have been a bond. In 1801 Beaumont admired his '*Bridgewater Seapiece*', complaining only that the sky was too heavy and the sea too brown; he would later change his mind, and in the course of the next few years was to deliver a stream of malicious similes to describe the works of an artist he had turned against, irrevocably and with unprecedented passion. The sea in *Calais Pier* (Pl. 66) was successively likened to 'veins in a marble slab' and 'pease soup',[43] and the brilliant tonality of *The Opening of the Vintage at Macon* upset him the same year — 'borrowed from Claude but all the colouring forgotten'.[44] The gradation of finish in Turner's work offended him, for the middle and far distances were finished 'upon a scale that requires universal pre-

cision throughout his pictures, — but his foregrounds are comparative blots, & faces of figures without a feature being expressed'.[45] In 1806 he was still more damning about *The Goddess of Discord* and *Echo and Narcissus* — 'like the work of an *old man* who had ideas but who had lost the power of execution'[46] — and worse would follow as he developed his views on Turner, seeing him first as another victim of the 'influenza in art' and then as its primary germ. From time to time Constable, Northcote, Hearne and other conservative spirits admitted agreement, but others of the younger generation were soon full of protest. They thought his prejudice perverse and inappropriate, and it would rebound. Beaumont's pungent criticism of painters for spurning the lessons of the past identified him as the main proponent of reactionary views, and, worse, it seemed unpardonable for a connoisseur to take so forceful and public a stance. It was ironic that, for all his love of genius, Beaumont now seemed to threaten its liberty, and his resistance to Turner would place him conspicuously at the centre of powerful debates about the proper sources of patronage and the true nature of professionalism in the arts.

It would all have mattered less if Beaumont's views had not become increasingly institutionalised by the middle of the decade. Early in 1802 he had been invited, with friends including Knight, Long and Townley, to join the Committee of National Monuments assembled to select and finance the sculptured monuments to national heroes in St Paul's Cathedral. The appointment to the 'Committee of Taste' gave official recognition to his position in the art world, although it was said to be Knight who dominated the group. The committee was soon resented bitterly by the Royal Academy, Farington losing no time in telling Beaumont that there was an Academy committee already appointed for just the same purpose, and although Beaumont assured Farington that he could keep Knight under control, this merely replaced one individual's opinion with another. Beaumont was in any case as known for his dogmatic views as Knight and his close participation in the founding of the British Insitution in June 1805 seemed to expose him more clearly as one determined to enforce those views officially, in competition with the Academy.

Founded by Thomas Bernard, with the Earl of Dartmouth as President, and Beaumont, Knight and other gentlemen-patrons among the Directors, the Institution held its first exhibition in 1806, in the Pall Mall rooms that had formerly housed Boydell's Shakespeare Gallery. The Institution's intentions were spotless — the encouragement of art in Britain through exhibitions and, a little later, purchase, as well as displays of the old masters so that young artists might learn from them. But far from earning their gratitude it put artists on their guard immediately, for unlike the Academy, which they ran themselves through elected representatives, it was in the hands of the connoisseurs and thus subject to the whims of patrician taste. Although even Turner sent to the opening exhibition, it is possible that one of his contributions, *The Goddess of Discord choosing the Apple of Contention in the Garden of the Hesperides*, with its accompanying verses about 'future woes', was in part a prediction of conflicts ahead, and Turner's relations with the Institution would later partake further of his disagreements with certain Directors.

The Institution's proposals for exhibitions of old masters and recently deceased artists were to prove especially contentious, being seen as tending towards unfair competition. A rearguard action was organised at once. Even at the earliest exploratory meetings, which Farington attended, and before any deep split occurred, painters were determined that the Institution should not win any kind of 'Royal approbation', and informed artists were heard to mutter that 'it had the appearance rather of desiring to get the patronage into its own hands than to benefit the arts';[47] only West, now unpopular in the Academy and under pressure to resign his Presidency, seemed in favour of the new Institution. Beaumont's own views were practical: all ways of supporting the arts were to be encouraged, although as Lady Beaumont trenchantly observed after reading Martin Archer Shee's provocative analysis of modern connoisseurship, *Rhymes on Art*, 'The public was not to be bullied into patronage of the arts.'[48]

To Beaumont, the maulings he was to suffer as a result of his involvement with the Institution must have seemed cruel and ungrateful indeed, but it is helpful also to enter the artists' minds. In 1813, provoked beyond endurance by Beaumont's jibes at his pictures, Callcott declared that the Directors of the Institution were 'not patrons of artists but breeders of artists'.[49] There was some truth in this as he was in a position to know, for around 1805 he had been briefly taken up by Beaumont and even more by Knight, who had bought a picture of his from the Academy that year. After Turner, Callcott was one of the most promising landscapists to have appeared in recent years, and his upright *Water Mill*, also in the 1805 Academy whence it was bought by Sir John Leicester, was an essay in just the kind of elegiac pastoral Picturesque, paying full respect to the tradition of Ruysdael and Waterloo, that Beaumont was likely to admire.[50] However, Callcott and some of his friends believed that the patron's approval concealed a devious intention to raise him 'at the expense of Turner', and altruistically admitted his reputation 'too much owing to this'.[51] By the following year, with what must have seemed deliberate perversity, Callcott had adopted Turner's manner in two marines exhibited at the Academy,[52] and had been heard making critical remarks about Beaumont and Knight. That April, Beaumont visited the painter's studio at Kensington Gravel Pits and found the pictures like Ruysdael's, but 'worn down and then worked upon in a fuzzy manner, but...there were silver grey skies well imitated, and good colour'.[53] In a matter of days, however, he reconsidered; on subsequent viewing the pale tones and crisp handling bothered him, and it was of Callcott's two Academy marines that he first used the term 'white painter' that he would so often direct against Turner and his followers.[54] Callcott, who felt on less certain ground than Turner himself, would not be slow to react, and Beaumont, while he could respond to Coleridge's ardent advocacy of Wordsworth, could never understand this talented painter's thrall to the greater man, nor allow them the privilege he accorded the poets — and Canova later — of creating the taste of their public.

* * *

Beaumont's own Academy exhibits of 1806 were more interesting than usual. Besides *Peele Castle*, there was *The Thorn*, perhaps the picture that Farington described as 'a Landscape with Children in imitation of Rubens',[55] a study near Coleorton, and a *Lake of Albano* that Beaumont later gave to Lawrence and whose appearance may be partly gathered from Constable's memorandum on the back of one of his own views of Borrowdale drawn the same year: 'a very beautiful clear effect on all the distance — very much like that in Sir George Beaumont's picture of the Lake...the heavy clouds remained edged with light'.[56] All doubtless owed something to the influence of S.W. Reynolds, whose help and advice in touching and finishing pictures Beaumont now freely acknowledged and whose habit of sketching broadly from nature on millboard he was now to emulate in the Lakes.

Beaumont seems to have been particularly anxious about the hanging of his pictures in a year in which, as Farington's diary makes clear, the Academy arrangement proved rather more contentious than usual, and some explanation for Beaumont's sudden turn against Callcott may be deduced from the diarist's laconic note on 10 April that Callcott had received a letter from Beaumont 'desiring that any of his pictures that could not be *conveniently hung* might be returned. A heavy dispute took place today.' The implication that Beaumont expected good positions for his pictures was all too easily read into his request, even if this was not really what he meant; Callcott may even have jumped to the conclusion that Beaumont proposed to trade his patronage for the influence that he, as a rising star and newly elected Associate, could wield in the hanging — influence that might well have been more beneficial, and certainly more discreet, than older members could bring to bear. Callcott never forgave Beaumont, and although the baronet himself was to deny it, a personal antipathy was always to lie behind their suspicion of each other's work.

It was also in the April of 1806 that Beaumont confided to Farington some wider views on contemporary painters including Turner. Hoppner, though soon to paint his portrait, was 'more remarkable for *peculiarity* than for *originality*, or any great power, considering Him upon the whole'; Lawrence, 'respectable, but not of a high order', was to Reynolds in painting much what Kemble was to Garrick on the stage; the watercolourists were obsessed by mannerism; and Turner was 'perpetually aiming to be extraordinary, but rather produces works that are capricious & singular than great.

His colouring has become jaundiced. His former pictures were better.'[57] Some hope had appeared in the form of young Moysey, in his twenties and a tutor to Charles Bowles at Christ Church, Oxford, who was showing a sea storm in the Academy and 'may become as good as *Brooking*, or better';[58] and that November he brought news of the still younger John Linnell who had painted 'scenes of Courts & Alleys — also a Stump of a tree all painted with extraordinary fidelity, — upon a small scale' and seemed 'most delighted with the pictures of Canaletti'.[59]

Beaumont had heard of Linnell from two other beginners to the art, David Wilkie and B.R. Haydon, who, with their friend John Jackson, were now to share his patronage. In his support of all three he was joined by Mulgrave, who in 1805 had been brought back to the centre of political life as Secretary of Foreign Affairs, and two years later would become First Lord of the Admiralty — although the very smell of ropes and tar made him sick. Jackson had been discovered on Mulgrave territory at Lastingham and was the first to enter the fold when Mulgrave and Beaumont, seizing the opportunity to share in the nurture of genius as they had not done since the death of Girtin, bought the remainder of his apprenticeship in his father's tailor's shop and brought him to London to study. With Jackson, a bluff Yorkshireman who loved jokes and stories and whose laziness threatened always to stifle his promise, Beaumont was at his most heavy-handed; he missed none of the young man's peccadilloes, and on a matter so compelling — though often frustrating — his letters to his fellow patron came thick and fast. Jackson had 'great feeling for the simplicity of nature', he told Mulgrave, but should 'abate his velocity & aim at correctness';[60] the first recommendation seems to have proved more congenial than the last.

Beaumont had thought it better 'to let him trust to his own genius' than to go to a teacher, provided he drew regularly at the Academy and got the Discourses by heart. As Jackson's ambition was portraiture, he was set to copy a Van Dyck, but the result was a failure and Beaumont could allow him little respite, sending him 'another dose, but made rather more palatable than the last', still, however, 'chaining him to the oar'.[61] At the end of the year he wished he could 'report progress in as great a degree as I expected, I will not say his case is desperate but if he does not with all his strength and unremitting diligence strive and struggle...he will never succeed according to our expectations...I am loathe to say so much, and I fear I have put off the unpleasant task too long, but it is unfair to palliate when you are at such trouble and expense'.[62] Mulgrave himself now lost patience and in the New Year read Jackson so stiff a lecture that Beaumont felt guilty: 'perhaps however I was too severe, and indeed I did not expect you would have administered the dose all at once, but by degrees as you found the patient would bear it'.[63] He did not think they had overestimated Jackson's promise: 'all I fear is a want of energy — of enthusiasm...the merest blockhead in the Academy can draw better than he can at present'. In sum, 'he wants a touch of the torch of Prometheus'.[64]

By 1806 Beaumont was delighted to hear from Mulgrave that Jackson had improved: 'I dare say I shall exclaim d-m me Amazing! when he comes to town'.[65] But he should still strive harder, 'not fiddling at what he can do with ease...but fairly putting his neck to the collar'.[66] He wanted him to paint Dame Rachel at Dunmow — though this commission went instead to William Owen — for 'I would not have him empty himself too much on landscape — his object is the human figure'.[67] But although Jackson continued to progress and in 1816 painted a group of Beaumont and

67. David Wilkie: *Self-Portrait*, c. 1804–6 (Edinburgh, Scottish National Portrait Gallery).

Mulgrave with Edmund and Augustus Phipps (Pl. 83), as well as copies of Reynolds's portraits of the Beaumonts, in future the two patrons were more concerned with Jackson's friends Wilkie, dedicated to narrative painting, and Haydon, who aspired to history.

Tired of the Yorkshireman's 'indolent apathy',[68] Beaumont saw a clearer light of genius in Wilkie (Pl.67), however shy and provincial the young Scot appeared in his first days in London. When introduced by Jackson in 1806, Wilkie was practically starving, although his *Village Politicians*,[69] his first exhibit, was a sensation in that year's Academy. Having visited his lodgings in April, Beaumont and Mulgrave assumed his rescue as a bounden duty, and Mulgrave was the host at Wilkie's first venture into 'high company', a dinner when the painter observed his fellow guests so assiduously that by the end of the evening 'he was as well bred as any man in England'; Farington, who was also there, drily observed that Jackson was 'little noticed' in the 'admiration of this young genius'.[70] It was not always Beaumont's custom to back his judgement with an immediate commission, but to Wilkie both he and Mulgrave gave one at once, although Beaumont no more expected to receive a masterpiece than when Wordsworth had told him of *The Prelude*, writing to Mulgrave of their 'earnestly wishing to serve the artist as well as please ourselves',[71] while leaving Wilkie in no doubt that 'although I shall have great pleasure in possessing the picture. . .I have ten times more, in the prospect of seeing you improve your talents to the utmost'.[72]

Wilkie unlike Jackson proved industrious, without need of the rod, and Beaumont

68. David Wilkie: *The Blind Fiddler*, 1806 (London, Tate Gallery).

was impressed by his modesty over money. He had been so delighted by the first sight of the picture that would become *The Blind Fiddler* (Pl. 68) that he had thought to give more for it than first agreed — 'all the money in my breeches pocket, together with the pocket and breeches into the bargain' — until caution prevailed, for if the artist should be 'thereby induced to ask a larger price for his pictures than the present state of patronism in this country would encourage, I should eventually injure him instead of serving him — he would in a short time paint out all those willing to give such price, and be obliged to lower his topsails, which is always a mortifying and injurious thing'. Mulgrave, who had 'indeed been a Maecenas' and was soon to propose a scheme to collect all Wilkie's sketches as an heirloom, should not offer more for his picture either, for although 'when we are all gone these pictures will treble in value, yet...I am inclined to think Wilkie will find but few who will give such large prices during his life'. The extra he proposed instead to give to Haydon for a sketch, for he 'improves upon me exceedingly...I have seen enough to prove to me his genius'.[73]

In fact Beaumont did offer Wilkie more, but was sufficiently moved, when the painter refused with tears in his eyes, to realise 'I was preventing him from doing a noble and disinterested thing'.[74] When Jackson told him Wilkie was 'very *Oeconomical*',[75] he feared grasping for money would after all prove his undoing, but

158

after Mulgrave told him how highly the picture had been praised in *Bell's Weekly Messenger*, he repeated his larger offer — actually 50 guineas — and this time Wilkie gave in. Farington told Beaumont Wilkie's 'pictures are Gold, and He should reap all the advantages He is entitled to';[76] and hard as Wilkie had been to help on this occasion — doubtless reminding Beaumont of Wordsworth — the painter proved a tougher bargainer with Lord Mansfield for whom he painted another picture. It had in fact been wise not to encourage Wilkie to over-price his work so early in his career lest other patrons should be put off, and although Haydon would soon accuse Beaumont and Mulgrave of meanness over the sums they had paid for their first commissions, they had been scrupulously fair by the standards of the day.

The Blind Fiddler was finished in what was for Wilkie a remarkably short time, even though it seems to have been based on an earlier, smaller version. Commissioned in April 1806, it was ready by August. Beaumont had given Wilkie a little picture by Teniers as a model to work from, though he probably sensed a Hogarthian as well as Netherlandish background behind the composition as it began to develop — he had already compared Wilkie to a superior Morland — and perhaps a Shakespearean echo too, for the various ages of Wilkie's characters, ranging from infancy to near dotage, recall Jacques's ruminations on the seven ages of man, Beaumont's favourite passage in *As You Like It* which he had perhaps by now read to his new friend. Wordsworth, besides, had written that same April of a blind fiddler in Oxford Street — perhaps the very musician on the Poland Street corner who had inspired Wilkie — in his poem 'The Power of Music', which he was soon urging Lady Beaumont to show to the painter; while William Bowles was soon to celebrate the picture in one of his sonnets. Surrounded as it was by a tissue of personal associations, Wilkie's picture nevertheless stood firm on its own merits, at once striking a new note in Beaumont's collection and in contemporary painting. Regrettably, Beaumont seems to have made no very specific comment on the picture's iconography, and there can be no way of knowing whether he associated its contrast between tattered and ragged poverty, and humble self-sufficiency — so potent a force in the work today — with the debates that had surrounded the condition of the poor during the long years of war.

In February 1807 the *Fiddler* was sent briefly to Dunmow before being returned in time for the Academy. Wilkie, like Wordsworth, was the hero of the hour. Beaumont could not stop talking about him and, 'in a fever about Wilkie's extraordinary merits',[77] spared no solicitude as to the picture's reception, hoping it would not be hung near any vulgar 'Boiled Lobsters' that might overshadow it.[78] When the exhibition, which included his own *Keswick Lake*, opened, he was constantly taking people to see Wilkie's picture, and it is certain that Wilkie's early fame owed much to his enthusiasm, now running at full tide. Sometimes his eagerness overstepped the bounds of good sense, as when he suggested that the Academy suspend custom and elect Wilkie an Academician without first being an Associate. This was rash, even had everyone agreed with his estimate, and hardly more tactful were the comparisons by which he was promoting his protégé, announcing that he would 'beat our artists out of their slapdash manner' — for 'a little colouring and effect will not make up for ignorant blunderhead drawing'[79] — and, telling Wordsworth of Wilkie's dedicated draughtmanship, trusting 'his assiduity will shame our artists into attention'[80] provided only those 'whose hope is at present to drive him out of his line and Fuzzeli him into a mongrel M. Angelo' did not get their way.[81]

Beaumont's response to Wilkie was genuine and sensitive. Of the *Fiddler* he told Wordsworth: 'he has finished each character with its appropriate expression so exquisitely that I believe few are able even to conceive the subject so well...he is indeed an extraordinary young man'.[82] He fully recognised that Wilkie's bent did not lie in an academic direction, nor, as his remark about Fuseli showed, towards history painting, and though he was soon reassured, he had been a little afraid in 1806 that he might make the peasant figures in his *Alfred reprimanded by the Neatherd's Wife*,[83] a tentative experiment in history, too frivolous for a subject containing a monarch and a hero. Perceptively, he directed him to Rembrandt, Ostade and later to Watteau at Dulwich, and did all he could to wean him away from temptations to lucrative portraiture, as well as from the siren lure of moderns like William Havell who had briefly attracted him, back to the 'work of your *heart*'. He was concerned, too, about Wilkie's reading, recommending Cervantes as well as English novelists. The correspondence between the two men reveals a deep, and deepening, understanding. Yet Beaumont's public pronouncements could sound unhealthily like infatuation, or exaggeration. To Mulgrave he spared no 'scruple to declare my *conviction* that he will become equal and perhaps greatly superior to every artist who has followed his line since the creation',[84] but not everyone took such rhapsodies seriously. Hoppner stemmed the flow by retorting that he had already 'heard enough of *Young Roscie*';[85] Northcote was reminded of Handel's remark about a musical prodigy who might be a great genius but played damned badly at present — he preferred Miss Spilsberry's pictures, for at least 'her thoughts are *her own*'[86] — and the actor Kemble, hearing Beaumont's latest claim that *The Blind Fiddler* was worth 200 guineas, demanded of a dinner party: 'wd. He give it? or as He had employed Wilkie pay proportionally?', adding that Beaumont 'never endeavoured to raise one man but to put down another. He said He knew Him and called Him "a Wretch".'[87]

It was true that Beaumont had not endeared himself by condemning Kemble's acting — though the two men were to reach an agreeable-enough accommodation later in life — but such remarks seemed to call the baronet's whole taste and judgement into account. His weathervane character was now widely observed. In the spring of 1807 William Daniell had finished a picture for him, but gossip had it that the patron had not even been to see it, being bored with the painter; and after Beaumont had been particularly scathing about a drawing by Robert Smirke the previous autumn, Farington complained of 'those Critics, who run abt. & in many respects do much harm to the Professors'.[88] Now, with that rather chilling even-handedness that sometimes borders on disloyalty, he began to compile a mounting catalogue of aspersions on his old friend. An article by Northcote in *The Artist*, criticising patrons for bringing young painters too far too fast and giving them rides on a 'flying coach', clearly referred to Beaumont, and when its victim thought of sending a piece in reply, arguing that 'to a certain extent at least, persons not professional might be proper Critics on works of art',[89] Farington approved — not for Beaumont's sake, but because it might determine '*What they are not judges of, & by so doing stop their presumption*'.[90]

Beaumont and Farington had discussed this very point once before, when the baronet had seemed to accept that the professionals had the better judgement. Artists began not to trust him. He had developed, if he had not always had, an irritating habit of saying different things to different people if only to avoid an argument.

160

69. William Owen: *Rachel, Lady Beau-mont*, 1808 (Melbourne, National Gallery of Victoria: Felton Bequeat 1955).

Farington noticed he would 'oppose alone, in company never',[91] public dispute being anathema to his old-world values, and preserved William Sotheby's comment that Beaumont 'had not a strong mind & could not bear to be pressed down deeply upon any subject . . . he always had a novelty to support, but never seemed to dwell upon the merits of those who were established'.[92] Alas, it seemed only too typical of him that he was now beginning to voice some private criticism of Wilkie, although this in itself was hardly unwelcome to those not in favour themselves. *The Blind Fiddler* was as yet sacrosanct, though this too would spend a brief spell in the wilderness, but Beaumont was much less enthusiastic about *The Rent Day* that Wilkie had painted for Mulgrave, and to Farington he expressed the fear that the painter might 'fall into manner'.[93]

Such then were the shifting moods of the elegant aesthete whom Hoppner — who privately thought Beaumont's taste 'most villainous'[94] — painted in 1808. Owen might well feel apprehensive when he went to Dunmow to paint Dame Rachel (Pl. 69) in the style of his recent and admired portrait of Lady Heathcote, although Farington observed that he seemed to be Beaumont's '*Eleve*'[95] this year and he was to feel the full sunshine of the patron's charm. Wordsworth on the other hand was under a cloud that May when was rash enough to send the baronet to the Water Colour Society to look at a Havell. He received a stern rejoinder, for although Havell's exhibit was 'one of the

70. David Wilkie: *B.R. Haydon*, 1815, pencil (David Brown).

best there', still he had been 'retrograde' and the 'general taste of the room [was] deplorable'; Beaumont foresaw

> a manner arising in this country which if not checked in time will effectively extinguish the remaining sparks of taste which exist. . . it is really enough to check the few stout and masculine spirits who still persist in the line of genuine art in spite of criticisms and senseless patronage.[96]

Meanwhile, Beaumont's admiration for Haydon (Pl. 70) at least had prospered. As 'assiduous' as Wilkie, he told Wordsworth, he 'draws admirably, is very modest and as far as I can judge at present promises great things'. Mulgrave, prompted mainly by Jackson and Wilkie — Haydon's constant companions in London — had given the aspirant his first commission, for a large picture of *The Assassination of Dentatus* (Pl. 71); and Beaumont also had been encouraging. But Haydon was soon to observe that while it was Beaumont who fanned the flames of fashion, it was Mulgrave who stumped up the cash; and when he proposed sending his *Flight into Egypt*,[97] a trial of strength before *Dentatus*, to the Academy, Beaumont, who had privately declared it 'very poetical, and quite large enough for anything',[98] told him it would be wiser not to show it — 'People were unused to any thing of this sort, it might be ridiculed, in short it was a dangerous experiment. . .better wait another year, &c, and all the feelings of timid imbecility' — but Haydon had already made up his mind. When the picture was a success and was bought by no less a person than Thomas Hope, it was Lady Beaumont who consigned doubt to the past with an airy wave — 'It was lucky,

71. B.R. Haydon (engraved W. Harvey): *The Assassination of Dentatus*, 1809.

Mr Haydon, you did not follow our advice'[99] — and with her husband she now proceeded to fall hopelessly for Haydon's monstrous claims for his own genius. He had survived the ordeal of dinner at Grosvenor Square — for 'I will *not* drink Lady Beaumont's health in porter' — although the whole affair put him 'in a cold perspiration', and the hostess had been entranced by his 'antique head'.[100] There would be some awkward moments when Haydon disagreed with Beaumonts, Mulgraves and Wilkie alike over Milton, but such debate was the stuff of life at the Beaumonts' table. Poor Wilkie, as Jackson had been before him, was somewhat eclipsed and Beaumont, frustrated as ever in his quest for a saviour of landscape — and for a while forgetful of all he had claimed for West — now concentrated on his conviction that 'A great historical painter would at last arise'.[101] The stirrings of his birth, awkward, painful but heroic, he saw in Haydon.

To Wordsworth, knowing 'you and yours interest yourselves in the progress of genius in every shape', Beaumont wrote in February 1809 that Haydon fulfilled Coleridge's criterion for genius, 'the power of labouring long and with pleasure to accomplish the end', and Haydon had impressed him by declaring thorough knowledge of landscape painting essential to a 'great historical painter'; he would not rest until 'all nature bow to his purpose'. Beaumont was certain he would 'turn out the best historical painter this country has ever produced', for he possessed so many requisites, all of them 'proceeding from an enthusiastic love of his art'.[102] 'How success or a prospect of success operates on men's minds', Haydon would soon reflect bitterly, but early in 1809, returning from the Beaumonts or the Mulgraves with the glitter of candles still dancing in his eyes and the echo of party chatter carrying him through the dark streets, he felt all before him. *Dentatus* was finished, and promised a fine place in the Academy, and he could not resist a sneaking pleasure at the 'prospect too of the People becoming tired of W.',[103] a trend to which Beaumont himself was contributing. Growing suddenly bored with *The Blind Fiddler*, he had sent it to Mulgrave telling him 'he knew not where to hang it, it being so ill-coloured'. Somewhat surprised, Mulgrave had shown Jackson some of his friend's letters in which 'he went to the utmost length of expression in praise of the picture, and that it would be a perpetual companion and society to him, or words to that effect'. Mulgrave 'remarked on the contradiction here manifested. Haydon is now Sir George's hero, who is with him every day. Wilkie is on the decline in favour.'[104]

As with Wilkie's picture, Beaumont was determined Haydon's *Dentatus* should be well placed in the Academy, but this time his intervention rebounded, partly because the Academy was beginning to resent his interference, partly because people were developing a certain resistance to his fickle fancies; as for the picture, its straining heroics bordered on the ridiculous. In the event, what Haydon was to call the 'rascality of West' resulted in *Dentatus* being placed in the Octagon Room at Somerset House, a distinguished but not pre-eminent position, and Haydon smarted under the supposed slight for the rest of his life, while that May he was put out to find Wilkie's star rising once more — 'Wilkie, who two months ago was neglected'.[105] In fact he could have taken comfort from his patrons' loyalty, for Mulgrave added 50 guineas to the price as a compensation, while Beaumont told him that 'the man who fancies attainment easy, has a circumscribed mind', adding a palliative that Haydon surmised to be an allusion to Lawrence but more probably referred to Turner:

> It, at first thought, seems rather hard that such a Birmingham gentleman should, in the multitude of his converts, proceed without difficulty and with great exaltation, whilst you meet with struggles...yet when you recollect the object of his vanity — that it has little to do with mind...that it is scarcely more valuable than the applause a rope-dancer receives for his monkey-tricks — he certainly ceases to be an object of envy.[106]

Privately, however, Beaumont and Mulgrave agreed Haydon must be taken in hand: he must stop swearing and offending his colleagues, and his manners had to be 'regulated'. For this Beaumont looked to Wilkie. The strange intimacy that existed between the pragmatic, passionless Wilkie and the headstrong Haydon was not unfamiliar, and if he were reminded of the poets, Wilkie would prove the Wordsworth, Haydon the Coleridge of this no less curious partnership. It was in apprehension as well as affection that Beaumont now wrote to Haydon: 'I contemplate the friendship which subsists between yourself and Wilkie with peculiar pleasure. Long may it last, uninterrupted by misunderstandings of any sort.'[107]

XI
PAMPHLETS AND CONTROVERSIES

BEAUMONT'S ENTHUSIASM FOR Haydon and his *Dentatus*, and the anticlimax of the picture itself, had not gone unnoticed. Nor had his poor opinion of Turner. Perhaps he had been unwise or blinkered, but just as he felt it his duty to advance genius where he saw it, so too he felt bound to speak out against a false taste. He was, as he was soon to insist defensively, entitled to his opinions, but in both cases he had put himself out on a limb. Resentment was mounting, but he still had little sense of it, for the first shot, though elaborately prepared, seems never to have been fired. It came not from Turner, who had been his prime target, but from Turner's friend and disciple, Callcott.

Just how Turner's and Beaumont's ways had parted so early in the artist's career is as tantalising a mystery as how Turner would later so bitterly offend his much younger admirer, Ruskin. While, as we now know, Ruskin told Carlyle the truth of his own brush-off from his hero, Turner seems to have confided in no one about Beaumont, the latter always insisting his opprobrium was all for the good of art. Perhaps Callcott knew a deeper truth, for Turner was capable of being brusque and rude; but if Beaumont could put up with Coleridge or Haydon, Turner should have been plain sailing. In any case, Callcott, who since 1806 had adopted Turner's style and even tended to anticipate his idol's cool palette and atmospheric effects, had drawn much of Beaumont's fire to himself and felt the more injured by it. For him the spectacle of Beaumont trumpeting so pretentious and clumsy a picture as *Dentatus* had turned out to be was the last straw. Incensed, he drafted a long and vitriolic letter to an editor, disguising himself as a naive guest at an Academy reception who had been first buttonholed by Beaumont in full flight about Haydon, and then warned by a 'friend' against paying attention to so biased a guide. By this pretext he put all his loathing of Beaumont, for such it had become, into another's mouth.[1]

Callcott's letter is too long to quote in full, but the salient features of his malicious invention are worth preserving. His innocent in the Academy was soon spotted by Beaumont who, 'catching me by the arm dragged me into the anti room' and standing before *Dentatus*, '"There said he is a picture as admirably painted as it is infamously treated...It is full of Energy and Enthusiasm and would have received its due...if the envy and malice of the council had not thought it necessary to suppress such merit".' The visitor was 'quite astonished' and 'should have imagined I had singled out the artist himself if his age had not set me right'. Luckily the wise friend arrived to put matters into perspective, condemning *Dentatus* — '"the enthusiasm is mere caricature, the composition contemptible"' — and Beaumont too at much greater length:

the gentleman is esteemed by the world at large as the first connoisseur of the day . . . The praise you have heard bestow is none other than what I have heard him regularly bestow upon the whole race of existing artists at their first appearance. He has deemed every one the greatest in his turn as long as he only promised well but the moment he began to fulfill his promise . . . he had made a point of pulling him to pieces, and for this simple reason, that while an artist remains below mediocrity, it is a display of his judgement to point out his beauties but directly he is above par then the tables must be turned . . . as this Gentleman has become the Demagogue of the picture Cricks so he conceived himself under the necessity of making the artists feel the weight of his power. In no instance therefore can any one of them receive his commendation but at the expense of some of his contemporaries and if he once condemns and the public do not follow his direction (as in the case of Mr. Turner whose works must ever be considered as a national Honor) he pursues his purpose with that determination and bitterness in which a galled and disappointed mind ever indulges.

Then followed a diatribe against Beaumont's own painting as being too inept to justify his claim to criticise others:

tell us upon what solid principles that man's judgement rests who out of at least fifty annual attempts can scarce find one that in its design is entitled to completion as a sketch . . . who never yet formed to himself the plan of a single picture but who constantly sits down at his easle [*sic*] with a particular picture before him to work from . . . let his most celebrated gallery picture in the gallery at Oxford be exhibited by the side of the picture by Artaud in his own possession.

This accusation of plagiarism, at least, is hard to justify, even if Callcott had confused Artaud with Arnald. Having thus quoted his 'friend', Callcott's Academy visitor concluded his letter with an appeal that, should it 'meet the eye of Sir G.B. the person accused . . . I should hope that in that consciousness he cease under the title of the first of connoisseurs to be the first of Persecutors.' Wisely, Callcott never sent his letter, or it was never published, but it represented an extreme statement of views that were gaining ground among his colleagues. It was ironic that Haydon himself would soon be saying many of the same things; even Hearne was complaining that his old friend 'sweeps away those Artists who at the time are not His objects';[2] Farington, who, one suspects, could be something of a snake in the grass, was beginning to take a sneaking pleasure in collecting such opinions; and Turner was probably getting his own back when, in a sketchbook of this very period,[3] he drew a caricature of an amateur artist staring with manic intensity at a canvas of his own:

Pleased with his work he views it o'er and o'er
And finds fresh beauties never seen before

— while all around stand old masters to borrow from (Pl. 72). It is highly likely that this refers to Beaumont, while the young assistant in the background who 'cares not for taste beyond a butter'd roll' might be any one of his disappointing protégés. In the same year, 1809, Turner is said to have had the 'proud pleasure of refusing to sell' *Fishing upon the Blythe-Sand* (Pl. 73) to Beaumont out of his own exhibition.[4] Beaumont perhaps intended to heal a now conspicious breach, but the artist made it

72. J.M.W. Turner: *The Amateur Artist*, c1809, pencil, ink and wash (London, Clore Gallery for the Turner Collection, Tate Gallery).

73. J.M.W. Turner: *Fishing upon the Blythe-Sand, Tide setting in*, 1809 (London, Clore Gallery for the Turner Collection, Tate Gallery).

clear he was not to be trifled with — and, worse, that Beaumont's patronage did not matter to him. However, to his sketchbooks and notebooks now and for several years, Turner would confide a number of sarcastic verses and epigrams about misguided patronage and narrow-minded connoisseurs, indicating that he may have been more hurt and provoked than he admitted in public.

Otherwise, Beaumont was still protected by a familiar caucus of painter-friends. That May the old dining club of Dance, West, Bowles, Farington and himself had re-formed, now christened the Peter Martyr Society after Farington, at one of his rare dinner parties, produced the drawing West had made at one of their original meetings in 1784 to show them the composition of Titian's celebrated altarpiece. West was to produce an emblem for the society and Beaumont was delighted, telling Farington, who glowed with unctuous pride, that his hospitality always produced something 'to make our meetings singularly pleasant.'[5] Farington was being pressed to Coleorton, and a visit to Leicestershire was now expected of all Beaumont's friends. Hearne came in September, old, ailing and in need of cheer; Beaumont had tried to organise support for him, 'a place in the Hawker's & Pedlar Office or some such thing', but had been told 'public money was not intended for Charity'.[6] There was much talk of painters and painting, and no doubt of Turner, for Hearne, who shared Beaumont's dislike of him, returned to London protesting at the 'established false taste...that were an Artist to produce pictures like those of Claude Lorrain they wd. not be admired'.[7]

* * *

At Coleorton Beaumont lost no time in getting to work on his friends. Outside the hothouse atmosphere of London, with the old masters brought from Grosvenor Square, he hoped the old values would reassert themselves. Haydon and Wilkie, tired and unwell though they were, seemed to respond splendidly to the magic when they came on a visit the following August. Their visit had been mooted for some time, Mulgrave jokingly blaming some of the failings of *Dentatus* on his friend's own failure to show Haydon some Coleorton rocks that might have helped him with his background. Beaumont had been rather alarmed when Haydon threatened to stay a month, but a fortnight was the perfect span and began happily, the host's charm and warm encouragement smoothing away all tensions. They sketched and painted, and in the evenings ruthlessly criticised each other's work. Haydon, deprived of the marbles, models and casts of the metropolis, came off worst in landscape but triumphed with a head of Beaumont's favourite horse, 'full of fire and life' — 'bringing it in when the party were waiting for dinner, I had the satisfaction of demolishing their little bits of study, for the size of life, effectively done, is sure to carry off the prize' — and then had to share the honours when Wilkie, already busy with an interior of the gardener's cottage, produced a fine study of an old woman from the village ('but they all allowed that nothing could exceed the eye of my horse').[8] Fascinated by the shadows of the hall they 'lingered on the stairs in going up to bed and studied the effect of candlelight upon each other', and one evening Wilkie and Haydon drew Lady Beaumont's maid at the turn of the steps, posing as Lady Macbeth (Pl. 74). Wordsworth was expected any moment and Beaumont cautioned the young men against his 'terrific democratic notions', but their minds were on art. Haydon recalled that they 'dined with the

168

74. David Wilkie: *Lady Beaumont's Maid on the Staircase at Coleorton Hall*, 1809, pen and wash (David Brown).

Claude and Rembrandt before us, breakfasted with the Rubens landscape, and did nothing, morning, noon or night, but think of painting, talk of painting, dream of painting and wake to paint again'.[9] Wilkie wrote to Beaumont for them both: 'to us it has been a constant and inexhaustible subject of conversation, since our return, and for my own part, I do not recollect any time I have spent with more pleasure'.[10]

But fatal seeds had been sown. Beaumont had read Holinshed's account of Macbeth one evening after dinner, the sketches had been made that night on the stairs, and Beaumont had already given Haydon a commission for a subject from the play. Riding one day in the park he broached the question of its size. Haydon replied 'Any size you like, Sir George', Beaumont casually asked if whole length would be large enough, and so it was agreed, Haydon returning to London afire to paint 'the finest picture ever executed...to colour it like Titian, to terrify like Michel Angelo',[11] leaving his patron in the country to forget the matter. Thus began in all innocence the saga of *Macbeth*, a protracted tragicomedy that would do little credit to any of its principal players.

Haydon had been promised a commission for some time, although Beaumont had hitherto managed to avoid committing himself, and whenever it had been discussed, 'with hesitation and perplexity, would quiver out "ah, yes, indeed, ah", or some such unmeaning observation'.[12] Now he was caught. Haydon chose to depict the moment after the murder of Banquo and would soon put 'the effect of the staircase' into the picture which Wilkie thought 'suits it amazingly well'.[13] Back in London in January, Beaumont found it well advanced, but he was unhappy about the scale. Looking at the figures he asked: 'This is the full size of life?' and Haydon admitted they were a little smaller. Beaumont brought General Phipps for a second opinion and 'they both abused, and even ridiculed, saying, "Figures less than life look dwarfish"'.[14] It was meant frivolously but was fatally wounding for a man of Haydon's gigantic ambitions, and now Beaumont, overcome with doubts, made matters worse by a typical change of mind, asking for a smaller picture instead; he would take the larger, if he liked it, on completion. He later claimed to have always had in mind a work of the same size as West's *Pylades and Orestes* that he could hang as a companion, and proposed just this as a solution to the deadlock, but in fact he found Haydon making the figures 'a size which he particularly disliked, — something less than the size of life, & looking like a race of little men', or as Constable put it, 'approaching too near the natural height of a man witht. being it'.[15] Haydon, he added, 'pleads the example of Titian & retorts by saying if these are of a dwarfish size those by Nicolo Poussin are Lilliputians', to which Beaumont could only reply that it was 'the first time he had heard the works of Poussin compared to Puppets'.

Haydon had by this time refused to compromise with his patron over the smaller picture and was pressing on with the large. Mulgrave had urged him to yield, but Jackson had told him he would be 'equally woretted, small or large', while Northcote had added to the conflict by blaming Beaumont himself for being difficult in order to get out of the commission altogether. At first Haydon had agreed to the smaller version, 'tormented into acquiescence, and frightened into concession by Wilkie's timidity and inclination to bowing' to produce 'a pretty furniture Picture for the dining room of Sir George';[16] but after this humiliating sacrifice Beaumont had seemed evasive and had rushed out to dinner and then to Dunmow, and it was useless for Wilkie to say that Beaumont had behaved just as oddly when he was finishing the *Fiddler*, for the damage was done and Haydon's mind made up. Now he managed to persuade Beaumont to defer his decision until the picture was finished, nevertheless offending him further by forbidding him to see it until then. If Beaumont was not satisfied then he would paint another, of a different subject; but he resolved, 'if Sir George had a spark of feeling, to vanquish him'.[17]

Beaumont, who hated arguments, had been avoiding Haydon, and the dispute had been conducted by correspondence that had become so acrimonious that he had broken it off thinking the artist 'deranged in mind'; but then, afraid he 'might commit some desperate act upon Himself', Beaumont wrote a few last lines. 'Haydon during this controversy neglects his business', Constable tersely observed.[18] Sometimes in a fever of activity, sometimes prostrate awaiting a fresh tide of patronage, Haydon passed some anxious weeks, meanwhile confiding all his frustrations to the pages of his diary. Day after day he indulged his fury with his elusive patron, telling and retelling the story of how he had been 'fascinated by his affability, his smiles, his flattery' and 'believed none could have such fundamentally wicked propensities as to be gratified with seducing youthful inexperience, for the mere purpose of abandoning it at the first blast of unsuccess'. Once he had looked up to Beaumont, but after watching him with 'a wary eye' he saw him plain, mean, vindictive, treacherous, 'one year in raptures, the next in horrors', so parsimonious that 'he fixed his talons' on Mulgrave to buy, 'while he only praises' or criticised as an excuse for not buying. 'Time', he wrote one day, 'could tell a tale of many a Man of Genius elevated & depressed, harassed and ruined, the victim of Sir George's seduction', and he could but hope that 'having laid open the secret of his quackery and exposed the hollowness of his intentions — inexperience will be on its guard against his plausibility'. 'You are a lamentable instance, Sir George, how much cunning is an overmatch for sincerity. . .Oh Sir George — I have no hope of putting a stop to your conduct — I only wish to check its influence, by laying open the secret spring of its motions'.[19]

This was hysterical of course, and Beaumont did best to leave Haydon alone, but eventually the martyr felt neglected, and so far forgot decency as to start showing his correspondence with Beaumont, while writing to Mulgrave as his 'real patron'.[20] To this solecism Beaumont responded subtly and with tact, inviting Haydon to dinner with a 'brilliant company' and remarking as he pushed the wine towards him that he had the strangest aversion to people showing private letters — 'nothing, you know, is so indelicate' — while Lady Beaumont, gently patting his arm, rallied him 'on the propriety of docility in early life'.[21] But in vain, for Haydon had merely added yet another strip to his canvas and resumed work. Haydon was convinced he 'had caught Sir G. and his Lady completely — they were in terror — they dreaded the exposure of their letters — they knew they stood on hollow ground — and it was in my power to plunge them through it'.[22] Calling a day or two later to see the picture, Lady Beaumont was adamant: 'We have no room'; but Haydon had stated his final terms and 'never did two People slink off as they did — instead of the chattering, impudent insolence that used to characterise her manner — Lady B. never spoke a syllable. Sir G. trembled as he caught the bannister — and once more quivered out "Good morning".'[23] Haydon thought him afraid, but for once he may have been trembling with rage.

*   *   *

Wilkie had sat silent and apart at the recent dinner party. Haydon believed 'Sir George was tired and wanted another extraordinary young man, for Wilkie was an old story and I was a nuisance.'[24] In fact Wilkie was in agonies of embarrassment, and whatever his motives for sending the *Fiddler* to Mulgrave, Beaumont had lost none of his affection for this most rational of men. Beaumont had just painted a landscape for him, lavished advice on *The Ale-House Door*,[25] then in the painting, and given him a small picture by Teniers as a guide,[26] while also offering him another commission. This was exactly the kind of intelligent consideration that Haydon had frozen in his would-be patron, determined as he was to see only the other side. Yet Wilkie too would suffer a reversal at Beaumont's behest that spring, though it was done with the best of intentions; for it was Beaumont who, on his own behalf and that of some Academicians, chiefly West, advised Wilkie to withdraw his *Wardrobe ransacked*[27] from the Academy on the grounds that it was inferior to his other work. Beaumont himself had provided an alternative title for this humorous subject of an elderly man donning a girl's cap, 'No Fool like an old Fool', and was as upset as the artist by its poor reception, which was largely owing to the success of a genre piece by the Bristol artist Edward Bird in the same exhibition. Though manifestly based on Wilkie, this picture, *The Village Choristers*,[28] was thought to put him in the shade and had

75. David Wilkie: *The Dunmow Gamekeeper*, 1811 (Private Collection).

moreover been bought by the Prince Regent. Although Wilkie afterwards improved his own picture and made a good sale, the incident distressed him and his illness later that year, as Haydon was quick to point out, sprang partly from nervous reaction.

Perhaps salving an uneasy conscience, Beaumont sent Wilkie a cheque for £50 after the Academy exhibition opened, conscious, he claimed, of possessing in the *Fiddler* a picture worth more than he had paid for it. Wilkie was touched but, having himself made a profit on the engraving by Burnet that his patron had recently allowed him to have made, refused, 'for acceptance would be an absolute act of injustice in me'.[29] Instead, Beaumont sent 'a few bottles of such as you cannot get at the retailers', for an artist laboured in vain 'if his port wine is not good'.[30] But Beaumont's port could not prevent a breakdown, and that summer, recognising his was a nervous case, he consigned Wilkie to the care of Dr Baillie at Hampstead, discreetly offering to fund a winter's recuperation in Madeira. When even Coleorton seemed too taxing, the patient came instead to Dunmow, and here, at last, Wilkie's strength crept back. Lady Beaumont was a constant nurse and Sir George encouraged some modest work — 'interesting heads to which he has great adroitness in giving such interest that "more is meant than meets the eye"'.[31] Wilkie borrowed his host's colours for a small oil of the Dunmow gamekeeper (Pl. 75), Beaumont paying £100 for it, a gesture that 'overpowered' the painter and called forth the reassurance that 'I had no other motive . . . but a real regard and esteem for you. . . I will not. . . suffer you to talk of obligation'.[32]

Haydon was still perplexing them both. The giant forms of Macbeth and Duncan were looming on his canvas and Haydon felt his genius taking flight. To Beaumont the thought of him suggested less the 'wings at the heart' of the painter's future motto, taken from Tasso, than a millstone from which he yearned to be free. But it was not easy to rid himself of his personal feelings for Haydon and with his support the British Institution awarded *Dentatus* its £100 premium for historical painting early in 1810, thus assisting him officially but indirectly, for socially he remained *persona non grata*. Haydon would make more trouble before he was done and only later would he realise that he was fighting a losing battle, and had misjudged a loyal and patient friend by mistaking caprice for wilful malice, uncertainty and prevarication for meanness of heart. Meanwhile *Dentatus* had met a harder fate than its prize-winning status suggested. Tactless as ever, Haydon had called on Mulgrave to see where it was hanging but was refused admission. Returning with Jackson, he was again turned away, and soon 'it was discovered that the much admired picture of Dentatus, is now in its *case* placed in his Lordship's stable'. Hearing the sorry tale from Constable, Farington was moved to moralise: 'So much for capricious patronage', blaming Haydon's self-opinionated presumption on 'over-commending'.[33] None knew better the arguments on both sides, but it was a foretaste of troubles ahead that Farington's loyalty lay first with the artist. To stress solidarity he called on Haydon and 'strongly exhorted him...not to give up his own observation & feelings to adopt the ideas of those who occasionally make remarks on his pictures'.[34]

*　　*　　*

Recovering in new lodgings in the Kings Road, Wilkie looked forward to a visit from Beaumont. Instead, he was sent the most gentle of prods to give the *Gamekeeper* 'the very little more' that would 'render it perfect', though he should 'burn this letter' if he did not agree with Beaumont's suggestions; the frame, carved by Charpentier, also must be replaced, as it had 'put out some of the *fire*'.[35] Thus improved, it appeared in that year's Academy exhibition, Wilkie now being elected Royal Academician and Beaumont writing to 'wish you joy. The honour is mutual.'[36] The summer found Wilkie in Scotland seeing his ailing father, and Jackson and George Arnald taking his place for long visits to Coleorton. Little more was heard of Wilkie until the following year when he resurrected an earlier project for a one-man exhibition in which, he pointedly told his patron, he had been 'more regulated by the opinion of my friends than by my own judgment'.[37] Beaumont replied cautiously, warning him the show might be less successful than if it had taken place when 'the public were under the influence of their first surprise, for "there is a tide in the affairs of men"'. Wilkie should also beware of 'a morbid or unreasonable effort to excell what you have done before'.[38] Beaumont now showed not only his deep sensitivity to Wilkie's work, but that fear of evolution in art and artists that would always limit him:

> believe me, there is in the first feelings of a man of genius a simplicity and truth which, as he advances in practical skill, will, without continual attention, be very apt to be lost in the struggle to excel; simplicity is the vital principle of the line you have chosen. Deep pathos, though I think you are quite equal to it, you do not appear to aim at; satire and broad humour are not perhaps congenial to your

feelings; what remains then is the amenity of humble life...It appears to me that you can never improve upon the simplicity of your first intentions; the notion of endeavouring to improve upon them by an introduction of more taste or refinement is extremely dangerous.[39]

Such observations from Beaumont might well have surprised Constable and others for whom greater taste and refinement were his constant hopes. But if Wilkie was a special case, Beaumont ended his letter to him on a familiar paternal note, justifying criticism but also showing a new awareness of criticisms levelled against himself:

I have been accused by high authority of having injured you by indiscriminate praise. I hope such is not the case, for I am well aware that it is as much the duty of a real friend to find fault as to commend; and as it is certainly less pleasant, perhaps it is the most meritorious of the two.[40]

This was however scarcely the spirit in which Beaumont had continued his campaign against Turner who, of all living artists, had departed furthest from his 'first intentions'. Among Turner's four Academy exhibits that year, *Mercury and Herse*[41] was specially praised by the Prince Regent at the Academy dinner, and his reference to 'landscapes which Claude would have admired'[42] must have urged Beaumont to reassess his view of the artist, for here certainly was a Claudian composition in the grandest manner, but treated with a brilliance all Turner's own. But try as he might, Beaumont could neither admire nor remain silent, and that June Callcott, still making capital out of a connoisseur's blind spot, told Farington of his 'continued cry' against Turner.[43] Beaumont had admitted Turner 'had merit, but it was of a wrong sort & therefore on acct. of the seducing skill displayed shd. be objected to',[44] and Beaumont's own words a year later were still stronger: Turner had 'done more harm in misleading the taste than any other Artist. At His setting out He painted some pictures, "The Plagues in Egypt", that gave great promise, but He had fallen into a manner that was neither true nor consistent.'[45] As for Callcott, he was 'merely a follower of Turner & seems to look at nothing else';[46] and Beaumont would 'never scruple to express [his] opinion because...it is proper to do so when a bad taste is prevailing'.[47]

All this Farington heard at Coleorton. His visit in 1812 was one of reconciliation, for the previous year a coolness had arisen, the two old friends hardly seeing one another and meetings of the Peter Martyr Society having apparently ceased. Who was avoiding whom is unclear, for if there was a wistful note in Farington's report of Charles Bowles's remark following his father, Oldfield's, death at the beginning of the year, that Beaumont would feel the loss, but had 'acquired many new acquaintances who engrossed his attention',[48] yet it was Beaumont who complained that Farington 'would not talk to Him abt. painting'.[49] There were too many sensitive issues between them just now, Farington sharing the Academicians' worst fears about the rising status of the British Institution and being friendly with the Callcott clique of Turner admirers, and probably Beaumont also suspecting him of taking Haydon's part too much in the continuing muddle over *Macbeth*. But, as ever at Coleorton, the tensions evaporated and their talk ranged wider than it had done for years, Beaumont being in mellow mood as he spoke of his ancestors, the estate and the future of his collection — already a matter of deep consideration — of his new-found admiration for George Barrett after a visit to Norbury Park, of how he would like to know Lawrence better,

174

of poets, neighbours and old friends — he had had a strange dream of Lord Aylesford just before he died at Packington. Nothing served better as a *sal volatile* than such a flow of nostalgia and goodwill — it was indeed true that Beaumont was a different man in the country — and, complaining that neither J.R. Cozens nor Jefferys had received proper biographies, Beaumont and the other guest, William Owen, flattered Farington further by suggesting that he write Wilson's before it was too late. Just before departing, Farington and Owen witnessed the inauguration of the monument to Reynolds, inscribed with Wordsworth's lines expressing their host's fondest sentiments:

> Admiring, loving, and with grief and pride
> Feeling what England lost when Reynolds died.

*   *   *

Haydon's name had been avoided during this rural idyll, and Beaumont had already given Farington his own account of what had passed between them back in the spring. By the winter of 1811 Haydon had finished *Macbeth*, and had written to Beaumont asking leave to show it at the British Institution. Beaumont had told him he could do as he pleased as he no longer considered the picture his, although he reserved the right to buy it if he liked it. When it was exhibited Beaumont still found it too large but offered Haydon 100 guineas in compensation for a lost sale, or 200 for another picture of a size mutually agreed. Under the circumstances these were generous terms indeed, but inevitably Haydon refused, again threatening to publish his correspondence with his patron. Haydon had intended *Macbeth* for the Institution's competition for its historical-painting premium, having already been the victor with *Dentatus*, and Beaumont, returning to London from Dunmow especially for the vote, was fair-minded enough to admit Haydon stood the best chance. True to form, however, this most impossible of painters now ruined his chances.

On 26 January there appeared in the *Examiner* the first installment of a long letter signed 'An English Student', in fact Haydon's work and a violently sarcastic attack on Knight — who had already roused his anger by his failure to appreciate the Elgin marbles — for his hostility to the history painter, James Barry. Two further passages were printed, this time denouncing the Academy. Only a Haydon could have produced an alliance, however unholy, between the Academy and the Institution. It was from the latter that he now had most to gain, but Knight was one of its most influential Directors. Beaumont wished only to distance himself from the whole affair and in any case was sadly disappointed when he saw the Institution's spring exhibition, pronouncing it 'a wretched display, & that it wd. be better to admit not more than a dozen respectable pictures than such a heap of bad'; wiser altogether not to offer premiums at all but to buy 'at liberal prices' the better pictures 'but not as from Candidates for Premiums'.[50] This policy, calculated to frustrate Haydon's prospects, was indeed soon to be adopted by the Institution. In fact Knight, Haydon's target though he was, was charitable enough to propose *Macbeth* for a premium, the Directors having discussed and rejected the idea of abolishing them, but he too was outvoted and the first and second premiums were withheld that year, the third and smallest going to a negligible picture, *The Procession to Mount Calvary*, by George Francis Joseph.[51]

Haydon's ill-timed resort to the press might well have put him out of court for good, but meanwhile Beaumont, swept away by one of his sudden enthusiasms, had disastrously compounded the problem. At the watercolour exhibition in Bond Street he and Mulgrave had fallen headlong for a picture by Henry James Richter, *Christ healing the Blind*, and amid a torrent of 'violent praise' and 'extravagant eulogiums' had declared he had 'never before seen the Divine Character so well expressed'.[52] Moreover, he had persuaded the Institution to buy it for 500 guineas, thus giving Haydon the perfect opportunity to tell everyone that the usual premium funds had been diverted to satisfy a whim of one or two Directors. Furious at seeing 'another placed before him', Haydon was indeed 'confounded' and by June had fallen ill with 'anxiety of mind'.[53] Beaumont of course had intended only to assist Richter, but the result was a furore. Nobody supposed *Macbeth* a particularly good picture or its painter other than an embarrassment, but there was no lack of people eager to orchestrate the whole affair into a glaring example of the fickle antics of connoisseurs and the incompetence and interference of the Institution, as well as of the false heroics and overweening ambition of artists who themselves had been unduly encouraged. A variety of opinion had now converged to make Beaumont the scapegoat of it all, and none other than West felt it time for a word in his ear — this was no doubt the 'high authority' of which Beaumont had written to Wilkie — warning him at Lord Ashburnham's against 'His criticizing the works of Young Artists and His praising one Artist at the expense of another'.[54] Beaumont told him roundly that it was 'not His fault that the Artists did not paint better',[55] but West was not easily settled, 'sensible of the extreme to which Lord Mulgrave and Sir George had gone in their unlimited praise . . . & of the want of judgement shewn in thus purchasing a mere work of promise for a purpose for which works of established merit only should be procured'.[56]

*　　*　　*

Beaumont had by now been introduced by Coleridge to another aspiring history painter of more manageable temperament than Haydon and greater talent than Richter, the American, Washington Allston. By the end of 1811 Lady Beaumont was telling Wordsworth that her husband was off to London from Dunmow eager to see the prodigy's *Cupid and Psyche*,[57] and a portrait of Coleridge was soon ordered, a mask and a chalk drawing by George Dawe being sent to Dunmow for Allston to work from.[58] Painter and potential patron had met by the following April. However, Wordsworth, who was at Grosvenor Square at this time, was surprised that 'Sir G. does not think so highly of A's picture as I expected'. Allston's conversation at dinner had also been disappointing, although Lady Beaumont had excused him by explaining that Coleridge 'will let nobody talk but himself'. Wordsworth 'heard an artist say Allston paints too timidly',[59] but, nevertheless, in August Beaumont visited the young American's studio and was greatly taken with a sketch for *The Dead Man restored by touching the Bones of the Prophet Elisha*,[60] hoping that Allston would finish it for the Institution where the Directors might buy it. By the summer of 1813, when the picture was advancing, he was as avid as ever in his enthusiasm for his new protégé and was 'very importunate' with Charles Long, pursuing him to his office to try to organise Institution support for the new American genius. He seemed again unwilling to learn from his mistakes, although he later admitted to Farington that the Institution 'might

76. Washington Allston: *The Dead Man restored to Life by touching the Bones of the Prophet Elisha*, 1811–13 (Pennsylvania Academy of the Fine Arts, Academy Purchase).

do much harm by exciting hopes in young men of little talent', and should foster only those 'manifestly promising...to prevent an accumulating number of inferior talents'.[61]

Coleridge had warned Allston both of the 'excessive meanness of Patrons, of the malignant Envy & Brutality of the Race of Painters'.[62] Allowing for the poet's paranoid exaggeration, he had a point, for Allston was about to receive similar treatment to Haydon's at the hands of the Institution, although this time it would be a fellow painter who was most to blame. With the *Dead Man* completed, Allston had planned a private exhibition and had hired rooms in Pall Mall, but Beaumont had insisted the picture should go to the Institution and in the 1814 exhibition it did not disappoint (Pl. 76). The Directors awarded it — unlike Haydon's picture — their

200 guinea premium, and were on the point of buying it, but suddenly lost their nerve, carried partly by a wave of anti-Americanism, but more particularly by Allston's fellow American, West, who in his old age was jealous of rivals. Allston lost his sale for the time being, and instead the Directors bought William Hilton's *Mary annointing the Feet of Jesus*[63] for 500 guineas — confirming the worst fears of Coleridge who wrote furiously: 'Mr Allston has been cruelly used. Good God, did I not hear Sir George Beaumont say, with my own ears! Nay, he wrote to me after a repeated examination of Allston's great picture, declaring himself a complete convert to all my opinions of Allston's paramount genius.' Obsessed by what appeared to him a 'wicked system of calumny and detraction', Coleridge was brooding 'a series of Essays on the principles of General Criticism concerning the Fine Arts'.[64] By its treatment of Allston the Institution seemed yet again to have played into the hands of its critics. Beaumont softened the blow by giving him a commission of his own for an altarpiece for Coleorton church, and the painter bore him no malice.

*　　*　　*

The Institution was now holding exhibitions of deceased artists and old masters as well as living painters, and this too was proving controversial, for the work of the former could be used as a stick to beat the moderns. It seemed the Institution could do nothing right, and even Beaumont's longstanding hope for a retrospective exhibition of Reynolds, realised in its galleries this year, came in for its share of protest. Careful as he was to tell Farington of the Directors' plans for a special reception for Academicians, and although 800 visitors were reported each day that May, artists began to find fault with the pictures and Callcott, still spokesman for the most resentful among them, resumed his complaints about the Institution in general and Beaumont in particular. He had not shown at the Academy this year, not having sold a picture in the last three because of 'persevering abuse' from Beaumont, who had cut him at the last private view. Turner, who 'suffered from the same cause', had told him he too would abstain, although he had later changed his mind.[65] It was true that Beaumont had been increasingly critical of both Turner and Callcott, lumping them together as 'white painters' on account of their pale colouring, but Callcott was more worried about Beaumont's role in the Institution than as an independent critic, telling Farington 'the active Directors will gradually assume a controuling power over Artists, and should they obtain the application of any funds granted by the Government for promoting the Arts will sink the importance of the Royal Academy'.[66] In his view their conduct of the Committee of Taste had already proved the unwisdom of setting up 'a body of Amateurs as Critics of the People'.[67] Farington, who sympathised with much of this, tried to make peace, but although Beaumont now bowed to Callcott when he met him at the Academy and assured Farington he 'personally liked' him, he still 'did not approve His manner of colouring his pictures, nor his imitating Turner; indeed there was no knowing the pictures of one from those of the other'.[68]

The Institution's premiums for modern painting, offered with the best intentions, had caused enough trouble with Haydon and Allston, and the preface to the catalogue of the Reynolds exhibition, written, it was generally supposed, by Knight, contained what Constable called 'a manifest allusion to the arrogant pretensions of Haydon'.[69]

77. J.M.W. Turner: *Apullia in Search of Appullus*, 1814 (London, Clore Gallery for the Turner Collection, Tate Gallery).

The following year, 1814, when the Institution included works by Wilson, Gainsborough, Hogarth and, at Beaumont's instigation, Zoffany, Turner threw his own challenge to the Directors, submitting his *Apullia in Search of Appullus* (Pl. 77), late and without apology, for the competition for history painting. A noble extrapolation from a Claude in the collection of Beaumont's fellow Director, Lord Egremont, and realised in a sober palette, it was exactly the kind of picture Beaumont had wished him to paint, but Turner had made it as impossible for the Institution to award him the premium as Haydon had done before. His apparent solecism, together with his subject itself — Ovid's tale of the transformation of the Apullian shepherd into a wild olive tree with bitter berries as a punishment for mimicking the nymphs — surely amounted to an exercise in Institution-baiting, especially as his other exhibit that year, *Dido and Aeneas*,[70] significantly sent to the Academy, was a more characteristically free interpretation of Claude, thus proving that art was not a matter of mimicry alone.

Whatever Beaumont made of Turner's ploy, Haydon was again his immediate concern, for although the painter himself had been unusually quiet, he was winning some dangerous friends. This spring Beaumont found in the *Examiner* a piece 'in which though not by name He was stated to have acted towards Haydon unjustly'.[71] According to Farington, the piece was written by Robert Hunt, elder brother of John and Leigh, the editors of the paper, which, a thorn in Academy and Institution flesh alike since its inception in 1809, had already published Haydon's 'English student' articles. A devoted Haydonite, Hunt had berated the Institution's Directors over the fate of *Macbeth*, but Haydon's art was about to speak for itself for at Spring Gardens the painter now exhibited his huge *Judgement of Solomon* (Pl. 78), begun in poverty and despair, 'without sixpense in His pocket for the purchase of a Candle',[72] in the dark

179

days after the failure of *Macbeth*. That it was a major work none could deny: sonorous and noble, a tribute to Raphael and Poussin, it was one of the major pictures of a year that also produced Turner's *Apullia* and *Dido and Aeneas*.

Haydon was certain he had 'knocked down the British Institution', and so it proved for the picture's fame spread like fire. For Beaumont it was a chance to show his real feelings for the painter without fear of rebuff. With Holwell Carr he rushed to buy the *Solomon* for the Institution collection, only to find it already sold, which was 'very provoking'; but still he could clasp Haydon's hand and tell him he was 'astonished' and promise to call.[73] To Farington he declared himself 'reconciled' to Haydon,[74] while Haydon confided to his sketchbook two sketches of 'Sir G.B. expression, first time looking at Solomon' which 'said more than all praise' (Pl. 79). Frustrated of the purchase, Beaumont moved an *ex gratia* payment of 100 guineas to Haydon from the Institution, and would soon propose a further commission of 200 guineas with 50 on account. Lady Beaumont, meanwhile, wrote to Wordsworth to describe the 'extraordinary historical picture...a grand conception, but not made out, but the passion...and variety of emotions...richness of colouring, correctness of drawing, and architectural background, combine to make it a magnificent work, & accomplished under the pressure of poverty and various other distressess. When we called to wish him joy, he spoke with enthusiasm of the happy warrior...the privilege of thus sustaining the soul is given to few.'[75] This letter was surely the source of the lines poet addressed to painter — 'the highest honour that was ever paid, or ever can be paid to me'[76] — the following year ('High is our calling, Friend! — Creative Art'):

> When the whole world seems adverse to desert,
> And, oh! when Nature sinks, as oft she may,
> Through long-lived pressure of obscure distress,
> Still to be strenuous for the bright reward,
> And in the soul admit of no decay,
> Brook no continuance of weak-mindedness —
> Great is the glory, for the strife is hard!

*　　*　　*

Beaumont was to meet his own 'obscure distress' in 1815, and his pleasure at being associated with the first collected edition of Wordsworth's poems, and the poet's presence in London would be the few bright spots in a darkening sky. Even Waterloo would bring him scant joy in a year of bitter personal defeat and humiliation. Yet it began in a mood of confident optimism for Beaumont and his fellow Directors of the Institution, who had been busy planning a new project — what was in effect the first English exhibition of mixed old masters, a major display of Dutch and Flemish pictures from their own and other private collections. Though inevitably uneven in quality, the show was a noble achievement. The Academy, however, saw it otherwise, and in May the Academicians signalled trouble by refusing, almost *en masse*, invitations to a special evening opening. Upset, Beaumont took Farington to task at Grosvenor Square; perhaps the Institution's secretary, Robert Gillam, had offended them in his letter for it had been 'an ill written and foolish composition, but it could

78. B.R. Haydon: *The Judgement of Solomon*,
1812–14 (Private Collection).

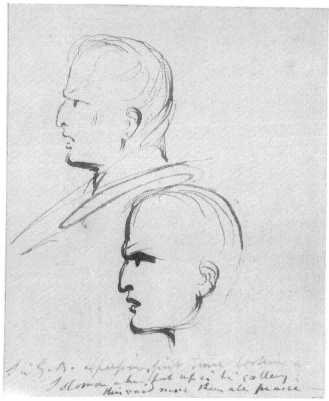

79. B.R. Haydon: *Beaumont looking at 'Solomon' in
the British Institution*, 1814, pen (London, Tate
Gallery).

not be supposed that the Directors authorised it, and it seemed not to be a sufficient cause to declare War against the British Institution'.[77]

Meanwhile the Hunts had fired a further shot in the *Examiner*, aimed at the Institution's conduct towards living artists. On 7 May they took up the case of their friend, the landscapist William Havell, whose *Walnut Gatherers* was now hanging in the Oil and Water Colour Society's exhibition, having been rejected by the Institution. They published Havell's letter of protest that described his significant desire to 'represent my own beautiful country without referring to other painters, ancient or modern', together with Gillam's reply that the Directors 'did not think it proper to enter into consideration of it'. 'Originality', declared the Hunts of these 'Patrons of British Art', always 'threatens to make them less, and they do not like it. To contradict their opinions is to let the world into the secret of their comparative insignificance'. Knight, Holwell Carr and Beaumont were alike despatched to obloquy, the latter, though 'a man of taste who really paints exceedingly well for an amateur', being asked how he could dismiss the painters of nature while thinking 'so highly of that very original and natural poet (we say it, in perfect gravity) his friend Mr Wordsworth?'

Beaumont would find there could be no divorcing his tastes among the old masters — let alone among the poets — from his strictures on the moderns, even if he might now sometimes wish to separate them. Some people were already aware that nemesis was about to descend, James Perry of the *Morning Chronicle* being heard to remark that there was 'a rod in pickle' for the Institution's Directors;[78] but meanwhile Beaumont was still laying down the law as strongly as ever. That June Farington heard one of his most extended critiques of living artists — it would also be one of his last — beginning with Turner, whose exhibits he had again disliked intensely. He had just had an unfortunate argument with Thomas Phillips over them, and Phillips had now joined Callcott in prickly disgruntlement, although Farington believed Turner's high prices were more detrimental to his sales than Beaumont's comments. In fact Beaumont well knew he was in a minority and had taken time to reconsider *Dido building Carthage* (Pl. 80) 'to satisfy Himself that He was not mistaken', only to be further convinced of its 'false taste' and 'discordant colouring' — like a mannered French imitation of Claude — while *Crossing the Brook* was 'weak and like the work of an Old Man, one who no longer saw or felt colour properly; it was all of *peagreen* insipidity'.[79] Defending himself he added: 'I have as good a right & it is as proper that I shd. express them as I have to give my opinion of a *poetical* or any other production.'[80] Lawrence too still came in for some stiff remarks for his 'tinselly touch', though there was now much to admire and he was 'very able', but only West, whose two versions of *Christ rejected* on exhibition that year were a sensation, showed 'the true quality of Art...that comprehensiveness and completeness which is found in the works of the great masters'. Beaumont urged Lawrence to look harder at Van Dyck, while everyone should study Reynolds and Wilson for 'true art, of the right character'.[81]

Just such opportunities it was the policy of the Institution to provide, and Beaumont was proud of it. His views were shared by Knight whose preface to the catalogue of the Dutch and Flemish exhibition stated its purpose as to 'excite in the British Artist the ardour of emulation', for though the 'great works now before us may seem the result of genius without the aid of study, no opinion can be more fallacious; and to the Artist, no mistake more fatal'. And in the year of Waterloo, Knight hoped Rubens

80. J.M.W. Turner: *Dido building Carthage; or, the Rise of the Carthaginian Empire*, 1815 (London, National Gallery).

would inspire painters to celebrate the Wellingtons of the future, a remark that seemed instinct with censure of his contemporaries, although the Institution accompanied its stick with a carrot by announcing for the next year a sum of 1,000 guineas to be divided as seemed best among artists submitting large sketches on the victories of the British army, instead of its usual premiums for history and landscape.

Most painters, however, were unimpressed. The Academy faction was poised to strike, and did so early in June. By the 9th Beaumont had received an anonymous pamphlet, *A Catalogue Raisonné of the Pictures now exhibiting at the British Institution*. Also published as a weekly serial in the *Morning Chronicle*, this was a spoof catalogue of the exhibits that, with a bitter and laboured irony, turned around the best intentions of the Directors in order to condemn them. An exhibition of bad and misattributed old masters, as the pamphlet falsely claimed, could hardly fail to promote the sale of modern art, and Beaumont, who had contributed the *Château de Steen*, was asked 'on what principle could we pretend to explain the abuse which the noble Director... pours forth on the greatest landscape painter of the present day, if he really was so deficient in taste and judgement as seriously to hold this up as an example of art'. It was none other than 'a piece of cunning', to induce a higher estimate of the artists he affected to despise by 'setting up as a specimen of great talent, a thing...that is infinitely inferior to any'. There followed a long piece on the difference between a 'Patron and one who is merely busied about the art' or those who 'buzz about the purlieus' of painting, and a bitter passage on the encouragement and destruction of 'child-wonders' that echoed almost word for word Callcott's letter of 1808.

Hardly had he read it but Beaumont had to play host to Farington and Wilberforce.

81. David Wilkie: *Distraining for Rent*, 1815 (Edinburgh, National Gallery of Scotland).

He was charming as ever, but the barbs had struck him to the heart. They were directed not exclusively at him but at the Institution as a body, but for one who genuinely loved painting and painters as he did — however unwise or rash he may have been in giving way to his enthusiasms — the satire was peculiarly cruel. Searching his conscience he thought first of Havell, embittered by the fate of his *Walnut Gatherers*, but Farington thought his authorship a 'great improbability',[82] and although Beaumont considered the catalogue libellous, neither he nor anyone else ever traced the writer. Indeed, there may have been several, for Phillips, Turner's friend Walter Fawkes — who had recently been haunting the Institution Galleries — Callcott and his friend Henry Thomson, and professional journalists like Fawkes's friend Perry, who now pretended to forget his forecast of 'a rod in pickle', or Haydon's friends the Hunts, had all said similar things for several years. Not knowing whom to trust was more painful than the insult itself. While some of his fellow Directors reacted like bulls to the goad, Beaumont suffered a setback from which he took many months to recover. Within days his appearance was shocking his friends — 'His countenance fallen, his spirits gone...fast falling towards dissolution.'[83] That summer he retreated to the Lakes, but there were melodramatic reports of his 'spitting of blood',[84] and early the next year Arnald, a loyal friend who joined him for Christmas at Coleorton, rightly judged that he had 'suffered mentally'.[85]

Meanwhile the Institution's critics were congratulating themselves that the catalogue had at least had the good effect of inducing it to purchase at last a modern picture of unquestioned merit, Wilkie's *Distraining for Rent* (Pl. 81) from that year's Academy exhibition. A counter to Beaumont's remark that Wilkie would not attempt

184

'deep pathos' — the painter may even have taken it as a challenge — the picture had in fact upset the land-owning classes as a 'factious' subject, by its reference to a punitive landlord. According to Haydon, Beaumont himself had been 'very sore... and said that Wilkie should have shown why his landlord had distrained; he might be a dissipated tenant'.[86] Whatever their motives for purchase, the Directors, 'frightened' by its implications, would soon hide the picture in a lumber room until, seven years later, they sold it to Abraham Raimbach to be engraved. Thus, what some claimed as a victory against the Institution, proved to be a notable example of what Callcott had called its 'controuling power'. For his part, Beaumont had been caught by the catalogue in one of his elated moods when he was taking himself rather too seriously; now he was on the defensive, preternaturally alert to anything that might reflect against his class as well as on himself, and of course there was also the painful memory of his own 'dissipated tenant' at Coleorton. As for Wilkie, he felt nothing but embarrassment at his unintentional blunder, and his biographer Cunningham would gloss over the whole affair.

Another catalogue appeared in 1816, more facetious than the last but perhaps less painful, for Beaumont was already wounded too deeply, and by now too indignant, to take further offence. The new one purported to be a history of the Academy and the Institution, transposed into a setting in Timbuctoo with the Directors of the latter cast as primitive chiefs, Beaumont appearing as 'Figgity — a man of some taste, and a tolerable painter; but uncertain, capricious, cowardly, and treacherous as a Hyaena, who entices the little children into his den, and then devours them', and Lady Beaumont, in her guise as vain enthusiast and lover of poetry, as 'soosee moosa...a little troublesome woman, very fond of Babies verses. She collects the eggs which Figgity uses in painting, and makes the vinegar herself':

> Oh! were she dumb, till Echo silence breaks
> Then would Sir George, and all his friends, be blest.

This would be the last catalogue from the 'Incendiary', who congratulated himself on the success of its predecessor. Of all his victims, he had no doubt Beaumont was laid lowest, 'so much undermined that the apprehension of an explosion, which might blow him and his eggs to atoms, operated so forcibly on his feelings, as to bring on an illness which nearly dispatched him to the land of his fathers'. Beaumont had recovered a little, 'but fears at every step, some impending mischief, and always sleeps with one eye open', and 'we cannot but think he lacks a little of that spirit which formerly animated him, and that he is perhaps awed into silence and precaution'.

82. Washington Allston: *The Angel releasing St Peter from Prison*, 1812 (Courtesy, Museum of Fine Arts, Boston. Gift of Robert William Hooper through the Worcester State Hospital).

XII
CHIAROSCURO

BEAUMONT HAD BEEN ill-prepared for the fury of his lampoonists. Even if the views expressed in the *Catalogues Raisonnés* were those of painters, the vitriol in which they were dipped could only have been poured from Grub Street, and it had been Wordsworth and Coleridge, both more used to the ways of *littérateurs*, who had helped to steel his nerves. Coleridge, whom Lady Beaumont still esteemed for his 'judgement' as well as his genius, had long ago assured her of his disdain for 'Reviews & the multiplication of newspapers', for they brought only superficial amusement,[1] and whereas Sir George had feared that 'the Bloodhounds will now be upon Wordsworth' when his two volumes of poems had appeared in 1807,[2] the poet had told him it was best not even to read them — a lesson he had learned at the unfeeling hands of Jeffrey of the *Edinburgh Review*. Perhaps it was no coincidence that only days before Beaumont received the first catalogue, Wordsworth had told him over dinner at Grosvenor Square that he never read the *Review*, not wishing 'to have the opinions and ribaldry...floating in His memory, for however much He may despise such matter He would not have it buz in His thoughts'.[3]

The Wordsworths had been in lodgings that spring of 1815, Lady Beaumont having made it clear to William that while she hoped to see dear Mary 'in a quiet way now and then', 'large parties would not suit her',[4] and there was a full house at Grosvenor Square. Summer, however, brought them together in the Lakes, there being no better place or company for Sir George to repair his shattered nerves. Only his commitment to Coleorton, and its expense, could have kept him away from his beloved mountains for a full seven years, but now, with the inheritance from his mother, he felt able to take a house in Keswick for three seasons from July to October, and it was distressing that this first holiday should be spoilt by a fever. During the long years of war the Lakes had become very popular and there was a large crowd for the peace celebrations in September. A bonfire on the summit of Skiddaw found old Lord and Lady Sunderlin making the ten-mile mountain walk to see fire balloons and fireworks, while Sir George, who in Mrs Coleridge's view had already 'imprudently' made the journey in the morning, watched thankfully from a window below. Meanwhile, he was considering the larger question of a national victory monument. With Knight, Long and the Marquess of Stafford he had been appointed to a committee for its selection and from Keswick he had written to seek West's views on a design, receiving in return rather more than he bargained for and offending his colleagues by jumping the gun. Evidently the catalogue, and his illness that summer, had not silenced him completely.

The Wordsworths were now comfortably housed at Rydal Mount, while the

Southey and Coleridge families continued at Greta Hall, and with the children now growing up, the Beaumonts enjoyed the company of both generations. Sara Coleridge, highly intelligent, was a favourite with them, and Hartley, though refusing his mother's suggestion of regular church attendance to create a good impression, delighted Sir George with his admiration of Shakespeare, while Lady Beaumont was gratified by his high opinion of *The Excursion*. It was her idea to bring a reluctant George Howland Willoughby under Hartley's influence; too conscious that he was 'no genius' she thought he could 'read Greek with Hartley and talk of mathematics and play with Derwent — and he will tell them something of their cousins. . .two of the cleverest boys at Eton School'.[5] She may have wished for some return on the £30 year she had offered towards Hartley's expenses at Oxford, but her prescription for her husband's dullard heir was too transparent.

In April of the previous year Lady Beaumont had been still more naive, tactlessly showing Wordsworth Coleridge's request for the return of his manuscript poem, forwarded at the time of their rift, to convince her of his devotion to his fellow poet. Unfortunately, Coleridge's letter also contained what Wordsworth considered 'comparative censure' of *The Excursion*. Greatly irritated by criticism from this quarter, Wordsworth demanded further explanation and asked Coleridge not to publish the poem in which he was addressed as

O Friend! O Teacher! God's great gift to me!

For once replying promptly, Coleridge did his best to justify himself — he had always thought *The Excursion* the 'finest poem in our language' of its own length, but 'I do not think, I did not feel' it equal to *The Prelude*.[6] Lady Beaumont learned her lesson sufficiently to conceal a letter that Price had intended for Wordsworth's eyes as well as her own, which reminded the Beaumonts that, on first reading the *Lyrical Ballads* at Benarth, they were 'both a good deal surprised at finding some 8 or 10 stanzas [in 'The Thorn'] employed in describing a little tuft of moss with a decayed stump upon it'. Price's verdict on *The Excursion* concurred with theirs: although too long, 'a person who does not admire its various beauties, can have no taste for the sublime, the beautiful or the picturesque', but it was 'too contemplative to be popular'.[7]

After staying with the Prices at Foxley in 1810, Wordsworth had complained of both the company — his hostess being too pleased with her old paramour, General Fitzpatrick — and the landscape, which was too contrived: wanting 'relish of humanity', it was 'a melancholy spot'. But there was respect between the two authors. Price was careful to encourage the poet's gardening interest at Coleorton, where they were both consulted, and such was his own enthusiasm that he set the labourers an example in under-lashing, and later, in 1813 even persuaded his host to work in the winter-garden quarry. All he asked was that the Beaumonts prove their friendship by a visit to Foxley, but the thought of his unfortunate daughter — resembling 'the bad sister who does all the mischief in a fairy tale' — and perhaps of Price himself, who was now reported to be so sunk in gluttony that all talk at table was deemed an interruption, was too much, and it was 1820 before Sir George made the journey — alone. Price could only dream of Lady Beaumont's 'lovely eager face' enjoying the 'picture galleries' of his grounds, and to vent his old complaints about Sir George's laxity as a correspondent, gave him a particularly severe 'crabbing' in September 1816 for taking no more interest in his eye, damaged by a branch, than 'in that of a dead whiting'. It was perhaps rough justice that the Beaumonts spent their last years longing for visitors to their own more restricted pleasure grounds.

Beaumont's illness in 1815 had left him weak and during the bitterly cold winter the following year he would excuse his 'habit of procrastination' to Wordsworth. Among other things his painting was suffering. There would be no exhibits until 1819 and he confessed his difficulty in concentrating, telling Wordsworth he had been painting Portinscale bridge, 'at least a composition founded upon it, & I think it is as well as I have done anything in this way — But I grow old & cannot sit to it long without fatigue'.[8] Southey, however, whom Beaumont had come to know better in the Lakes, rightly sensed that, at heart, his passion for art was undimmed. Later he would recall that Beaumont painted with 'more ardour' in his last years, although he sometimes complained that art overwhelmed nature in his work.

In hibernation after the first *Catalogue Raisonné*, Beaumont had not forgotten his friends. Wordsworth was by now the intimate of Haydon and Wilkie (though the latter had thought him patronising), as Coleridge was of Allston, and their concentric circles delighted and reassured the baronet as he found himself at their centre. Haydon was still a matter of general concern; Wordsworth, early in 1816, had sent the Beaumonts at Coleorton a 'description of Haydon & his enthusiasms' that was 'a true likeness', and Sir George, who had at last taken possession of *Macbeth* although its size was a painful inconvenience, was really 'sometimes alarmed for him' and had given him some more 'advice respecting his unbounded eagerness — but he is as tender as a "wincing colt" & I fear I have done no good'.[9] Beaumont had been distressed to read a piece in the *Champion* attacking Knight over the Elgin Marbles, 'which will of course be imputed to Haydon — by these means he throws obstacles in the way of those who value his talents & have his welfare & cause sincerely at heart'. He urged Wordsworth to take a hand, for 'He admires you — to adoration — perhaps a few lines of advice from you might be of service — you must be cautious however & not a word of what has fallen from me...for you I know are his sincere well wisher & rate his talents as they deserve & wish to serve him.'[10] Beaumont had hoped the article was not Haydon's work and even briefly attributed it to John Croker of the Admiralty, but he soon knew the truth and told Wordsworth he despaired that Haydon 'is daily making clouds of enemies & makes it almost impossible to serve him but you may as well talk to him...you have of course seen his attack upon Knight — it is in the Examiner as well as in the Champion & not content with that he has also printed it as a shilling pamphlet.'[11] Now he was even worried lest Wordsworth should prejudice his own reputation by publishing the lines he had written to Haydon the previous December, and perhaps it shook him a little that the poet chose none other than the *Champion* and the *Examiner* in which to do so.

Allston was also a topic between Beaumont and Wordsworth, and the latter's presence there must have been invoked when Beaumont tried to lure the painter to the Lakes, for although 'small pools would appear trifling to one accustomed to the extended lakes of America', still 'I think you would be much gratified with the sight of them, for the mountains are high enough to induce the clouds to repose upon their bosoms...the criterion by which I judge what is the proper height of a mountain'.[12] But Allston had disappointed him, and, more sadly, did so again in his *Angel releasing St Peter* intended for Coleorton church and sent to the British Institution in 1816 (Pl. 82). Beaumont was anyway horrified by the exhibition, declaring it 'universally bad' and what might be expected from students, but he had hoped for more from Allston, telling Wordsworth the picture was not equal to the sketch and 'not finished to my mind':

> It is certainly excellently conceived upon the whole but the angel is certainly too material — the garment is too like flannel, it should be of the consistency of a summer cloud — He will I dare say greatly improve it, but my main purpose which was to serve him is in some degree frustrated by his sending it forth so precipitately.[13]

Although he had originally preferred a Resurrection scene, Beaumont had come to take a highly proprietorial interest in Allston's picture and had wished him to exploit to the full its theme of the supernatural and miraculous — an interest he himself shared with both the painter and with Coleridge. The 'downy softness' of the angel's wings had delighted him in the sketch, but the finished picture seemed earth-bound by comparison. He had directed Allston to look as closely at Rembrandt as at Sebastiano del Piombo, no doubt so that he could develop his subject through qualities of light and texture. Now he felt a little guilty at having perhaps hurried Allston, or made him feel so beholden that he had exhibited before he was ready. At all events, on Coleridge's advice he acquired another work by him this year, a landscape now unidentified.

The bitter winter of 1816–17 took its toll among Beaumont's older friends. Alexander, who had spent Christmas at Coleorton, died the following year, and in May a mournful little party bumped its way down to Bushey church to bid farewell to Hearne, who had not long ago written to Beaumont recalling forty-four years of friendship that 'must be drawing to a close'. After a long day the Beaumonts entertainted Dr Monro, Richard Duppa, Edridge, Farington and Hakewill to dinner at Grosvenor Square. Ashburnham, a fellow Director of the British Institution and Hearne's chief patron in his last years, had fulfilled his obligations by sending a carriage to the funeral.

William Westall and the diminutive Edward Nash, whom the Beaumonts had met in the Lakes, had provided younger company at Coleorton, Westall painting a landscape and Nash copying the Rembrandt in small. Beaumont had delighted in introducing Westall to *The Excursion*, which 'astonished' him and, as he told the poet, 'brought you before me in such magnificent character that I cannot refrain from expressing the admiration I feel of your powers'.[14] There was good news also of Wilkie, who had visited the Netherlands the previous autumn, returning much struck by 'what you had prepared me for, the resemblance of everything to the Dutch and Flemish pictures', an impression Beaumont relayed to Wordsworth together with Wilkie's awe both on seeing the field of Waterloo — he had thought a model should be made of it — and on receiving a visit from the Duke of Wellington, who had suggested a subject of 'soldiers regaling with pipes & tobacco at an alehouse door recounting their feats' that would eventually become *Chelsea Pensioners reading the Gazette of the Battle of Waterloo*.[15] As for Haydon, Beaumont had received

> a letter from the seventh heaven. . . Wilkie says, & he confirms it, that he is going on 'gloriously' with his picture. . . he says he hopes not only to do much himself but also to innoculate a sufficient number of daring spirits who will complete what it

may be his destiny to leave undone &cet — now really if he is uniform in his application I think great things may be expected — but I own he alarms me & I wish his head were a little cooler.[16]

It was as well Beaumont did not know that Haydon, who hoped for state sponsorship for a painted celebration of victory and resented the assumption that it should be a sculpture or a building — even though he also ranted that there was no column to Shakespeare — was now confiding to his journal a secret wish that Beaumont and his fellow members of the monument committee would 'shrivel up as reflected from a dreadful mirror' or receive a mark as terrible as Cain's 'and be cursed like Cain to relieve their tortures'.

Beaumont had tried to persuade Haydon to safeguard his income by occasional portraiture which the painter thought 'timid', but the *Christ's Entry into Jerusalem*[17] that he now had in hand, on a characteristically huge scale, was promising very well and Farington reported Beaumont 'in raptures' with it, as well as with Haydon's 'excellent drawings'. Soon, however, the painter's ardour had abated, sapped by his ocular problems, and Beaumont told Wordsworth that he 'proceeds slowly...complains & I fear with cause, of his health',[18] but that the heads of the apostles were 'very fine indeed' and if only the Christ succeeded equally it would be a 'wonderful picture'. Haydon had, he told the poet, 'introduced you but not at present with success'. To Wordsworth also he reported that Allston had redeemed himself with 'an excellent sketch for a large picture of Belshazzer's dream' and one for Jacob's dream, 'which is very striking, instead of a ladder, flights of steps lead far into glory — the effect is poignant & grand'.[19] Wordsworth did not forget this account, nor the picture; they are echoed, and perhaps interwoven with allusions to Beaumont's recent distress over the *Catalogues Raisonnés*, and to Allston's fellow history painter, Haydon, and his motto 'Wings at the heart', in some lines 'Composed upon an Evening of Extraordinary Splendour and Beauty', written this year:

> And if there be whom broken ties
> Afflict or injuries assail,
> Yon hazy ridges to their eyes
> Present a glorious scale,
> Climbing suffused with sunny air,
> To stop — no record hath told where!
> And tempting Fancy to ascend,
> And with immortal Spirits blend!
> — Wings at my shoulders seem to play;
> But, rooted here, I stand and gaze
> On those bright steps that heavenward raise
> Their practicable way.

Sending him the poem, Wordsworth told Allston he could not know how far he was indebted to him for this stanza, and, he might have added, to Beaumont also. That autumn Allston visited France with William Collins and C.R. Leslie, and Collins's *Departure of the Diligence from Rouen*,[20] bought by Beaumont from the exhibition at Spring Gardens in 1818, perhaps alluded to a stage in their journey. This purchase, and that of *Fighting Dogs*[21] by Edwin Landseer, then one of Haydon's pupils, from the same exhibition and made on Haydon's advice, together with subsequent purchases from Wilkie and George Lance, another pupil of Haydon, show Beaumont still following the progress of the young. Nothing gave him greater pleasure than to watch the deserving rise to fame, and he felt almost cheated when Allston decided to return to America this year; 'I am convinced', he wrote, 'you are quitting this country at a moment when the extent of your talents begins to be felt, and when the encouragement you are likely to receive will bring them to perfection'.[22]

*　　*　　*

Beaumont's confidence in his own opinions, if it had ever been really shaken, had evidently by now been restored; or at least he felt less reluctant to express them. He had not forgotten the *Catalogues Raisonnés*, which he still attributed to members of the Academy, and Lady Beaumont was apt to complain of the 'prevailing tendency to calumniate persons',[23] but having shot their bolt, his critics seemed to have gone to ground. Beaumont himself had been conspicuous in London in 1817, planning an exhibition of deceased British artists for the Institution the following year, or accompanying Mulgrave and General Phipps as a 'flying squadron of the British Institution making their visits to painters'.[24] It was diplomatic of him to remark that he had seen great improvement in British art over the past forty years, but he could be as hasty and impressionable as ever. At the 1817 Academy exhibition he was smitten briefly with a picture by Henry Harlow of the Kemble family in character from *Henry VIII*, but on being advised that the artist's character left much to be desired — according to Farington he was a 'deliberate *lyar*' — Beaumont decided the picture was a work of 'vicious art, finery, & ostentation'.

Harlow's picture had been well timed, for on 23 June, Kemble celebrated his retirement from the stage. Beaumont had only slowly come to terms with the 'measured and artificial practice' and 'rigid passion' of Kemble and his school, but although he enjoyed his closing performance, he was irked that the farewell was so much more lavish than that Mrs Siddons had received in 1812, and in protest wasted his ticket for the banquet. Off stage, however, he had grown rather to like the Kemble family and had even tried to temper the animosity of his old actor-friend Smith, who wrote from his own rural retirement to tell him that Kemble was no more than 'a grand Imposter...a common stroler' who 'play'd Tricks of sleight of hand or other quaint conceits in Barnes & Hovels, Villages & market Towns'. Smith had been appalled by his success — 'How glorious are his Triumphs, D. of Wellington sinks under him...when I think of a Great Name, a true Roscius & luminary...I shrink at the prostitution'[25] — but although Beaumont fully sympathised with the reference to Garrick, who had indeed been impossible to follow, he was now an enthusiastic admirer of Kean, and was quick to congratulate Samuel Whitbread, who had just rebuilt Drury Lane, on his encouragement of the actor. Despite his poor physique, Kean was to earn, for the first time since Garrick, the tribute from Beaumont: 'he electrifies you'.[26] It had, however, been a disappointment to him that Kean had failed as Kitely in *Every Man in his Humour*, a role Beaumont himself had persuaded him to try, even demonstrating some of Garrick's touches in the part; and now Kean, following George Cooke, was completing the disillusionment by succumbing to Bacchus.

83. John Jackson (engraved William Ward): *The Earl of Mulgrave, Beaumont, and the Hon. Augustus and the Hon. Edmund Phipps*, 1816 (B.C.)

The theatre was still a ruling passion for Beaumont. In 1815 Jack Bannister, who would be the last link with the past when old Smith died in 1817, played his final performance in *The World*, displaying in the role of Echo all his mimetic gifts, which were as attractive in the tavern as on the stage. But it was not only fine acting that caught Beaumont's fancy. Quite late in life, Price was teasing him about the attentions he paid to a certain Mrs Wingfield, and in 1815 there was no mistaking his enthusiasm for 'the very child of nature', Miss O'Neill, a young actress with whom Mulgrave's son was so taken that, to the fury of his family, he looked to her for his wife, while Lady Beaumont considered her the original of Wordsworth's Lucy Gray. None of this, however, could quite allay the Beaumonts' fatigue with London as they grew older, and in 1817, 'fagged by perpetually gazing at brick walls' in a metropolis where the east wind blew the 'eyes full of dust and chopped hay', they decided to spend the later part of the summer quietly at Coleorton before visiting Mulgrave Castle for six weeks from October. The Lakes, where they had been too wet for comfort the previous year, suddenly did not attract them. Yet for all the beauties of Mulgrave, 'crowned by the glories of the ocean', and Beaumont's delight at having been accepted into the Phipps brotherhood and painted with Henry, Edmund and

Augustus in the family livery by Jackson (Pl. 83), by December he was telling Wordsworth that he 'languished' for the mountains. The poet had sent him his verses on 'The Pass of Kirkstone', sacred ground since they had shared that wonderful day in 1807. Beaumont later wrote:

I have lately read to Mrs Fermor the two first books of the *Excursion*...I enjoyed them more than ever — Your description of the glorious vision we saw together passing Kirkston astonished me. I remember how much struck you as well as myself were at the time, & I whispered to Lady Beaumont 'Mark how our comrade's rapt'. When you recovered from your trance you told me nothing could be done with it in words — & indeed I thought so — but you have proved to the contrary — such a complete blending of earth & heaven I never saw — a scene so full of matter & spirit...the solid mountains entrenched almost to their tops in burning masses of etherial clouds...equated in splendour by your wonderful description & as I read it I really thought I saw with my bodily eye the enchanting vision again.[27]

At long last, in January 1818, William and Mary Wordsworth came to spend a week at Coleorton on their way back from London. The winter garden had grown almost too well, the carriage road had been diverted to skirt it, Dance had inspired a lodge for the new entrance, and Sir George himself had supervised the area adjacent to the new church pool within sight of his dressing room which opened on to the *porte cochère*. He was proud of his new shower bath, installed on medical advice, and the heating had been improved; but 'in spite of hot air & plenty of coal fires', in 1825 Sara Hutchinson could still complain of being 'cold beyond endurance' during a freak cold spell in October, and the next generation of Beaumonts learned to winter elsewhere. Dance, made of sterner stuff, was apparently satisfied, for his were often winter visits, and he was soon to be active making the Grosvenor Square house more comfortable. A dear, sentimental old friend, he could be rendered speechless for half an hour by Lady Beaumont's reading of *The Excursion*.

The church at Coleorton now displayed Allston's altarpiece (Pl. 82), sufficiently imposing despite its patron's strictures to compete with the tomb of the last Lord Beaumont whose wife had haunted the earlier house. This Lady Beaumont had killed herself on account of her husband's infidelity, her ghost remaining a torment until the parson was inveigled into 'laying on her' and she was put into a bottle. Beaumont had already relayed to Wordsworth her gruesome tale, told by an 'old man who looks so much more than he is'[28] — a phrase that may give a clue to the poet's conversation, which Beaumont found so instructive, for it is echoed in the 'Afterthought' of the 1819 River Duddon sonnets:

> And if, as towards the silent tomb we go
> Through love, through hope, and faith's trandscendent power,
> We feel that we are greater than we know.

The Beaumonts were together in the Lakes for the last time that autumn. In London as usual from mid-March, Sir George appeared 'improved in health & size', but poor Lady Beaumont caught a chill at the theatre in May. At last she looked her age when she told William Owen that, for the first time in thirty years, either she or Sir George had felt too ill to breakfast together. Cutting short their London stay they paused during June at Coleorton where, having in January 1817 placed an enormous boulder

84. Francis Chantrey: *Bust of Wordsworth*, 1820, plaster (Oxford, Ashmolean Museum). The *modello* for the finished version in marble.

in the garden in tribute to Richard Wilson (the foreground stones in whose paintings it resembled), Sir George needed only a likeness of Wordsworth to complete his gallery of heroes. By good fortune, Francis Chantrey was at Keswick in August. Much taken with the sculptor, Beaumont commissioned for the following spring a bust to be taken in London, thus ensuring the bonus of the poet's company there.

William Collins, Beaumont's latest painter-protégé, also came up to the Lakes in 1818, and found it rewarding 'to sketch in his company and that of Wordsworth — to hear from the mouths of each the antiquarian and poetical associations connected with the scenes', accepting the lesson that the habit of reading led to 'new trains of pictorial thought'.[29] Collins was grateful, too, for the introduction to Mr Marshall of Leeds who became his patron after he had accompanied the Beaumonts for two nights to the Marshall family at Hallsteds on Ullswater. Sir George commissioned from him a small portrait of Sara Coleridge, now fifteen and 'elegant', as 'The Highland Girl' to occupy the many rainy days[30] and the Beaumonts kept Collins busy until they took him to Rydal Mount. Wordsworth considered Sara unsuitable for portrayal in this character from his poem — she would have made a better sylph — but Coleridge was delighted with the portrait, which Beaumont presented to him. On a rare family visit to Keswick, Coleridge enlisted Collins's attendance at his London lectures, and the two left the Lakes before the Beaumonts' grand finale in Borrowdale when, on a fine October day, they dined with the amateur painter, Miss Barker, the Wilberforce family, over a dozen strong, and the Wordsworths.

The 'soul of the poetry, but not the countenance of the man' was to be Coleridge's verdict on Chantrey's bust of Wordsworth (Pl. 84).[31] This was apt, but the Beaumonts no longer took him quite seriously. His boast of April 1816 that he had declined a Covent Garden advance for a 'dramatic piece' needing only slight alteration drew a unique trio of exclamation marks in Sir George's report to Wordsworth,[32] and his *Zapolya* was said by a friend of Lady Beaumont to contain 'some 30 lines of exquisite poetry and all the rest glorious absurdity'.[33] But then, just as they had consigned him to the limbo of which he had written so bleakly in 1817, his *Biographia Literaria* presented Lady Beaumont with as stern an intellectual test as she had ever had to face. Its penetrating analysis of poetic imagination — both his own and Wordsworth's — could not but be read and admired, even though Wordsworth turned his back on it. Coleridge's generous tribute to mystical writers like Jacob Boehme in the course of his account might well have surprised Lady Beaumont, to whom he had written in January 1810 that 'I must confess I never brought away from his works anything I did not bring to them'. Coleridge's book assured his friends that his mind was still intact beneath its dilapidated exterior, but his London lectures, which he had hoped Sir George would not attend, made his physical anguish all the more poignant. The Beaumonts, who still entertained him regularly, wished he would bring them more often the innocent amusement with which he greeted Sir George's little tale of the collector Sir Gregory Page Turner's seeing the French coast for the first time through a powerful spy-glass and exclaiming delightedly: 'France! France! How odd! — And which is Spain?'

*　　*　　*

In December 1818 Lady Beaumont was in sad disappointment at the difficulty of finding a house near Rydal Mount for the following season and she feared Sir George would take them to Greta Hall. Feeling sufficiently strong again to regret there were not more hours in the day, she was looking forward to entertaining the nine Buckland Beaumonts for Christmas. Thomas Beaumont having died the previous January, Sir George was responsible for the education of his ward and heir George together with that of the younger Thomas, whom Lady Beaumont found of 'very regular and docile dispositions' but indolent. A family Christmas now made it only too evident that, whereas the girls excelled at the pianoforte, the boys remained unresponsive to Sir George's enthusiasm. There had been talk of another trip to the Continent — only Bonaparte's escape from Elba had saved the Beaumonts a journey to Paris in 1815 — and they now planned to spend the summer in Switzerland, taking the two boys to continue their schooling there.

In March Lady Beaumont was ill again with chest trouble, dreading the journey and afraid the hot weather might bring a return of the fever Sir George had suffered on their Grand Tour. In the event all went well; they left England on 27 May, travelling through Montreuil, Abbeville and Rouen to Paris, and Edridge, accompanying them thus far, reported Beaumont 'a delightful companion but there is a perpetual fidget about him...very little has been done in the way of sketching and by him — not a touch'.[34] But when Beaumont did produce his sketchbook near Geneva in the third week of June, he responded with all his old vigour to the mountains and, although admitting he lacked patience to draw it, he was intrigued by the architecture of

Rouen, even if with all 'the richness of their surface', the buildings were 'over-wrought'. In Paris the Louvre answered his 'most sanguine expectations' though the pictures had suffered from overcleaning.[35]

Once they had reached Switzerland, even Lady Beaumont's spirits rose to match the mountains and, after repeating their 1782 journey to Chamouni on a cloudy day, Sir George was in raptures when suddenly 'Mont Blanc shone forth in all his majesty. I never saw so sublime a vision'.[36] Writing to Dorothy Wordsworth towards the end of July from Gex on Lake Geneva, Lady Beaumont believed her husband could be content 'to live in the sight of Mont Blanc for ever'.[37] Southey, who had taken solicitous interest in their trip and even recommended his guide, Hans Roth, had stressed how Switzerland 'excels as much in beauty as in grandeur' and instead of 'the magnitude of the mountains', had pleaded the 'softer scenery which may well be envied' in the Alpine valleys.[38] Renouncing the passage of the Simplon for fear of the heat, the Beaumonts did indeed spend their summer in the 'petits Cantons' before returning home up the Rhine and past Waterloo, their curiosity about the battlefield having been whetted by Wilkie and Mrs Phipps as well as by Jackson who had been at Coleorton during the winter painting Dance's portrait. Beaumont brought back sketches from Montreux, Neufchatel and the shores of Thun and Lucerne, and he had excelled himself with some large drawings on blue paper of Berne, Fribourg and Heidelberg. The climate had revitalised them both and for all their love of Cumberland, they determined to spend more time abroad.

That spring Beaumont had exhibited again at the Academy a landscape, *Jacques and the Wounded Stag* — a uniquely large variation on his recurrent theme of a pool beneath trees — that was presented to the National Gallery by Lady Beaumont after his death (Pl. 87). Home again at Coleorton at the end of October, having introduced his heir into Oriel College, Oxford, he was soon engaged trying to paint the Swiss mountains from his drawings, thus disproving his own 'concetto' that they were 'sketcheresque' rather than picturesque (Pl. 86). A view of the Vale of Chamouni and a nocturne of Lake Geneva and his beloved Mont Blanc appeared in the Academy exhibition of 1820, the latter a study for a larger picture. These were perhaps the works on which Price hoped he was engaged 'not only *con amore* but *con furia*', and a new freedom and spontaneity had indeed entered his style. His sketches were bolder than ever as he pursued what he once described as 'a reeking atmosphere'. To Wordsworth he admitted that he 'no longer suffered painting to tease him',[39] and there was more humour than sadness in his remark that he had begun a thousand pictures, but finished few. *Jacques* apart, age had tempered ambition and he now painted only for pleasure. There had recently been some coolness with Farington, although Beaumont had tried to induce him to Coleorton with the bait of his own painting room, for as so often he needed the stimulus of a companion of the brush. By now, however, S.W. Reynolds, William Westall and Collins had succeeded Farington in this not altogether enviable capacity before Beaumont transferred his allegiance briefly to R.R. Reinagle, from whom he took lessons in painting trees in 1820.

Painting had kept his spirits high during the previous winter, but in London in March there was bad news of Mulgrave sadly dulled by a stroke and Owen never to recover the use of his limbs; and on the 29th Beaumont served as a pall-bearer with Edmund Phipps and Lord Aberdeen at the funeral of West, the second president of the Royal Academy that he had seen to the grave. His melancholy and lassitude now re-

85. Beaumont: *'Top of Montanvert'*, 1819, pencil and wash (B.C.).

86. Beaumont: *Swiss Landscape*, c.1820 (Leicester Museum and Art Gallery).

87.   Beaumont: *Landscape with Jacques and the wounded Stag*, 1819 (London, Tate Gallery).

turned to haunt him and to Farington he complained of the gloom in which he awoke. He was fussed, too, by the state of the country — hardly surprisingly, when the conspirators of Cato Street nearly blew up the entire cabinet dining at Lord Harrowby's in Grosvenor Square; in his alarm he had finally been moved to write an overdue letter to Price, whose reply, couched in a torrent of simile, shared his friend's horror of anarchy and despotism alike, the one 'a roaring and a ravishing lion; the other, a serpent silently coiled up in his den. . .heaven preserve us from them both'.[40] The Beaumonts would have loved to leave it all behind, to return to Switzerland and to winter in Italy, but there were ructions also in Naples and, somewhat irritable and restive, they remained in London. This year it was the three Wordsworths, William, Mary and Dorothy, who crossed the Channel, making the Beaumonts' journey of the previous summer in reverse.

It was now that Crabb Robinson found Lady Beaumont's politics verging on the intolerant, and indeed she was virulent against Henry Brougham, who had not only opposed the Parliamentary interests of her friends the Lonsdales in the recent election, but also represented those of the erstwhile Princess of Wales. Following the death of the old King in January, Caroline of Brunswick was now Queen; her virtual trial in the Lords later this year promised to be a highly theatrical event and Beaumont, who could never resist such an occasion, took Wordsworth to watch the sessions. The

199

Beaumonts increasingly deplored any challenge to the establishment and even Farington for once permitted himself a smile when Lady Beaumont approved the election of Lawrence to the presidency of the Academy as 'very proper: he is not a democrat'. The painter had already found Sir George 'amazingly courteous' at a recent dinner, and now he made himself so agreeable that, after years of guarded acquaintance, he became an esteemed friend who, more and more, shared Beaumont's views in matters of taste and connoisseurship.

*　　*　　*

This summer Lady Beaumont was perhaps influenced by Wordsworth to take an enthusiastic view of Haydon's *Christ entering Jerusalem*, but Sir George was more guarded. He had sent Haydon £50 to help with his expenses but would have preferred to share with the British Institution in buying it. When this failed, he tried, with Sir George Phillips, to raise a public subscription to acquire the picture for a church, but this too proved fruitless, which did not entirely surprise him, for 'if success should follow it will raise my opinion of the liberality of mankind'.[41] The exhibition had brought some tense moments, Haydon himself describing the occasion when

> in walked, with all the dignity of her majestic presence, Mrs. Siddons, like a Ceres or a Juno. The whole room remained dead silent, and allowed her to think. After a few minutes Sir George Beaumont, who was extremely anxious, said in a very delicate manner: 'How do you like the Christ?' Everbody listened for her reply. After a moment, in a deep, loud, tragic tone, she said 'It is completely successful'.[42]

To Price and others Beaumont described the picture as a work of genius, but like everything of Haydon's it would be hard to sell, and his letters to Haydon struck ever more cautious tones as their discussions extended to the painter's school whose promising pupils, including the Landseer brothers, George Lance from Dunmow and William Bewick, were put through such rigours of drawing as Beaumont feared might lead to corresponding neglect of painterly qualities. Quick to reassure the prickly Haydon that he possessed 'an exquisite taste for this delicious ornament of art', he felt it was high time to turn the students' attention to painting for if they should lag behind, 'how would your animated foes (if you have any) presume upon it?' Wishing only for Haydon's 'success, your comfort, & your fame', he missed no opportunity to temper his encouragement with warnings or hints: of the tactful Wilkie who had taken full account of his suggestions over *Chelsea Pensioners* and whose *Irish Whiskey Still* had just delighted him, he wrote to Haydon how 'it certainly adds to the measure of seeing such works when to it is added a full & heartfelt approbation of the author'. This, he added, might be 'inculcated as a useful lesson to young painters',[43] for Haydon's behaviour had put him beyond such unreserved praise, and a year later when Beaumont could at least be pleased that the *Christ* had been acclaimed in its Scottish exhibitions and that Haydon was busy with a new picture, he wrote as firmly as he could:

> It makes me hope your attention is now devoted to your art & that you now follow the advice I have heretofore taken the liberty to give you — to paint down your enemies (if you have them) rather than attempt to write them down — which will

only multiply them — & believe me there is no man so insignificant as not to stand a chance of having in his power to do you a serious injury at some time or other.[44]

Meanwhile, it was Lady Beaumont, less gullible in her old age, who had an eye for some of Wordsworth's worst poetic extravagances, and when Crabb Robinson agreed with her, Wordsworth, now a little mellowed by success, removed from the reprint of Peter Bell, first published in 1819, the 'grotesque' description of Peter's perplexity as he looked at what was in fact a floating corpse:

> Is it a party in a parlour,
> Crammed just as they on earth were cramm'd;
> Some sipping punch, some sipping tea
> But, as you by their faces see,
> All silent and all damn'd.

Shelley and F. Mansel Reynolds had enjoyed themselves parodying lines such as these, and while sales might be boosted, religious readers were offended: in 1816 Lady Beaumont had felt obliged to reproach Martin Archer Shee for being 'unable to relish a certain poet because he wanted piety'.[45]

The Beaumonts in their turn had brought Wordsworth a few crosses to bear: a tragedy by Sotheby, one of those amateur poets 'of whom this Age produces such swarms', Miss Jones's poems, for which Lady Beaumont was 'very warm', then Price's work on the modern pronunciation of Latin and Greek — all these required his time. Price could be forgiven, for his comments on Wordsworth's prose work *Scenery of the Lakes*, published in 1820 and 1822 had been flattering. That it should be considered 'the Manual for Improvers in every part of the Kingdom' was praise enough to place Wordsworth high among the landscape professors,[46] and in 1820 Price was also advancing the rather humbler claims of William Sawrey Gilpin, who was offering just such a service at three guineas a day. Having known him as a painter and his father before him, the Beaumonts felt obliged to encourage Gilpin's new activities, and that autumn he received a handsome fee, with travelling expenses, for work at Coleorton. A legion of good works produced varied results, but there was sufficient talent shaping Coleorton for Lady Beaumont to dread leaving it, even for the charms of southern Europe.

The London season of 1821 was exceptionally busy, literally crowned by the coronation of George IV, of which Sir George wrote eagerly to Wordsworth: while Cheapside and the Exchange, 'as hush as death', might have inspired another 'exquisite sonnet on the sleep of the City', in Green Park 'a million human faces glittered before my eyes', 'every horse, poney, ass & pug dog if it could draw a wheelbarrow' having been 'put into requisition for 30 miles around'; and he was 'near crushed to death' watching the fireworks in Hyde Park.[47] There had been some important exhibition openings — Lord Grosvenor's and Sir John Leicester's collections as well as the sale of West's — and a last visit to Drury Lane for a performance of *The Coronation*, far more enjoyable than the actual event.

Quite suddenly in June, exasperated by George Howland Willoughby's lack of progress at Oxford, Sir George had decided to follow his tutor's advice to complete his heir's education in Europe, and the Beaumonts began preparations for a year abroad, conscious that, at their age, their return could not be certain. Sir George's final round

88.   Beaumont: *Stratford Mill, Essex*, 1819 (Private Collection).

took him to Frances Fermor at Worcester, at long last to Price at Foxley, and on a
'pious pilgrimage' to Stratford-upon-Avon to pay his respects to the Bard, having
earlier refreshed his memories of the Dedham district where he painted two versions of
Stratford Mill (Pl. 88) as presents for Knight and Constable,[48] whom he still treated
with casual affection. The tour had the distinct flavour of a farewell and *en route* he
searched in vain for his old school near Luton; only the churchyard remained and,
tickled by an epitaph, he wrote it out for Wordsworth, who was something of a
connoisseur of such matters.

*   *   *

Farington dined with the Beaumonts for the last time in August, on the eve of their
departure for Italy. Wilkie and Jackson were there too, all concerned about Mulgrave's
'creeping palsy'. It was ironic that the man who had generally enjoyed 'a state of high
preservation', the Phippses' jocular description of good health, was now too ill to
travel home to Yorkshire, and the Beaumonts broke their journey south to stay with
him at Riverhead in Kent. Sir George had promised to write to Farington from Italy as
he had done in 1782, but his earliest letters were to his ailing friend, the first, from
Milan on 2 October, reporting an unpropitious crossing on one of the new steamboats,
delayed no longer by tides but by waiting for passengers, many of whom were sick

202

despite a smooth sea. Surviving thus far, they caught cold travelling south of Paris in a carriage with open windows, and Sir George developed one of his low fevers, slowing their progress and holding them up a week at Sécheron for full recovery; fortunately entertainment was provided by an old acquaintance, Matthew Montagu, with his 'kind obliging duo decimo daughters who skip over the mountains like chamois' — doubtless more welcome to the young George than the serious business of Paris and the Louvre.

The Beaumonts had determined to enter Switzerland from the Dijon road, passing over the Jura, and by the shore of Lake Geneva they called on the Kembles living in happy retirement, Mrs and Miss Siddons also being there. They found Bonaparte's new road across the Alps 'amongst the noblest works of man', the descent from the Simplon Pass, 'almost entirely of the terribly sublime', now gentle and well guarded. In deference to Wordsworth who had directed him there, Sir George made one of his only two Swiss drawings at Lugano with Mont Salvador in the distance, and the party continued past Lakes Como and Maggiore to Milan, where the marble cathedral was disappointing, looking unfinished from afar and, close up, like the 'the vagaries of a frosty night'. The Beaumonts were delighted to find the Ashburnhams' two elder sons there, and at Verona Sir George went in search of old friends Mercutio and Friar Lawrence, although he had by now now fallen and broken his shin, a disaster of which he made the most, being unable to reach Capulet's house. In Vicenza, however, he 'hopped out', determined to see Palladio's Teatro Olimpico, and struggled up the hill of Madonna della Monte to renew his acquaintance with a picture by Veronese, and his elation was transparent when at last he caught up with 'old Rogers' in Venice. Lodged opposite S. Giorgio, Beaumont confessed to 'the lazy luxury of floating at one's ease in a gondola from church to church & palace to palace...the tints sweet enough...to give sensations to the eyes of the blind'.[49]

To Lawrence he was soon writing that he had gazed at Titian's *St Peter Martyr* 'until I verily believe I can recollect every touch & gradation in that wonderful picture', but, alas, it seemed 'the sacrilegious hand' of the 'abominable picture cleaner' had been at the *Assumption of the Virgin*, and 'in restoring the glazing, he has put the picture into a fever' and made the Virgin 'blood red'.[50] Lawrence could not agree and wrote that, even if the tone was 'too feverish and fierce — the clangour of the Trumpet is too long upon your Ear, but 'tis a glorious sound and only Titian could have breathed it';[51] he did however share Beaumont's preference for Titian over Tintoretto, of whom Beaumont had remarked when 'they told me he had stilettoed a man — this did not surprise me for when I think of the fuss of his execution I am surprised he did not stab somebody every day'. Venice was leaving him 'intoxicated' and 'tipsy with colour', but now he was pressing on to Rome 'with the ardour of a bridegroom'.

Reading Beaumont's letters from Italy, where he regained his youthful spirits, one senses both his joy and an old man's sense of elegy and nostalgia for the country that gave him the sunshine and the beauty he craved, but from which he had been parted by long years of war. To the Italophile Lawrence, whom he wished were beside him, he revealed his feelings as never before:

How ardently I have wished to renew the pleasure I received so long ago in this enchanting country. I have frequently dreamed of being here & I can hardly believe I am where I am, it has more than answered my most sanguine expectations already,

& I can assure you the pictures, the climate & the scenery have given me more pleasure than even when my pulse beat high & every object was an object of rapture. My relish altho' subdued is, I think, deeper & I flatter myself more rational.[52]

The Sublime was on his mind as he sang the praises not only of Venice but of the 'unbounded invention' of Giulio Romano at Mantua, which Lawrence had recommended him to see, and the 'great merits of a race of painters almost unknown' at Siena, where the Beaumonts were delayed by the young George's illness. Rome was his greatest rapture, however, and almost every day from their lodgings in *Piazza di Spagna*, he went to look at Claude's house, finding it one evening 'illuminated with the very same sun which gilded his pictures'; and Poussin and Salvator Rosa had lived in the same street.

Rogers, who had paused in Florence to see Byron and other friends, arrived in Rome in mid-November and most mornings he and Sir George met together. There were dinners with the banker Prince Torlonia, the Barings, the widowed Lady Abercorn, and Lady Westmorland, whose behaviour had divided the English community, while Madame Arponi, the wife of the Austrian minister, was at home to them all every Monday. But such pleasures were as nothing to those of the galleries and churches, or expeditions to old haunts like that one brilliant December day when he and Rogers set out for Frascati, and rode their donkeys as once Claude had done to Tusculum and Grotta Ferrata, 'through galleries or avenues of ilex and cypress', catching wonderful views of Rome and the campagna, pausing to drink Wordsworth's health in the good wine of Velletri before returning exhausted but enthralled. And Rogers had been the second bard to survive unharmed a fall from his mount under Beaumont's eyes.

In late February the Beaumonts were ready to rest, and set out for a few peaceful days in the hills around Albano to recapture the sights of the lake, the Galleria di Sopra and Castel Gandolfo. Sir George was surprised how little his choice of view had changed, and still finding the town of Ariccia exquisitely beautiful, he made a fine sketch from which he later painted a small oil. Thence they took the road for Naples, of which the stretch between Velletri and Fondi was still beset by brigands, but they survived with some anxiety but without an escort. Deprived of satisfactory lodgings in the city — a brick wall hid the view of Vesuvius, which had greeted them with 'the most magnificent firework' — they continued to Salerno and Pompeii before returning to the 'enchanted ground' of Rome where Sir George, basking in the sun, was content: on 18 February he headed his letter to Mulgrave: 'sun shining warm as June St Peters in a glow'. Such scenes brought Wilson to mind and his pictures to life, and it was sad indeed that it was in Rome that he heard the news of the death of their mutual friend Farington; in distress he wrote to Lawrence: 'As I used to tell him, C. Lorraine painted Elysium, N. Poussin ancient Greece, & old Wilson Italy.'[53]

But young artists, abundant as ever in Rome, could for a while assuage Beaumont's longings for the past. An amateur, Miss Catherine Fanshawe, introduced him to Charles Eastlake, Haydon's sometime pupil, from whom he bought a small picture of *banditti*, (little knowing that here was the future Director of the National Gallery, the dream of his remaining years); and one day in the Capitol he came across Joseph Severn, making a sketch of Rubens's *Romulus and Remus* with what the tyro admitted was 'outrageous boldness'. Invited to dinner with Rogers, Severn was impressed by Beaumont's 'lively, benevolent countenance' although during some talk of Keats,

89. Michel-angelo: *Tondo: the Virgin and Child with St. John*, marble (London, Royal Academy of Arts).

Rogers upset him by claiming the poet had asked him to lend him money — a slander, according to Severn, who 'flared up' and, appealing to his host, told Rogers poet should honour poet as Beaumont had been kind as one 'pittore' to another. Rogers apologised and the two became friends, while Severn went on to spend a week with the Beaumonts at Tivoli, hearing a wealth of stories from Sir George who was once again in flights of nostalgia, constantly referring to Reynolds, still his *ne plus ultra* although Lawrence had now won something of the same status. Lawrence had already flattered Beaumont by claiming him as 'an ally whose authority I may confidently oppose to the Enemies of Sir Joshua and the Truth',[54] and in May Beaumont would return the compliment by telling Lawrence he had been fortunate in 'the intimacy of two persons of exquisite taste' of whom he had 'enjoyed the esteem of the one, & possess the friendship of the other'.[55]

Lawrence had earned the accolade by connoisseurship as much as talent, a rare combination which Beaumont most of all people could appreciate. It was to Lawrence that he reported one of the last, and certainly the greatest, of his purchases for his collection, a work indeed out of all proportion to anything he had collected so far: Michelangelo's marble tondo of the Virgin and Child with St John, for which 'you may be sure I was made to pay' (Pl. 89).[56] Chantrey too heard the news, and Beaumont told him he could

almost imagine Sir Joshua had seen it; the child has much of that transient grace so common to children, the hitting of which he called shooting flying. I had always a veneration for Michelangelo. — I used to think Sir Joshua's comparison for him to Homer, and Raphael to Virgil, a little too strong; but now I am, to say the least, in doubt.[57]

Fascinated by its varied degrees of finish, displaying as he told Lawrence 'the whole of his process from the first hint to completion', and by its stylistic relationship to Raphael's holy families, he had acquired it through the good offices of Canova (Pl.

205

90. George Hayter: *Portrait of Antonio Canova* (British Government Art Collection).

91. Giovanni Paolo Pannini: *The Gallery of Cardinal Valenti-Gonzaga* (Hartford, Conn., Wadsworth Atheneum: Ella Gallup Sumner and Mary Catlin Sumner Collection).

206

90), who had become his greatest friend in Rome, precious not only for his genius but for his 'candor, his generosity, his freedom from jealousy & every selfish tendency'.

Canova was all that a great artist should be, as was proved by his constant charity to the young and his recent encouragement to aspiring colleagues like John Gibson, 'modest and assiduous, with much taste', whom Canova had recommended to the Duke of Devonshire, being too busy to undertake a commission himself. To Southey Beaumont wrote further of Canova's virtues, accepting as simple truth his remark that he was going to confession but did not know what to say. Few artists had ever so impressed him, and Canova's friendship, together with that of Vincenzo Camuccini, neo-classical history painter and Director of the Vatican museums, warmed the air of Rome still more.

Beaumont had also bought a large painting in Rome, Pannini's fantastic compendium of old masters, *The Gallery of Cardinal Valenti-Gonzaga* (Pl. 91),[58] which he thought 'very amusing'. Evidently, he was spending rather freely. He had described to Lawrence a clay model of *The Zephyrs raising Psyche to the Heavens* that Gibson was working on as 'one of the most beautiful groups I have seen'[59] (welcome praise indeed after Sir Watkin Williams Wynn, who would have preferred Gibson to carve an eagle, had advised the sculptor to replace Psyche with a timepiece and turn the group into a clock), and, prompted by Canova, he returned again and again to gaze upon the model. Gibson later recalled: 'At length he asked me what would be the price of the group in marble. I said that I would put a moderate price and let him know. The next time he came to my studio I was prepared, and named the price of seven hundred pounds; he then ordered the group in marble, to my great delight.'[60]

Chantrey had been afraid Rome would spoil Gibson, but Beaumont thought otherwise, and must have envied the ardent young man's wish to remain for ever in a city where daily he 'rose up with the sun, my soul gladdened by a new day of happy and delightful pursuit'. Their respect for Canova was their most abiding bond, and the classicism lightly veiled with sentiment that the work of the Italian now shared with that of the Englishman perfectly suited Beaumont's mood. He loved Canova, he told Southey, and, forgetting his own more critical past, was distressed to find 'the nibbling witlings of would be critics & men of taste' condemning him as meretricious, for 'The master passion of Canova is beauty — he is by no means destitute of dignity, or even Grandeur, but I think his forte is Pathos, & Beauty.' His greatness was surely for all time, for, as he added to Southey, 'like yourself, Wordsworth, Sir Joshua Reynolds & cet according to Coleridge's excellent expression, he has had the taste to create, by which he was to be relished'.[61]

So much for high art; but Beaumont loved Italy as much as its artists and the most touching memorial of his stay was of a humbler kind — the pine tree on Monte Mario that he bought to spare it from destruction so it could continue as part of the loveliness of Rome. Wordsworth found it years later and

> when I learned the Tree was living there,
> Saved from the sordid axe by Beaumont's care,
> Oh, what a rush of tenderness was mine!
> The rescued Pine-tree, with its sky so bright
> And cloud-like beauty, rich in thoughts of home,
> Death-parted friends, and days too swift for flight.

92. John Constable: *The Cenotaph*, 1836 (London, National Gallery).

XIII
GIFT TO THE NATION

AS THE BEAUMONTS set their faces north at the end of May 1822 to avoid the heat of a Roman summer, Sir George consoled himself with thoughts of an early return to what had become his spiritual home. These and the pleasurable anticipation of the tondo and *Psyche* arriving in England helped to sustain him during his last three months on the Continent. Through Canova and Camuccini, he had been elected — as a *pittore inglese* renowned for his *amore* and *cognoscenza* — to the Accademia di San Luca,[1] and his thoughts were still with recent friends when, from Berne on 1 July, he asked Gibson for news of his progress on his group, to be sent to await him at Geneva.[2] Nearly two months later he wrote introducing the Kembles, encountered at Lausanne and due to winter in Rome, where 'I almost envy the pleasure you will enjoy, to see him in his Toga at the Vatican, how much he will be at home among the Brutuses, the Caesars and the Pompeys, and how much he will look like one of their party.'[3] To Lawrence in London he bemoaned the deaths of old friends — the loss of his old sparring partner Farington was a grievous one — and he urged the President to take care of himself, for 'if I am allowed to return, let me not return to a desert'.[4] At Boulogne, Miss Barker, who had last entertained the Beaumonts in Borrowdale and now looked 'as plump & ripe as a prize gooseberry', had made them 'shudder' with a very exaggerated account of a recent accident to Wordsworth,[5] and Sir George, appalled to think he might have neglected the poet, hastened to repair the omission as soon as he was home. The resumption of their friendship did much to help him bear the blow of Canova's death in October.

Gibson too was a support. Next summer Beaumont wrote to him to describe the arrival in London of their departed friend's *Endymion*; he had examined it by day and by night, admiring especially 'the perfect distinction between sleep and death', and the group had 'roused all my enthusiasm, my admiration and my grief for the loss of the excellent author'.[6] The following May he wrote again to thank Gibson

> for the medal and the hand of our admired friend Canova, I cannot express my feelings, when I took hold of the latter; it reminded me strongly of the last grasp I received from the living hand, after he had taken the trouble, tho' very ill, or going over the Vatican with Lady Beaumont and myself. It was a pressure, warm from the heart, and affected me greatly, and when I looked up, and saw the langour of his countenance, I felt a sad foreboding. . . He departed the next morning for Naples, and I never saw him more. . .

And of himself he added: 'I cannot promise myself a sight of Rome and its inexhaustible treasures this year, indeed, I feel the weight of years creeping upon me;

consider this and let me have your excellent work, for I know it will be inestimable to me, as soon as you can.'[7]

Intimations of mortality, long an affectation of Beaumont's, now gathered around him with a grim reality, and the melancholy and introspective side of his mercurial temperament was often in the ascendant in his last years. The future of his collection was a constant pre-occupation in this condition, especially in view of young George's lack of soul which, as his Italian tour had demonstrated, was clearly incurable. Whereas his heir had been unmoved by his recent diet of history and art, Beaumont had returned from his last journey into Europe with a mission that, at long last, gave him a sense of purpose. Animated by a vision of 'fair Italy...in all her splendour, peopled with her poets, her painters & her philosophers',[8] he believed the one service he could perform for his country was to help the British public towards an appreciation of works of art, with the establishment of a national gallery as a first step. Once an assembly of great works became generally accessible — as they were in the Vatican and the Capitol — they would be 'not merely toys for connoisseurs but solid objects of concern to the nation'. His recent experience of France, which had enjoyed Bonaparte's plunder of many objects of beauty, had also made him more aware than the majority of his complacent countrymen that 'works of high excellence pay ample interest for the money they cost', for they led to improvement in taste and industrial design; and he had in mind 'the "Apollo", the "Venus" and the "Laocoon"' as well as pictures.

Beaumont regretted that, under the pressure of war, Pitt had failed to take advantage of a unique opportunity to acquire a collection for the nation when the French refugees put their pictures on the market at the turn of the century, and that the subsequent economic depression had given the government an excuse to do nothing. A growing body of opinion in high circles now considered the lack of a national gallery, when the French had a magnificent one, nothing less than a public disgrace and, with prosperity restored, it needed only one man of vision to inspire a campaign to force the government's hand. Beaumont had his own special incentive to take the lead: the safe keeping of his precious pictures, for he had seen too many collections, including Holker's, with its Claudes, ruined by 'ignorant persons' who 'rubbed, scraped & polished' paintings 'as if they were their family plate'.[9]

Before Beaumont had resumed his Continental travels, he had added a codicil to his will leaving his collection to the British Museum, which had already accepted some manuscripts, and in November 1822 he approached Long, now Sir Charles and a Trustee, wondering whether it was the right choice of location for pictures. Long could advise only that, as the Museum had nowhere to display them, the gift should be conditional on the donor becoming a Trustee in order to advocate the construction of a suitable gallery — 'for Lord Elgin who *sold* his marbles, is on that account a Trustee'.[10] As Paymaster-General and art adviser to George IV, Long knew what Beaumont may have heard rumoured, that the King was awaiting an opportune moment to give his father's magnificent library to the Museum, and that partial repayment of the Austrian loan might be used to provide the finance for the necessary rebuilding of the institution. 1823 proved to be the critical year: the King's library was offered in January and in February not only did the Prime Minister, Lord Liverpool, confirm that the principle of repayment had been agreed with the Austrians but the Chancellor, Frederick Robinson, in his Budget speech, felt able to boast of the country's new-found prosperity. In mid-April a Select Committee of the House of

Commons endorsed the Museum Trustees' wish to receive the King's library in an entirely new building and further suggested the provision of rooms as 'a fit receptacle' for any pictures which might be donated. This was the first mention of accommodation for pictures and, significantly, on 28 May Beaumont was enlisted to fill the first vacancy as Trustee, thus joining many old friends, including Stafford, Ashburnham, Aberdeen and Payne Knight, as well as such *ex officio* members as the Archbishop of Canterbury and the Speaker of the House of Commons.

In London Beaumont now appeared full of zest. There was suddenly much to achieve, and, with the tondo, as Wilkie wrote, 'the chief talk of all the artists' — Fuseli having restrained Mrs Damer from 'finishing' it[11] — a stream of callers came to pay homage at Grosvenor Square. When Wordsworth brought Crabb Robinson, the diarist was most impressed with his hosts —' amongst the most interesting by far of persons of quality in the country'. Beaumont was able to indulge his unrivalled loquacity on his favourite subject not only to the literati, artists and architects but also politicians. Amongst the rising generation of the latter were the Home Secretary, Robert Peel, a sensitive connoisseur then forming a splendid collection of Dutch painting, and George Agar Ellis, the future Lord Dover, a Whig supporter of Canning on the issue of Catholic emancipation, which, contentious though it was, the Beaumonts also believed long overdue. Beaumont was fortunate in that this young man, a member of the fashionable younger set of the Morpeths, Granvilles, Percys and Normanbys centred on Devonshire House, shared his ambition for a national gallery and had the ear of power. They had first talked seriously in 1821 at Lord Carlisle's drawn together by admiration for Zoffany's portrait of Garrick as Abel Drugger, a print after which they were later to commission from 'that not gay but sad deceiver', S.W. Reynolds[12] (together with another from Nathaniel Dance's portrait of the actor). Both men were abroad for a great deal of 1822 — Ellis on his honeymoon after his marriage to Carlisle's grand-daughter Georgiana — and it was May 1823 when Beaumont received Ellis at Grosvenor Square to admire not only the tondo but the Pannini, which he found 'quite wonderful', depicting as it did the world's finest pictures gathered in one gallery. Beaumont easily persuaded Ellis that it was time for him to talk again to the Prime Minister and to Aberdeen and Long about the gallery, but the catalyst was the death of John Julius Angerstein the following January, for within a few months Angerstein's son had decided to sell his famous collection of some thirty-eight pictures, nearly all of them old masters of the highest quality and in many cases chosen with the advice of Lawrence. Such works as the five Claudes, Raphael's *Pope Julius II*, paintings by Rembrandt, Rubens and Cuyp, Reynolds's *Lord Heathfield*, Hogarth's *Marriage à la Mode* and Wilkie's *Village Festival* would lay a fine foundation for a national collection, and again prompted by Beaumont, Ellis pressed the Prime Minister to acquire the pictures, repeating the baronet's bribe : '"*Buy* Mr. Angerstein's collection and I will *give* you mine"';[13] but despite fears of a foreign purchaser, the government still hesitated.

Meanwhile, on 30 March Beaumont wrote to Long, who alone knew of his bequest, anxious to know whether his pictures were deemed worthy, there being 'no place so secure & respectable as the Museum', for, 'not "to speak it profanely"', he doubted 'even Mr Pitt valued pictures as you & I do '.[14] Despite this sudden invocation of the great leader who had brought them together, progress remained slow. On 14 June at Beaumont's first Museum committee meeting he was chosen with Long and Henry

Bankes to form a sub-committee for the removal of some Egyptian antiquities into the building and for the placing of the statue of Shakespeare bequeathed by Garrick. The latter business, a matter to which he could relate, made an encouraging start to his trusteeship, but, far less enjoyable, six days later, was the all-party attack on the Trustees in the House of Commons when the Museum's future was discussed on a vote of £40,000 for housing the library. In a virulent and unexpected broadside, John Croker, who tabled one of two amendments, spoke scornfully of a disorganised and dirty establishment with the only fireproof extension reserved for marbles, and urged a more accessible location for the library. Long and the Museum's spokesman, Bankes, who objected that 'a very personal attack had been made upon him', defended the Trustees, leaving Ridley Colborne, himself a picture collector, as a lone voice rejoicing that 'the foundation stone of a national gallery of paintings' was about to be laid. After the government won the day, this point was immediately picked up by the Trustees and Beaumont was appointed to a sub-committee of seven 'to consider a proper Building for the Reception of the Royal Library and a Picture Gallery over it...such a building to form part of a General Plan'.[15]

Before this sub-committee could meet on 4 July to look over Robert Smirke's plans for a new museum, on the 1st there was a second debate in the House of Commons of even greater relevance to the national gallery, the money now being voted not only for 'the reception of the Royal Library' but 'for other purposes'. Croker dropped his objection to the Museum having the library but insisted that the position of Montague House in Great Russell Street was too remote for the display of pictures and models and, with great perspicacity, he moved that the design and expenditure on buildings come under the control of the Lords of the Treasury. As many of the Trustees were also Treasury Lords, this was a fine point but with the amendment carried, the seed was sown for a national gallery to develop outside the control of the Trustees. For the first time the debate focussed on the prospect of a national picture collection; Long, defending the Museum's budget, announced that Beaumont's gift had been turned down for want for space — a provocative over-simplification, since it was still offered subject to the availability of space — and Ellis made a decisive intervention, as recorded in his diary of 4 July:

> Went to the H of Commons, where I found Croker making a foolish & at the same time ill natured attack upon the Trustees of the British Museum — I spoke shortly in their defence — praised Sir George Beaumont for his generous intention...& gave notice of my intention early in next session to propose to Parliament a vote of a sum of money to buy Angerstein's collection for the public — Ridley Colborn — Alexander Baring — & Wortley supported me — & the House cheered, & seemed upon the whole favourably disposed.

Talking to Allan Cunningham many years later, Ellis gave Beaumont full credit for giving him the courage to make this bold proposal and he considered that this first formal announcement of Beaumont's donation caused the sentiment of the House to swing so sharply in favour of the acquisition that the government began negotiations during the long recess. Meanwhile, the Treasury Lords duly approved Smirke's Museum design, beginning with a new east wing for the library, and temporarily for pictures until the opposite wing with a first-floor gallery could follow. On 12 July Long presented his fellow Trustees with the provisional list of Beaumont's pictures

(Appendix II), the cream of his collection save for the Pannini, Wilkie's *Blind Fidder* — presumably omitted because the artist's *Village Festival* was amongst Angerstein's pictures — and Gainsborough's *Cottage Door with Peasant smoking*, which, sadly, he may have thought superfluous in view of Long's intention, executed before Beaumont's death, to donate Gainsborough's *The Watering Place*. On 21 July the Archbishop, Charles Manners Sutton, wrote as chairman his formal thanks for the gift.

By this time Beaumont was back at Coleorton, grateful that his pictures appeared to have a future 'under the guardianship of a body which never dies' in a building he had approved, but by November he was despairing of definite news and wrote to Ellis, worrying that Lord Hertford was 'in treaty' for the Angerstein Collection, though, he hoped, still willing to defer to the government. In fact, on 19 September the Prime Minister had told the Duchess of Devonshire: 'We are about to lay the foundation of a National Gallery, by the purchase of Mr Angerstein's Pictures — You know that Sir Geo Beaumont has announced his intention of leaving his Pictures to the Public & I am persuaded that when a Gallery is established there will be many bequests'.[16] While this letter confirms the significance of Beaumont's generous act, Liverpool quite failed to consult the Museum Trustees officially; he was, however, using Long as an intermediary with the vendors, and on 25 November wrote to inform him that the government was 'ready, on the part of the public, to purchase Mr Angerstein's collection of pictures for any sum between fifty and sixty thousand pounds which Mr Seguier and Mr Woodburn will state...a *fair & reasonable* valuation',[17] and the bargain was settled at £57,000. Long now saw to it that the Trustees reorganised themselves, establishing sub-committees to preside over the various collections, and on 14 February 1824 he, Beaumont and Lord Harrowby were chosen to supervise the department of paintings, prints and drawings. It was only on 27 January, after hearing from Payne Knight, that Beaumont had felt confident enough of the outcome to write congratulating Ellis for his part in the purchase of the Angerstein Collection.

While the Trustees presumed that the Museum would continue as the 'General Repository' for all gifts and a picture gallery was at last approved, the government remained conscious of strong opposition to the Museum serving as a national gallery. In his Budget speech of 23 February, 'Prosperity' Robinson, announcing the Angerstein purchase, referred to 'a valuable collection at present in the hands of a high-spirited individual of acknowledged taste and judgment' also 'likely to find its way to a National Gallery', and hoped that the example would be 'followed by many similar acts of generosity and munificence: the result of which will be the establishment of a splendid Gallery'. Its location remained to be disputed during another money vote on 1 March. Croker, this time abetted by the banker, Sir Thomas Baring, again pressed the claims of Somerset House while the Chancellor insisted that 'Sir George Beaumont had given his collection to the British Museum'. Baring knew better: 'Beaumont had not given his pictures to a building; but to the nation', and in vain Long explained that pictures would complement the Museum's other works of art.

Beaumont had appeared extraordinarily flexible, despite hoping that the Museum would prevail, and his ears should have been burning as Colborne once again acknowledged 'the noble gift of a beautiful collection of pictures'; but the Museum's battle for possession was virtually lost when, some three weeks later, Liverpool did the obvious and acquired the lease of Angerstein's house at 100 Pall Mall to enable the collection to remain *in situ*. In the subsequent debate of 2 April Ellis, learning that the Treasury

Lords were to be ultimately responsible for the Angerstein collection, sought a compromise acceptable to the Museum lobby by suggesting its Trustees be also Trustees of the National Gallery and that the government 'would so erect a gallery which would be no less beneficial to the taste, than it would be conducive to the glory of the country'. In an anonymous *Quarterly Review* article of November 1824 he pleaded for the gallery to be 'in the very gangway of London', meaning within easy reach of St James's, possibly in what is now known as Lancaster House. Like Beaumont, Ellis had no illusions about Englishmen's zeal — the gallery must be accessible *'without trouble or difficulty to themselves'*. While artists would benefit from being able to study models of real excellence, he also made Beaumont's point that it was equally important to improve *'the general taste of the public'*, who would provide the market.

In accordance with at least the form of Ellis's proposal, the government appointed a Committee for the Superintendence of the National Gallery from Museum Trustees. Thus Liverpool, Robinson, Aberdeen, Long, Lawrence and Beaumont became responsible for the national collection in Pall Mall at a time when only the Museum was committed to building a gallery: the ambiguity of the situation was to lead to considerable heart-searching over the next few years, and Beaumont, who had achieved so much, did not live to see the final fruit of his labours, a national gallery built for the purpose. For the time being he was obliged to retain his pictures. On 3 April he met Ellis by chance at Jackson's studio and had a long discussion on the management of the Gallery, and the next month there was the satisfaction of its opening in Angerstein's house. Although this merited only a few lines in *The Times* of 11 May, the public response was more gratifying, there being over 24,000 visitors by the end of November, despite the rooms being dark and cavern-like. Haydon, for once forgetting the histrionics, spoke for the artists: 'it was delightful at last to walk into the Gallery just as you felt inclined without trouble or inconvenience'. Ellis was pleased that entry without ticket worked perfectly, Seguier reporting the people 'very orderly and well behaved'.

Meanwhile, John Nash was transforming the West End of London with his 'metropolitan improvements', beginning with the creation of new residential terraces of grand stucco architecture in Regent's Park and spreading first down the new Regent Street to connect with the Mall, and now into the future Trafalgar Square. One scheme for the square presented to the House of Commons in 1826 allowed for a national gallery on the north side of this quadrangle near Charing Cross, with the Academy in the centre of the area, and an alternative plan proposed a new main street linking Charing Cross with the Museum. Ellis and Colborne visited the architect and 'liked his plans generally' for the first of these, but Long so committed himself to the scheme which reduced the isolation of the Museum that, when the government decision went against it, he resigned as Paymaster-General, accepting a peerage as Baron Farnborough. In many ways the choice of the Trafalgar Square option was bad news too for Beaumont: 1825 had seen a new financial crisis and the redevelopment of the Charing Cross area was postponed. In the debate of 21 March 1826 on the Charing Cross Improvement Bill, the Minister responsible could only express the wish that 'the quadrangle should contain a Gallery for our national paintings and statues'; and at this point the government abandoned the plan for Beaumont's pictures to be placed temporarily in the new wing of the Museum, although the Trustees were offered the sop of retaining the guardianship.

The government had fixed on the princely salary of £200 for the National Gallery superintendent, but it was the power not the pounds that attracted the first and most remarkable holder of the office, William Seguier, whom Beaumont insisted on calling 'Mr Segar'. Ellis, mainly in jest, had 'wished to know, who was to superintend the superintendent', but with long experience of picture dealing and restoration for the nobility — as early as 1814 Farington had complained of him being 'lifted up by the attentions shewn him' — the 'sneering Cockney', as Haydon dubbed him, was 'shrewd, witty and odd' enough to appeal to the most patrician connoisseur and all relied on his judgement. Haydon also described him as a member of the clique of Wilkie, Jackson, Beaumont and the Phipps brothers, seeking every opportunity to join them on occasions such as the weekly openings of Lord Grosvenor's collection, which he had helped to form.

Beaumont had consulted Seguier in 1808 before sending his pictures to Coleorton and in March 1828, anticipating the result of the Commons debate and rightly afraid he might not live to see them in a newly built national gallery, he enlisted him to hang them in Pall Mall. It was a momentous day when they left Leicestershire, but, once installed in London, his sole concern was whether they were worthy of their place alongside Angerstein's. On 5 April Ellis, who had never visited Coleorton, saw them for the first time before hanging and noted: 'A little Grey Claude is beautiful — & there are three others by the same master, all possessing merit — a beautiful little sketch by Rembrandt of the Crucifixion — a good Landscape by Niccolo Poussin — a good Landscape by Sebastian Bourdon...& the very fine Landscape by Rubens — these are his best — there are a few others Zoffanis etc.' The Zoffanys had never been intended for the national collection and on 18 April Beaumont wrote to Long, who had 'kindly consented to manage the business', requesting permission to withdraw 'pictures which appeared to discredit the purity of the collection': the Swaneveldt, 'a downright imitation of Claude & vastly inferior', and a now mysterious 'Titian or Giorgione', doubtless misattributed and certainly 'unmercifully cleaned'; instead he offered Wilkie's 'inimitable picture of the Blind Fiddler' and a 'very fine head' by Reynolds, that of the model for *Ugolino*.[18] The changes were agreed and soon Beaumont borrowed back his beloved Claude, the *Hagar*, unable to live without it — a sentiment that distinguished him from the grand collectors whose pictures meant prestige and possession, disposable like surplus acres. As Colborne had already pointed out in debate, it was liberal to bequeath a collection but 'doubly liberal to give it during his lifetime'.

Wilkie, who heard the news of the Gallery when in Venice, wrote to congratulate his patron on his 'sacrifice': Beaumont would be regarded as its founder 'as Lorenzo the Magnificent was of the gallery of Florence'. The opening had 'made a stir even in Italy' where dealers were 'on the alert',[19] and in fact Beaumont had already engaged Wilkie to give his advice on the colossal statue of Antinous from the Braschi Palace, thought to be for sale. Manoeuvreing to augment the sculpture collections was no part of his brief and it was perhaps fortunate that the matter went no further. On 2 May Beaumont was purposely absent from the Extraordinary General Meeting at the Museum when it was resolved to request the Lords of the Treasury to reconsider the proposal to remove the pictures, a part of the Museum's collection, bearing in mind how this might affect future donors. A stronger memorandum establishing the Trustees' obligations, possibly the work of Lord Colchester, accompanied the motion.

His lordship, with Long and Howley, now Bishop of London, feared the surrender of Beaumont's pictures could lead to the removal of the Townley and Elgin marbles, and next day he agreed with Long on the compromise that Beaumont's pictures, which had cost the baronet only £4,000 and were not yet deposited, were 'far differently circumstanced from other collections belonging to the Trust' and might, 'with the consent of the donor', be placed anywhere in the metropolis under the care of the Trustees. It was not, however, thought advisable to put to the government Beaumont's wish 'to become a joint trustee of the Museum'.[20]

Thus, two old politicians, survivors from Beaumont's own parliamentary days, judged how far to carry the fight, without jeopardising Liverpool's acceptance of the Trustees' resolution. Beaumont, regretful to lose his point of joint trusteeship, could not foresee how soon the omission would be significant. When he died the next year and Liverpool became too ill, the two were replaced on the Committee of Gentlemen for the Superintendence of the National Gallery in June by Peel and Ellis; neither had any connection with the Museum, and the sub-committee ceased to be informed of National Gallery developments, a state of affairs recognised in 1828 when the Museum Trustees formally relinquished control of Beaumont's gift. The National Gallery had emerged with its own identity, and Beaumont's two swordbearers remained to continue the battle for proper accommodation, though Ellis was seldom in accord with Long. With retrenchment again the political cry, there were to be many disappointments before Holwell Carr's legacy helped to concentrate minds in 1831. Following Beaumont's example, he bequeathed his pictures to the nation on condition that suitable accommodation was available, and the National Gallery 'Gentlemen' were not sorry to point out that saturation point had long ago been reached (Seguier did fit in one or two of Carr's pictures but only at the cost of relegating Beaumont's Both and Canaletto to the stairs). Beaumont's last act on the management committee had been to approve the purchase in 1826 of Titian's *Bacchus and Ariadne*, Poussin's *Bacchanalian Feast* and Annibale Carracci's *Christ appearing to St Peter* for £9,000, acquisitions that signalled the policy, adumbrated by Long in Parliament, of obtaining 'the best works of any considerable master'. Long's policy would hold for nearly thirty years, but the initial announcement elicited a letter from 'Alfred' in *The Times* of the same day, 23 March, criticising the cost and calling the committee ciphers, save for Long and 'the picture-cleaner' Seguier, the 'absolute rulers of the Gallery'. Beaumont, condemned as one who 'talks too much, to think upon the subject', might well have been more careful with his own money, but he was rightly excited about such noble additions and glad as ever to leave finance to others.

In May Beaumont was embarrassed to receive from his old friend Jack Taylor some effusive lines 'on his splendid contribution of Pictures to the National Gallery'. His gift had received a better press than the opening of the Gallery, the small Claudes, the Wilsons, the Both and the Canaletto being especially commended in *The Times* of 25 April, which complained bitterly of the gloom in which they were all exhibited. Beaumont's response to Taylor that he could wish only that 'every genuine & pure picture by the classics of the art were destined to be placed in this asylum'[21] shows him quite satisfied for the future, and he was also pleased generally with William Young Ottley's catalogue describing his paintings, even if Poussin's trees were wrongly given as evergreen oaks. It was fortunate that he could not foresee the day when a select committee would hear evidence from David Roberts and other artists to the effect that over-cleaning had removed the tiles from the stonemason's yard in his Canaletto.[22]

In the last two years of his life, Beaumont's message was simply the importance of preserving the past as an example to the future, while he was able to enjoy the best of the present as much as ever. Without Farington to report, there are fewer glimpses of him, but in May 1825 Ellis took Beaumont to Greenwich, the annual outing that he had made first with Hearne and Woollett, later with West, Dance, Farington and Wilkie and, in 1815, with William Bowles, who had subsequently written 'The Chelsea Pensioners'. On this occasion they were joined at Greenwich Hospital by Long and continued on to his estate, Bromley Hill Place, to be entertained in its picturesque gardens with Croker, Lawrence, Seguier, Holwell Carr and Edward Hawke Locker, the Hospital Governor, not reaching home until eleven at night. Ellis records, too, a dinner the following June when the Aberdeens, who had taken over Stanmore Priory at Abercorn's death, received Liverpool, the Longs, Lawrence, Rogers, Chantrey, Miss Berry and Beaumont. This was the last time that the men who had done most to achieve the National Gallery would meet together and it was a fitting finale to Beaumont's London life.

*   *   *

To please Lady Beaumont, the last years were spent mainly in Leicestershire. Coleorton had prospered under the baronet's care and aided by the advice of a Dorset land surveyor, Edward Knight, who now lived locally, the estate had grown to some 2,400 acres. This, together with lands at Dunmow, Haverhill and a small patch in Clerkenwell, represented the Beaumont wealth which, modest by comparison with that of fellow patrons — Farington in 1804 guessed at an income under £8,000 — had increased sufficiently to enable Sir George not only to make his boldest art purchases in his last years but to present his heir with £15,000 on his marriage in 1825.

In contrast to London there was little society at Coleorton, apart from the Mereweathers, the Revd Francis having transferred from Haverhill in 1815 to build a new rectory at Coleorton, where he survived to bury three baronets. As Wordsworth had perceived when he planned her winter garden, Lady Beaumont, increasingly neurotic, needed this tranquillity; her letters from Italy had revealed more than a hint of desperation as she yearned for her home in the cool north, and never again did she feel up to a long absence. Sir George, too, tried to convince himself that the country suited him better in old age than '"the busy haunts of men"': in 1823 he was complaining to the poet that there was 'no time for anything rational in this *Rattle* of a town', but he hated the cold and the gloom, and 'the adjustment of the flue between Sir George's love and my dread of heat' was not the solution that his wife hoped. In February 1823 Wordsworth came with Mary to spend three weeks at Coleorton, returning with Dorothy for the same month of the following year, during which visit he composed 'A Flower Garden'. No one could have done more to see Beaumont through the long winters when he ardently wished himself in Rome.

The two old friends had much to discuss, not having met since the Wordsworths stayed at Coleorton in December 1820 on their return from their Continental tour. Wordsworth could now report the success of his *Guide to the Lakes*, published in 1823 'with Additions and illustrative remarks upon the Scenery of the Alps', including

Beaumont's theory — which, to his prejudiced eye, Turner had failed to dispel — that 'the colouring of Switzerland' was 'ill-suited to the pencil'.[23] Starved of stimulation, Sir George was a demanding host, while Mary, longing for her own home, gave pleasure by reading to Lady Beaumont; and it was a remarkable tribute to their friendships that Wordsworth, now much sought after, was so generous with his time.

Over the years the Beaumonts had quite a variety of visitors: Mrs Coleridge with Sara, who, already secretly yearning for the man who was to become her husband, was deemed by her hostess 'to look so delicate I should tremble at her becoming a wife or mother'; Lady Susan Percy, who became very close after the death of her mother, Lady Beverley; the Ashburnhams; the Lonsdales; the Howleys; Whitbread; Mrs Siddons; and the artists, S.W. Reynolds, Edridge, and William Young Ottley, who would be working on the National Gallery catalogue; and in October 1823 Constable came for a happy six weeks after Beaumont had completed 'a long Devon ramble'.

It was ironic that, while Beaumont was pressing for a national gallery, he was spending more and more time with an artist who had misgivings about its influence, although he truly appreciated living amongst the 'Ancient Masters'. From Coleorton Constable wrote: 'I am almost choaked in this breakfast room. Here hang 4 Claudes, a Cousins & a Swanevelt. The low sun in the morning sets them off to great advantage.' He was also full of admiration for his host: 'It is delightful to see him work so hard — painting like religion knows on difference of rank.'[24] The relationship had long been affectionate — when Constable's health was poor in 1811, Beaumont had advised a daily walk to Grosvenor Square to copy a picture and rewarded him with Wilson's oil sketch, *Lake Avernus*. The cure, however, had been marriage and the two men became close again only in 1820 when Constable, just elected Associate, had a success at the Academy with his *Stratford Mill*, and Beaumont noted approvingly 'the boy undergoing the agony of a bite'. The next year, on his round of long-familiar places, Beaumont painted the same subject, presenting a version to the artist, who received it kindly: 'a Rembrandt, full of tone and chiaroscuro'. In 1823 Beaumont, back from Italy, was greeting Constable's newly toned 'large wood', identified by Leslie as *Helmingham Dell*, with '"well done". We shall in time drive the "Albanians" from the field.' He must have returned to his old hobby-horse, for Constable goes on to comment that 'the civil war is at its highest in the Academy, the *white* & the *black Rose*. Collins & the Sculptors & the portrait painters are for Turner but it won't do.' That autumn, Constable, aware that Beaumont's best pictures were only awaiting space in the National Gallery, decided he owed it to himself to study them at Coleorton. He arrived still feeling a sense of social inferiority, but he thought the arrival of a letter to him from Bishop Fisher helped raise him in the Beaumonts' estimation, and, by the second week, he had 'lost all uncomfortable reserve and restraint.'

Constable gives a picture of a happy day at Coleorton: Beaumont rising at seven to walk in the garden, feeding the birds during breakfast at nine, then working in his painting room, full of anecdote — 'he laughs, sings, whistles & plays with his dog' — side by side with his visitor. At two the horses are at the door and Lady Beaumont 'hunts' them out. Fortunate with the weather, they ride to the ruins at Ashby or 'the mountain streams and rock (such Everdingens)' at Gracedieu or to Lord Ferrers's old convent, Beaumont holding the horse while Constable sketches some trees at Staunton

Harold. After an hour or so they return to dinner and hear Lady Beaumont read the news in the *Morning Herald*; then to the drawing room for tea, and Constable is 'furnished with some beautifull portfolio. . .and Sir George reads a play, in a manner the most delightfull — far beyond any pronunciation I ever heard'; on one memorable evening it was *As You Like It*, with Jacques ruminating on the Seven Ages, on another *The Excursion*, 'beautifull but has some sad melancholy stories. . .to harry you up without a purpose'.

Released at eleven, Constable, taking pictures and portfolios to his room, 'slept with one of the Claudes every night'. He copied both the small ones, the 'Grove', (probably *Narcissus and Echo*), which he really wanted, not at first being available. Never had he been so readily exposed to such riches, nor so tempted to see nature through art. Not a moment was wasted as he devoured not only the Claudes but also Alexander Cozens's sky studies and his sixteen landscape etchings entitled *Various Species of Composition of Landscape*, copying both the etchings and some metrical verses that old Charles Davy had written many years ago to help Beaumont himself remember Cozens's landscape system. In the last week, when Constable was working against the clock, there was the pleasant interruption of Southey's arrival with his daughter, in whose album Constable sketched *Coleorton Hall with Flag flying* (Pl. 93). He also found time at the very last minute to sketch the Reynolds memorial — at Wordsworth's suggestion to be known as the Cenotaph — and Wilson's stone which, Beaumont noted, had taken twenty-three horses to place in position. Sadly he declined the one small commission offered by the Beaumonts, retaining all his work, including a small oil of the view towards Bardon Hill, some local sketches and the copies he made in the evenings from Beaumont's own early East Anglian drawings (Pls 94 and

93.   John Constable: *Coleorton Hall with Flag flying, 1823*, pencil and wash (Bristol, Avon County Reference Library).

94. Beaumont: *The Mill (adapted from Rembrandt)*, pencil and wash (B.C.).

95. John Constable: *The Mill (after Beaumont)*, 1823, pencil and wash (Oxford, Ashmolean Museum).

95). At the end of his stay — 'one of the epocks of my life in taste, industry, pride and so on' — his host congratulated himself that it had all been 'of great mutual service', quite oblivious of the pressure under which Constable had been working to complete his tasks — not quite all of which had been self-imposed. Although the artist was now almost one of the family, there was no consideration for his poor wife, who might still have been bereft at Christmas had the Beaumonts had their way and she not been goaded into writing: 'it was complimentary of Sir George to ask you to remain over the Xmas, but he forgot at the time that you had a wife'. Kindly as the baronet wrote when Constable was back in London that 'unless you take more air & exercise you will never reach my age', he rather missed the point that the painter's visit had ended in an illness — probably some kind of neuralgia from the victim's description — brought on by nervous exhaustion.

The following year, when Constable's pictures were causing a sensation in the Paris Salon, he was enjoying the benefit of being in Beaumont's good books, but the baronet's 'flying coach' was no joy-ride. Constable narrowly avoided having to undertake the trial of a Venetian process devised by a Miss Cleaver in which the British Institution's Directors were taking an interest, despite his having made it clear that they might as well set themselves up to adjudicate on church or legal matters as on artistic ones, and there were a legion of small jobs: the son of the Beaumonts' former cook with ambitions to art whose drawings must be examined; canvases to prepare and holes to repair — jobs which at least Constable could pass on to his assistant John Dunthorne. The master himself, renowned for his sarcasm, let his old friend off lightly even though the reward was often only 'a nice little sketch' and a few shillings for Dunthorne.

On 3 June Beaumont called on Constable and 'helped a good deal in toning & improving' *Stratford Mill*, which he thought one of the artist's best pictures, 'admirable in colour & light & shade'. The next day Constable called at Grosvenor Square and 'did a good deal to his [Beaumont's] picture then on the easel which he could not get on with'. A month later Constable took Dunthorne to 'overlook' the pictures Beaumont was leaving behind in London at the end of the season, and took some home, including 'his lovely little Rubens & the Teniers', and 'did up' one. Constable's touch may well have contributed something to the masterly breadth and boldness of the view in the lakes (Pl. 96) that Beaumont now sent as a present to

Beaumont: *View from Southey's House, Greta Hall*, 1824 (Private Collection).

Southey. It was a view from the poet's house Greta Hall, and on 10 July Southey wrote perceptively that Beaumont had 'dealt with this landscape as a poet does with a historical tale: modifying it to his purpose, and supplying whatever it wanted to make it suitable to his art'; more privately he observed that 'scarcely an object in the picture resembles the reality. His aim was to give the character, the spirit of the scene. But whoever may look upon this picture hereafter, with any thought of me, will wish it had been a faithful portrait of the place.'[25]

The famous anecdote of Constable laying an old Cremona fiddle on the grass to show Beaumont that brown was not the proper colour for trees and grass in painting has tended to suggest that the differences between the two men, such as they were, centred on colour. In fact Constable, like Wilkie, by now had much sympathy for Beaumont's preference for a sombre and old masterly effect and, if pushed on the point, would have ranked himself with him against the 'Albanians' in the debate that Wilkie would call 'the great and leading question of modern art'.[26] Beaumont for his part had at last found the collaborator and assistant he needed in the painter he had kept at a respectful distance for so many years, and that autumn Constable might well have returned to Coleorton at the behest of Lady Beamont, who well knew what was best for her husband, but for Mrs Constable's writing tartly: 'I think it much better for you to resist Lady B you have plenty to do at home.' If he refused an invitation it was probably just as well, for that autumn Beaumont was too ill to 'touch a pencil' and 'lost all relish for the art', but by December the baronet was 'endeavouring (according to your excellent metaphorical expression) to "whip up" one or two of my old pictures' and hoping not to 'whip them to sleep'. He had chosen *Jacques and the Wounded Stag* (Pl. 87) to represent him in the exhibition of British Masters at the British Institution the following year. It had probably begun life as his Academy exhibit of 1819 and depended also on an oil sketch that may be rather earlier. Although it was to attract some cruel criticism in the *London Magazine*[27], *Jacques* probably holds the key to some of Beaumont's closest artistic dealings with Constable, for the younger man seems to have adopted some features from the oil sketch, including a particular distorted tree, for his own Helmingham Dell subjects begun in 1823, and Beaumont may well have been moved to work up his large version of *Jacques* for the 1825 exhibition by seeing Constable toning his pictures; moreover, he added to it impasto highlights that are very reminiscent of Constable's. Constable was later to treat the same subject, his watercolour exhibited in 1832 being based in reverse on Beaumont's oil sketch.

Beaumont's *Jacques*, and his readings from *As You Like It* at Coleorton help to explain Constable's inclusion of a stag in *The Cenotaph* (Pl. 92) which he sent to the Academy in 1836, wishing 'to see Sir Joshua Reynolds' name and Sir George Beaumont's once more in the catalogue, for the last time in the old [Somerset] House', and little knowing it was to be his own final contribution. It was based on his drawing of the Reynolds memorial at Coleorton, with the addition of the two pillars supporting the Coade busts of Raphael and Michelangelo, and the stag which, far from being wounded, looks out alert and expectant. Constable had never carried out his intention of publishing an account of Beaumont, tempted though he had been to redress Allan Cunningham's brief life — 'a trumpery affair. . .he seems to have known nothing about him (or of the art of censure)',[28] but he apparently sent a draft to Leslie, who mislaid it, or perhaps incorporated it in his biography of Constable in a manner too diffuse for us to recognise its source. But he said all he wanted in this final tribute. His relationship with Beaumont had been as it was for many — exhausting, sometimes exasperating, but above all inspirational; as Leslie put it, Beaumont had throughout 'assumed the character of a teacher', but despite strictures and disagreements, Constable had found friendship and emerged more nearly his true self. Constable and Beaumont had shared many debates on brown trees and in *The Cenotaph* the russet limes take their natural place in an autumn setting, confirmation of the artist's sympathy with the old masters, while the stag shows there is no cause for melancholy.

*   *   *

In the autumn of 1824 Beaumont had suffered a bad attack of the bilious fever that had pursued him since 1782 and rendered him so sympathetic to the illness of others — soon it was again to be Wilkie who needed enouragement, moral and financial, to travel to Italy in pursuit of health. Old age had caused Beaumont to forego his dream of accompanying Wordsworth to the South, but he consoled himself by giving his friend, long past protest, £100 for the family to make the journey, hoping that Dorothy, whose poems the Beaumonts had encouraged, might produce another journal. This gift doubled Frances Fermor's legacy — she died at Worcester in December 1824 — and Wordsworth found it easy to write some tributary lines for her kindness had been proverbial. That year Beaumont confessed to having travelled a thousand miles post, all on sad errands, and he missed the chance of joining the Wordsworths in Wales or seeing them at Coleorton.

Frances Fermor's death was a sad blow to the Beaumonts but fortunately the spring brought the joyous news of young George's engagement to Mary Howley. The dull young man, in whom they had failed to animate 'decisive taste', had chosen, in Price's words, 'with his mind's eye' rather than for looks, a delightful girl, and the alliance not only put an end to the 'unpleasant reserve' between Sir George and his heir but removed the Beaumonts' fears for the future of Coleorton. Young George suddenly appeared quite '"a Giant"' in his exertions, his cousin's inverted commas drawing attention to the bridegroom's unfortunate lack of stature (which presumably did not worry him, for he was to appear as an English jockey at a Roman masquerade on his honeymoon). The relief was sufficient to restore Lady Beaumont 'in health and strength', although she remained 'in such a perpetual motion both of mind & body' that her husband feared no constitution could long sustain' it.[29] The wedding took place at St George's, Hanover Square and was an emotional occasion for the old Beaumonts, who could look back nearly fifty years since they had set out together from the same church.

Coleridge was present in the 'downright Broil' of that June day and Wordsworth had been delighted to receive the rarity of a letter written in 'a happy state of mind'. He implored Beaumont to be 'thankful to Providence...and Gratitude is the hand-maid to Hope, and hope the harbinger of Faith'. His old friend knew it well, for he had lectured Wilkie on the attainment of tranquillity from 'a true sense of the importance of religion & a firm reliance on that Providence who is constantly watching';[30] yet at times nothing could relieve his melancholy, nor persuade him that he had fewer sins to exculpate than most men. Susceptible as ever to novelty, he had been fascinated by Wilkie's friend, the Revd Edward Irving, who, according to Hazlitt, was spouting Shakespeare from the pulpit at the same time as preaching hell and damnation. In 1824 Constable, having suffered a surfeit, hoped to hear no more of Irving, but the preacher may have fed Beaumont's darker side, though the only outward result was the observance of Sunday as a day of rest, even from painting, and the introduction of daily family prayers.

Coleridge, who had once been able to lift Beaumont out of his depression, was now valued mainly for his conversation, and even he was outmatched one evening by the scintillating Lady Dacre, Byron's favourite 'blue'. Coleridge probably preferred such company as the editor Jeffrey or his friend, the educational pioneer, Dr Andrew Bell, whose Madras system, whereby senior pupils instructed their juniors, was, thanks to the Beaumonts, adopted at Dunmow and Coleorton schools.

Davy, now Sir Humphrey and rather grand, came on other occasions. He was full of new ideas as befitted a man of science, alarming Lady Beaumont who, after a dinner at the Sothebys in 1825, described despairingly his vision of England as a great manu-facturing country leaving agriculture to the peasants of Europe. Her intellect was as keen as ever and she was a voracious reader: Coleridge's *Aids to Reflection*, published that year, she anticipated would be 'too deep' for 'the world of London' but was delighted when the Howleys and Blanco White, impressed by the new work, wished to meet the author. She had written amusingly to Wordsworth of Coleridge 'talking to his ladies in Mrs Gilman's parlour, on Spurgeum's mistake with regard to his skull,

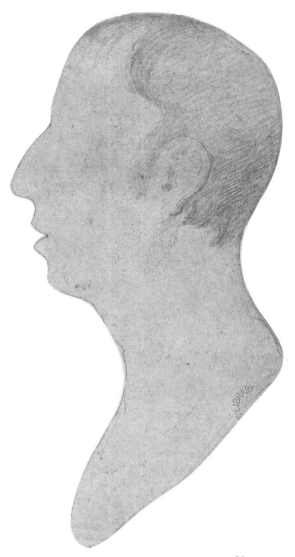

97. Beaumont: *Head of Wordsworth*, 1815,
pencil, cut to outline (Exeter, Royal Albert
Memorial Museum).

which he pronounced possessed the organ of locality in an eminent degree';[31] it was
not often that she was caught out, but obviously Spurzheim's theories had escaped her,
although her husband sufficiently shared Haydon's phrenological interests to send him
a cut-out profile he had drawn from Wordsworth's head when the painter had proposed a bust of the poet (Pl. 97). Meanwhile, Sir George, through the good offices of
Ellis, saw Coleridge to a fellowship of the new Royal Society of Literature, worth £100
a year, and on the poet's behalf showed his gratitude to Ellis by sending him Coleridge's lines, 'made almost extempore many years ago at the house of Bowles, his
brother poet, on hearing one of the Linleys play on the violincello'.[32]

It was Ellis amongst others, in particular Davy, who persuaded Beaumont to
become a founder member of the new club for men of artistic, literary and scientific
distinction,the Athenaeum. While Lady Beaumont was grateful to stay quietly at
home, Sir George was as social as ever, frequently with Rogers, whose table was
unmatched for intellect, and where he met the poet, Thomas Moore, and, with far

greater pleasure, Scott, now Sir Walter. Scott appreciated Beaumont's exquisite sensitivity and looked to him for helpful advice to the young Scottish artists who tried their luck in London, such as he had given Archibald Skirving in 1812 and his namesake, David Scott, in 1825.

Wilkie, exhausted by his labours, was at this time preparing for a long rest on the Continent and Beaumont wrote to recommend 'Dr. *Horse* & Dr. *Cow*' and not too much work; he urged him to be patient with 'the Gothic rudeness of Cimabue and his compeers' while in Italy, and to learn to appreciate the full majesty of Michelangelo, 'the most wonderful, sublime, and original of them all'. He too still longed for 'beloved Italy' and kept 'the most sanguine hopes of seeing it again', but both he and Lady Beaumont were failing and 'it would be a presumption to run the risk of being one or both of us laid up at an inn', although the thought of spending the winter with Wilkie was a temptation hard to resist.

In October 1825 the Wordsworths fulfilled, Mary rather reluctantly, 'the half-promise' to pay Coleorton an annual visit. This began with quite an invasion of visitors, including the Master of Trinity and three Hutchinsons, Sara staying on with the Wordsworths to report 'so much has been done by good taste that one can scarcely wish for any residence...being more delightful — But the Master & Mistress are the charm of the whole — never was there such a well assorted pair — or one so full of enjoyment at such an advanced period of life'.[33] Not only had the grounds been greatly improved — Chantrey's bust of Wordsworth had joined the garden monuments, most of which were a tribute to the owner's economy — but Sir George had insisted that the cottages were restored with picturesque thatch instead of the local slate, and Lady Beaumont had been persuaded to carry out some ferocious surgery on the winter garden, which was constantly threatening to became a jungle, following Price's advice that it was kind to be cruel.

On this visit Wordsworth was suffering great discomfort from his eyes and, although he hid it well, they must have been on his mind when he responded to Lady Beaumont's request for a sonnet, Mary posting the following version in December:

> Lady, what delicate graces may unite
> In age — so often comfortless and bleak!
> Though from thy enfeebled eye-balls break
> Those saintly emanations of delight,
> A snow-drop let me name thee...

These woeful lines were greatly improved in the published version:

> Such age how beautiful! O lady bright,
> Whose mortal lineaments seem all refined
> By favouring Nature and a saintly Mind
> To sit purer and more exquisite
> Than flesh and blood...

In both, Lady Beaumont was 'that child of Winter', a revealing epithet.

At the end of the 1826 season Beaumont determined to pay one more visit to the Lakes while Dorothy Wordsworth came to keep his wife company at Coleorton. Rogers was his companion as he set off in early September for a first night at Matlock, visiting *en route* Chatsworth, which, for all its Canovas, pleased less than Haddon.

Soon he was once again at the Lowood inn with its magnificent views across Windermere to the Langdale Pikes which, according to Rogers, he sketched 'from morning till night',[34] then moving on to the inn at Lodore on Keswick Lake. Here Sir George wrote to Mary Beaumont, of whom he was obviously very fond:

> My mental diet has been so much confined to Clouds & Mountains, washed down with waterfalls that if you should find me a little visionary I hope you will excuse it...many days splendidly fine & the others only sufficiently charged with storms to set off the Mountains to the best advantage, with intervals of brilliant sunshine to give a poetical zest to the whole & a Poet at each elbow & one behind me with eyes in fine frenzy rolling to give these airy wonders form and shape, to turn all this as occasion required into sonnets & elegies.[35]

Once again he was in his element and with the added bonus of the company of Wordsworth, Southey and Rogers, who was touched by such enthusiasm: 'Sir George is always going to the window and looking earnestly out as if he saw somebody he knew, though it is only a cloud or a gleam of light on the water.' From Rogers, too, comes quite a surprising picture of the Lake poets during this social season: 'masses of callers' at the Wordsworths, who produced a very good dinner at Rydal Mount, and sixteen — 'quite usual' — taking tea at the Southeys. After three weeks on Derwentwater and a few days at Lowther Castle with Wordsworth, who had spared every minute he could for his friends, Rogers accompanied Beaumont somewhat reluctantly to Castle Howard and Mulgrave Castle. 'Rubens and Guido and Claude and Poussin, and Haydon, and Lawrence'[36] had been so much in his ears that he was not sorry to have the excuse of toothache for a direct journey home, while Beaumont, who had been relieved to find Mulgrave in better health, returned after a second call at Castle Howard which was in the hands of a younger generation, the present Earl of Carlisle being Ellis's brother-in-law.

Beaumont had a miraculous escape shortly after leaving Mulgrave when his carriage left the road on a bridge, but he appeared none the worse for the fright. The journey across Yorkshire, his last excursion, was an emotional one, pregnant with thoughts of friendship and art as he 'plunged into the moors'. To Lady Mulgrave he wrote of the scenery: 'What a change! Yet their desolation is sublime, & I can imagine a composition might be formed from them...with awe and not unpleasing melancholy — But then the painter must be a poet — a mere matter of fact man can never give sentiment to his landscapes'.[37]

In November he wrote to Rogers in excellent spirits, and Ashburnham, who now spent the winter at his Florentine villa, wished Beaumont's health might continue 'to be such as you have for many years enjoyed and complained of'. The baronet was nagging Jackson to add Chantrey's portrait to those of Dance and Smith, and besides family portraits there was also Beechey's *Mulgrave*, but otherwise the walls of Coleorton were now largely occupied by Beaumont's own work. Despite a slightly shaky hand, his enthusiasm was as great as ever and he was painting happily when overcome by a sudden fainting fit at the end of January 1827; erysipylis set in and he barely regained consciousness before he died quite peacefully on 7 February, only three months short of his fiftieth wedding anniversary.

EPILOGUE

EATH, LONG ANTICIPATED by Sir George, had at last stolen up on him. Lady
Beaumont was thankful that he had been spared 'the final parting from one who
had shared his joys & sorrows for near half a century', and 'the more awful conflicts of
the soul trembling on the verge of Eternity in which Fear might have participated'.
With great strength of mind she resolved to prepare for their reunion by devoting the
rest of her life to expiating 'the sins of the past',[1] for her husband had refused to
believe that repentance alone sufficed. His early neglect of Coleorton and its people
weighed on him to the end, hard as he had worked to lay the foundation for the
Beaumonts to enjoy over a century of prosperity, which was brought to an end only by
the Second World War — and this was the least of his achievements.

Beaumont had always been spurred by the family pride instilled by his mother
during his isolated childhood and by a sense of obligation that seemed distinctly old-
fashioned by the end of his life. Possessive by nature, he had felt her remarriage very
deeply: indeed the blow could have nurtured the depressive streak that only his wife
and Wordsworth seem to have appreciated fully and from which Coleridge himself
suffered. In his salad days, when he was content to exploit his talents as a gentleman-
painter and actor, Beaumont might have settled for playing the dilettante, glass in
hand, for the rest of his life, but, after his marriage, he had to justify his wife's faith in
him and match her enthusiasms. Given the support of such a loving companion who
intensified his commitment, he began to take himself seriously and, filling the
vacuum left by Reynold's death, he became a spokesman for art with the uncomplicated approach of his generation which never fully understood the creative forces
of the new century.

His short years in Parliament gave him the confidence and connections for his new
role and none would deny that he proved a good friend to the arts. From the modest
society of Dunmow to intimacy with the moving spirits of the day, ranging from
Reynolds, Wilson and Gainsborough to Wordsworth, Coleridge, Constable, Wilkie
and Canova, had been a remarkable progress. If a man may be judged by his friends,
Beaumont must rate high indeed. His enemies, vociferous as they were, did not really
know him. But in his early sixties this basically modest man was riding for a fall with
his growing conceit that he should direct the tides of genius. The few who understood
him realised that increasingly Beaumont swung between bouts of depression that
rendered him almost incapable, and elation, when his enthusiasm and didacticism
were unnatural. In his state of mind lies the clue not only to his excessive praise for
fresh faces — be it of man or picture — but to the virulence of his attacks on Turner
and other innovating artists who did not respond to his direction. It is understandable
that he could not accept Turner as a successor to his beloved Claude, especially when

artists of that faction bated him with the comparison, for in technique Turner was an entirely different painter. Beaumont, who 'always hated the turbulence of contention'[2] and was, like Price, not 'a good hater',[3] might have been expected to take a benign view of a dissident; instead, his volatile temperament sometimes admitted no contradiction on matters he considered to be within his jurisdiction. In such a mood he had to be right and could not stop talking, opening the way for so-called friends like Farington to make the most of his provocation and sting him to self-justification. In between the extremes, Beaumont was a delightful companion, as Walter Scott testified: 'the most sensible and pleasing man I ever knew, kind, too, in his nature, and generous — gentle in society and of those mild manners which tend to soften the causticity of the general London tone of persiflage and personal satire.'[4]

Beaumont had sometimes appeared too much the defender of the traditions of the old masters, both privately and through the British Institution directing painters and collectors to their example. It was a cruel irony that cast him as the enemy of promise as well as its supporter, but resentment — even hatred — of Beaumont was perhaps the only thing sworn enemies like Callcott and Haydon ever had in common, while Turner, less vocal and characteristically circumspect, relieved his feelings in private comments and verses in his sketchbooks. Yet, while lesser spirits vented their spite in the *Catalogues Raisonnés*, it was Turner who, in a great decade of painting, seems to us today to have most nobly defended 'the Art' that Beaumont sought to protect. Constable, for his part, was too loyal to reflect how far his own career might have been advanced had Beaumont been as enthusiastic in his cause as he had been in Wilkie's. Their friendship had begun in obligation rather than admiration, and only gradually blossomed into intimacy, but Beaumont had never commended him for his genius — always his highest praise.

Beaumont's eighteenth-century mentality was most pronounced in his attitudes to the theatre, and it was no accident that he sometimes likened performers such as Kemble to their painter contemporaries, in adverse comparison to the age of Garrick. On the other hand his championship of the intimate genre of Wilkie or the elegant and sentimental neo-classicism of Canova or Gibson, is proof enough that he had adapted to the finer sensibilities of the Romantics. Quality, as well as power of feeling, was always his requirement in the arts, and thus his commentaries on painting old and new, with their felicitous turns of phrase and based on personal response, are among the finest expressions of old-world connoisseurship before the onset of scientific approaches to such matters as date or attribution. He judged with his heart as well as his eye: both the critic and the painter must be a poet. Wilkie was referring not only to Beaumont's own painting but to his whole mode of thought when he wrote that his was 'an aim the most elevated and enlarged': 'The beautiful style of art he professed was abstract and general, — a poetical recollection rather than a minute detail of nature, full of sentiment and feeling.'[5] Beaumont had a horror of all that struck him as pretentious and meretricious or of extremes of fantasy or realism that might diminish the poise and equilibrium of recollected emotion. After Wilkie had completed *The Blind Fiddler* Beaumont wrote: 'Save me from myself is as rational a petition in painting as in morals...some peculiar colour is always striving to get the better of an artist — some finesse in pencilling, under the pretence of neatness, splendour, or despatch, is for ever ready to take possesion.'[6] When he saw such things, he added: 'I shall not fail to act the part of a flapper'. Nor had he, but in old age he had mellowed, impressed perhaps by Coleridge's heroic view of genius as being above criticism and creating its own taste; to Wilkie he wrote in 1825:

> Whenever a man is anxious to discover small faults, it is all over with him: I never knew one of those cavillers come to any thing. Faith is as necessary in art as in more sacred subjects. If we begin with doubting, we shall never be certain: we must take something for granted, and, above all, receive with reverence the decided opinions of ages.[7]

With his poet friends, Beaumont's aesthetic judgement was not involved and he was quite relaxed, and Coleridge's powerful advocacy at the beginning of their friendship had confirmed the respect that his own literary forebears had given him for their calling. Coleridge had written to Lady Beaumont: 'To be incapable of a feeling for poetry, in my sense of the word, is to be without love of human nature and reverence for God',[8] and imbued with the eighteenth-century belief that art elevated Man, Sir George was bound to approve such proselytising. Even if he did not always share his wife's passion for the new nature poetry, he found himself moved by passages such as those in 'Tintern Abbey' that reach out beyond everyday experience. Poor Coleridge proved a disappointment, but Beaumont's admiration and affection found fulfilment in Wordsworth, who had stated early in their correspondence: 'There can be no valuable friendship where the parties are not mutually capable of instructing and delighting each other',[9] thus putting Beaumont on his mettle to contribute more than his patron's pounds — which indeed were not welcomed. Allowing for a degree of mutual flattery — 'Thus do these persons bepraise each other', Farington once wryly remarked[10] — it was a remarkable friendship, and, if Beaumont gained more than he gave, he and Lady Beaumont have to be credited not only with practical and moral encouragement, but above all for wasting no time in bringing the Lake poets to the notice of the London world and stimulating the interest of artists and intelligentsia, to the benefit of the Romantic movement in this country.

Beaumont's letters to Wordsworth, full of quotations, are soul-searching, whereas in those to Mulgrave, his other great friend and support in later life, the lighter vein must reflect the genial peer's refusal to allow Beaumont's depressions to intrude. Mulgrave's infectious vitality was probably the best palliative and it was doubly fortunate that the Phipps family, which virtually became Beaumont's by adoption, should have been headed by a man of such achievement who rose to unexpected political heights and could keep Beaumont in touch with the world of power, while sharing his love of painting and joining him in patronage. Beaumont was ever conscious of the need for such friends, not least during the long winters at Dunmow and Coleorton when he suffered from the *ennui* that was the curse of the comfortably-off and it was hardly surprising that he sometimes returned to London with rather too much to say. It was his year on the Continent in 1821–22 that gave him a new lease of life and a wider perspective, and rallied his strength for his final and most important contribution to the art he cherished: the creation of the National Gallery. It is by this and his efforts to 'serve' the artists he loved that he would wish to be remembered. Wilkie said it all in his letter of condolence to Lady Beaumont:

> your Ladyship well knows how warm and steady has been the friendship with which he has honoured me. In the time of sickness, as well as in health, how kind, how

unwearied have been his attentions! And in the time of adverse fortune, which he has tried to alleviate, as well as in the prosperity to which he has so much contributed, how sympathising and how generous has he been in his conduct towards me! I may indeed boast other advantages — the society and contact with a mind so endowed for the elevation of one's views, and for giving a favourable bias to one's character, has influenced, and I hope improved, my conduct and pursuits![11]

*   *   *

Grosvenor Square was under dust sheets in the September after Beaumont's death when Haydon wandering through the deserted gallery reflected: 'here have assembled more men of real genius, and more pretenders to it, than in any other room perhaps in Europe'.[12] In the spring of 1828, full of dread at facing London alone, Lady Beaumont had been relieved to find 'the solitude of a great city as profound as a wilderness'.[13] She was fortunate to be visited by young Sara Coleridge, who found her conversation more interesting than ever and was happy to share the religious readings. There was much business, particularly carrying out the many bequests, which included those to Wilkie, Wordsworth, Southey and Mrs Coleridge (but not her husband, although Lady Beaumont left him £50 in her own will to compensate for what Charles Lamb considered an insult); and the godchildren were remembered, including Beverley's youngest son, Charles Beaumont Percy, the next legatee should the Beaumont line fail. Less pleasant was the emergence of a claimant to the baronetcy in the unattractive shape of a ribbon-maker from Coventry who had five children and appeared at the funeral. Redesdale once again rallied to Lady Beaumont's side — it transpired that a pretender had already been seen off in the early Dunmow days — and the case never came to court though the threat looked great throughout that July.

That month the new baronet and his wife came to Coleorton to see it for the first time in summer and found the old lady busy 'improving' the grounds, encouraged by Price, who had lost his wife in 1826, and Wordsworth, who was a tower of strength and brought Mary to stay in the autumn. The dowager had tried through friends to obtain a fellowship at Merton College for the Wordsworths' son, John, but he was reduced to accepting a curacy under Merewether at Whitwick, a rough parish four miles from Coleorton, where his aunt Dorothy came to share his dull existence during the winter of 1828–29. That April, Dorothy was seriously ill and Mary came to join them. Dorothy and John had been frequent visitors to Coleorton, on one occasion finding Lady Beaumont surrounded by young Beaumonts, including the new heir, George Howland, born 12 September 1828.

A compulsive learner to the last, the old lady was taking organ lessons on the instrument in the hall, which became perishingly cold in winter, and even she noticed 'the freezing blasts' of her favourite breakfast room. She had decided to fulfil Sir George's wish to leave the Michelangelo tondo to the Academy, and a copy was commissioned from Sarti for the staircase, where it remains today (the house, divided into offices, is maintained well — and warm — by its owner, British Coal). The Pannini and the Gibson were named as heirlooms in the will, and, although Beaumont never saw it, the *Psyche* (Pl. 98) was the last work of any consequence to arrive at Coleorton, having been exhibited at the Academy of 1827, the same year as Constable's *Cenotaph*.

230

98.   John Gibson: *Psyche and the Zephyrs* (present location unknown).

Succeeding generations spent their increasing wealth on improving the amenities and extending the house — another storey was added by Frederick Pepys Cockerell in 1862 — until, around the turn of the century, the pressing demands of a Parisian love-nest caused the tenth baronet to step up the sales of family treasures.

Lady Beaumont's was a brave performance and it was a just reward for her many acts of kindness to the Wordsworths that she should see so much of them in the long two years she lived on alone. Despite delicate health, her mind was as active as ever and her last letters to the poet pleaded the cause of Catholic emancipation. It was the end of a great family friendship when she died on 12 July 1829, but they rejoiced, for 'she was ripe for the change'.[14]

Wordsworth visited Coleorton again in November 1830. Much needed improvements were in train — the Grosvenor Square lease having been sold to provide funds — but he found the new baronet, who had already served as High Sheriff for Leicestershire and was proving capable in business affairs, dreading another winter, having lost his second son the previous month after family illness. Despite the welcome, Wordsworth left feeling quite desolate: as he rode home through Derbyshire in a storm, the words for which he had long been searching in order to do justice to his old friend, came to him at long last and he composed the 'Elegaic Musings':

> With copious eulogy in prose or rhyme
> Graven on the tomb we struggle against Time,
> Alas, how feebly ! but our feelings rise
> And still we struggle when a good man dies.
> Such offering BEAUMONT dreaded and forbade,
> A spirit meek in self-abasement clad.
> Yet *here* at least, though few have numbered days
> That shunned so modestly the light of praise,
> His graceful manners, and the temperate ray
> Of that arch fancy which would round him play,
> Brightening a converse never known to swerve
> From courtesy and delicate reserve;
> That sense, the bland philosophy of life,
> Which checked discussion ere it warmed to strife:
> Those rare accomplishments, and varied powers,
> Might have their record among sylvan bowers...

The lines were inspired by Beaumont's inscription for his memorial tablet in the church at Coleorton: 'Enter not into judgement with thy servant, O Lord!' — a choice that might appear ironical, but was in fact his own humble and heartfelt acknowledgement of his own inadequacies. Wordsworth caught the essence and the best of Beaumont, who, for all his faults, must rank as one of the greatest of connoisseurs, and the most enlightened of British patrons — a benign and gifted man who could obstinately, sometimes misguidedly, stick to his guns, but, at the end, so justifiably in his consistent advocacy of a national gallery.

APPENDIX I
Plan of Coleorton Hall and Grounds

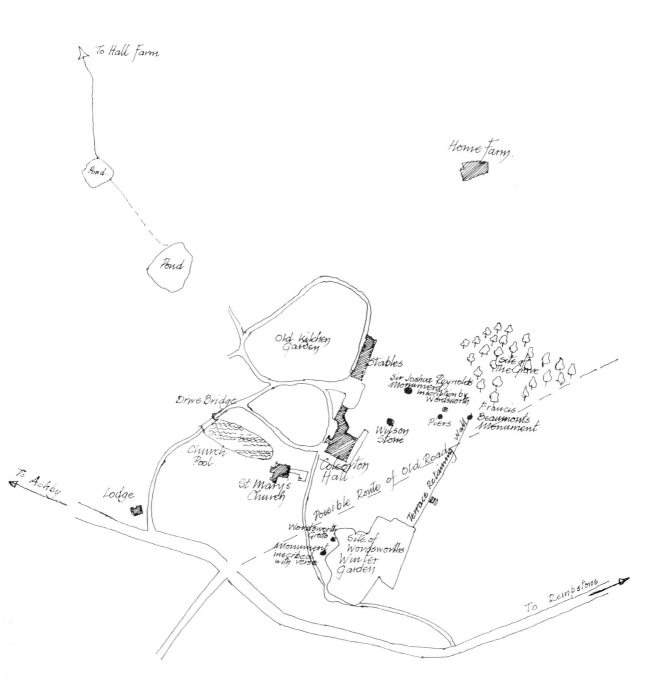

APPENDIX II
THE BEAUMONT GIFT

Titles and attributions given in parentheses are those of the original presentation. Unless otherwise stated, works are in the National Gallery, London.

Inventory No.	*Artist*	*Title*
19	Claude	*Landscape: Narcissus* (Narcissus and Echo)
40	Poussin	*Landscape: A Man washing his Feet at a Fountain* (Landscape with Figures)
43	Rembrandt	*The Deposition*
51	Ascribed to Rembrandt (Rembrandt)	*A Seated Man with a Stick, 'A Jew Merchant'*
55	After Claude (Claude)	*Landscape: The Death of Procris*
58	Claude	*Landscape with a Goatherd and Goats*
61	Claude	*Landscape: Hagar and the Angel* (Landscape with Figures)
64	Bourdon	*The Return of the Ark*
66	Rubens	*The Château de Steen* (Autumn — The Château de Steen)
71	Both	*A Rocky Landscape with Herdsmen and Muleteers* (Landscape — Morning)
99	Wilkie	*The Blind Fiddler* (Tate Gallery, London)
106	Reynolds	*A Man's Head* (Tate Gallery, London)
108	Wilson	*Tivoli, Ruins of Villa of Maecenas* (Tate Gallery, London)
110	Wilson	*The Destruction of the Children of Niobe* (Transferred to Tate Gallery in 1919. Destroyed by enemy action 1944)
126	West	*Pylades and Orestes* (Tate Gallery, London)
127	Canaletto	*Venice: Campo S. Vidal and S. Maria della Carità* (The Stone Mason's Yard)

BIBLIOGRAPHICAL REFERENCES

Unless otherwise stated, all letters from Wordsworth and Coleridge quoted in the text with their appropriate dates are taken from Wordsworth Correspondence and Coleridge Correspondence (Griggs) respectively (see below).

Unless otherwise stated, place of publication is London.

Angelo	H. Angelo, *Reminiscences of Henry Angelo*, 2 vols, 1828.
Builder	The issue of 5 May 1867, pp. 307–8, carried an article, signed P.C., quoting George Agar Ellis and reprinting four of the five letters from GB to Ellis now with the Trustees of the Chatsworth Settlement.
Clayden	P.W. Clayden, *Rogers and his Contemporaries*, vol I, 1889
Cunningham, *Lives*	A. Cunningham, *The Lives of the Most Eminent British Painters*, 3 vols, revised edition 1879.
Cunningham, *Wilkie*	A. Cunningham, *The Life of Sir David Wilkie*, 3 vols 1843.
Griggs	E.L. Griggs ed., *Collected Letters of Samuel Taylor Coleridge*, vols II and III, 1956 and 1959.
Haydon, *Autobiography*	B.R. Haydon, *The Autobiography and Memoirs of Benjamin Robert Haydon*, ed. T. Taylor; new edition revised by A. Huxley, 3 vols, 1926.
Haydon, *Diary*	*The Diary of Benjamin Robert Haydon*, ed. W.B. Pope, 5 vols, Cambridge, Mass. 1963.
Jones, *Memoirs*	*The Memoirs of Thomas Jones*, ed. A.P. Oppé, *Walpole Society*, vol. XXXII, 1946–8.
Knight, *Memorials*	W. Knight, *Memorials of Coleorton. Being Letters from Coleridge, Wordsworth and his Sister, Southey, and Sir Walter Scott*, 2 vols, Edinburgh, 1887.
JCC	*John Constable's Correspondence*, ed. R.B. Beckett, Suffolk Records Society, 6 vols, 1962–68, and *Further Documents and Correspondence*, ed. Leslie Parris and Conal Shields (documents) and Ian

	Fleming-Williams (correspondence), Suffolk Records Society and Tate Gallery, 1975.
Leslie, *Constable*	C.R. Leslie, *Memoirs of the Life of John Constable*, ed. J. Mayne, 1951.
Whitley	W.T. Whitley, *Artists and their Friends in England 1700–1799*, 2 vols, 1968 edition.
Wordsworth Correspondence	Ernest de Selincourt ed., *The Letters of William and Mary Wordsworth*, 2nd edition, vol II revised by Mary Moorman and Alan G. Hill, 1969–70 and vol III revised by Alan Hill, 1978.
FD	*The Diary of Joseph Farington*, 14 vols, New Haven and London, 1978–84; vols I–VI ed. Kenneth Garlick and Angus Macintyre, vols VII–XIV ed. Kathryn Cave.

The following personal and archival abbreviations are used throughout:

GB	Sir George Beaumont
LB	Lady Beaumont
STC	Samuel Taylor Coleridge
DW	Dorothy Wordsworth
MW	Mary Wordsworth
WW	William Wordsworth
BC	Beaumont Collection
BL	British Library
BM	British Museum
DCT	Dove Cottage Trustees
MCA	Mulgrave Castle Archive
PML	Pierpont Morgan Library, New York

NOTES

INTRODUCTION

1. Leslie, *Constable*, p. 98.
2. Haydon, *Diary*, I, p. 143.
3. *Ibid.*, p. 125.
4. Constable to WW, 15 June 1836. DCT.
5. GB to Gilpin, 4 September 1802. Bodleian Library, Oxford.
6. Wilkie to LB, 12 March 1827, in Cunningham, *Wilkie*, II, p. 397.
7. Severn, recollections of Rome; transcriptions in Whiting collection.
8. Haydon, *Diary*, I, p. 146.
9. Haydon, *Autobiography*, I, pp. 405–6.

CHAPTER I

For Dunmow history we are indebted to Dr Castleden for lending Dorothy C. Dowsett, *Dunmow through The Ages*, Essex Record Office (no date).

1. Cooper's Memoir in A.F.J. Brown ed., *Essex People 1750–1900*, 12 June 1759. Essex Record Office 1972.
2. Amongst documents remaining with the Beaumonts' Essex lawyers and agents, Wade & Davies of Dunmow, are the 6th baronet's will and marriage settlement and the lease from the Bishop of London for Parsonage Farm. In 1799 the 7th baronet bought its reversion for £7,701.10s.
3. Miss Isabella Howland. Collection Mrs McLane van Ingen, New York.
4. Angelo, I, pp. 212 and 217. For Eton, see Sir Thomas Frankland, *Nugae Etoniensis*, 1765–66, *Etoniana* X, 1907 and A. Austen Leigh ed., *Eton College Lists*, 1678–1790, 1907.
5. On Cozens, see Kim Sloan, *Alexander and John Robert Cozens, the Poetry of Landscape*, 1986.
6. Langham Hall was advertised as to let in the Ipswich Journal, 20 March 1773, and in 1779 Gates was taxed for three servants there (Beaumont had four at Dunmow). He also owned the Higham millhouse. We are indebted to John Bensusan-Butt for this and much other information about Essex life.

7. GB to Dr Monro, 30 September 1816. Victoria and Albert Museum Library.

CHAPTER II

For information on amateur theatricals we are indebted to Sybil Rosenfeld who kindly lent her notes. See her *Temples of Thespis*, 1978, X, pp. 146–53 for 'The Theatricals of Two Country Squires'.

1. Davy to GB, 7 May 1773, in Charles Davy, *Letters addressed chiefly to a Young Gentleman upon Subjects of Literature*, 1787, II pp. 479–80.
2. J. B. Malchair, 'Observations on Landskipp Drawing with many and various Examples intended for the use of beginners'. Ian Fleming-Williams Collection.
3. Ashmolean Museum, Oxford.
4. The oval *River Landscape with Rustic Lovers*; John Hayes, *The Landscape Paintings of Thomas Gainsborough*, 1982, I, p. 489, see no. 128 repr.
5. Davy to his son Frederick, 21 April, 1777, in Davy, *op. cit.*, II, p. 540.
6. Jones, *Memoirs*, p. 32.
7. *Ibid.*, p. 31.
8. *Ibid.*
9. FD, 25 June 1797.
10. Price to GB, 3 June 1795.
11. Jones, *Memoirs*, p. 26.
12. *Ibid.*, p. 35 (23 January 1775). The picture is unknown today.
13. For the other drawings, see Benedict Nicolson, *John Hamilton Mortimer*, catalogue of an exhibition at Eastbourne and Kenwood, 1968, nos 29, 31, 60, 61, 64, 65, 72, 87, 88, 90, 93, 111.
14. Angelo, I, pp. 148–50.
15. The drawings were the *Rosa* and *Lairesse* already mentioned and *Monsters* (Nicolson, *op. cit.*, cat. nos 87, 88).
16. Yale Center for British Art, New Haven.
17. Whitley, I, p. 380.
18. National Museum of Wales.
19. GB to Gilpin, 9 November 1802. Bodleian Library, Oxford.
20. Angelo, I, p. 255.
21. J. T. Smith, *Nollekens and his Times*, 1829, II, p. 149.

22. GB to Bannister, 20 November 1820, in G. A. Adolphus, *Memoirs of John Bannister*, 1828, II, p. 278.
23. GB to Cradock, 9 February 1826, in Joseph Cradock, *Literary and Miscellaneous Memoirs*, 1828, IV, p. 257.
24. GB to Ellis, 9 February 1824, in the *Builder*.
25. Woollett's drawing from that day, inscribed with the names of the party, is in the BM.
26. GB to Smith, 27 January 1805 and 19 December 1805, Houghton Library, Harvard. (BL MSS fiche, RP 541.) We are indebted to Mr Frank Simpson for drawing this correspondence to our attention.
27. Cradock, *op. cit.*
28. GB to WW, 20 February 1821. DCT.
29. Smith to GB, 28 January 1805. BL MSS fiche, RP 541.
30. GB to Bannister, 20 November 1820, in Bannister, *op. cit.*
31. Sold Sotheby's, 30 June 1948. Both lot 44.
32. Tate Gallery, London.
33. LB to DW, 1 May 1808. DCT.
34. James Boswell, *Life of Johnson*, 1831, IV, p. 514.
35. Given in Clayden, p. 514.
36. FD, 1 June 1808.
37. A. Graves and W. V. Cronin, *History of the Works of Sir Joshua Reynolds*, 1899, p. 70.
38. C. R. Leslie and Tom Taylor, *Life and Times of Sir Joshua Reynolds*, 1865, I, pp. 112–13.
39. Haydon, *Diary*, V, p. 575.
40. Brooke in John Nichols, *Illustrations of Literary History of the 18th Century*, 1831, VI, p. 382.

CHAPTER III

1. National Portrait Gallery, London.
2. Northamptonshire Record Office.
3. Mary Hartley to William Gilpin, 29 July 1786. Bodleian Library, Oxford.
4. STC to WW [23 July 1803], Griggs II.
5. Plate 31, *Antiquities of Great Britain*, 1807, I.
6. Whereabouts unknown.
7. *Observations, relative chiefly to Picturesque Beauty, made in the year, 1772, on Several Parts of England especially the Lakes etc.*, 2 vols, 1786.
8. *A Description of the Lake at Keswick*, 1770, partly reprinted in Thomas West, *Guide to the Lakes*, 1789 (4th edition), p. 194.
9. West, *op cit*, p. 5.
10. Derwent Bay House, dated 15 August in sketchbook. DCT.
11. Leeds City Art Galleries.
12. Robert Southey to Allan Cunningham, 3 June 1833, in C. C. Southey ed., *Life and Correspondence of Robert Southey*, 1850, IV,

p. 215. Hearne's panorama is lost.
13. Charlotte Burney to Fanny Burney, June 1780. Charlotte Barrett ed., *Diary and Letters of Madame D'Arblay*, 1876, I, p. 298.
14. Walpole to Harcourt, 10 June 1780, W. S. Lewis ed., *Horace Walpole's Correspondence*, 1973, XXXV, p. 503.
15. Houghton Library, Harvard.
16. Sold Sotheby's, 15 April 1953, lot 14.
17. Private Collection.
18. Private Collection.
19. Sold Sotheby's, 21 November 1984, lot 15, now Private Collection. Thirty-six views.

CHAPTER IV

1. Sir Nathaniel W. Wraxall, *Historical Memoirs of my own Times*, 1884, II, p. 319.
2. Anon., *A Tour to Spa*, 1774.
3. Lady Theresa Lewis, ed., *Extracts of the Journals and Correspondence of Miss Berry*, 1865, I, p. 31.
4. 'An English Woman' [Lady Anna Miller], *Letters from Italy*, I, p. 59, Letter VIII dated 3 October 1770, and Letter IX, 16 October 1770, p. 97.
5. Earl of Ilchester ed., *The Journals of Elizabeth, Lady Holland*, 1907, II, p. 67.
6. Reported later to Wilkie. Cunningham, *Wilkie*, III, p. 219.
7. GB to Price in Uvedale Price, *Essays on the Picturesque*, 1810, II p. 406.
8. National Gallery, London.
9. More to GB, Edinburgh University Library, Laing MSS, IV, 25, f. 25.
10. We are indebted to Dr Gertrud Seidmann for information regarding Marchant.
11. Ramsay, Diary, 18 December 1782, 26 February 1783. National Library of Scotland, MS 1833.
12. John Moore, *A View of Society and Manners in Italy*, 1781, II, p. 79.
13. GB in conversation, in E. V. Lucas, *Charles Lamb and the Lloyds*, 1898, p. 250.
14. Jones, *Memoirs*, p. 121 (11 March 1783).

CHAPTER V

1. Malchair to Skippe, 12 February 1784. We are indebted to Ian Fleming-Williams for drawing this letter to our attention.
2. Ashmolean Museum, Oxford.
3. Henry Crabb Robinson, MS Diary, VIII, p. 35 (26 April 1820). Dr Williams Library.
4. FD, 15 May 1809.
5. Price to GB, 12 February 1802. PML.
6. *An Account of the Remains of the Worship of Priapus lately existing at Isernia, in the Kingdom of Naples...*, 1786.
7. Annotated copy of C.R. Leslie's *Life of Constable*, 1843, Yale Center for British

Art, Library, ND 497 C7 and L47, copy 2.

8. Cunningham, *Lives*, I, p. 273.
9. GB to Henry Briggs (painter, 1791–1844), 11 November (?)1829. Birmingham City Art Gallery.
10. GB to unknown correspondent (Gilpin?), in Cunningham, *Lives*, III, p. 4 (MS now in the PML).
11. *Ibid.*, p. 5.
12. GB to Southey, (?)1821, Huntington Library, San Marino.
13. Whereabouts unknown. The subject was evidently a woodland landscape with a pool.
14. GB to Gilpin, 9 November 1802. Bodleian Library, Oxford.
15. More to GB. Edinburgh University Library, Laing MSS, IV, 25, f. 25.
16. More to GB. *Ibid.*, f. 70.
17. National Gallery, London.
18. More to GB. Edinburgh University Library, Laing MSS, IV, 25 ff. 70; 27–8; also 25.
19. National Trust, Anglesey Abbey.
20. Yale Center for British Art, New Haven.
21. Gilpin to Mary Hartley, 8 July 1786. Bodleian Library, Oxford, Eng. Misc. d 572.
22. Mary Hartley to Gilpin, 29 July 1786. Bodleian Library, Oxford, Eng. Misc. d 572.
23. Dulwich College Gallery, London.
24. Constable to John Fisher, 20 September 1821, in *JCC*, XII, p. 74.
25. Constable, in *JCC*, XIV, p. 80.
26. James Northcote, *Life of Sir Joshua Reynolds*, II, 1878, p. 214.
27. Reynolds to GB. 28 August 1786. Yale Center for British Art, MS Reynolds 19.
28. Leslie and Taylor, *op. cit.*, II, p. 419.
29. National Gallery, London.
30. Leslie and Taylor, *op. cit.*, I, p. 478.

CHAPTER VI

1. Haydon, *Autobiography*, I, p.49 and FD, 9 January 1795.
2. Mulgrave to Windham, 1 December 1792, Earl of Rosebery ed., *The Windham Papers*, 1913, I, pp. 107–9.
3. Beaumont's bank account at Hoare's shows payments to Hakewill of £200 in 1790, £40 in 1791 and £160 in 1792. Mr Howard Colvin kindly provided the information about Playfair. See also Colvin's *Biographical Dictionary of British Architects 1600–1840*, 1978.
4. Cunningham, *Lives*, III, p.4.
5. FD, 5 November 1795. Mitford's letters of 25 January and 14 February are in the Public Record Office, London (30/8/170).
6. *Monthly Magazine*, August 1800, p. 37.
7. FD, 4 April 1794.

8. FD, 11 April 1794.
9. *A liberal critique on the present exhibition of the Royal Academy*, 1794 (new edition), referring to no. 126, Beaumont's landscape.
10. Price to GB, 2 February 1795. PML.
11. Price to GB. 5 September 1797. PML.
12. Price to GB, 4 December 1794. PML.
13. Price to LB, 2 February 1795. PML.
14. FD, 6–15 December 1794.
15. FD, 29 December 1794 and 9 January 1795.
16. FD, 26 January 1794.
17. GB to Lady Inchiquin; transcription in Whiting collection.
18. *Conversation of humorous characters*, whereabouts unknown.
19. Price to GB, 2 December 1797. PML.
20. Price to LB, 2 February 1795. PML.
21. Constable, Letterpress to frontispiece, *English Landscape Scenery*.
22. FD, 19 August 1795.
23. GB to Gilpin, 7 December 1801. Bodleian Library, Oxford.
24. FD, 11 November 1795.
25. FD, 22 and 24 November 1795.
26. FD, 29 and 24 November 1795.
27. Tate Gallery, London.
28. FD, 10 February 1796.
29. *Ibid.*
30. FD, 3 June 1796.
31. FD, 22 March 1797.
32. FD, 18 May 1796.
33. Rose to Pitt, 11 April 1796. Suffolk Record Office, Ipswich, Tomline MSS, HA119 T108/44.
34. FD, 18 May 1796.
35. FD, 23 April 1796.
36. FD, 2 May and 5 June 1796.
37. Price to GB, 8 March 1798.
38. FD, 11 and 26 March 1797.
39. GB to Mulgrave, 30 November 1806. MCA.
40. GB to Lady Mulgrave, 8 October 1811. MCA.

CHAPTER VII

1. FD, 20 February 1796 and 17 July 1797.
2. FD, 26 June 1796.
3. FD, 22 May 1796.
4. FD, 26 and 28 February, 9 and 11 March 1797.
5. Whereabouts unknown. See FD, 25 June 1796.
6. FD, 9 April 1797.
7. FD, 10 December 1797.
8. FD, 15 and 28 April 1797.
9. FD, 12 May 1797.
10. FD, 16 July 1797.
11. FD, 5 April 1797.
12. FD, 17 July 1797.
13. FD, 25 June 1797.
14. FD, 7 April 1798.

15. National Gallery, London.
16. FD, 17 July 1797.
17. *A Scene from Foote's Comedy 'Taste' — Lady Penteazle* and *A Scene from 'The Taming of the Shrew'*, both Sotheby's, 30 June 1948, lot 44. GB originally paid £50 for the pair.
18. FD, 14 July 1796. GB paid 8 guineas.
19. FD, 2 May 1797.
20. FD, 16 November 1797.
21. FD, 9 April 1797.
22. FD, 16 November 1797.
23. Price to LB, 21 December 1818.
24. FD, 28 October 1812.
25. Price to GB, 7 December 1797. PML.
26. Price to GB, 28 January 1798. PML.
27. Price to GB, 8 March 1798. PML.
28. Price to GB, 18 December 1797. PML.
29. Price to GB, 15 January 1798. PML.
30. Price to GB, 28 November 1797. PML.
31. Price to GB, 20 December 1797. PML.
32. Price to GB, 28 January 1798. PML.
33. Price to GB, 8 March 1798. PML. The description of Wouverman's picture appears in the preface of *Essays on the Picturesque*, 1798, II, p.v.
34. Price to GB, 8 March 1798. PML.
35. FD, 6 June 1798.
36. FD, 9 July 1798.
37. FD, 7 November 1798.
38. Whitworth Art Gallery, Manchester. After GB's death LB gave this album to Bowles's daughter, Anne Sturges Bourne, who had seen many of the drawings made at Benarth in 1802. Another album was given to Lady Susan Percy, and has since been split up.
39. For the recipe, see FD, 10 September 1800; also GB to Ibbetson, 15 December 1799 in R. M. Clay, *Julius Caesar Ibbetson*, 1948, p. 83.
40. The sketch is in the Huntington Library, San Marino.
41. Only eight can be identified today: *Keswick, Derwentwater* and *Culloth Force* (private collections); *Wathenlath* (Eton College); *Borrowdale* (DCT); *Grange Bridge* and a sepia *Coastal View* (BC) — all after pencil sketches by GB; and *Conway Castle*.
42. Leslie, *Constable*, p. 5.
43. FD, 1 February 1796.
44. 28 May 1798. Mrs. Henry Baring ed., *Windham's Diary*, 1866, p. 397.
45. MCA, dated 1799.
46. 17 May 1799, Miss Berry to Mrs Cholmeley, in Lady Theresa Lewis, *op. cit.*, II, p. 92.
47. *Ibid.*, 23 May 1799.
48. Colman to GB, 2 June 1812, PML 2803.
49. FD, 2 March 1799.
50. FD, 13 April 1799. Smirke and Farington's drawings were presumably those of scenes from *The Merry Wives of Windsor*, exhibited Bolton, Hastings and Oxford; *Joseph Farington*, 1977, nos 81, 82 repr. Smirke's subject is untraced.

51. FD, 24 May 1799.
52. FD, 10 June 1799.
53. *Landscape with the Father of Psyche sacrificing to Apollo* and *Landscape with the Arrival of Aeneas at Pallanteum.* FD, 12 May 1799.
54. FD, 12 June 1799.
55. FD, 20 May 1799.
56. John Mander, acting for GB, signed on 16 August a one-year lease of Benarth from 7 October 1799 (Caernarvonshire Record Office, Poole 2934). We are indebted to Michael Pidgley for this information.

CHAPTER VIII

1. For Boultbee's accounts up to 1797, see Beaumont *v* Boultbee, Public Record Office, London, C 35/504. For court proceedings, see Vesey Jnr., *Cases in Chancery*, V, pp. 484–96 (15 July 1800), VII, pp. 599–617, (10 August 1805) and XI, pp. 358–60 (8 August 1805). See also FD, 16 December 1805 for GB's estimate of only £12,000 received in compensation.
2. John Throsby, *Select Views in Leicestershire*, II, 1790, p. 427.
3. FD, 7 September 1800.
4. FD, 21 September 1800.
5. Price to LB, 27 April 1802. PML.
6. FD, 26 October 1800.
7. Granville Leveson Gower to his mother, Lady Stafford, 7 February 1801., in Castalia Countess Granville, ed., *Lord Granville Leveson Gower Private Correspondence, 1781–1821* 1917, I, p. 289.
8. GB to Mulgrave, 28 July 1802. MCA.
9. GB to Gilpin, 4 September 1802. Bodleian Library, Oxford.
10. Dance Papers, Soane Museum, London.
11. Dance to Soane, 2 August 1802, Soane Correspondence, Soane Museum, London. Soane had built Tyringham Hall, Buckingham, which was an influence on Dance's final design.
12. Price to GB, 31 May 1803. PML.
13. Price to GB, August 1803. PML.
14. FD, 21 March 1804.
15. GB to WW, 24 October 1803. DCT. GB paid £100 for three old houses and two small fields, thus making Wordsworth a freeholder of Cumberland.
16. Crabb Robinson's diary, 4 March 1811, quoted in P. P. Howe, *The Life of William Hazlitt*, 1922, reprinted in Penguin Paperback, 1949, p. 95.
17. Coleridge to WW, 23 July 1803. Griggs, II, p. 500.
18. STC to John Rickman, 13 February 1804, in Griggs II and Kathleen Coburn ed., *The Notebooks of Samuel Taylor Coleridge*, II, 1983.
19. FD, 25 March 1804.
20. Coburn, *op. cit.*, I, 1731 and note.
21. GB to Coleridge, April 1804.

22. GB to WW, 24 October 1803. DCT. This poem, 'Anticipation. October 1803', appeared in the *Poetical Register*, III, p. 340; the others sent were 'Degenerate Douglas' and 'Vanguard of Liberty'.
23. GB to WW, 5 February 1805. DCT.
24. FD, 21 March 1804.
25. GB to WW, 3 March 1805. DCT. Both LB's portrait of 1808 and Dame Rachel's exhibited RA 1801 are unknown today.
26. GB to WW, 23 March 1805. DCT.
27. GB to WW, 24 October 1803. DCT.
28. Price to GB, 9 June 1804. PML.
29. Price to GB, 24 August 1804. PML.
30. Price's portrait remained with Dance (Price to GB, 9 June 1804.); Hodgkinson is still BC; Beaumont is National Portrait Gallery.
31. Price to GB, 9 June 1804. PML.
32. Throsby, *op. cit.*, p. 427.
33. GB to Whitbread, 13 and 20 October, 1805. Bedford Record Office, W1/4073–4, by courtesy of S. C. Whitbread.
34. See William Wordsworth, *Guide to the Lakes*, 1835, p. 66.
35. GB to WW, 25 November 1805. DCT.
36. Price to LB, 24 August 1804. PML.
37. FD, 30 March 1806.
38. GB to WW, 5 February 1805. DCT.
39. FD, 12 December 1804.
40. Smith's published letter dated 13 February 1805 is in the Houghton Library, Harvard.
41. FD, 18 March 1805.
42. FD, 19 April 1806.
43. FD, 22 July 1806.
44. FD, 8 July 1806.
45. GB to WW, 21 July 1805. DCT.
46. GB to WW, 21 July 1805. DCT.
47. GB to WW, 5 March 1806. DCT.
48. GB to WW, 25 November 1805. DCT.
49. GB to WW, 5 March 1806. DCT.
50. GB to WW, 5 March 1806. DCT.
51. GB to WW, 29 June 1806, DCT.
52. GB to WW, 5 March 1806. DCT.
53. FD, 28 March 1809.
54. GB to WW, August 1806. DCT. Wordsworth had already sent in October 1805, 'Yes! hope may with strong desire keep pace' and, in September 1806, 'No mortal object did these eyes behold', both translated from Michelangelo.

CHAPTER IX

1. WW to GB, 6 November 1806.
2. The poem was addressed to WW: 'Composed for the greater part on the same night after the finishing of his recitation of the Poem in thirteen Books, on the Growth of his own Mind.' See Knight, *Memorials*, I, p. 213 for the version given in a letter to GB, January 1807.
3. GB to Coleridge, 8 February 1807, and again early that year (undated) in reply to Coleridge's letter which is lost.
4. Translated Jeremy Collier, 1701, 'Meditations', p. 8. See Evelyn Mitchell's M. A. thesis, 'Sir George Beaumont and his Contacts with English Romanticism', 1938 (London University.)
5. Line 27, 'Earth helped him with the cry of blood.' GB had sent WW his ancestor's poems 21 July 1805.
6. FD, 17 June 1809.
7. GB to WW, 25 February 1808. DCT.
8. Southey to GB, 4 January 1808, Duke of Northumberland's Archives, MS 725.
9. J. Simmons, ed., *Robert Southey. Letters from England*, 1951.
10. 'The Thorn' is in a private collection, *Peter Bell* belongs DCT.
11. GB to WW, 25 February 1808 and 4 July 1814 refer to GB's wish for an engraving to accompany WW's poems. DCT.
12. GB to WW, 19 July 1814. DCT.
13. FD, 12 January 1808.
14. FD, 9 August 1808.
15. LB to DW, 22 November 1822. DCT.
16. LB to DW, 11 May 1808 DCT.
17. FD, 1809.
18. GB to WW, [autumn 1807]. DCT.
19. FD, 7 June 1809.
20. GB to WW, 13 November 1810. DCT.
21. Whereabouts of the picture is not known. WW wrote 28 August 1811: 'the images of the smoke and the Travellers are taken from your Picture'.
22. Before this poem was published in 1842, Wordsworth added another, 'Upon Perusing the Foregoing Epistle Thirty Years after its Composition', together with a note explaining Loughrigg Tarn's resemblance to Lake Nemi or *Speculum Dianae* and his regret that Beaumont did not build there, and set an example of a house suited to its setting. The land was sold in 1819, see GB to WW, 23 March 1819. DCT.
23. This poem was cut in stone and placed near the cedar tree close to the winter garden. The tree was blown down in 1854 but the tablet has been restored.
24. GB to WW, 4 November 1811. DCT. The small niche in the winter-garden bank remains without any inscription.
25. GB to WW, 28 October 1811, querying the first person; WW replying on 16 November with the alternative version. DCT.
26. GB to WW, 10 August 1806. DCT. In 1810 Alexander Chalmers published *Works of English Poets* including poems by Sir John, thus forestalling Sir George.
27. GB. to WW, 4 November 1811. DCT.
28. GB to Southey, 5 August 1809. PML.
29. GB to WW, 28 October 1811. DCT. WW's comments followed, 16 November to GB. Wordsworth Correspondence.

30. FD, 16 and 17 October 1812.
31. Hon. Edmund Phipps ed., *Memoirs of Robert Plumer Ward*. 1850, I, p. 477 (17 April 1812), dining with Sir John and Lady Swinburne with William Wilberforce present.
32. Lady Theresa Lewis, *op. cit.*, II, p. 92 (12 May 1809).
33. LB to WW, 2 June 1814. DCT.
34. FD, 6 May 1806.
35. GB to Lonsdale, 5 March 1809. Lonsdale Papers, Carlisle Record Office.
36. GB to WW, 28 October 1811. DCT.
37. Price to GB, 18 March 1815. PML.
38. GB to WW, 20 November 1814. DCT. WW relayed to his brother Christopher on 26 November 1814 GB's news of the Bishop of London's approval. The letter from GB to WW of November 1814 is lost.
39. GB to WW, 30 November 1814. DCT.
40. GB to WW, 30 November 1814. DCT.
41. LB to WW, 4 July 1814. DCT.
42. LB to WW, 17 January 1815. DCT.
43. GB to WW, 20 August 1821 calls Reynolds's work 'a libel'. LB to WW, 17 January [1815] and [29 April 1815] also refers. DCT.
44. GB to WW, spring 1815, in reply to the dedication (DCT); WW's letter to GB dated 1 February 1815 was prefixed to the 1815 edition.

CHAPTER X

1. FD, 7 May 1799.
2. Sydney Smith, *Wit and Wisdom*, new ed., 1888.
3. FD, 1 June 1808.
4. FD, 3 May 1803.
5. GB to Bowles, 21 February 1808. PML 1854 v.
6. Constable, 2nd Lecture to Royal Institution, 1836.
7. GB to Lawrence, Royal Academy of Arts, London, letter VII.
8. FD, 26 January 1808.
9. FD, 4 December 1807.
10. 'On a Landscape by Rubens', *Poetical Works of William Lisle Bowles*, 1855. I. p. 142.
11. GB to Ibbetson, 8 March 1804, in Clay, *op. cit.*, p. 84.
12. FD, 19 May 1803.
13. J. G. Lockhart, *Life of Sir Walter Scott*. 1839, IX, p. 79.
14. Sir John Soane's Museum, London.
15. Manchester City Art Gallery.
16. FD, 15 April 1803.
17. Buchanan to Irvine, 6 June 1803, in Hugh Brigstocke, *William Buchanan and the 19th Century Art Trade: Letters to his Agents in London and Italy*, 1982, p. 82.
18. Mrs Anna Jameson, *Companion to the Most Celebrated Private Galleries of Art in London*, 1844, p. 383.
19. Buchanan to Stewart, 24 February 1804, in Brigstocke, *op. cit.*, p. 142.
20. *Ibid*.
21. FD, 1 June 1803.
22. GB to Gilpin, 6 December 1802. Bodleian Library, Oxford.
23. Lawrence to GB, 22 November 1821. PML 3288.
24. FD, 19 May 1803.
25. The picture is in the Ashmolean Museum, Oxford. The other exhibit was a 'moonlight'.
26. Callcott to an unknown 'Editor', from papers on deposit in the Ashmolean Museum, Oxford.
27. FD, 21 March and 3 May 1802.
28. FD, 6 April 1804.
29. FD, 25 March 1804.
30. FD, 24 January 1803.
31. FD, 5 May 1804.
32. BC, with a drawing.
33. FD, 2 December 1803.
34. FD, 23 May 1803.
35. FD, 7 September 1800.
36. BC.
37. GB to Gilpin, January 1802. Bodleian Library, Oxford, Eng, misc. C. 389, ff. 40–41.
38. FD, 8 May 1807.
39. FD, 13 March 1801.
40. Constable to Dunthorne, *JCC*, II, pp. 31–2.
41. FD, 1 April 1804.
42. FD, 25 March 1801.
43. FD, 3 May 1803 and 1 April 1804.
44. Sheffield City Art Gallery; FD, 3 May 1803.
45. FD, 3 May 1803.
46. Turner Collection, Clore Gallery, London and Turner Collection, Clore Gallery, London/National Trust. Petworth.
47. Callcott, Diary for 1805 (on deposit in the Ashmolean Museum, Oxford, records this discussion with Hoppner, Henry Thomson and William Owen.
48. FD, 12 May 1805.
49. FD, 16 April 1813.
50. Private Collection; see David Brown, *Augustus Wall Callcott*, Tate Gallery, 1981, no. 2 repr.
51. Callcott, 1805 Diary.
52. *Sea-Coast, with Figures bargaining for Fish & Calm, with Figures; Shrimping* (Private Collection); see Brown, *op. cit.*, nos 3 and 4 repr.
53. FD, 5 April 1806.
54. FD, 13 April 1806.
55. FD, 3 April 1806.
56. Constable's drawing (Thomson Collection, Canada) is dated 23 September 1806.
57. FD, 26 April 1806.
58. FD, 26 April 1806.
59. FD, 9 November 1806.

60. GB to Mulgrave, 10 January 1802. MCA.
61. GB to Mulgrave, 28 July 1802. MCA.
62. GB to Mulgrave, 16 December 1802. MCA.
63. GB to Mulgrave, 6 January 1803. MCA.
64. GB to Mulgrave, 23 January 1803. MCA.
65. GB to Mulgrave, 14 November 1806. MCA.
66. GB to Mulgrave, 30 November 1806. MCA.
67. GB to Mulgrave, 30 November 1806. MCA.
68. FD, 12 April 1806.
69. Collection of the Earl of Mansfield, Scone Palace.
70. FD, 12 April 1806.
71. GB to Mulgrave, 14 November 1806. MCA.
72. GB to Wilkie, 15 June 1806, in Cunningham, *Wilkie*, I, p. 118.
73. GB to Mulgrave, 14 November 1806. MCA.
74. GB to Mulgrave, (?) November 1806. MCA.
75. FD, 7 November 1806.
76. FD, 7 November 1806.
77. FD, 9 April 1807.
78. FD, 8 April 1807.
79. GB to Mulgrave, (?) November 1806. MCA.
80. GB to WW, 15 March 1807.
81. GB to Mulgrave, (?) November 1806. MCA.
82. GB to WW, 15 March 1807.
83. M.C.C. Armitage Collection; see Cunningham, *Wilkie*, I, pp. 123–4.
84. GB to Mulgrave, (?) November 1806.
85. FD, 14 November 1806.
86. FD, 6 May 1806.
87. FD, 21 June 1806.
88. FD, 12 November 1806.
89. FD, 12 April 1807.
90. FD, 15 April 1807.
91. FD, 24 May 1807.
92. FD, 19 May 1807.
93. FD, 29 November 1807.
94. FD, 1 June 1806.
95. FD, 12 June 1808.
96. GB to WW, May 1808. DCT.
97. GB to WW, 15 March 1807. DCT.
98. Haydon, *Autobiography*, I, p. 42.
99. Haydon, *Diary*, I, pp. 63–4.
100. Haydon, *Autobiography* I, pp. 42–9.
101. *Ibid.*, p. 86.
102. GB to WW, 26 February 1809. DCT.
103. Haydon, *Diary*, I, p. 60.
104. FD, 3 April 1809.
105. Haydon, *Diary*, I, p. 61.
106. GB to Haydon, 28 February 1807, in Haydon, *Autobiography*, I, p. 47.
107. *Ibid.*, p. 48.

CHAPTER XI

1. Callcott to an unknown 'Editor', from papers on deposit in the Ashmolean Museum, Oxford.
2. FD, 6 July 1809.
3. Turner Collection, Clore Gallery, London, T. B. CXXI-B.
4. Walter Thornbury, *Life and Correspondence of Turner*, 1862, I, p, 297.
5. FD, 15 May 1809.
6. FD, 15 May 1809.
7. FD, 5 July 1809.
8. Haydon, *Autobiography*, I, pp. 96–7.
9. *Ibid.*, p. 96.
10. Wilkie to GB, 16 September 1809. PML M.1851. 7.
11. Haydon, *Diary*, I, p. 135.
12. *Ibid.*, I, p. 134.
13. Wilkie to GB, 16 September 1809. PML M.1851. 7.
14. Haydon, *Autobiography*, I, p. 98.
15. FD, 1 March and 7 May 1810.
16. Haydon, *Diary*, I, p. 138.
17. Haydon, *Autobiography*, I, p. 101.
18. FD, 1 March 1810.
19. Haydon, *Diary*, I, p. 145, and *passim*.
20. FD, 7 May 1810.
21. Haydon, *Diary*, I, pp. 151 *ff*.
22. *Ibid.*, p. 155.
23. *Ibid.*, p. 157.
24. Haydon, *Autobiography*, I, p. 102.
25. Now known as 'The Village Festival' (Tate Gallery, London).
26. The Teniers in untraced. Its composition is recorded in two copies by Constable on the backs of oil sketches.
27. (?) Destroyed 1934.
28. Royal Collection.
29. Wilkie to GB, undated, in Cunningham, *Wilkie*, I, p. 304.
30. GB to Wilkie, *ibid.*
31. GB to WW, 13 November 1810. DCT.
32. GB to Wilkie, undated, in Cunningham, *Wilkie*, I, p. 322.
33. FD, 15 January 1811.
34. FD, 15 January 1811.
35. Cunningham, *Wilkie*, I, pp. 326–7.
36. *Ibid.*, p. 331.
37. *Ibid.*, p. 342.
38. *Ibid.*, pp. 343–4.
39. *Ibid.*
40. *Ibid.*, p. 344.
41. Private Collection.
42. The Prince Regent was thought to have been interested in purchasing the picture.
43. FD, 8 June 1811.
44. FD, 8 June 1811.
45. FD, 21 October 1812.
46. *Ibid.*
47. *Ibid.*
48. FD, 6 January 1811.
49. FD, 26 April 1812.
50. FD, 30 March 1812.
51. Whereabouts unknown.
52. FD, 7 June 1812.
53. FD, 7 and 18 June 1812.
54. FD, 27 May 1812.

55. FD, 27 May 1812.
56. FD, 7 June 1812.
57. Whereabouts unknown.
58. See STC to GB, 7 December 1811. The mask is perhaps the one in the Chanter's House, ascribed to Spurzheim.
59. WW to MW, 29 April 1812, in B. Darlington ed., *Love Letters of William and Mary Wordsworth*, 1982.
60. Beaumont had perhaps seen a clay modello, of which Allston made several for this work.
61. FD, 5 June 1813.
62. STC to Allston, Griggs, III, p. 508.
63. Whereabouts unknown.
64. STC to D. Stuart, 12 September 1814, in D. Stuart, *Letters to the Lake Poets*, 1889. p. 230
65. FD, 8 April 1813.
66. FD, 8 April 1813.
67. FD, 16 April 1813.
68. FD, 15 April 1813.
69. FD, 24 May 1813.
70. Turner Collection, Clore Gallery, London.
71. FD, 20 May 1814.
72. FD, 15 May 1814.
73. FD, 20 May 1814.
74. FD, 20 May 1814.
75. LB to WW, 2 June 1814. DCT.
76. Haydon to WW, in C. Olney, *Benjamin Robert Haydon*, 1952, p. 87.
77. FD, 21 May 1815.
78. FD, 22 June 1815.
79. FD, 5 June 1815.
80. FD, 5 June 1815.
81. FD, 5 June 1815.
82. FD, 2 June 1815.
83. FD, 2 June 1815.
84. FD, 30 June 1815.
85. FD, 30 January 1816.
86. Haydon, *Autobiography*, I, p. 254.

CHAPTER XII

1. FD, 25 October 1812.
2. FD, 13 May 1807.
3. FD, 21 May 1815.
4. LB to WW, 29 April 1815.
5. S. Potter, *Minnow among Tritons*, 1934, pp. 39–44. Letter of 20 September 1816.
6. STC to WW, 30 May 1815.
7. Price to GB, 18 March 1815.
8. GB to WW, 8 January 1817. DCT.
9. GB to WW, 24 November 1815. DCT.
10. GB to WW, 24 November 1815. DCT.
11. GB to WW, 17 April 1816. DCT. The article was Haydon's famous diatribe, *On the Judgment of Connoisseurs being preferred to that of Professionnal Men*.
12. GB to Allston, in J. B. Flagg, *Life and Letters of Washington Allston*, 1892, p. 93.
13. GB to WW, 17 April 1816. DCT.
14. GB to WW, 8 January 1817. DCT.
15. Apsley House. See Wilkie to GB, 12 December 1816. PML MA.1851; also GB to WW, 8 January 1817. DCT.
16. GB to WW, 8 January 1817. DCT.
17. St. George's Seminary, Cincinnati, Ohio.
18. GB to WW, (?)1817. DCT.
19. GB to WW, (?)1817. DCT. *Belshazzar's Feast*, only completed in 1843, is in the Detroit Institute of Arts; *Jacob's Dream* is at Petworth.
20. Whereabouts unknown.
21. Whereabouts unknown. Purchased after Beaumont had been shown Landseer's sketches by Haydon.
22. GB to Allston in E. H. Gerdts and T. E. Stebbins, '*A Man of Genius*', *The Art of Washington Allston*, Boston, 1979, p. 111.
23. FD, 26 March 1817.
24. FD, 2 April 1817.
25. Smith to GB, 26 July 1817. PML 1581. 3.
26. GB to WW, 2 June 1814.
27. GB to WW, 15 December 1817 DCT.
28. GB to WW, 11 February 1816.
29. W. Wilkie Collins, *Memoirs of the Life of William Collins by his Son*, 1848 (reprinted 1978), p. 131.
30. *Ibid.*, p. 129.
31. STC.
32. GB to WW, 17 April 1816. DCT.
33. D. Terry to Scott, 8 May 1816, in W. Partington ed., *Sir Walter's Postbag*, 1932, p. 121.
34. Edridge to Monro, 17 July 1819. Victoria and Albert Museum Library, London.
35. GB to Mulgrave, 9 June 1819. MCA.
36. GB to WW, 20 February 1820. DCT.
37. LB to DW, 29 July [1819].
38. Southey to GB, 8 February 1819, in Knight, *Memorials*, p, 185.
39. GB to WW, 20 February 1821. DCT.
40. Price to GB, 2 April 1820. PML.
41. GB to Haydon, 18 August 1820. Huntington Library, San Marino.
42. Haydon, *Autobiography*, I, p. 283.
43. GB to Haydon, 29 February 1820. Huntington Library, San Marino.
44. GB to Haydon, 14 February 1821. Huntington Library, San Marino.
45. T. Sadler ed., *Diary, Reminiscences and Correspondence of Henry Crabb Robinson*, 1869, 14 June 1816, V, p. 186.
46. Price to LB, 6 August 1820. PML.
47. GB to WW, 4 August 1821. DCT.
48. GB to WW, 27 December 1821. DCT.
49. GB to Lawrence, 21 October 1821. Royal Academy of Arts, London.
50. GB to Lawrence, *ibid*.
51. Lawrence to GB, 22 November 1821. PML MA.3288.
52. GB to Lawrence, 21 October 1821, Royal Academy of Arts, London.
53. GB to Lawrence, 14 May 1822. Royal Academy of Arts, London.
54. Lawrence to GB, 22 November 1821. PML MA.3288.

55. GB to Lawrence, 5 May 1823. Royal Academy of Arts, London.
56. GB to Lawrence, 14 May 1822. Royal Academy of Arts, London.
57. GB to Chantrey, in Cunningham, *Lives*, III, pp. 10–11.
58. Beaumont thought the gallery Cardinal Colonna's. Canova had told him the picture was Pannini's masterpiece; see Cunningham, *Lives*, III, p. 10.
59. GB to Lawrence, 14 May 1822, Royal Academy of Arts, London.
60. Lady Eastlake ed., *Life of John Gibson R. A.*, 1870, pp. 56–7.
61. GB to Southey, 9 October 1822. Transcript from Whiting collection of letters.

CHAPTER XIII

All quotations from Parliamentary Debates are taken from Hansard, New Series 1820–30.

1. Francesco Massimiliano(?) to GB, 29 April 1822, PML 1851.1 His painting deposited with the Accademia is of a familiar subject, *Pool with Trees*, and has recently been attributed to 'John Parcher' following an inscription *verso*.
2. T. Matthews, *Biography of John Gibson RA.*, 1911, pp. 56–7.
3. *Ibid.* The letter is dated 28 August 1822.
4. GB to Lawrence. Royal Academy of Arts, London.
5. GB to WW, [September 1822]. DCT.
6. GB to Gibson, 24 August 1823, in Matthews, *op. cit.*, pp. 58–9.
7. GB to Gibson, 10 May 1824, in Matthews, *op. cit.*, pp. 59–61.
8. GB to WW, [September 1822]. DCT.
9. GB to AE, 27 January 1824, in the *Builder*.
10. Long to GB, 8 November 1822. PML.
11. Price to GB, 20 August 1820. PML.
12. GB to Ellis, 27 January 1824, in the *Builder*. The prints were published in 1824 by Colnaghi. Ellis in his diary, 20 May 1821, called the Zoffany 'the best of the Monster' (G. A. Ellis, Diary, Annaly of Holdenby Collection, Ref. X1384, Northamptonshire Record Office).
13. *Builder*.
14. GB to Long, 30 March 1823. PML. GB asked for copies to be provided for his descendants.
15. General Meeting, 26 June 1823. British Museum Archives. The other committee members were Abercorn, Knight, Long, Bankes, Tyndale and Lord St Helens.
16. Liverpool, British Museum Add MSS, 38475/79.
17. Whitley, II, p. 69
18. GB to Long, 18 April 1826. British Museum Archives.
19. Cunningham, *Wilkie*, II, p. 399; Wilkie to GB, 14 May 1826. PML.
20. 24 May 1826, in *Diary of Lord Colchester*, ed., his son, Lord Colchester 1861, II, p. 435.
21. GB to Taylor, 26 May 1826, in Whitley, II, pp. 106–7
22. Whitley, II, p. 108.
23. 1835 edition, paperback edition 1971.
24. Constable to John Fisher, 2 November 1823. This and other quotations from Constable's letters are published in *JCC*, XII (the Fishers) and VI (Early Friends and Maria Bicknell (Mrs Constable)).
25. Southey to GB in Knight, *Memorials*, p. 217, and Southey, *op. cit.*, VI, p. 217.
26. Wilkie to LB, 12 March 1827, in Cunningham, *Wilkie*, II, p. 399.
27. Whitley, II, p. 127.
28. Annotated copy of Leslie's *Life of Constable*, 1843, Yale Center for British Art Library, ND 497 C7 and L47, copy 2.
29. GB to WW, 29 May 1825. DCT.
30. GB to Wilkie, 1825/6, in Cunningham, *Wilkie*, II, p. 298.
31. LB to WW, [1825]. DCT.
32. GB to Ellis, 13 March 1824, in the *Builder*.
33. Sara Hutchinson to Edward Quillinan, [24] October [1825], in Kathleen Coburn ed., *The Letters of Sara Hutchinson*, 1954, p. 307.
34. Rogers to Sarah Rogers, 12 September 1826, in Clayden, pp.430–34.
35. GB to Mary Beaumont 9 October 1826. PML.
36. Rogers to Sarah Rogers, 12 September 1826, in Clayden, pp. 430–34.
37. GB to Lady Mulgrave, 1826. MCA.

EPILOGUE

1. LB to WW, 8 [February 1827]. DCT.
2. GB to WW, 20 February 1821. DCT.
3. Price to GB, 10 August 1811. PML.
4. Quoted in Whitley, II, p. 125.
5. Wilkie to LB, 12 March 1827, in Cunningham, *Wilkie*, II, p. 397.
6. GB to Wilkie, 1806, in Cunningham, *Wilkie*, I, p. 132.
7. GB to Wilkie, 8 December 1825, in Cunningham, *Wilkie*, II, p. 204.
8. STC to LB, in Griggs, II.
9. WW to GB, 14 October 1803, in Wordsworth Correspondence.
10. FD, 12 December 1807.
11. Wilkie to LB, 12 March 1827, in Cunningham, *Wilkie*, II, p. 397.
12. 17 September 1827. Haydon, *Autobiograpy*, p. 349.
13. LB to Lady Mulgrave, 2 April 1827. MCA.
14. WW to Sir George Howland Willoughby Beaumont, 19 July 1829, in Wordsworth Correspondence.

INDEX